D0436919

Cambridge Studies in Chinese History, Literature and Institutions
General Editors Patrick Hanan and Denis Twitchett

THE GREAT WALL OF CHINA
From History to Myth

The Great Wall of China
From History to Myth

Arthur Waldron

The right of the
University of Cambridge
to print and sell
all manner of books
was granted by
Henry VIII in 1534.
The University has printed
and published continuously
since 1584.

Cambridge University Press

Cambridge

New York   Port Chester

Melbourne   Sydney

Published by the Press Syndicate of the University of Cambridge
The Pitt Building, Trumpington Street, Cambridge CB2 1RP
40 West 20th Street, New York, NY 10011, USA
10 Stamford Road, Oakleigh, Melbourne 3166, Australia

First published 1990

Printed in Great Britain at
the University Press, Cambridge

British Library cataloguing in publication data

Waldron, Arthur
The Great Wall of China: from history to myth
1. Northern China. Fortifications:
Great Wall of China, ancient period
1. Title
931

Library of Congress cataloguing in publication data

Waldron Arthur.
The Great Wall of China:
from history to myth / Arthur Waldron
p.   cm. – (Cambridge Studies in Chinese history,
literature, and institutions)
Bibliography.
Includes index.
ISBN 0–521–36518–x
1. Great Wall of China (China)
1. Title.   II Series
DS793.G67W25   1989
951 – dc19   88–32689 CIP

ISBN 0 521 36518 x

BOMC offers recordings and compact discs, cassettes
and records. For information and catalog write to
BOMR, Camp Hill, PA 17012

To the Memory of

Arthur T. Nelson (July 13, 1880–May 4, 1959)

&

Arthur T. Nelson, Jr. (March 17, 1922–May 2, 1945)

In studying the Chinese world order it
is important to distinguish myth
from reality wherever possible.
Both can be influential.

Lien-sheng Yang

Contents

Illustrations

Acknowledgments

Thanking the many people who have helped with a project such as this is usually a pleasant task. It is therefore painful to record the death in 1984 of my teacher Joseph F. Fletcher, Jr., at the age of only 49. We talked about the book's broad outlines before he died, and it is hard to accept that he will never read the final version, which was intended, above all, for him.

But I owe much gratitude as well to my other thesis adviser at Harvard, Philip Kuhn, and to my colleagues in the History and East Asian Studies departments at Princeton, among them Frederick Mote, James T. C. Liu, Marius Jansen, and James Geiss. Denis Twitchett in particular read and painstakingly criticized two versions of the manuscript. Others who have helped in one way or another include Thomas Allsen, Thomas Barfield, Thomas Bartlett, K. C. Chang, Shan Chou, Hung-lam Chu, Rafe de Crespigny, Robert Darnton, Edward and June Dreyer, Carney Fisher, Tom Fisher, Clive Foss, Peter Golden, Howard Goodman, Anthony Grafton, Robert Harrist, Keith Hazelton, Philip De Heer, Roland Higgins, Ray Huang, Eric Jones, Yu-kung Kao, David Keightley, Anatoly Khazanov, Gari Ledyard, Wai-fong Loh, Li Liu, John T. Ma, Michel Masson and his colleagues at *China News Analysis*, Victor Mair, Louise Marlow, Roy Mottaheddeh, the late Jeannette Mirsky, Scott Pearce, James Polachek, Gerta Kennedy Prosser, James Pusey, Hyong Gyu Rhew, Morris Rossabi, the late Father Henry Serruys, Jonathan E. B. Shepard, Kwan-wai So, Jonathan Spence, Van Symons, Hai-t'ao T'ang, Winifred Vaughn, and Bob Wakabayashi. I am also grateful to Professors Tung-hua Li and Hong Hsü of National Taiwan University, Professor Ling-ling Kuan of Soochow University, and Professors Yü-ch'üan Wang, K'o-wei Ch'en, and P'ing-fang Hsü of the Academy of Social Sciences in Peking, for their assistance, and to Alta Walker, Bob Wallace, and Tom Hanks of the U.S. Geological Survey.

The Gest Oriental Library at Princeton and the Harvard-Yenching Library have provided or obtained most of the materials I have needed, and I would like to thank in particular Dr. Min-chih Chou, Mr. Jae-hyun Byon, and Professor Ch'iu-kuei Wang, all formerly on the Gest staff, as well as Diane Perushek, the curator. Thanks are also owed to E. Adger Williams for help chasing books, to Peter Kolk for photography and general counsel, and to Sonja Lindblad and her colleagues at Lindblad Travel. Finally, I would like to express my profound gratitude to the scores of people who, knowing of my interest, have taken the time to send me relevant materials they have come across. I am extremely grateful to all of them, and hope readers of this book will not hesitate to do the same.

Versions of this research have been presented to many groups, and their criticisms have, I hope, improved the final work. The errors are all my own.

This work was supported by a research grant from the Joint Committee on Chinese Studies of the American Council of Learned Societies and the Social Science Research Council, with funds provided by the Andrew W. Mellon Foundation.

Arthur Waldron
Princeton, N.J.
June 1988

Note on romanization

The Wade-Giles system of romanization has been used throughout this book, with one exception. When, as with the names of contemporary figures mentioned in the last chapter, Pinyin forms are more familiar, we have used them.

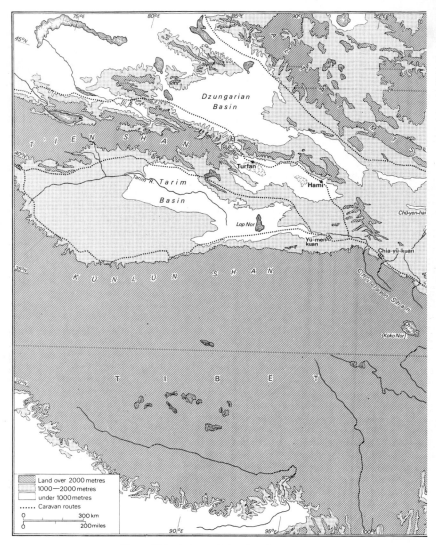

Map 1 China's inner Asian frontiers

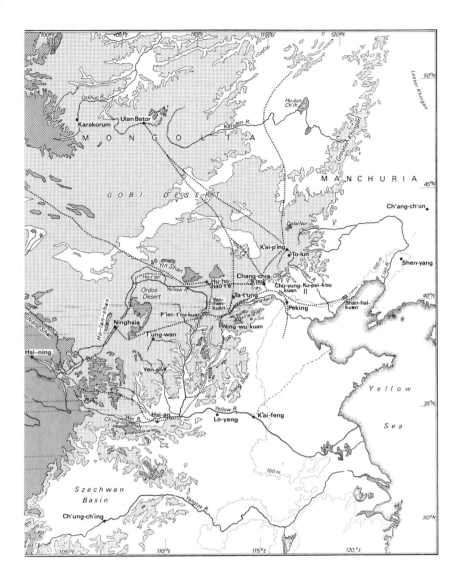

1
Introduction: what is the Great Wall of China?

In September of 1984 Deng Xiaoping himself inscribed the characters that launched a new campaign in China. Loosely translated, they said "Let us love our country and restore our Great Wall."[1] In the months before, the Chinese press had been carrying many stories about the famous Great Wall, and they made unpleasant reading. Although wind and weather over hundreds of years had eroded much of it, man, it seemed, had done the worst damage, particularly during the years of the "Cultural Revolution" when everything old had been despised. Then hundreds of kilometers of wall had been destroyed, and the material sometimes used for road, reservoir, and building construction.[2] Now the Chinese government was going to restore and preserve what remained, and rightly so. As a journalist active in the new campaign put it, "The Great Wall is the symbol of the Chinese nation," and "loving and repairing the Great Wall will reflect the patriotic feelings of the Chinese people."[3]

But what exactly was this "Great Wall" that China was now setting out to repair and why had it been built in the first place? The need to answer these questions led to the writing of this book, and the task has proved far less straightforward than might have been thought. This may seem surprising. The Great Wall of China, after all, has been known in the west for centuries, and seemingly definitive descriptions of it are not hard to find. A dictionary, for example, tells us matter-of-factly that it is a structure "over 1,500 miles long, extending from Kansu in the west to the Yellow Sea in the east, constructed between 246 and 209 B.C., and defining the historical boundary between China and Mongolia."[4] Somewhat more romantic is the description found on the dust-jacket of a recent illustrated book on the subject. The Great Wall, it tells us, is "the most awesome structure ever devised by man," one that "lies across the northern borders of China like some great sleeping dragon, stretching and sunning itself on the peaks and ridges of some of the most beautiful mountain scenery in the world. An astonishing 6,000 kilometres long," it continues, "the Great Wall of China was more than 2,000 years in the building, and the only way man can look upon the sum total of his handiwork is by viewing it from outer space."[5]

Certainly both general surveys and specialized monographs on Chinese history make frequent reference to this Wall. The commonly accepted account tells how the emperor who first unified China, Ch'in Shih-huang (r. 221–210 B.C.), incorporated early walls built by the preceding Warring States into a first "Great Wall" constructed at his command. Subsequent dynasties repaired and rebuilt his original work ever after, so that a Great Wall originating in ancient times was, as William McNeill puts it, "maintained throughout most of subsequent Chinese history."[6] This account of the history of the Wall is presented to visitors at its best-known section, along the Pa-ta-ling ridge not far from Peking. There a Chinese-language sign describes the wall of Ch'in Shih-huang, and adds that after his death "many dynasties carried out rebuilding. The present Great Wall was rebuilt in Ming times on the ancient foundations."[7] Guidebooks say the same, as do journalists. At the time of Richard Nixon's visit to China in 1972, for instance, the *New York Times* explained the Wall by noting that "Beginning in 221 B.C., construction of the unified stone, earth, and brick barrier took 15 years and employed a million men."[8] Other writers add the assertion that the Great Wall is the only man-made object visible from outer space.[9] Generally speaking, some version of this idea of the Great Wall of China today forms part of the common knowledge of most ordinary Chinese and Westerners.

The idea of such a Wall has furthermore become a major ordering concept for students of Chinese history, and a major source of cross-cultural comparisons. Its construction and renewal figure in theories of Chinese society and foreign relations, while its route is thought of as defining that country's traditional northern boundary. Karl August Wittfogel (1896–1988), for example, takes the "periodic reconstruction" of the Wall as powerful evidence of the "continued effectiveness" of the hydraulic economy which he argues makes China's society an "oriental despotism."[10] Owen Lattimore (1900–89) asks if there is not "something inherent in the historical processes of the state in China" that "favored the evolution of walled frontiers."[11] As for foreign policy, Frederic Wakeman is one of many scholars who make the Wall embody traditional Chinese attitudes toward the outside world. It was, he explains:

[...] more than a defense line. To the Chinese it marked the border between civilization and the barbarian hordes of Huns, Turks, Khitan, Ju-chen, and Mongols that successively threatened native dynasties. To the nomads it was a barrier that challenged and beckoned ... [12]

In 1969, the U.S.S.R. brought this wall into the territorial dispute with China, officially suggesting in *Pravda* that "The Great Wall was the northern boundary of China."[13] The Wall has even been assigned a key role in world history. The scholar Joseph DeGuignes (1721–1800) suggested the theory, since widely accepted, that its construction by Ch'in Shih-huang forced the people known in Asia as the Hsiung-nu to begin a migration across the Eurasian continent that ultimately brought them to Europe where, as the Huns, they contributed to the fall of Rome.[14]

When, as a graduate student at Harvard, I began thesis research into the military policy of the Ming dynasty (1368–1644), I too believed in this Great Wall. Like my teachers and fellow students, I had known about it since childhood, and never doubted its existence. It formed, furthermore, part of the setting for my chief interest, Chinese foreign policy in traditional times, and specifically the wars between the Ming Chinese and the Mongols. To me the significance of those wars was chiefly the way that, over decades, they drained much of the wealth of the Ming state, thus causing, indirectly, the collapse of that last Chinese-ruled dynasty. The Great Wall, which in nearly every account of these wars is described as marking the limits of "China proper," through which nomads are said to break, and from which Chinese armies are described as exiting at the start of northern campaigns, I took completely for granted. The Wall for me was as close to being a part of China's natural geography as any man-made feature conceivably could become. As for the Wall's significance, I tended to agree with my teacher, the late Joseph F. Fletcher, Jr., that its existence over millennia was important above all because of what it seemed to demonstrate about the fundamental incompatibility of the agrarian society of China with the nomadic world of the steppe.

But as I pursued my research in Chinese documents of the Ming period, I began to feel doubts about much that I had taken for granted, and slowly to realize that my assumptions about the continuous existence of a Great Wall simply did not fit with what the Chinese texts told me. Much attention is devoted in traditional Chinese writings to problems of border defense, and fortifications of many different kinds are described. But nowhere did I find a clear mention of "The Great Wall" as I understood the concept and supplied it almost instinctively to my texts: what was more, some passages seemed impossible to reconcile with its existence. My reading also raised doubts about the larger question of the compatability of nomadic and agrarian ways of life. Chinese sources record in considerable detail debates carried out by successive dynasties over policy toward the Hsiung-nu, the Turks, the Mongols, and other nomadic groups. These discussions disclosed a far wider range of points of view on policy than I had expected. Some Chinese, to be sure, wanted exclusion and at various times advocated wall-building to accomplish it. But others argued for trade and diplomacy, or in effect for peaceful coexistence with the nomads. It occurred to me that rather than being a given, almost an aspect of Chinese culture, wall-building was a policy about which people disagreed, and ought to be studied as such. Thus the first outlines of the present work began to take shape.

Initially my plan was to limit my scope to policy discussions regarding wall-building in the Ming dynasty. For the history of the Wall in earlier periods I would rely on secondary literature. But when I attempted to resolve my doubts about its pre-Ming history in this way I began to realize just how vast the topic I was stumbling into was. It did not take much investigation to discover that no standard or definitive work on the Great Wall exists in any language. Joseph Needham had earlier found out the same thing: In the section called "Walls and the Wall' in *Science and Civilization in China*, he complains that studies of the Wall "based on modern historical scholarship" are "few and far between, whether in Chinese or Western languages," and adds in a footnote that he had "not been fortunate enough to find one."[15] The period since Needham made his survey had not filled the gap, and I realized that I would have to begin at the beginning in my investigation of the Wall, the topic to which I shifted my research as soon as my Ph.D thesis was completed. This book is an account of what I found out, and its conclusions conflict at nearly every point with what I thought I knew when I began. The Great Wall of China, it turns out, is a fascinating vision, and one not surprisingly now deeply imbedded in learned and popular imaginations, in both China and the west. Yet at the root of the commonly accepted idea of the Wall lie some fundamental misunderstandings. The reality is quite different from the vision, and the whole topic is in need of comprehensive reexamination.

The first problem that anyone setting out to study the Great Wall of China encounters is that of evidence. Most of the information upon which descriptions of the Wall are based comes from the Chinese written tradition: the *Shih chi* and the other standard histories, various encyclopedias, scattered literary references, some specialized works on border policy, and particularly for the late imperial period, local gazetteers. The total amount of material (except for the Ming) is not forbiddingly large, but the sources turn out to be rather difficult to interpret at key points. Chinese, and to a lesser extent Japanese, scholars have taken an interest in these sources since the early decades of this century, and a modest literature in those languages now deals with them.[16]

But the written record has definite limits, and in the Chinese case the kinds of cartographic and archaological work that have made it possible for students of comparable topics in the west to fill in its omissions and resolve its inconsistencies have not yet been carried out. One has only to compare the studies of the Chinese walls with those of Roman frontiers to realize this point. The sixty-eight miles of wall built by Hadrian (r. 117–38) in northern Britain, for example, have been far more thoroughly studied than have the many hundreds of miles of wall that exist in China. We know the exact dimensions of that Roman wall and of the moat that lay in front of it, as well as the precise location of every tower and gate along its length.[17] The wall-ruins in China, by contrast, have never been surveyed.[18] Even today, one cannot be sure exactly where wall-ruins are, not to mention make enumerations of gates, towers, precise lengths, etc.

Even the route of the Great Wall shown on most maps today is uncertain. It appears to derive not from recent surveys but rather from charts first prepared by three Jesuit fathers for the Ch'ing emperor K'ang-hsi (r. 1661–1722), presented to him in 1708, and subsequently published in Europe. These were almost certainly not based entirely on firsthand investigation.[19] The detailed maps in the latest historical atlas from Peking suffer from the same flaw: the wall routes shown in them are based on literary sources and not on fieldwork.[20] Even the best maps, those prepared by the U.S. government using aerial and satellite photography, are not free from errors.[21]

In recent years, and particularly since the late 1970s, a limited amount of archaeological investigation has been undertaken in China, which is highly promising, though still in its initial stages.[22] Better maps are also likely to appear before long: a systematic survey, using "aerial remote sensing techniques (including infrared photography) is now underway."[23] But it will nevertheless be decades before specialists on the history of Chinese frontiers reach a level of sophistication comparable to that of their colleagues in Roman studies today.

Furthermore, the difficulties of interpreting the limited evidence we have are compounded by the existence of a large body of misinformation and unreliable analysis found in the substantial popular literature about the Wall, which continues to confuse scholars and ordinary people alike. One example of the problem is the abundance of conflicting yet exact figures that can be turned up for the length of the Great Wall. Joseph Needham cites an "officially accepted" Chinese estimate from 1962 of 3,720 miles.[24] When Richard Nixon visited China in 1972, the *New York Times* gave the figure as 2,484 miles while *Time* magazine favored 1,684.[25] A few years later, in 1979, the New China News Agency announced that there were 31,250 miles of wall, without making clear the exact meaning of the figure, while Orville Schell, writing in the *New Yorker* in the autumn of 1984 gave the length as 4,000 miles (though it should be noted that when Schell's article appeared in book form the Wall had shrunk to only 1,500 miles).[26] Yet clearly, in the absence of surveys and reliable cartography, it must be admitted that the figure cannot be known. A similar problem arises with

5

other statements about the Wall's size. Its volume, for example, was calculated almost two centuries ago by Sir John Barrow (1764–1848), the celebrated explorer who would later found the Royal Geographical Society of London, and who accompanied the first British mission to the Ch'ing court in 1793–4. Assuming the Wall to be throughout of the same construction that he had observed near Peking, Barrow estimated the stone in it was equivalent to "all the dwelling houses of England and Scotland" and would suffice to construct two smaller walls around the earth at the equator.[27] These impressive, but utterly unfounded, extrapolations are regularly quoted, down to this day, by scholars and popularizers of the Great Wall alike, as are similar dubious assertions about the history of the Wall's construction, its cost, the manpower involved, its visibility from outer space, etc. They form part of a popular legend of the Great Wall that has proved so enduring and influential that our final chapter will be devoted entirely to its history.

Clearly, the problem of evidence is fundamental to any study of the Wall, and this book differs from its predecessors chiefly in the way it deals with it. A number of Western authors have studied the Wall.[28] Even the best of them, however, those who recognize and acknowledge the severe evidential problems (Joseph Needham is a good example), nevertheless present accounts in which something like the notion mentioned above of an ancient and continuously existing Great Wall forms the framework, despite the lack of evidence for it. The validity of that larger concept is never subjected to questioning.

My approach has been rather different. I have tried to examine the evidence, in the first instance, without any fixed prior idea of what it ought to add up to. When one does that, certain fundamental, and I think insurmountable, problems with the ordering concept of "The Great Wall" itself become clearly evident. Then, rather than attempting somehow to fit recalcitrant evidence into it, I have chosen instead to discard the concept. The basic conviction that has thus emerged from my research is that the idea of a Great Wall of China, familiar to me since childhood, and with which I began my work, is a historical myth.

It is important to understand what is meant by this. The phrase "historical myth" is not intended to suggest that the Chinese did not build walls, or that accounts of their northern frontier fortifications are fanciful or invented. Chinese have been constructing border walls of various kinds since the seventh century B.C. The enterprise has been recorded in the histories, and travelers, and more recently archaeologists as well, have described some of the remains of these walls. The problem is not with the existence of walls in Chinese history, but rather with the way that we understand and interpret them.

6

In the past, the numerous questions posed by the evidence about how and why walls were built, what they looked like, and how long they survived, as well as, most basically of all, about what significance they should be given in any general understanding of Chinese civilization, were resolved by reference to a single Great Wall thought of as having a unified history and a single purpose. It is that concept, and the many ideas based on or derived from it, that I am convinced is myth. Removing it from our historiography will require us to reconsider much that we thought we already knew. But just as importantly, it will reveal the existence of important questions, hitherto concealed by belief in the myth, that must be considered.

This book cannot hope to treat definitively all the issues raised by these two processes. Its three parts will carry the processes of rethinking evidence, subtracting myth, and reassigning significance through several stages with varying degrees of detail. First it will present what we know about wall-building in Chinese history, and then suggest a general framework for understanding it: a framework that is partly new and partly a rediscovery of a longstanding Chinese tradition of interpretation that has been largely lost sight of during the last century. Second, it will attempt to present the wall-building of the Ming period, when most of what today we call "The Great Wall of China" was in fact built, in terms of that framework. And finally, it will try to explain, once again in general terms, both what, if anything, the heritage of wall-building really tells us about Chinese society and politics, and how the mythic misunderstanding of it originated and spread. That last task will involve consideration of some basic questions about the nature of Chinese civilization, and about the relationship of Asia and Europe.

The two chapters in Part I seek to define the issue. Chapter 1 will survey the evidence bearing on the border fortifications built by Chinese rulers since the first millennium B.C The narration should make clear how important it is to replace the notion of a single Great Wall existing over time with an understanding that while a number of Chinese dynasties built border fortifications, these did not form a single structure. Among the more important northern fortifications were those built by the Ch'in (221–207 B.C.), the Han (202 B.C. – A.D. 220), the Northern Ch'i (A.D. 550–74), the Sui (A.D. 589–618), and the Ming (A.D. 1369–1644). But rather than being aggregated under one rubric, and considered as parts of a single phenomenon, these walls must each be examined and understood in their own historical contexts. Recognition of this fact, however, leads to a new and basic interpretative question: namely, why did some dynasties build walls while others did not?

Chapter 2 will suggest some ways of thinking about that question, by proposing that we understand wall-building as one possible response to the problems presented by the interaction of a largely agrarian Chinese state with the nomadic peoples of the steppe. Using the anthropological understanding of this relationship as our basis for analysis, we will suggest that successive Chinese courts had no single foreign policy, but rather could choose from a variety of possible approaches to the steppe, ranging from peaceful coexistence based on trade and diplomacy, to outright conquest, to attempted isolation. Understanding this range of possible policies, however, is only the beginning of real understanding of the origins of walls. For choice among policies was not a straightforward process. It involved not simply strategic analysis, but also political, bureaucratic, and cultural factors. To understand a dynasty's wall-building then will require considering a larger picture: essentially, the strategic and political origins of what today we might call its "national security policy."

Of course such a study could be made for every dynasty. But to do so at more than an impressionistic level even for those that built walls is beyond the capacity of a single researcher and the scope of a single book. Therefore Part II will attempt to begin the task for only one: the Ming, whose wall-building was the most extensive in Chinese history. Ming politics are fairly well documented, and use of contemporary sources, notably the *Veritable records*, the somewhat-edited daily chronicle of palace activities and decisions, makes it possible to reconstruct the arguments about that dynasty's national security, and for and against walls, with a high degree of confidence.

The six chapters of Part II will attempt to tell the story of Ming wall-building as it was understood at the time, as a question of policy choice in a highly charged political atmosphere. Beginning with an analysis of the specific issues of strategic geography on which Ming policy discussions focused, they will narrate the strategic debates, and in particular a celebrated series of court arguments over "the recovery of the Ordos," the territory of the great bend of the Yellow river, into which the Mongols moved in the mid fifteenth century, and which form the background for Ming decisions to build the vast system of border fortifications which in retrospect have been named "The Great Wall."

Part III returns to more general questions. Chapter 9 attempts to relate wall-building to basic questions of Chinese history and foreign policy. It argues specifically that the Ming had economic and diplomatic options for dealing with their nomadic adversaries that might have obviated the need for walls, but which were scorned for political reasons. It furthermore suggests that such damaging unwillingness to compromise, of which the Ming case is a clear example, is part of a larger pattern in Chinese foreign policy. Chapter 10, the conclusion, turns away from the real Wall and looks at the evolution of the myth of the Great Wall, specifically at the process by which the Great Wall became one of modern China's national symbols. The chapter will show how Chinese and Western elements were combined to produce the mythical account of the Wall. And it will argue that on some level territorial definition through wall-building, and national definition through the creation of cultural symbols, are both aspects of a single, ongoing process.

That process is of course the definition of China itself, which removal of the Great Wall myth reveals to be even more complicated than we have previously understood. Basic to the process is the definition of the civilized, Chinese *hua* and its negative counterpart, the *i*, or barbarian. Although the actual size of Chinese states has varied greatly from one dynasty to another, the question of what was "Chinese" territory, and what constituted "China proper" is still often thought of as having been answered long ago by the Great Wall, or in modified form, the "line of the Great Wall." But without any such line to rely on, the full magnitude of the problem of defining China becomes clear.

In the Ming, for instance, the question facing the first rulers after the Mongol Yüan had been overthrown was not, as is sometimes thought, how once again to hold the Great Wall, because there was no Great Wall then. Rather, the problem was where the Ming dynasty's own territory should end. Should it stretch to the north, and try to encompass at least some of the territory that its predecessor, the Mongol Yüan, had held? Or should it adopt a line closer to the ecological boundary of Chinese-style agriculture? Debate over this issue simmered for most of the dynasty's nearly three hundred years, without definitive resolution, as Part II will relate. But because historians have assumed that a pre-existing, ancient Great Wall marked the dynasty's northern boundary at the start, most have missed both the existence and significance of this debate.

And the Ming case is but one example of the problem. Dynasty after dynasty has faced the question of where China should end, because for most of her history China's northern frontier has not been walled, but rather quite open. Since no Great Wall has ever supplied a ready-made boundary for them, each dynasty has had to define for itself where its political sway would end. Far from agreeing on a single line, they have made a great variety of choices.

Some dynasties have chosen broad, inclusive definitions, and attempted to place their frontier far in the north. To encompass the diverse peoples who live there, they have had to adopt rather cosmopolitan definitions of Chinese culture and Chineseness. Other dynasties have been more narrow and exclusive, and have either drawn, or been forced to draw, the line in the south. Sometimes these boundary lines have been marked by walls or fortified frontiers that can still be traced. But as the great variety of the lines suggests, the route of China's northern frontier has always been a question (and indeed it remains so today).

So considered, the full intellectual significance of the idea of a single Great Wall begins to become clear, as do the possible effects of revising it. Obviously, the first idea fits into a way of thinking about China that sees that state not only as clearly bounded, but also as culturally cohesive, and historically continuous. Given the very real continuities in the Chinese past, such an idea clearly contains more than a kernel of truth. But studies of Chinese culture and society have reached a stage of sophistication which finds scholars increasingly disassembling their subjects into component parts, whether regional populations, philosophical schools, or marketing networks, before once again combining them into some sort of Chinese unity. Disassembling "The Great Wall" in much the same way, over both time and space, will show us more completely than before the range of implications that the issue of boundary demarcation has had, and continues to have, in the Chinese world.

PART I

First Considerations

2

Early Chinese walls

The first walls in Chinese history were probably between households, and marked an important stage in the evolution of the traditional Chinese home, with its blank outer walls and its inner courtyards, that continues to exist into the present. Next, it seems, came walls around villages and towns. Some settlements of the prehistoric Lung-shan culture, for example, were surrounded by earthen walls built by the same *hang-t'u* or tamped earth method used for domestic architecture, while the famous seven kilometer long wall of Erh-li-kang, near Cheng-chou in Honan and dating from Shang (1766? B.C.–1122? B.C.) times, still more than nine meters high in places, is perhaps the most impressive example of such construction to survive from ancient times. In the tamped-earth method, "planks were erected on both sides of the wall, earth (*t'u*) was poured to fill the space between the planks, and the earth was then tightly pounded (*hang*), layer by layer, with a heavy pounder." Layers ranged in thickness from three to twenty centimeters, and cared for properly, such tamped-earth walls could survive for a very long time.[29]

In the period before the Ch'in dynasty, when political power in the Chinese cultural area was still divided effectively among the rulers of regional kingdoms, the tamped-earth method was adopted to build state border walls as well.[30] Our first textual reference is to a wall of 656 B.C., built by the state of Ch'u in what is today the southern part of Honan province, of which some 1,400 meters have recently been excavated.[31] Later, during the Warring States period (403–221 B.C.), other kingdoms followed suit. In the fifth century B.C., the state of Ch'i built walls, and ruins of some of these have survived in modern Shantung.[32] The state of Wei built a western wall, against the Ch'in, which was completed in 361 B.C., and an eastern wall in 356 B.C. Ruins of the former are visible today in Han-ch'eng county, Shensi.[33] The state of Yen built two walls, one in modern Inner Mongolia (311–279 B.C.) and the other in northern Hopei (334–311 B.C.) Ruins of the former are visible at Mt. Shih-fo, Chao-wu-ta league, Inner Mongolia, and of the second in Hsü-shui county in Hopei.[34] The state of Chao built a southern wall (333–307 B.C.) in what today is

Fig. 1. Many modern writers confuse the border walls of the Ch'in and other early dynasties with the much more elaborate ones built 1,500 years later by the Ming. The beautifully rendered illustrations from Leonard Everett Fisher's children's book *The Great Wall of China* (New York: Macmillan, 1986) are a good example.

northern Honan, and extending to beyond Yen-men-kuan at the base of the T'ai-hang mountains; a northern wall (300 B.C.) in the Yin-shan area, extending to modern Pao-t'ou and beyond, almost to Chang-chia-k'ou; and a third wall even further to the north, from Kao-ch'üeh almost to Pai-ling-miao, north of the Ordos.[35] Non-Chinese built walls as well: the I-chü people, for example, built a wall to protect themselves from the Ch'in.[36]

These early walls, however, are not usually thought of as being a Great Wall. Most writers suggest that the enterprise of wall-building, along with many other aspects of Chinese life, was qualitatively transformed in the third century B.C., when the first unified Chinese state came into existence. It was created when one of the earlier states, the Ch'in, defeated its rivals, and its king adopted the newly-created title of *huang-ti* ("emperor") of the Ch'in dynasty (221–207 B.C.). Among the many achievements of this dynasty, the construction of a new border defense system, a *wan-li-ch'ang-ch'eng* or "ten thousand *li* long wall," into which some of these earlier walls were incorporated, is usually numbered as one of the most important. (One *li* equals approximately one third of a mile.)

The story of the Ch'in wall continues, as we shall see in more detail in our final chapter, to hold a powerful fascination. Popular Chinese written materials recount again and again the sufferings of the hundreds of thousands of soldiers, convicts, and peasant *corvée* laborers who are said to have been sent to the northern border to work on the project, as do songs and ballads, some very ancient. Western sources do the same. Images of this wall-building are particularly vivid in children's books, where one regularly finds illustrations that show masses of laborers hauling great stone blocks to the northern frontier, and a wall built of them, complete with crenellations, gates, and towers, snaking over the hills until it disappears in the distance.[37] From such a concept of the Ch'in achievement follows the idea, already mentioned in the Introduction, that the Ch'in laid the foundation for the present Great Wall. The *China Daily*, for example, describing recent rebuilding work, explains that "The 6,000-kilometre-long wall was built more than 2,500 years ago, running from the coastal town of Shanhaiguan pass in northeastern China to Jiayuguan pass in northwestern China."[38] And many learned writers concur. The eminent scholar C.P. Fitzgerald, for example, has written, "The Great Wall, though often repaired and refaced, was planned and linked together by Shih Huang Ti; although probably only the core of the modern wall is Ch'in work, the design and trace of the wall were planned by the great Emperor, and subsequent generations have only restored or maintained his monument."[39]

Despite its great importance, however, our knowledge of the exact history of this Ch'in wall-building is by no means exact. It is beset by the sorts of problems with evidence and interpretation that we have already mentioned in general. Even today, scholars do not agree about what exactly the Ch'in dynasty did, despite the expenditure of much painstaking effort in analyzing the sources. What we make of the Ch'in, however, is of such great importance to our interpretation of everything that follows, that we must pay more than passing attention to exploring it.

The conventional story is that after conquering his rivals among the Chinese, Ch'in Shih-huang (r. 246–210 B.C.) turned to face the challenge from nomads to the north. To subdue them he sent his trusted general Meng T'ien with 300,000 men, who, after the successful conclusion of a campaign that drove the nomads out of the north and beyond the Yellow River loop, put his men to work constructing frontier fortifications to guard the newly-won territory.

The work was not completely from scratch. Most authorities agree that Meng T'ien did not build an entirely new wall, but rather worked with pre-existing Warring States walls which he repaired and connected. But nevertheless, the consensus is that this was an awesome feat. *The Cambridge History of China*, for example, speaks of "the colossal nature of the wall."[40] Owen Lattimore evokes its grandiosity.[41] Scholars speculate that the Ch'in work went on for perhaps ten years, and was in many respects far more complex even than "building a pyramid, dam, or other stationary monumental structure," for one had to reckon with "the long stretches of mountains and semi-desert it traversed, the sparse populations of those areas, and the frigid winter climate."[42] It involved, according to some, moving more then 1.3 billion cubic meters of stone and earthwork, and mobilizing perhaps 400,000 men.[43]

Such writing, however, seems to reflect not so much hard evidence as it does a general fascination with Ch'in Shih-huang, the great and cruel first unifier of the Chinese cultural realm, who remains still vividly alive in the historical imagination. The building of the Great Wall is but one of his legendary feats: he also is said to have burned classic books and buried alive the Confucian scholars who studied them, even while standardizing weights, measures, and axle widths, and knitting his empire together with a network of roads and canals.

If we examine the evidence alone and uninterpreted, however, it quickly becomes evident that we know very little about the celebrated Ch'in wall, and that in reality it almost certainly differed very much from what we have imagined.

The evidence is rather limited. In the written record we have only two primary accounts of any length, and they are both inexact. Chapter 88 of the *Shih chi* records that:

After Ch'in had unified the world [in 221] Meng T'ien was sent to command a host of three hundred thousand to drive out the Jung and Ti along the north. He took from them the territory to the south of the [Yellow] river, and built a Great Wall, constructing its defiles and passes in accordance with the configurations of the terrain. It started at Lin-t'ao, and extended to Liao-tung, reaching a distance of more than ten thousand *li*. After crossing the [Yellow] river, it wound northward, touching Mount Yang.[44]

A parallel passage in Chapter 110 is very similar:

[The emperor] dispatched [his general] Meng T'ien to lead a force of a hundred thousand men north to attack the barbarians. He seized control of all the lands south of the Yellow River and established defenses along the river, constructing forty-four walled district cities overlooking the river and manning them with convict laborers transported to the border for garrison duty [...] Thus he utilized the natural mountain barriers to establish the border defenses, scooping out the valleys and constructing ramparts and building installations at other points where they were needed. The whole line of defenses stretched over ten thousand *li* from Lin-t'ao to Liao-tung and even extended across the Yellow River and through Yang-shan and Pei-chia.[45]

These two texts, and a number of other short references in the *Shih chi* and *Han shu*, constitute the written evidence for the Ch'in wall.[46]

These passages provide very little in the way of specific information. They do not tell us when Meng T'ien's campaigns took place, nor do they make clear the precise route of the fortified frontier he created. They say nothing about the possible use of earlier fortifications. And perhaps most striking is their lack of any description of the kind of massive work – cutting stone, hauling building blocks, etc. – that one would expect if the Ch'in wall was at all like our popular vision of it.

Even historians who accept the idea that the Ch'in built a great and mighty wall have been puzzled by this lack of information about it in the Chinese historical record. Professor Bodde calls the written evidence "casual and brief to an extreme,"[47] while Jonathan Fryer observes that "Ssu-ma Ch'ien [treats] the building of the Great Wall like a summer picnic."[48]

Unfortunately, archaeologists can add only a very little to this written evidence. Sections of wall said to be of Ch'in date may be seen in Heng-shan county, Shensi; Ku-yüan and Hsi-chi counties, Ning-hsia; Lin-t'ao county, Kansu; and Yü-lin and Shen-mu, in Shensi; as well as near Ch'ih-feng in Liaoning province and near Chang-chia-k'ou, in Hopei.[49]

Both this written evidence and the results of archaeological investigation have been subjected to considerable interpretative efforts by a variety of scholars.[50] In examining the topic here, we will consider three interrelated questions. The first inquires about the relationship of the Ch'in fortifications to earlier walls, built during the Warring States period. The second, whose answer depends upon how we deal with the first, asks what the Ch'in dynasty itself created. And the third wonders what relationship, if any, the Ch'in wall had to later fortifications. Tentative answers to all these questions can be fitted together in a way that eliminates most of what would otherwise be discrepancies in the evidence. The price of consistency, however, will be a downward revision in our estimate of the scale and importance of the Ch'in wall.

Let us begin with the question of earlier walls. We have seen that the Warring States built many walls, both between themselves, and along the northern frontier against the nomads. And a number of historians, of whom Chang Wei-hua is perhaps the most notable, have argued that the Ch'in in fact made extensive use of already extant frontier lines.[51] One important component seems to have been a wall, built by the Ch'in in modern Kansu and Shensi provinces, during the reign of King Chao-hsiang (r. 306–251 B.C.) before the state conquered the rest of China. As far as scholars can tell, this wall's route corresponds to that described for the northwestern portion of the fortified line of Ch'in Shih-huang, which began at Lin-t'ao, near Min county in Kansu, and ran via the southern edge of the Ordos desert to the vicinity of Chia county in northern Shensi. The Ch'in seem also to have incorporated into their frontier some walls built by other states. The northern section of Ch'in Shih-huang's defense line corresponds to the line of a wall built by King Wu-ling of the state of Chao (r. 325–299 B.C.), which runs beyond the Yellow river and north of the Yin shan from the neighbourhood of Kao-ch'üeh east to a little south of Chang-chia-k'ou. And the northeastern stretch of the Ch'in dynasty wall may be associated with the northern of the two defense lines of the state of Yen, which extended from near Hsüan-hua almost to the Korean border.

An obvious objection to such a reconstruction, however, is that it places the Ch'in dynasty wall south of the Yellow river loop and the Ordos desert, while the historical texts describe how Meng T'ien drove the nomads out of that area and made the river the frontier. A number of scholars, notably Huang Lin-shu, have challenged it on this basis, and argued that the Ch'in wall ran to the north of earlier frontier lines, in particular in the northwest where it lay outside of the Yellow river loop rather than south of the Ordos desert. One corollary of such an interpretation is to increase the amount of wall-building that must be attributed to Ch'in Shih-huang, and this Huang does. "The portions of the wall where

Ch'in Shih-huang followed others," he concludes, "are short; those which he built [himself] are long."[52]

Clearly, a great deal hangs on our reconstruction of the route of Ch'in Shih-huang's wall. If we take it as having been outside the Yellow river loop, then much of it must have been new work, which would have required vast numbers of men and years of effort to complete. If, on the other hand, we follow Chang Wei-hua, we can argue that Ch'in Shih-huang did little more than consolidate and strengthen an already existing defense line, a task nowhere near so great.

What we decide will depend, to some extent, on how we punctuate a single line of Chinese. The words in the *Shih chi* passage quoted above, about the "forty-four walled district cities overlooking the river" can be read two ways. If one puts a break between the two words *hsien* and *ch'eng*, which occur in succession, then the first, which means district, can be taken as referring to new geographical divisions in the captured territory, while the second, which can mean a wall either around a city or along a border, stands alone and becomes a wall which was built along the river. If one reads the words together, however (as Watson, whom we have cited, does) then *ch'eng* becomes part of a compound term with *hsien*, and refers the district towns, having walls, which were built along the frontier. With such a reading, the Great Wall north of the Ordos along the Yellow river disappears.[53]

Our choice of reading may be affected by consideration of time constraints. To have built a "Great Wall" – especially one that followed the Yellow river frontier, and thus involved much new construction – would have been a monumental task. Yet the entry in the *Shih chi* describing the creation of the river frontier refers to the year 214 B.C. Ch'in Shih-huang died in 210 B.C., and it is hard to imagine that would have been enough time to build a very substantial wall.

Probably the most reasonable way to reconcile these seemingly conflicting pieces of evidence is the one suggested by Professor Rafe de Crespigny. In its early period, he believes, the new Ch'in dynasty maintained its northern frontier along more or less the same line that the earlier state of Ch'in had followed – that is, south of the Ordos and the Yellow River loop, where King Chao-hsiang had built his wall, and not far from where the ruins of Ming fortifications can be seen today. But according to Professor de Crespigny this border-line was shifted north in 215, when Meng T'ien was ordered to drive the Hsiung-nu out of the Ordos region. When he had done that, he established a new frontier line beyond the loop of the Yellow River, probably not far from the older wall of the state of Chao mentioned above. If we accept that Ch'in incorporated that wall, and read the texts in the way that Watson and de Groot do, making of *hsien* and *ch'eng* "walled

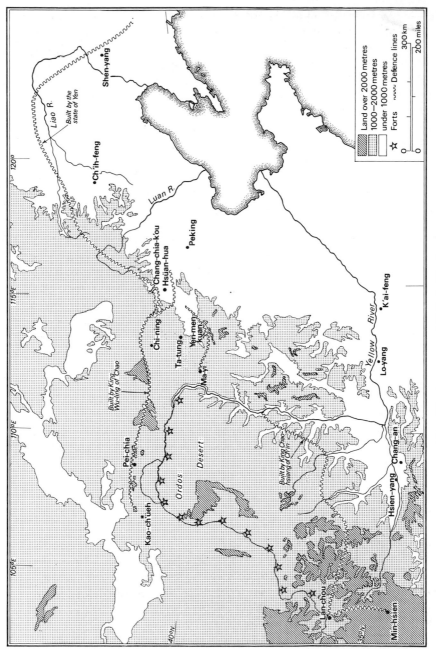

Map 2 Warring states and Ch'in fortifications

Land over 2000 metres
1000–2000 metres
under 1000 metres
Forts
Defence lines

300km
200 miles

Built by the state of Yen

Liao R.

Shen-yang

Ch'ih-feng

Luan R.

Chang-chia-kou
Hsüan-hua
Peking

K'ai-feng

Chi-ning

Ta-tung
Yen-men
kuan
Ma-yi

Lo-yang

Yellow River

Built by King
Wu-ling of Chao

Pei-chia

Ordos   Desert

Kao-ch'üen

Built by King Chao
Hsiang of Ch'in

Chang-an

Hsien-yang

Lan-chou

Min-hsien

district cities," then there is no need to imagine Ch'in as having built an entirely new wall in the region. According to de Crespigny's interpretation, the completion of the task of moving the frontier forward was signaled by the emperor's tour of inspection in 212 (see Map 2).[54]

This interpretation has many advantages. If the Ch'in, in its early stages, continued to maintain the frontier line that had been established by King Chao-hsiang about fifty years earlier, then it is not surprising that the historical texts do not stress Ch'in wall-building. And the suggestion that only limited new construction followed the conquest of the northwest by Meng T'ien accords with the time available. A less monumental Ch'in wall is also in keeping with the limited archaeological evidence. Most importantly, this interpretation clears the way for a sounder understanding of wall-building in the period that followed.

If we believe that the Ch'in indeed built an awesome Great Wall, then it is puzzling that we find little mention of it in the immediate post-Ch'in period. Scholars of the Ch'ing dynasty noted how the Ch'in wall seemed to drop out of the historical record as one entered the succeeding Han dynasty. Then, and in records of the Chin dynasty that followed it, armies are described as leaving outposts or crossing mountains, but not walls. Places now impressively fortified receive modest descriptions: Chü-yung-kuan, where the Wall is most commonly visited today, is a "mountain pass," while Yü, the older name for Shan-hai-kuan, is mentioned only as the "name of a river" in the geographical section of the Han history.[55] The Han did build fortifications, as we shall see, but contemporary sources suggest that they were not continuations of the Ch'in's Great Wall. Thus, a gloss in the *Ku-chin chu* of Ts'ui Pao (fl. 290–306) makes an explicit distinction between Ch'in and Han work in explaining the origin of the poetic term, "purple barrier":

The Ch'in built *ch'ang-ch'eng*. The color of the earth was reddish purple (*tzu*). The *sai* of Han times were the same way. Hence they were called *tzu-sai*.[56]

Indeed, throughout the whole middle period of Chinese history there is very little mention of a Great Wall. When the Mongols invaded China in the thirteenth century, no Great Wall slowed their advance. They were briefly held up at Chü-yung-kuan by the Chin, who had used molten metal to seal the gates at the pass and spread caltrops about the surrounding countryside.[57] But there was no wall: a few decades later Wang Yün (1227–1304) wrote a poem about the place in which he evoked the Ch'in wall (which did not in fact pass through it) but mentioned no existing wall.[58] Marco Polo, who is said to have visited China in the late thirteenth century, never mentioned the Great Wall either, an omission that led to much puzzlement (and which was remedied with lavish scenes shot along the Wall in the Chinese–American joint television production, "Marco Polo," aired in 1982).[59] Sir George Staunton, who traveled with Barrow and Macartney on the first British Mission to China, even doubted "whether the wall was really in existence in the thirteenth century when that celebrated Venetian went to the court of the Tartar sovereign of China."[60] Nor was the Wall ever a subject of traditional Chinese painting. The closest approximation may be a series of scenes from around Peking by the early Ming artist Wang Fu (1362–1416) which includes several of Chü-yung-kuan, where the most impressive walls stand today. But Wang's paintings show only a famous ceremonial arch, the Yün-t'ai, built by the Mongols, and not a Great Wall.[61]

Against such negative indicators, however, we should consider some of the positive evidence. To begin with, there are treaties between the Han and the nomads which seem to declare that the boundary between their two realms shall be marked by the Great Wall, and this evidence is strong enough to persuade Professor Loewe that during the Han dynasty "the Great Wall continued to serve as the line of demarcation between Han and Hsiung-nu."[62] Then there are the references to wall-building which are found in the histories of several subsequent dynasties, notably the Northern Wei, the Northern Ch'i, and the Sui. It is these records which give rise to the common suggestion that successive dynasties "rebuilt" the Great Wall. What they say seems further confirmed by maps. Our oldest Chinese maps, the Sung *Hua-i t'u* of about 1137, and the *Ti-li chih t'u* of about 1155, both show walls,[63] as does the so-called "Mongol map" of about two hundred years later.[64] Here and there in the Chinese record there are also general statements which seem to require the existence of a wall to be intelligible, for example the description of how the wall divides the lands of civilization from those of barbarism, in the *Liao shih*.[65] And finally, there is the tradition, which one can trace in poetry and folklore, that tells the story of the Great Wall. What are we to make of this evidence?

The assertion that the Ch'in "Great Wall" survived into the Han is primarily based on three incidents in the histories. The first was in 198 B.C., when the Hsiung-nu and the Han dynasty concluded a treaty which is usually stated to have had four provisions, of which the last was that "neither side would venture beyond the frontier as marked by the Great Wall."[66] In fact, the entries in the Chinese records describing the treaty-making of 198 B.C. do not mention the provision about the Wall; that appears to have been supplied by various authors on the basis of a second incident, which occurred about thirty years later. In 162 B.C. the

Han emperor Wen sent an envoy to the Hsiung-nu with a letter which Burton Watson translates as follows:

According to the decree of the former emperor, the land north of the Great Wall, where men wield the bow and arrow, was to receive the its commands from the *Shan-yü*, [leader of the Hsiung-nu] while that within the wall, whose inhabitants dwell in houses and wear hats and girdles, was to be ruled by us.[67]

The third case in which the idea of the wall as a line of demarcation occurs is from the year 8 B.C., when the Han asked for a strip of valuable Hsiung-nu land that stretched into the Han frontier commandery of Chang-i. The Hsiung-nu leader turned down this request by saying that according to the agreement between Hsüan-ti (r. 7–49 B.C.) and the *Shan-yü* Hu-han-yeh, "all the lands north of the Great Wall belonged to the Hsiung-nu."[68]

Reading these passages uncritically it would be easy to accept that they demonstrate the continued importance of the Ch'in wall, at least as a line of demarcation, well into the Han dynasty. But while they do suggest the existence of an idea of boundary between Hsiung-nu and Han lands, they do not appear to make the Ch'in wall that boundary. This is certain in the case of the third of them, the one dealing with Chang-i [or Chang-yeh] commandery, for that place was well out in the Kansu corridor, and the Ch'in never controlled it.[69] It seems reasonable to assume that as the Han moved into that area, and built fortifications, they might have agreed with the Hsiung-nu that at least in certain places those new walls should form a line of demarcation. But those walls were not the Ch'in "Great Wall."

The case of the text from 162 B.C., however, poses more problems. It comes from a time before Han expansion had gotten underway; and is phrased with a generality that makes it appealing to associate it with the Ch'in wall. And in fact it does appear to refer to a Ch'in fortification, but not to "The Great Wall."

It is important to remember that the boundaries of the early Han state lay within those of the Ch'in at its height. Both in the north and in the northwest the new dynasty proved unable to hold the frontier that its predecessor had taken, and the Hsiung-nu recovered their lost territories. Indeed, the treaty of 198 B.C., which is said to have established "The Great Wall" as the line of demarcation, was itself the result of the near-defeat of the Han emperor by the Hsiung-nu at a place called Mt. Pai-teng, not far from P'ing-ch'eng (modern Ta-t'ung) in what today is Shansi province. This territory is well within what both literary and archaeological evidence suggest was the line of the late Ch'in frontier, the presumed route of the Ch'in wall. And it seems highly unlikely, to say the least, that having established their military ascendancy south of that line, the Hsiung-nu would have agreed to a treaty which then conceded the very same territory back to the Han.

The phrase *ch'ang-ch'eng*, or "long wall" in the text, then, most probably does not refer to the original Ch'in frontier line which in 198 B.C. (and still in 162 B.C., when we find our first textual reference) was firmly within Hsiung-nu territory. It must refer to something else, and there are two obvious possibilities. One is that it refers to the line of the Ch'in frontier as it ran before Meng T'ien's conquests: that is, to the line of the wall built by King Chao-hsiang of Ch'in. As Liu Ching, the Han emperor's envoy noted, "The Hsiung-nu in the Ordos region south of the Yellow river [...] are situated no more than 700 *li* [approximately 233 miles] from Ch'ang-an [the Han capital]."[70] For a nomadic cavalryman, this was only a few days' ride. Clearly the Han would have been concerned about the threat, and plausibly would have sought to establish a frontier along the early Ch'in line. But another possibility is favored by Chinese scholars. They maintain that the treaty refers to a short stretch of wall east and west of Ma-yi, in Shansi to the south of P'ing-ch'eng: i.e. in a place that would make perfect sense. According to Yen Shih-ku's gloss in the entry for Yen-men county in the treatise on geography in the *Han shu*, a book of Chin date attributes the building of a stretch of wall south of the important pass at Yen-men-kuan, at Ma-yi, to the Ch'in. This is a place of great strategic importance, controlling access to central Shansi. It is not far from the place where the Hsiung-nu nearly defeated the Han founder, and is also where, early in the Han, general Han Hsin fought with the Hsiung-nu. Chang Wei-hua argues persuasively for this interpretation, and it makes perfect sense of the passage.[71]

But some of the passages mentioned above do seem to refer unmistakably to something like a Great Wall. That is the case with the passage from the Liao history; it is also true for the three early maps mentioned. Here the case against accepting such a wall's existence based on them must rest on problems with their possible sources. It is not at all clear, for example, where the early cartographers got their ideas. The first two maps mentioned date from the Sung dynasty, and show a wall passing almost entirely through territory which that dynasty never controlled, thus making it unlikely that the map-makers had any first-hand acquaintance with the region in question. Probably the two maps, and the Mongol map (which was compiled at a time when investigation would at least have been possible) were compiled on the basis of written records, and the wall-line they show is perhaps drawn (like nearly all of the wall-lines on maps right up the the present) not on the basis of a survey, but rather according to written records and tradition. Much the same can be said of the comments in the Liao history. They are not specific or empirical, but rather appear to

Fig. 2a,b Said to have been built by the state of Chao, this stretch of wall near Pao-t'ou in Inner Mongolia is virtually indistinguishable from the natural contours of the landscape. The layering which is visible where the road cuts through, however, shows that it is man-made. (Photo: author.)

come out of a legendary concept of a Great Wall. In our last chapter we will attempt to trace the development of this imaginative tradition which, incidentally, seems to have gained some strength in Sung times. From time to time thereafter it seems, as perhaps in these cases, to have invaded the realm of history.

The argument that the Ch'in fortifications did not survive long is further strengthened by consideration of what early Chinese walls were really like – something that is easy to forget if one is standing on the magnificent stone fortifications at Chü-yung-kuan. Walls built by earlier dynasties bore little resemblance to them. They were, as far as we can determine, ramparts of earth, and today peasants give their remains such names as "earth dragon."[72] The author has visited one, attributed to the state of Chao, near Pao-t'ou [Baotou] in Inner Mongolia. Its surface blends into the contours of the surrounding land, but where the road cuts through, the layers of earth that prove it to be man-made are clearly visible (fig. 2*a*, *b*).

Such walls were built quickly, in a season or two by troops or *corvée* labor. One passage tells that a man could build such a rampart eighteen feet long in a month.[73] And they made use of diverse materials. The Han walls that Sir Aurel Stein discovered in 1906 in western Kansu near the Han fortress of Yü-men were composed of layers of bundled twigs, six-or-so inches thick, alternated with thinner layers of coarse clay or gravel.[74] While pounded or layered earth was commonest, stones were used as well, for example in the wall north of Chang-chia-k'ou that is said to be of Ch'in date.[75] Such rough and ready constructions eroded easily. In Han times, one objection raised to giving up border defense in return for peace with the Hsiung-nu was that the fortifications would decay without maintenance.[76] In the early Ming, walls built of earth in the traditional way disappeared in a few decades and had to be rebuilt. Ming sources are full of memoranda from officials illustrating this.[77] The walls visited today, that are built or faced in stone, date from only the sixteenth century, and they required years for the completion of even short stretches.

Far from constituting permanent additions to a single Great Wall, then, few of these early Chinese walls even survive (though some, even mud brick, have lasted), and there are few mentions of their remains in the written record. In addition to the evidence already mentioned, remnants of the Ch'in wall have been listed since T'ang times in the sections of gazetteers devoted to ancient sites (*ku-chi*), while other references are found in the *T'ung-tien* (801), an ancient encyclopedia.[78] In the *Kuei-hsin tsa-shih* (ca. 1298) people living near old walls are described as pulling durable wooden stakes out when portions collapsed in the rain, and the author records his astonishment that the wood could have lasted over 2,000 years.[79] A Yüan traveler describes coming across a section of wall in the north, at modern Dalai Nor in northwest Heilungkiang.[80] (This must have been part of the Chin wall, which is today the best preserved of the pre-Ming works: over 5,000 kilometers can be traced.)[81] In 1752, the emperor Ch'ien-lung happened upon a stretch of ancient wall in Hopei and had a stele erected to commemorate the occasion, which was smashed in 1966 but has now been repaired.[82]

Even many of the walls built by the Ming have greatly decayed. In July 1980 a fortified complex was discovered, apparently associated with the pass at Ku-pei-k'ou, and elaborate enough to be declared a "new Pa-ta-ling" after the most celebrated section of the Wall. Although it was built only in the Lung-ch'ing period (1567–72), apparently little more than foundations remained.[83]

Final confirmation of our contention that no single Great Wall ever existed in China, and that the idea of one can only confuse us, however, is found in the evidence of the Chinese language itself. If an ancient Great Wall had existed, it almost certainly would have had a single, fixed name, just as mountains, rivers, temples, etc. do, which would have been used consistently. When dynasties restored or repaired that Wall, as we are told they did, they would have used that name. Yet when we turn to the vocabulary used by Chinese to describe wall-building, we find not a single name, but rather a range of terms and usages that are utterly inconsistent with such a situation. Unfortunately, the existence of this range of terminology is often obscured by the use of the English term "The Great Wall" to translate a number of different Chinese words and phrases, as well as by the problem created in modern times by the translation of that Western term back into Chinese.

The commonest of the Chinese phrases usually translated as "Great Wall" is *ch'ang-ch'eng*, a term which can be found in the *Shih chi* (1st century B.C.). But since the words are used there to refer to a variety of walls, built both by Chinese and by nomads, they cannot mean "The Great Wall."Rather they must be read literally as "long wall" or "walls."[84] Other words often rendered as "The Great Wall" include *yüan* (a rampart less elaborate than a wall), *sai* (which means "the frontier," but which may be used for walls, especially in poetry), *chang* (barrier) and *ch'eng* (the wall of a city, hence a frontier fortress). In Ming times, when many walls were built, the term *ch'ang-ch'eng* was not used. The frontier was then usually referred to by the phrase *chiu-pien-chen* ("the nine border garrisons"), which specifies commands and men, not fortifications, and when fortifications were mentioned the Ming never applied the phrase *ch'ang-ch'eng* to them; rather they called them *pien-ch'iang* or "border walls" because, it is said, the memory of the tyrannical first emperor of Ch'in was so loathed that the Ming preferred to avoid a term so intimately associated with him.[85] Yet if the Ming had been repairing an ancient and well known "Great Wall" it seems likely they would have had little choice but to continue to use its traditional name. Apparently no word or phrase in the traditional Chinese lexicon corresponds exactly to the modern Western term "Great Wall."

In modern Chinese, of course, there is a phrase, *wan-li ch'ang-ch'eng* ("wall ten-thousand *li* long"), which, unlike the classical terms just mentioned, does convey exactly the same idea as "The Great Wall" does in English. The phrase furthermore occurs in pre-modern writings. However, it seems reasonable to suspect that its wide use, as an equivalent of the English phrase, is a modern phenomenon, and that its meaning has been modified, like so many other ancient Chinese terms, by its modern uses.[86]

Certainly taken as a whole, the use of language suggests that Chinese in the past thought about walls and border defenses rather differently than they, or we, do today. The phrases we have examined appear to be generic terms, used to designate a type of defense, and not (except in certain poetry and allusion) references to a particular historical work. In fact, the concept of a single "Great Wall" appears to be both misleading, and relatively modern. Unfortunately, it is now being implanted even in Chinese historical texts, where it is not uncommon to find the phrase "Great Wall" supplied in brackets where the text may say something quite different. And in today's standard Peking edition of the dynastic histories, the phrase *ch'ang-ch'eng* is side-scored, as if it were a proper noun. Examination of historical texts, however, confirms the linguistic evidence that (outside of certain literary contexts) it is not. We find many fortifications, but no "Great Wall."

What are our main conclusions from this evidence? It should be clear, first of all, that no "Great Wall" anything like our modern conception of it existed in ancient times. Before the sixteenth century, walls in China were of modest scale, and eroded easily. Furthermore, they followed no single route, but rather a series of different ones, according to the defense needs of the dynasties that built them. One makes sense of them by looking at each against the background of the strategic and political challenges of the dynasty that built it, not by linking them all together in to single mythical structure.

Furthermore, almost all of these early walls, as the modern geographer Pai Mei-ch'u has observed, have long since disappeared. The walls that exist today were built by the most active wall-builder of all dynasties, the Ming.[87] But the questions raised by this fact have scarcely begun to be addressed. This is because, as the historian Chu Tung-jun writes, "Most people know that Ch'in Shih-huang built a Great Wall, but do not know that the present Great Wall is a border wall built by Yang I-ch'ing, Yü Tzu-chün, Weng Wan-ta, Yang Po and others."[88] Yet this fact opens up the questions with which much of this book deals. Given that no ruined wall existed when the Ming came to power in 1368, and that even precedents for wall-building were rather limited, why did this last native Chinese dynasty decide to spend vast sums of money to close what had been for centuries an open border? Few answers are near at hand, for the question itself has scarcely been recognized.

We will try to answer the question, to the extent that the evidence permits, in the middle chapters of this book. But first we must know something about the military challenge from steppe nomads faced by the Ming, in common with many of its predecessors, and about the prescriptions for dealing with that threat which were provided by the Chinese tradition. For even though the Ming did not inherit a Great Wall from the past, it did inherit a large body of wisdom about wall-building as one possible way of dealing with national security problems.

3

Strategic origins
of Chinese walls

Our analysis of the purposes of wall-building in Chinese history will take as its points of departure two ideas. The first is that the primary purpose for which Chinese states built border walls was to cope with nomadic attack, while the second is that such wall-building was undertaken only sporadically, and should not be thought of as representing a consistent Chinese policy, or one necessarily having deep cultural roots. Before proceeding, we should note that many scholars appear to dissent from each of these seemingly innocuous assertions.

The idea that Chinese border walls were really defensive in intent received its most searching challenge beginning in the 1930s, and chiefly from Owen Lattimore, who in a series of articles and a highly influential book, *Inner Asian Frontiers of China*, first published in 1940, espoused the idea that the origin of wall-building should be sought not in China's foreign relations, but in changes in her society. Specifically, he argued that wall-building was a manifestation of the transition from a feudal to a centralized regime in China that got underway in the Warring States period, and which he saw as the political consequence of the economic differentiation of a previously mixed society into two incompatible components, the first and more "Chinese" of which was based on intensive agriculture, and the second on nomadism. According to Lattimore it was inconceivable that a regime based on the former type of production could rule one based on the latter: for the Chinese to attempt to control territories more suitable to nomadic life involved "the anti-historical paradox of attempting two mutually exclusive forms of development simultaneously." Yet the nomadic realm offered possibilities to individuals within the Chinese realm, who from time to time migrated out or defected. To deal with this problem, "the statesmen of China" were prompted "to build walls that limited their own expansion as well as defending them against attack."[89] This Chinese-initiated process of demarcation in turn created nomadic hostility by cutting off trade with them, and the general conclusion is that walls were built for "keeping in, not keeping out," and hostilities with the nomads are not so much their cause as their consequence. A few lines, of course, cannot do full justice to Professor Latti-more's theory: certainly his approach contains much of value, and has been adopted even by so eminent a scholar as Professor Chaoying Fang.[90] Never-theless, as we shall show in more detail below, it is not true to the latest understanding of the origins and dynamics of nomadism, as explained, for example, in the recent work of Professor Anatoly Khazanov.[91]

The second commonplace about wall-building with which this chapter will take issue is the idea that wall-building, as a consistent policy in Chinese history, reflects some sort of basic Chinese foreign-policy orienta-tion: a "Middle Kingdom complex," or a desire to exclude, or to distinguish "inner" from "outer," or whatever. The Wall understood in such terms often turns up playing a supporting role in accounts of China's traditional foreign relations in which stress is laid on the belief that a single set of attitudes unites them. Usually these are seen as summed up in the Wall, and in the Tribute System, a pattern of ritual relations in which nomadic states and even such foreign countries as Korea and Vietnam accepted a sort of Chinese suzerainty. This is thought of as having given Asia a framework for political order. Such a system existed (at least in the minds of the Chinese) by late imperial times, though it should be noted that most authors take as their model the system of the Ch'ing, at a time when the most troublesome peoples (the Mongols, for example) had been conquered.[92] Like Lattimore's approach, this view has merit, but has recently come in for some questioning.[93] Certainly adopting it is of little use in understanding why the Chinese built walls.

For that purpose, perhaps the most useful starting point is not a belief in China's cultural unity, but rather a recognition of the profound internal discontinuity that was created by the advent, for the first time in the middle of the first millennium B.C, of true mounted nomads on the northern frontier of the Chinese cultural world. The early states, which had created a vast but loosely-knit Chinese empire, and laid down the basic cultural orientations that held it together – the Hsia, the Shang, and the Chou – had all come into existence before these nomads appeared. These states achieved a high degree of integration and unity, but one that was based, as recent studies have argued, not so much on military power and bureau-cratic coercion, as on common culture and ritual.[94] This cultural realm, in which military power was relatively unimportant, produced most of the classics that would orient later generations of scholars. These texts, in turn, expounded a theory of government that reflected the values of the world that had created them, and stressed not force, but rather culture and virtue as the bases of effective rule. Such ideas had worked when dealing with earlier "barbarians" along the Chinese border. But they were utterly inadequate to the problem of the new nomads.

The arrival of true horse-nomads posed a total challenge to this empire. The earlier "barbarians," we should stress, had lived in more or less fixed areas, often virtually intermixed with Chinese. The horse-nomads, by contrast, lived in the steppe, and were extraordinarily mobile. They were able to move rapidly on horseback from place to place, choosing when and where to attack, and by virtue of their speed, able almost always to concentrate superior forces against the Chinese, whose slow-moving armies were necessarily scattered along a lengthy perimeter. In addition, the nomads possessed superior military technology, and they followed a way of life that was radically different from that of the Chinese states. They could not be controlled or gradually incorporated by any of the means that had previously proved effective in the steady expansion of the Chinese world. The traditional Chinese texts thus could offer little guidance. Most of them did not even contain the character *hu*, which was adopted to denote and distinguish true mounted nomads.[95] Thus, beginning in the centuries just before the creation of a unified Chinese empire by the state of Ch'in in 221 B.C, and almost until the nineteenth century, Chinese states faced unrelenting nomadic challenges. During those centuries, the question of how to deal with the nomads became a defining theme of Chinese history.

Response to the challenge was of two types: one idealistic, with a rationale drawn from well-defined but unrealistic views defined in the early classical texts that antedated the arrival of the nomads, and the second more realistic, and reflecting a real but uncodified body of experience in dealing with nomads, many of whose most important points were incompatible with the former intellectual framework. Almost from the start, then, the deep architecture of Chinese culture and its thought produced difficulties in dealing effectively with the chief threat to its own continued existence.

The threat was posed by a succession of nomadic peoples. Before China's unification we hear of the Hsien-yün, while from the second century B.C to the second century A.D., the Ch'in and Han warred intermittently with the Hsiung-nu. In the period of disunion that followed, north China witnessed the rise and fall of a whole series of states that to one degree or another combined nomadic and Chinese elements, and which culminated in the second period of Chinese unification. With this, in the sixth and seventh centuries, came the rise of a great Turkish empire in the steppe whose history was intimately bound up with that of the Sui and T'ang dynasties. In the twelfth and thirteenth centuries the nomadic Mongols extended their control over all of China. The Ming, who eventually overthrew the Yüan, faced an almost continual challenge from the steppe, first from the Mongols, and then toward the end of the sixteenth century, from the Manchus, a partly nomadic people who in 1644 overthrew the Ming and established the last dynasty of imperial China, the Ch'ing.

As we have suggested, the arrival of the nomads opened up a sort of fault-line in the previously undivided Chinese culture. It posed questions at many levels: military men and politicians had their hands full attempting to cope with the threat, while philosophers, who were wedded by and large to inclusive concepts of culture, and to the idea of cultural assimilation as the moral and practical basis for state formation, found it difficult to accommodate anything as different as nomadic life in their world. This fault-line, with universalistic conceptions on one side, and the more particularistic on the other, can be traced through almost every area of Chinese life and thought. Here, however, we are concerned only with defense.

Walls were one possible way of dealing with the problem, and they were favoured by certain dynasties: the Ch'in, the Han, the Northern Ch'i, the Sui, and the Ming in particular were notable wall-builders. But walls were by no means the only, or even the favored, expedient. Other strategies included attempts to divide or conquer the nomads militarily, or to control them peacefully by such means as diplomatic relations, royal marriages, and subsidies. None of these strategies proved entirely satisfactory, however. Diplomatic relations and trade could be criticized as humiliating and expensive; offensive warfare was both costly and extremely risky; while wall-building consumed tremendous resources without in most cases proving very effective. Just as importantly, wall-building conflicted, in its attempt to exclude certain peoples and territories, with the universalistic tendency in Chinese culture.

Not surprisingly, the choice among these policies proved extremely controversial, and in dynasty after dynasty first one, and then another, was adopted. Sometimes decisions were made rationally, after relatively disinterested consideration of the policy choices. At other times, internal political questions and power struggles took command. And always lurking in the background was the issue posed by the arrival of the nomads and never definitively answered: what, exactly, was China? Was it a country? Or was it a civilization? It was almost a moral issue, and one that had great emotional resonance.

This chapter will suggest that we take wall-building as a strategy and a policy choice as our focus in trying to understand the origins of the fortifications that today are thought of as the Great Wall. Just as we will no longer think of China as having had a single, enduring border established in antiquity and marked by a single Great Wall built millennia ago, so we may think of her as having no single fixed security policy, but rather as having adopted at various times a whole series of different and often mutually incompatible policies. We will therefore recognize the periodic bouts of wall-building as a sign of the ascendancy of one of them.

Wall-building was simply one of several Chinese policy alternatives, and what follows in this chapter will outline its vicissitudes in Chinese history before the Ming period. We will show what the other alternatives were, and try to explain, at least in rough terms, under what sorts of circumstances wall-building was selected from among them. That will mean saying something about political and cultural developments in addition to purely military factors. But perhaps the most important factor to assess before turning to the question of policy choice, is the origin and nature of the nomadic threat itself. Policy discussion within China was framed by examples, usually taken from the written tradition and often from the very distant past, of how nomads should be treated, and of what sorts of policies toward them would work. Although there are kernels of truth in this Chinese tradition, there is also much that is subjective, ignorant, or stereotyped. Before proceeding, we must consider the nature of the relationship between nomadic and settled peoples as it is understood today.

Nomads are peoples who follow a pastoral way of life, subsisting on the products of their flocks, and usually moving with the seasons from one place to another. Their society usually lacks much organization over and above small herding units loosely linked to one another, and certainly has no fixed permanent structure. Yet until modern weaponry finally shifted the balance, nomads possessed a powerful military advantage over settled peoples, and from one end of Eurasia to the other, they were feared as the most dangerous of adversaries.

Nomadic military prowess was based ultimately on their way of life. Warfare or activities related to it were such a natural part of Inner Asian existence that neither the Turkic nor the Mongolian languages have a native word for soldier, nor generic terms for war and peace.[96] Ssu-ma Ch'ien, speaking of the Hsiung-nu around 200 B.C, told how "The little boys start out by learning to ride sheep and shoot birds and rats with a bow and arrow," lessons which eventually made of them fine mounted soldiers.[97] Nomadic horses and weapons were outstanding. The Przhevalski horse is a "relatively small, pony type animal" but its "toughness and wantlessness" as well as "its relatively good speed and exceptional endurance caused it to be the most formidable single factor of Inner Asian military power."[98] With their bows and bone-tipped arrows, the Hsiung-nu could lay down a barrage "like rain," an image used in both Chinese and western sources.[99]

34

Discipline and organization were also strong. The story was told of how Mao-tun, the son of a Hsiung-nu ruler, trained his soldiers to shoot at whatever target he did. "In succession he aimed at his best horse, his favorite wife, his father's best horse, and after each exercise he executed those who had failed to follow his example. Finally he took aim at his own father," and his men followed his example. Thus he killed the ruler and secured the throne for himself.[100] Later, the Mongols were celebrated for their operational skills. They planned their campaigns with great care, and were able to synchronize the movements of their forces with great precision, even when large distances separated them.[101] While it is true that some authors have exaggerated the military prowess of the nomads,[102] nevertheless ancient Chinese writers were quite correct when they pointed out the disproportionate military effectiveness of nomadic forces when compared with the Chinese.[103]

Against the threat posed by the nomads, the Chinese, like other settled peoples, had no reliable military solution. To fight the nomads on their own terms was difficult. Horses did not flourish in China, and peasants made poor cavalrymen. A professional army would be expensive, and by no means certain to succeed. Yet defense was also not a fully satisfactory option. It is futile to attempt to hold a long perimeter in the face of a mobile foe, who is able to concentrate large numbers quickly, where and when he chooses. Realistically, one must ask whether there are ways of managing the nomadic threat by other than military means. Are there nomadic needs which settled peoples can use as a source of leverage? Are there ways of drawing nomadic societies into some sort of political structure? Can a settled society hope, by using economic and diplomatic means, at least to reduce hostility with the nomads to a point at which it can be tolerated and coped with? If the answers are no, then exclusion and wall-building make a certain amount of sense. But if the response is yes, then wall-building will appear as an unnecessary, wasteful, and even provocative, choice of policy. Ancient Chinese writers debated these questions, and modern anthropologists continue to do so.

Traditional Chinese writers usually portrayed nomads as making war on settled societies simply because it was their nature. The *Shih chi* notes of the Hsiung-nu that "It is their custom to herd their flocks in times of peace and make their living by hunting, but in periods of crisis they take up arms and go off on plundering and marauding expeditions. This seems to be their inborn nature."[104] The *Han shu* described the same people as "covetous for gain, human-faced but animal-hearted."[105]

In modern times, other explanations have been advanced for nomadic attacks on settled societies.[106] They fall roughly into three categories. The first group stresses ecological factors: overpopulation in the steppe, or the

35

gradual drying-out of the land and a consequent decrease in available fodder. The second category looks to economic causes to explain hostility: refusal by settled communities to trade, its advocates argue, prevented nomads from obtaining goods needed to supplement the low-level productivity of their limited pastoral economy; or in another version, made it impossible for nomads to dispose of their surplus production of livestock. A third approach is more political and psychological: it sees raiding not as an economically or ecologically determined fact, but rather as an activity which facilitates the formation of supra-tribal confederations, one tool an ambitious leader can use to reward his followers, and ensure their loyalty. The choice among these explanations is not straightforward.

Today, however, a consensus is beginning to emerge which finds the explanation not in one society or the other, or indeed in a single factor, but rather in the entire relationship. It used to be thought that nomads followed a self-sufficient way of life and that "the steppe economy [could] manage on its own better than the economy of sedentary societies." Today that view is less widely accepted. Nomads, it turns out, are far from self-sufficient.[107] They need grain, which they do not produce themselves, and must obtain by trade. Metals and craft products, as well as medicines and luxury goods, are also required. Less tangible needs also tie the nomadic world to the settled. Demographic equilibrium among nomads appears to be linked, in some cases at least, to a steady rate of sedenterization.[108] Meeting this wide range of needs seems to be the driving force behind nomadic raiding.

Indeed, it now seems clear that the linkage with the settled world provides the impetus that brings nomadic states themselves into existence. They develop not because of changes within themselves, but rather in response to external developments, in particular the appearance of wealthy, sedentary neighbors. They are organized in order to obtain wealth from settled societies, a process that reflects both genuine needs and an awareness of the opportunity for plunder that a developed agrarian society presents.[109]

These facts about nomadic–settled relations are basic to understanding the dilemmas of Chinese military policy. They make two facts clear. The first is that the rise of an organized state in China will inevitably create at least the possibility of military problems by leading, before long, to the creation in response of a nomadic state whose purpose is to exploit it. The second, however, is that this exploitation can be managed, and need not take the form of prolonged warfare. Recently anthropologists have outlined the elements of a so-called nomadic "outer frontier policy," an approach to China whose purpose was to use force or the threat of force to win agreement to provide subsidies, in return for which hostility will be abandoned.[110] This means that to the extent that the settled society is able and willing to meet nomadic needs, the threat of warfare may be averted, or at least limited in scale. But the measures necessary to carry out such successful management on the Chinese side are often at odds with fundamental cultural norms, and as a result difficult to sustain.

The pattern of Chinese wall-building is the product of the interaction of these factors. As we survey its history, we see a process repeatedly unfold in which an initial stance of accommodation of the nomads, which meets many of their basic needs, is gradually displaced by a more uncompromising attitude. That usually leads to hostility, and with further accommodation ruled out as a means of dealing with the danger, the choice is reduced either to attempted conquest, or defense and exclusion. Since offensive warfare is extremely dangerous, the ultimate choice, at the end of this cycle, is usually wall-building – which of course, to the extent to which it is successful in cutting off the nomads, simply exacerbates the problem, stimulating them to form larger and more powerful confederations with which to attack China.

Many Chinese military men had some understanding of this process, and thus not surprisingly favored a rather high degree of accommodation of the nomads. To understand why, in spite of their urgings, counterproductive measures such as wall-building were nevertheless adopted, requires looking beyond the border and the soldiers stationed there, to civilian politics, and in particular to the role of fundamental cultural orientations in defining them. Basically universalistic Chinese beliefs had been well established long before the nomads appeared, and they provided no intellectual framework that could deal with people as different in every respect as the nomads. Furthermore, they simply could not accommodate the degree of equality and reciprocity required for the smooth working of the nomadic–settled relationship. These concepts lay – or were placed – at the heart of Chinese concepts of morality and cultural self-definition. And as a result, while accommodation could be practised as a tactic, it could not legitimately be raised to the level of a strategy without violating moral norms. Rational frontier policy, in consequence, could be practised only by an individual who both understood what it should be, and who possessed the personal power to put it into effect – usually an emperor or an extremely powerful prime minister. The possibility of its implementation was, ultimately, a function of politics, as our analysis of the Ming case will demonstrate. But the Ming dynasty came late in the evolution of Chinese frontier policy. To understand its experience requires examination of the precedents for border policy on which it drew.

Any reasonably well-educated official of later imperial China would have commanded at least as much information about the Chinese relationship with the nomads as the most learned modern anthropologist, but it would have been organized and understood in a quite different way. The background for policy decisions in China was provided by strings of incidents, often identified by a name or a catch-phrase, which exemplified alternatives, and their merits or demerits. Encompassing them all was a basically stereotyped and moralistic understanding of the relationship in general.

Consideration of wall-building in this intellectual world might well have begun with a citation from the collection of verses called the *Shih ching* or *Classic of Songs*. One of the early poems it preserves, perhaps from the seventh century B.C., tells of General Nan Chung and his campaigns against the Hsien-yün:[111]

> The King charged Nan Chung
> To go and build a wall in the [disturbed] region.
> How numerous were his chariots !
> How spendid his dragon, his tortoise and serpent flags!
> The son of Heaven has charged us
> To build a wall in that northern region,
> Awe-inspiring was Nan Chung;
> The Hsien-yün were sure to be kept away.

Much about this passage is unclear. It is not even certain that it refers to the building of a wall. (The words are ambiguous: *ch'eng*, translated above as "build a wall," can simply mean to build a fort.) And the identity of the Hsien-yün is also a problem. Modern scholars believe that they were probably the first true horse-nomads to confront the Chinese, and were most likely related to the Scythians of the west. Their base may have been in the Ordos region, around the great northwestern loop of the Yellow River, and their attacks were concentrated on the Ching and Lo rivers north of the Wei valley, near where the first Chinese capitals were located. Scholars place the attacks, and the Chinese campaigns into the northwest, in the reign of King Hsüan of Chou (827–782 B.C.).[112]

But the Chinese understanding would probably have been rather different. Although much careful work on the names and origins of border groups was done by Chinese scholars even in early times, an ordinary literatus would probably have thought of the Hsien-yün, the Hsiung-nu, and other groups in stereotypical terms, indeed often using distinct names interchangeably. We have already seen how they were considered to be "human-faced and animal-hearted." Just as their nature marked the limits of human character, their homeland was thought of as the edge of the world. The Hsiung-nu were believed to inhabit the north "where the land is cold and the killing frosts come early." The *Shih chi* repeatedly calls the Hsiung-nu lands "unfit for habitation; they were nothing but swamps and saline wastes. In military skirmishes, when 'chased' by Chinese troops, the Hsiung-nu hid 'north of the desert in a cold bitter land where there is not water or pasture.' "[113]

Later literati would also have approved of Nan Chung's mission, to overawe the nomads and drive them away, for which purpose a huge army was raised.[114] Particularly in the early period, before the Chinese had gotten to know the nomads very well, offensive warfare was a favorite option. Often it involved adopting some of the nomads' techniques. Several hundred years after Nan Chung another Chinese campaigned in much the same northwestern territory. Wu-ling was king of Chao, one of the Warring States that existed before the Ch'in conquest, from 325 to 299 B.C. His territory was in the northwest, partially in modern Inner Mongolia. Realizing the effectiveness of steppe fighting ways, he and his warriors adopted both nomadic clothing and tactics, and campaigned with some success in the northwest, in the territory from which the Hsien-yün may have come, along the Yin-shan mountains and in the Ordos loop of the Yellow River.[115] The emperor of Ch'in, who had already conquered the other major Chinese states, in 215 B.C. ordered his general Meng T'ien to conquer the same northwestern territory in which King Wu-ling had campaigned. 300,000 soldiers are said to have taken part in the expedition, which cleared the Hsiung-nu nomads from the whole Ordos area, which was then fortified. Offensive warfare had a powerful appeal, particularly when campaigns were thought of as punitive expeditions, undertaken for the moral purpose of chastising barbarians who had rebelled against the universal authority of the Chinese emperor.

But these early offensives proved ultimately futile. Those of the emperor of Ch'in had been the most ambitious, yet after his death in 210 B.C., the Hsiung-nu reclaimed their territory. Several hundred years of warfare demonstrated that offensive campaigning was not very effective, and could be risky. This latter point was driven home in the very early Han, when the founder of the dynasty, Kao-tsu (r. 202–195 B.C) decided to emulate his predecessors and smite the nomads. He came very near to disaster in 200 B.C., when the Hsiung-nu encircled him and his army at Mt. Pai-teng, near Ta-t'ung (then called P'ing-ch'eng) in modern Shansi. The siege lasted seven days before Kao-tsu escaped and abandoned the campaign.[116] The Han did not turn to the offensive again until 133 B.C.

The realization that the nomads could not simply be defeated led the Han to develop policies that sought to manage the threat either by economic and diplomatic means alone, or by using these in combination with military measures. The Han practised this approach throughout the first half of the second century B.C.

There were precedents: as early as 568 B.C., the *Tso chuan* tells us, the Marquis of Chin had wanted to attack the Jung and the Ti tribes, but had been dissuaded by the objections of his minister Wei Chiang, and instead adopted a more pacific approach.[117] But the Han policy, which was adopted more than 300 years later, became a model.[118]

The new approach was called *ho-ch'in*, literally "peaceful and friendly relations," and was followed for nearly sixty years.[119] It combined the establishment of kinship and political ties with the opening of markets on the borders and the payment of subsidies to the nomads by the Chinese. A treaty made in 198 B.C. between the Han and the Hsiung-nu provided that a Chinese princess was to be married to the nomadic ruler, the Shan-yü. In addition the Chinese were to make annual payments to the Hsiung-nu, including silk, wine, rice, and other kinds of food, each in fixed amounts, and the Han and Hsiung-nu were to be equal ("brotherly") states.[120]

Ho-ch'in was not a complete success. Hostilities continued while it was effect. The Hsiung-nu "used violent raids, or the threat of violent raids, as a tool in negotiations with the Han court," and proved adept at alternating "periods of war with periods of peace in order to extract increasingly higher benefits from China."[121] The policy also had an economic cost to the Han. Substantial quantities of grain, wine, silk floss, finished cloth, suits of clothes, etc. were regularly delivered to the Hsiung-nu. It is sometimes said that the payments the Han made to the nomads were a grave burden, but this appears not to have been the case. Nevertheless, a clearly increasing trend is evident in the first century B.C., with the amount of silk floss presented, for example, increasing fivefold, from 6,000 to 30,000 *chin*, or about 7,800 pounds to 39,000 pounds, between 51 B.C. and 1 B.C..[122]

But it is clear nevertheless that for more than forty years relative peace along the borders was maintained by means of *ho-ch'in*, in large part because it succeeded in reconciling the economic and political interests of the two sides. Markets were opened on the northern frontier beginning in the reign of emperor Wen (179–157 B.C.), and the ordinary Hsiung-nu "flocked to them in large numbers to trade pastoral products of the steppe for Han goods."[123] This trading relationship proved so workable that "by the time of Emperor Ching [156–141 B.C.], the northern border had become peaceful, and frontier communities suffered only minor raids. Old hostilities were forgotten, and 'from the Shan-yü on down all the Hsiung-nu grew friendly with the Han, coming and going along the [long walls].'"[124]

In later periods, the name *ho-ch'in* became shorthand for almost any attempt at accommodation of the nomads, for which the Han case became the classic example. By and large it was viewed with deep disapproval: to recognize the leader of the nomads as a brother, to marry even a very minor royal princess into his line, to deliver Chinese goods to the "barbarians" – all flew in the face of attitudes about Chinese culture that were deeply entrenched even in this early period of the imperial state. When later authors criticized such appeasement-minded policies, they would almost always quote from a famous memorial by Chia I (201–160 B.C.) which criticized the *ho-ch'in* policy followed by the emperor Wen (r. 179–157 B.C.) of the Han.

Chia began by treating the power of the nomads rather dismissively. "In your minister's evaluation," he wrote

The population of the Hsiung-nu does not exceed that of a large Chinese *hsien* or district. That a great empire has come under the control of the population of a district is something your minister feels must be a source of shame for those who are in charge of the affairs of the empire.

Furthermore, it upset the whole natural hierarchy of the empire. As Chia put it,

The situation of the empire may be described as like that of a person hanging upside down. The Son of Heaven is the head of the empire. Why? Because he should remain on the top. The barbarians are the feet of the empire. Why? Because they should be placed at the bottom. Now, the Hsiung-nu are arrogant and insolent on the one hand, and invade and plunder us on the other hand, which must be considered as an expression of extreme disrespect toward us. And the harm they have been doing to the empire is boundless. Yet each year Han provides them with money, silk floss and fabrics. To command the barbarian is the power vested in the Emperor on the top, and to present tribute to the Son of Heaven is a ritual to be performed by the vassals at the bottom. Hanging upside down like this is something beyond comprehension.[125]

Although Chia adduces economic objections to *ho-ch'in*, what really concerns him is its incompatibility with Chinese ideas of hierarchy.

Criticisms such as Chia's, and a general feeling that as the Han dynasty grew stronger it no longer made sense to be so accommodating with the Hsiung-nu, led to a reversal of the policy, and in 133 B.C., a new series of Chinese offensives. In that year "The Martial Emperor" Wu-ti (r. 140–87 B.C.) began a series of campaigns designed to outflank and ultimately defeat the Hsiung-nu, first driving into the Ordos and the Yellow River loop in the northwest, and later, far more ambitiously, out along the Kansu corridor and into the Tarim basin.[126] Wu-ti's campaigns were an attempt to do, under Chinese auspices, what the Hsiung-nu had done: to organize the steppe and its peoples within an economically and politically coherent structure. They proved over-ambitious, and their intentions beyond the capacity of the dynasty to finance. Ultimately they had to be abandoned.

Just as *ho-ch'in* became a synonym for appeasement, so Wu-ti's campaigns became a byword for militarism and the empty pursuit of glory which gradually exhausted the state with prolonged warfare – *ch'iung-ping tu-wu*.

If trade and diplomacy were politically unacceptable, and conquest was impossible, then perhaps, some literati argued, fixed and secure defensive frontiers could somehow be established militarily. One early and enduring proposal was for the settlement of troops along the borders where they would support themselves by growing their own food at so-called *t'un-t'ien* or military farms. First proposed by Ch'ao Ts'o (d. 155 B.C.) and Chao Ch'ung-kuo (137–152 B.C.) of the Han, this idea of substituting self-sustaining defensive power for offensive thrusts each of which required special mobilization, would prove to have a strong appeal for the rest of Chinese history (today we find an echo of it in the use of the People's Liberation Army to raise food) even though it never worked quite as well in practice as it did on paper.[127]

Associated with the idea of sending defensive troops went the delimitation of frontiers and the construction of defensive works. It should be noted, however, that the idea of clear boundaries is not, in the earliest period of history, a particularly strong one in the Chinese tradition. Early texts were rather vague about China's borders: they described not a single frontier, but rather a series of zones. Relations between the court at the center and the ever more distant peoples were governed, according to early theories, much as the relations between the Chou king and his various vassals was, by ritual, in a way that foreshadowed the later theory of tributary relations. Differences among the peoples were not of quality, but of degree, and the early texts, written before the nomads appeared, are full of descriptions of how a virtuous ruler could, by virtue and observance of ritual alone, bring the rude and uncultured peoples to submission.[128] Such frontiers as there were had been established by Heaven. But faced by nomads who refused to remain in the gloomy wastelands where nature had clearly intended to contain them, the Chinese had to begin to think about improving on the natural map. Thus wall-building was thought of, in the first instance, as a supplement to what nature had created.

Later writers would frequently quote Ts'ai Yung (133–192) who stated that

Heaven created the mountains and rivers, the Ch'in built long walls, and the Han established fortresses and walls. These all aim to divide the interior from that which is alien, and to distinguish those of different traditions.[129]

Such authors considered knowledge of natural boundaries, and the ability to take advantage of them, to be one of the basic components of sound military strategy. To make the point, they would repeatedly refer to the

Classic of Changes which stated; "The ruler holds strong points to defend his kingdom."[130] This, indeed, was how the authors of the *Shi chi* and *Han shu* seem to have thought of the fortifications built by Meng T'ien in the Ch'in. Instead of describing the kind of brute engineering that some have imagined to build a Great Wall, the *Shih chi* tells us he "Utilized the natural mountain barriers to establish the border defenses, scooping out the valleys and constructing ramparts [...] where they were needed."[131]

Wall-building was thought of as a way of providing boundaries where Heaven had neglected to make them clear. Because the difference between civilization and the barbarism was ultimately a moral one, boundary drawing and defense were impossible without morality as well. This point is made clear by the Ming commentator Ch'iu Chün (1420–95, *chin shih* degree [hereafter cs], 1454) in his great compendium on questions of government, the *Ta-hsüeh yen-i pu*. Ch'iu echoes the classical understanding of the frontier: mountains, rivers, passes and other natural boundaries have been created by Heaven. To supplement them by building walls is no fault according to Ch'iu, but it must be remembered that all such measures are futile if virtue does not rule government.[132] That, of course, was the lesson that later writers usually attached to the legend of the Ch'in wall.

Later commentators who advocated wall-building would often cite Nan Chung, as well as the Ch'in (though the emperor's bad reputation made his policy an unattractive example) and the Han. But for a thorough and complete exposition of the virtues of wall-building as a policy, they turned not to such examples, but rather to the Northern Wei dynasty, and minister Kao Lü's memorial "In favor of long walls."

The Han had collapsed into civil war in A.D. 220, and its rather feeble heir, the Western Chin, had expired in A.D. 311. By the end of the fourth century, however, a new power was being established in North China, that of the Hsien-pei. This people, whose language seems to have combined Turkic and Mongol elements, gradually became dominant in Mongolia from the Kansu corridor to the Liao river in the period following the end of the Han, and incorporated elements that had previously belonged to the Hsiung-nu federation. Repulsing their rivals, the Joujan and the Kao-chü, and moving south into northern China, they established, at the end of the fourth century, a partially sinicized monarchy, with its capital at P'ing-ch'eng (modern Ta-t'ung), which exercised power both over the southern steppe and much of the north China plain. The military power of this new Northern Wei (386–534) state was based on huge cavalry armies, many of which were based in six fortresses to the north along the steppe margin. Economically, however, it came to depend more and more on settled agriculture, both that carried out by its Han Chinese subjects, and by its former tribal adherents, who were forbidden nomadism, and forced to settle on land allocated to them.[133]

As a result the state was pulled in two directions, and the question arose whether it should remain basically steppe-oriented, or attempt to transform itself into a sinified state, on the Han model. By the late fifth century, the second approach had become dominant, and the Hsien-pei court came increasingly to face the same sorts of problems dealing with nomads that had plagued their sedentary Chinese predecessors. Along with those of the Han, the debates over policy that emerged in the late Northern Wei court later came to constitute an important part of the classical canon of precedent regarding frontier policy.

Earlier the Northern Wei had maintained its position in the north both by active military campaigning, and by the occupation of fixed positions. Campaigns into the steppe were mounted almost yearly during the reign of T'ai-wu (r. 424–52). A huge and successful expedition was undertaken against the Joujan to the north in 429, while to the west, the Hsiung-nu Hsia, whose capital was at T'ung-wan, were destroyed in 431. Meanwhile, defense lines are recorded as having been built in 423 and 446. Neglect of the steppe during the next two reigns, however, prepared the way for the active sinicization that followed. And this sinicization of the Northern Wei dynasty meant that the problems of the northern frontier came to be viewed increasingly from a Chinese, rather than a nomadic perspective.

Kao Lü was an important official of the Chinese-born Dowager Empress Feng and her step grandson, Hsiao-wen-ti (r. 466–99). Addressing this court, whose origins were nomadic, he contrasted the strengths and weaknesses of settled and steppe peoples in words that show not a trace of nomadic influence. The "northern barbarians" (*ti*) he stated were

fierce and simple-minded, like wild birds or beasts. Their strength is fighting in the open fields; their weakness is in attacking fortified places [*ch'eng*]. If we take advantage of the weakness of the northern barbarians, and thereby overcome their strength, then even if they are very numerous, they will not become a disaster for us, and even if they arrive, they will not be able to penetrate our territory.[134]

Kao Lü's explanation of how the tables might be turned on these stereotyped nomads drew in similarly stereotyped ways on purely Chinese approaches to border policy. The six garrisons (*liu chen*) of the Northern Wei caused a dispersal of military power. But in the histories, we learn how

In former times the Chou ordered Nan Chung to build a wall in the northern region; Chao Ling and Ch'in Shih built long walls; while Emperor Wu of the Han followed these precedents.[135]

And such a strategy appeared to be endorsed not only by historical precedent, but by philosophy as well. In the *Classic of Changes*, Kao notes, reference is made to how "the ruler holds strong points to defend his kingdom." Can this be a reference, he asks, "to the building of long walls?"[136]

The policy that Kao Lü outlines seems rather like that of Ch'in Shih-huang. First he urges a military expedition. Some sixty thousand men should be sent north to clear the nomads from the territory to be held, and he devotes considerable attention to the training, equipping, and command of this force. But the real point of his argument is to render any further such expeditions unnecessary, by

following precedent and constructing a long wall to the north of the six garrisons, in order to protect against the northern barbarians. Even though this will require a short term expenditure of labor, it will have permanent advantage. Once it is completed, its benefit will be felt for one hundred generations.[137]

Kao has a schedule for the campaign and for the wall construction:

In the seventh month, send out six divisions of soldiers, or sixty thousand men [...] to the northern garrisons. In the eighth month, [...] display our might north of the desert. If the barbarians descend, then we should engage them in a decisive battle. If they do not, then the army should be dispersed over the area, to build long walls. I calculate that the area of the six garrisons is no more than one thousand *li* [approximately 333 miles] from east to west, and if one soldier can build three paces of wall in one month, then three hundred men can build three *li* [about 1 mile], three thousand men can build thirty *li* [about 10 miles], and thirty thousand men can build three hundred *li* [about one hundred miles], so that a thousand *li* [about 333 miles] would take one hundred thousand men one month to complete. The grain for a month is not sufficient to amount to a lot. And because the men would understand long-term advantages of the wall, they would work without complaining.[138]

Kao Lü concludes his memorial by summarizing the "five advantages of long walls," a phrase which has informally become its title:

We calculate that building long walls has five advantages. First, it eliminates the problems of mobile defense. Second, it permits the northern tribes to nomadize [beyond the wall] and thus eliminates the disasters of raiding. Third, because it enables us to look for the enemy from the top of the wall, it means we no longer wait [to be attacked, not knowing where the enemy is]. Fourth, it removes anxiety about border defense, and the need to mount defense when it is not necessary. And fifth, it permits the easy transport of supplies, and therefore prevents insufficiency.[139]

Kao's recommendations were repeatedly cited by later writers, though apparently not acted on at the time. Striking about them is their failure to refer to the Ch'in wall as anything more than a precedent. The use of the

45

phrase *ch'ang-ch'eng* by Kao Lü further confirms that in this early period, it had not yet acquired its later meaning. And it is also interesting to imagine what kind of wall Kao is considering. It is one that can be built in a month. Probably the Ch'in wall was built rapidly in much the same way, and that accounts for the seemingly short time it took to build. But even if Kao's recommendations had been implemented, they probably would have worked no better than other earlier and later attempts somehow to solve the nomadic problem for once and all by conquest and defensive construction carried out in sequence – a policy that appealed to Chinese because it would allow them to disentangle their culture and politics from that of the steppe. The Northern Wei attempted to disentangle itself by moving its capital to Lo-yang, an action which greatly undermined the dynasty, and led to its collapse within a few decades.[140]

Although the end of the Northern Wei dynasty underlined the weaknesses of policies of sinicization within accompanied by wall-building and exclusion on the frontier, variations of that approach continued to be followed for the next two centuries by Chinese states unable or unwilling to deal with the nomads. We cannot be absolutely certain even of the broad outlines of the policies of the states that arose during this period, which lasted until the beginning of the T'ang. The written records are brief, while archaeological work is virtually nonexistent. Wall-building activity, however, is widely referred to. It is recorded that in 545 the Eastern Wei state (524–49) strengthened its defenses by building forts at strategic places.[141] The Northern Ch'i (550–74), the more sinicizing of two states that contested power in North China in the mid sixth century, seems to have adopted wall-building on a larger scale. In 552 that dynasty is recorded as having built 400 *li* (about 133 miles) of wall,[142] and 900 *li* (about 300 miles) more in 555, including some at Chü-yung-kuan, where the *Shui-ching chu*, a text of the 6th century A.D. mentions a gateway of stones and lookout towers.[143] Two years later the Northern Ch'i built a secondary wall inside of the main one.[144] By 556 it was calculated that the dynasty had built 3,000 *li* (about 1,000 miles) of wall, extending to the sea.[145] In 580, the Latter Chou (557–80) apparently repaired some of these fortifications.[146] And a similar policy was followed by the far more secure and powerful Sui dynasty (589–617). It built walls in 581,[147] 586,[148] 587,[149] and 588.[150] In 607–9 the Sui built a frontier barrier from near Yü-lin to near Hu-ho-hao-t'e.[151]

These frontier fortifications from China's middle period are very little studied. In accounts of the history of the Great Wall, however, they play an important part. Historians, for example, who recognize that the present, Ming-dynasty walls have no relation to the fortifications of the Ch'in, nevertheless often assert that those Ming walls were built on the foundations of Northern Ch'i and Sui dynasty walls, though without presenting any evidence for this claim. Recently however, some Chinese historians have begun to express doubt about this. So little is known about the fortifications in any case that nothing can be said for sure, but a stretch of what is identified as Northern Ch'i wall exists near Peking, and perhaps significantly, it is not associated with Ming walls. There are few references in modern literature to either Northern Ch'i or Sui walls, even though the historical record describes them as having been rather extensive. Indeed, one puzzling aspect of the archaeological work now being carried out in China is that nothing has been published about walls from these periods. Most of the works described are dated to the Han or earlier. Since most dating of these early walls is done by looking at their routes, which are in fact close to those of later walls, one wonders whether perhaps walls of the Northern Ch'i and Sui are being mistakenly attributed to earlier periods. If not, it would be interesting to know what has become of the apparently numerous later walls (some of which are shown in Map 3).[152]

The widespread use of frontier walls ended abruptly, however, with the victory of the T'ang dynasty (618–906). For reasons that are still not altogether clear, the T'ang was able to break the destructive stalemate between nomadic and settled polities which had led its immediate predecessor, the Sui, to carry out massive defensive work. With Turkish tribal auxiliaries, and light cavalry which displaced the heavily armoured mounted forces of the earlier period, the T'ang was able to take control of large sections of the steppe. Walls were no longer necessary: building them became, in retrospect, a sign of military weakness. T'ang T'ai-tsung (r. 626–49) for instance, remarked in appreciation of his general Li Chi (584–669) that while Emperor Yang of the Sui had needed to build long walls, he himself needed only to appoint Li Chi to Ping-chou, the strategic territory of the northwest, mostly in today's Shensi.[153] The T'ang was able to discard the tactic of wall-building because its fundamental strategic approach to the nomads differed from that of its predecessors, as the dynasty's early rulers clearly recognized. Modern scholars stress increasingly the many nomadic elements, including ancestry, in the T'ang ruling group. This cosmopolitanism clearly affected their foreign policy – even making it possible for early T'ang emperors to be accepted simultaneously as qaghan by the nomads. T'ang T'ai-tsung, for one, was proud of his achievement, and understood the reason for it. When he was asked by his ministers why his foreign policy surpassed that of all previous emperors, he replied that "since Antiquity all have honored the Hua ["Chinese"] and despised the I and the Ti ["non-Chinese," "barbarian"]; only I have loved them both as one, with the result that the nomad tribes have all held to me as to father and mother."[154] In the early T'ang, as well, the dynasty controlled grasslands in the northwest upon which a nomadic-style army could be based.

This situation changed when the dynasty lost its authority over the Turks, and its territory contracted, in the late seventh century. Eventually forts were built in the northwest to hold the frontier, as we will see in the next chapter. But these forts were not walls, and indeed so little seems to have remained either of actual walls or of traditions about walls in T'ang times that it is hard to specify what concept of frontier an educated Chinese of that dynasty might have had.

Certainly unambiguous references to walls as such are scarce in T'ang times. In the important T'ang geographical source, the *Yüan-ho chün-hsien chih* of Li Chi-fu (758–814) the phrase *ch'ang-ch'eng* occurs four times, but in reference to two Warring States walls and two of the Sui. The Ch'in wall is never mentioned.[155] Indeed, a T'ang commentator glosses a reference to *ch'ang-ch'eng* in the *History of the Latter Han Dynasty* by referring to the *locus classicus* of the Ch'in wall in the *Shih chi*. This would scarcely have been necessary for a commonplace reference.[156] Border service is a common theme in T'ang poetry, but a Great Wall figures in it only rarely, which suggests that people of the time had rather different stereotypes of the border than they do today.[157] Legends about the wall, such as that of Meng Chiang-nü, developed in the T'ang as well, as we shall see in the Conclusion. But of a real Great Wall the T'ang seems to have had as little notion as it had intention to build one.

If the T'ang scorned walls out of strength, the next major dynasty, the Sung (960–1279), built no walls out of weakness. The change from T'ang to Sung is one of the great shifts in Chinese history. The T'ang had a strong Central Asian flavor, and a ruling class of polo-playing aristocrats. But the Sung was administered by literary bureaucrats, at home in the refined landscape of southeast China's paddy land. This change in setting and mores was accompanied by a change in basic orientations. In the T'ang, legitimacy had still rested on loyalty to the ruling house, while by Sung times the idea of legitimacy had become more philosophical and abstract – enough so that it could serve as the basis for independent criticism of the actual ruler, a fact that had much to do with the way decisions about military policy would be made. In particular, it made it far more difficult for the Sung to deal pragmatically and tolerantly with the nomads than it had been for the T'ang. Confronted by first the Liao (947–1125) and then the Chin (1115–1234), stronger and better-organized adversaries in the steppe than any earlier Chinese dynasty had faced, the Sung lost their original foothold in the north (which had never included the area of the future Peking), and in 1134, pressed by the Chin, concluded a treaty ceding away roughly the territory north of the Huai river.

The reaction among many of the literati to this treaty was reminiscent of the bitterness of Chia I in the Han, and underlined how much basic assumptions about politics and culture had been altered since the T'ang. Most intellectuals were highly critical. The treaty's author, Ch'in Kuei (1090–1155, cs. 1115), was opposed by a faction that rejected compromise, whose hero was the military commander, Yüeh Fei (1103–41), who argued for resistance. Yüeh Fei was eventually executed, but as happened with some of the other opponents of compromise in Chinese history, he has been made into a hero of modern Chinese patriotism. To this day Ch'in Kuei is execrated as a traitor, while the heroism of Yüeh Fei, "loyal to the last" continues to be powerfully admired.[158] Yet, given what we know about the threat the Sung faced, Ch'in Kuei probably had little choice but to make peace. Even some Chinese scholars have recognized this. The Ch'ing intellectual Wang Fu-chih (1627–79) argued that by forcing Yüeh Fei to retreat from the north in 1140, Ch'in Kuei had actually saved him from a defeat, and Chao I (1727–1814) agreed.[159] A modern scholar argues that the "peace policy and the treaty which embodied it would seem to have been validated by the later history of the Southern Sung."[160]

While the Sung retreated south, to territory that was not easily conquered by nomads, the states that followed it in the north and occupied the transition zone between settled lands and the steppe proper, were faced themselves by the threat of nomads like themselves, but less sinicized, from further to the north. As a result, first the Liao (against the Chin) and then the Chin (against the Mongols), found themselves adopting wall-building as one strategy for dealing with the threat. The Sung did almost no wall-building.[161] But the Liao (947–1125) did quite a bit, mostly in central Manchuria, though compared to the work of its successors, it was limited.[162] The Chin kingdom (1115–34) built many walls. Some of their extensive work was begun before 1138; large-scale work was carried out in 1181; and additional construction was completed in 1198. Liao-Chin work is notable for a variety of technical improvements introduced into fortifications. Some Chin walls follow a pattern of outer moat, outer wall, inner moat, and main wall, with the inner moat ranging from ten to even sixty meters in width. Beacon towers, at irregular intervals, are associated with Chin walls, as too are semicircular platforms on the outside of the wall, called "horse faces," or *ma-mien* in Chinese. Battlements and parapets are also new features of Liao and Chin walls.[163] The longest Chin walls, known as *wai-pao* in Chinese, *öngü* in Mongolian, and *yoqurqa* in Turkish were in modern Inner and Outer Mongolia, far to the north of the present wall.[164]

49

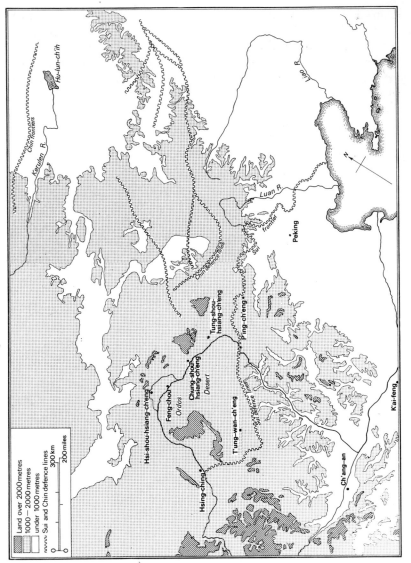

Map 3 Later pre-Ming fortifications

Less than a century later, the Chin, the Sung, and their western neighbor, the Ta Hsia, had all been swept away by the Mongol conquest, which brought China, traditionally set apart, into a world empire that stretched from Europe through Russia and the Middle East to the Pacific. In such a multinational polity, frontier walls lost any usefulness. It was not until the Mongol empire began to fragment, and its components to redifferentiate themselves, that wall-building was once again undertaken by Chinese.

PART II

The making of the of the Great Wall

Application of the general approach to wall-building already sketched out can cast considerable light on the process of defensive construction undertaken by the Ming dynasty (1368–1644), which created the system whose ruins today give us our common idea of the Great Wall of China. We have suggested that walls in Chinese history are above all the products of policy decisions; the study of their ruins, therefore, can be a kind of archaeology of foreign policy. Certainly the ruins of the border fortifications that remain from the Ming provide, when properly interpreted, a record, in earth and stone, of changes in that dynasty's military strength, strategic thinking, and even palace politics.

The Ming began in the fourteenth century with an open frontier, and ended, almost three hundred years later, having the most carefully closed border in pre-modern Chinese history. To understand how and why this transformation occurred will require considering all the factors already mentioned in the introductory chapters, and then one more: geography. We have said little so far about the particular physical features of the northern territories through which the various Chinese borders have passed. Yet larger questions of strategy often came to focus on rather specific questions regarding the precise course of boundaries. The history of other societies provides many examples of this. In Roman history, there was the question of where the eastern border in Europe should lie: whether on the Rhine, as Augustus found it, or roughly on the Elbe and the Danube, where he would have placed it had it not been for the loss of Varus and his three legions in A.D. 9.[165] And in modern France, as we shall mention again below, there was, between the two world wars, great controversy over the future of the Rhineland. The national security debate of the Ming in China, out of which emerged the decisions to build walls, also had such a geographic focus: namely, the question of the future of the Ordos, or territory of the great bend of the Yellow river in the northwest, which the dynasty repeatedly considered occupying, but never did.

The Ordos is an anomalous area. No clear physical boundary such as a mountain range marks the division in north China between the lands that

55

are just about hospitable to farming, and those that properly belong to the nomad.[166] But since settled agriculture depends for its existence upon a minimum amount of rainfall each year, on maps the 15″ isohyet, or equal-rainfall line, marks this limit, and in a rough way, border fortifications follow it. Because the Ordos lies outside this line, it might seem by rights to belong to the world of the nomads. But the loop of the Yellow river, which cuts it off from the steppe proper, also makes irrigation possible in certain places, and in these the Chinese have planted colonies since ancient times. Economically, such settlements have been barely self-supporting at best. But they have always had a compelling strategic rationale. As Ku Tsu-yü (1631–92) explained in his treatise on geography, the *Tu-shih fang-yü chi-yao*, the Ordos lies just to the north of the modern province of Shensi, and thus commands the valley of the Wei river to the south, the location of the early Chinese capitals such as Ch'ang-an; while the later imperial city of Peking lies not far to the east, and is also easily accessible to horsemen dwelling there. Unless the territory is held, the capitals become vulnerable.[167] Owen Lattimore makes much the same point. Normally he lays great stress on the distinct ecological bases of nomadic "barbarian" and settled "Chinese" societies, writing, for example, that the economic logic of Chinese history dictated an exclusion of the former, because generally "it was best to administer as 'Chinese' only territory in which it was possible to promote the increasingly intensive agriculture on which the new standard of empire was based," and that did not include the steppe.[168] But this was not true of the Yellow river loop. "The Ordos," he writes, "a reëntrant of the steppe – a wedge pointing southward into China – was an exception: the Chinese needed to take it over for strategic reasons."[169] Ming officials understood this point as well. The problem for them was how to act on it.

Like the Rhineland for France, the Ordos has repeatedly proved beyond the capacity of the Chinese to hold permanently; indeed it was brought firmly under the control of Peking only in the Ch'ing dynasty. Before that it was contested, and in the Ming, it lay outside of the state's borders. The question of whether it should be allowed to remain there, or should be conquered and "recovered," framed a political debate that lasted more than a century, and whose outcome led to the building of the first walls. That debate in turn drew on precedents that went back to before the Han. The chapters of Part II will treat that debate as the key to understanding Ming military policy, and therefore wall-building.

Broadly speaking, that Ming strategic policy passed through three phases. The first of these lasted, we will suggest, roughly from the founding in 1368 until a catastrophic defeat of a Ming expeditionary force by the Mongols at a place called T'u-mu in 1449. During this phase the northern frontier appears to have been open: the dynasty's security rested not on any tangible defense system, but rather on the military prestige the early rulers built up by active campaigning in the steppe. Ming military policies of this early period resembled, in their broad outlines, those of its Mongol predecessors.

But during the second phase, which we will suggest began after the T'u-mu defeat, and which lasted for most of the fifteenth century, the Ming lost the skill and the wherewithal to continue to project power into the steppe. At the same time, the Mongols, who had been greatly disrupted by Ming policies in the early phase, began to regroup and reorganize, and to pose a growing threat to the dynasty. This became particularly acute when they moved into the Ordos, in which neither Chinese nor nomads had previously established any sort of enduring presence. To the new threats of the late fifteenth century the court was able to adopt no consistent response: instead, it shifted intermittently from offensive to defensive approaches.

The third phase began after the defeat, in the late 1540s, of proposals that the security problem should be solved once and for all by means of a massive campaign to conquer the Ordos and re-establish a position of power in the steppe. Unfortunately, by this time the Ming no longer had an army that could carry out such a campaign, as was clearly demonstrated in 1550, when a Mongol raiding party reached the gates of Peking virtually unhindered. So instead of trying to fight the nomads on their own terms, as they had in the early years, the dynasty tried simply to exclude them by ever-more-ambitious wall-building.

Each of these periods has left remains of its characteristic defense system. In the first period the northern frontier was not clearly defined. The Ming placed garrisons both in the steppe itself and along the steppe margin, and began to fortify important passes. But these defenses were not continuous; rather they were dotted through the whole steppe transition zone, the area from which Ming armies set out into the steppe itself.

After the Ming position in the steppe border was lost at the beginning of the second period, however, the dynasty began to build walls, initially of earth, and greatly to increase defensive deployments. The first major wall was built south of the Ordos desert in 1474 in an attempt to contain the threatening Mongol presence in the Ordos itself, while later in the period work was begun on a defense line from the eastern edge of the Ordos to the capital region.

In the third period, wall-building changed in character. Stone began to be used in addition to earth, and from simple ramparts, walls at key places were transformed into elaborate structures having watch-towers and crenellations. This climax of wall-building, which occurred in the late sixteenth century, produced the most impressive stretches of the "Great Wall" we know today.

Behind this move toward wall-building lay deep shifts in military, institutional, and political factors. The early Ming rulers and their commanders had both the knowledge and the forces to campaign in the steppe: indeed, they came close to capturing the Mongol capital at Karakorum. But by the second quarter of the fifteenth century Ming military capacity was declining. Toward the end of the fourteenth century the founding emperor had purged and killed his most skilful generals, and in the fifteenth century the strength of the Ming army declined, as it became apparent that the institutions the founder had created to supply an effective steppe fighting force were not doing their job. At the same time the political balance at court between emperor and officials was also changing. From being a matter the emperor alone decided, military policy became a subject for bureaucratic controversy, and an arena for competition among the politically ambitious – whether generals, eunuchs, or scholar-officials. Unlike the strong rulers of the early period, the later Ming emperors proved indecisive, and courtiers sought their favor by advancing, among other things, competing strategies for dealing with the nomadic threat.

Indeed, by the mid and late Ming, domestic political interests were taking control of the debates over what basic approach to adopt toward the nomads. The terms of the debate shifted as well, as it began to involve not only military questions, but also sensitive and fundamental questions of Ming, and Chinese, national and cultural definition. As the Ming differentiated itself culturally from the Yüan, it became more difficult for it to follow Yüan-style policies.

The Yüan dynasty had demonstrated that successful management of the steppe was more than a matter of occasional military intervention there. To pacify the frontier, the Yüan had channeled Chinese resources to the north, establishing order "in the steppes of Mongolia by imposing upon it a non-indigenous apparatus of control which was largely supported, directed, and supplied from outside."[170] The Ming might have been able to do the same, by maintaining diplomatic ties with the nomads, trading and providing subsidies, occasionally sending a military force out to help an ally, or a Chinese princess to wed a steppe noble. But most educated Chinese of the Ming thought of the steppe peoples who had been kin to the Mongols as "barbarians," and strong currents of thought opposed every sort of tie with them. Distinguishing between the "civilized" and the "barbarian," the *hua* and the *i*, was after all one of the central themes of the system of thought that, by defining a common culture, gave a degree of coherence to the vast lands of China. Anything that muddled the distinction might threaten that unity, and would be looked on most unfavorably by most of the educated class, even if it made good sense as security policy.

Of course a strong emperor would have been able to enforce a Yüan-style policy, but at a court over which a weak emperor presided, principled opposition to dealing with the nomads was bound to be strong, and politically influential. At the Ming court, from the mid-fifteenth to the late sixteenth century, such opposition successfully vetoed successive attempts to implement a steppe policy more like the Yüan's. Nomadic attempts to trade or establish diplomatic ties were rejected, which meant that the steppe peoples had no choice but to raid China to obtain the goods they needed. Warfare worsened, and brought with it an increasing need for walls.

The change in policy toward the steppe reflected the way the character of the Ming dynasty changed as it grew older. The Mongol style of rule evident in its early years was supplanted by ways that had more clearly Chinese origins. The early Ming rulers had a style sometimes more reminiscent of the nomadic khans who had been their immediate predecessors than of more distant and culturally Chinese figures such as the late Sung rulers. But by the sixteenth century they were succeeded by emperors reared in the inner palace who knew nothing of the steppe or warfare. And these changes brought about changes in the way military options were defined and understood, and in the ways choices among them were made.

Cultural change shifted the nature of political competition at the Ming court, and this shift in turn was the ultimate cause of the changes in strategy that by mid-Ming made the Mongol threat unmanageable, and led to adoption of the costly and futile expedient of wall-building. To a very large degree, then, the origins of the "Great Wall of China" of the Ming are found not so much in ecology, or even in strategy, as in politics. Part II will tell a largely political story to make sense of them.

4

Geography and strategy:
the importance of the Ordos

Much of our political story will focus on the Ordos, and perhaps the best way to understand the importance of this territory to China is through the analogy we have already mentioned to the importance of the Rhine and the Rhineland for France. Potentially the Rhine forms a natural and militarily advantageous eastern frontier for France in much the same way that the great loop of the Yellow River defines a possible and highly logical northwestern boundary for China. Each of the rivers forms a natural barrier, while the territories that they enclose are salients into the lands of the potential enemy. Both of these territories also have economic significance: the steppe-lands of the Ordos could provide an economic base for nomadic-style warfare in a way China proper could not, while the Saar with its industry could supply modern mechanized combat. So it made sense for the Chinese to try to incorporate the Ordos, as it did for the French to try to draw their frontier on the Rhine.

Furthermore, the Ordos played a very special strategic role in the steppe world. It was one of the handful of places dotted through that arid realm where lakes or rivers provided a water supply which made farming possible. For nomads contending for power in Inner Asia, control of such virtual oases could be of critical importance, utterly out of proportion to their size. Several such places have shown their importance repeatedly in Eurasian history: in addition to the Ordos, they include the Liao river valley, the Orkhon river valley, and the Tarim basin. Any dynasty or nomadic state evaluating the strategic situation in the northern region would consider these territories first, for with the possibility they offered of settling self-supporting garrisons, carrying out limited manufacturing, raising grain, etc. they could help assure that command of resources which was the surest key to military and political control of the steppe,

As map 1 illustrates, attacks by nomads based in these river valleys would be further channeled geographically, by mountains and deserts, on to three main invasion routes: from the west past the Yü-men and Chia-yü passes, from the north through Chang-chia-k'ou and Chü-yung-kuan, and from the east past Shan-hai-kuan. Control of these river valley territories was therefore crucial to strategic control of the frontiers.

In fact, one can analyze the whole pattern of steppe warfare with reference to such places. Three of them, the Tarim, the Orkhon, and the Ordos, form the corners of a critical triangle. When nomads have waged war against one another in the steppes north of China, they have repeatedly sought to occupy these base areas and to deny them to their adversaries. For without access to at least one of these areas, from which to obtain grain, a nomadic horde would grow hungry and weak, while without metal for weapons, also a product of such settled areas, it would become militarily vulnerable. Control of such regions is the basis for control of the steppe itself. According to Professor Larry Moses, no power which did not hold at least two of them has ever managed to achieve hegemony in the steppe.[171]

For China, not primarily a steppe power, the Ordos has always been the most important of these three territories, and one to which a substantial amount of attention has been devoted in traditional Chinese writings.[172] This is because the Ordos is not only important to potential Chinese influence in the steppe. It is also of potential importance to the security of China proper. Since earliest times, Chinese strategists have been aware of the territory's commanding position in relation to the Chinese heartland. And history shows that Chinese states which have failed to control it have inevitably found themselves on the defensive in relation to the steppe.

This was what happened to the Ming. When the Mongols withdrew in the fourteenth century, the new dynasty did not occupy the territory, but rather left it vacant. In the fifteenth century, however, the Mongols began to move back into the Ordos, creating a threat on the border. After about 1450, this problem with the Ordos became Ming China's most basic security issue, and the one that defined the debate about wall-building.

Geographically, the Ordos is defined by a loop of the Yellow River. The river originates in southeastern Ch'ing-hai, flows east and northeast through Kansu, past Lan-chou, where it becomes navigable, and then turns north. Beyond Ning-hsia (called Yin-ch'üan today) it runs parallel to, and within, the line of the Ho-lan mountain range, but about 140 miles north it turns east at the barrier of the Yin-shan mountains. In this northernmost part of the loop, south of the mountain barrier and north of the desert, it meanders through a plain, creating a potential agricultural region in the midst of what would otherwise be desert. This is the *Ho-t'ao* area, where the river has changed its course repeatedly over the years, entering its present bed in the early Ch'ing.[173] Fertile and rich, this plain is called the one blessing of the Yellow River, source of a thousand sorrows.

Beyond it to the east, the river begins to turn south, passing the important city of Hu-ho-hao-t'e, founded by the Mongols during the Ming, and reaching T'ung-kuan, in Shensi province, where it turns eastward toward the sea.

Enclosed within this Yellow River loop is the Ordos desert, today called the *Mao-wu-su,* an expanse of some fifty thousand square miles, nearly the size of New England. Bounded to the north and west by mountains and river, to the east by river alone, and to the south by high bluffs that mark the beginning of the loess country, it is a compact and easily defended territory hospitable only to nomads. Today these lands are divided between the Inner Mongolian Autonomous Region and the Ning-hsia Hui Autonomous Region. Under the Republic the Ho-t'ao and Pao-t'ou plains were included in Sui-yüan province, and the Ning-hsia area in Ning-hsia province.

Ecologically, the territory is mixed. Parts are pure desert. Just how barren these are comes through clearly in some of our best descriptions, those provided by early-twentieth-century explorers and geographers, such as Ferdinand von Richthofen, William W. Rockhill, and George B. Cressey.[174] According to Cressey:

The greater part of the Ordos is an arid desolate plain, parched by a blazing sun in summer and swept by icy blasts in winter. Shifting sands held here and there by low scrub or wiry grass makes the region an inhospitable waste where nature offers but little to man, and yields that little grudgingly.[175]

But other parts of the Ordos are ideal for nomads, with good grazing land, where:

natural vegetation is comparatively more luxurious, so that it nearly carpets the ground. Short grasses afford some feed for animals and make this area better for nomad and farmer. The western limit of this semi-humid area is along a line roughly connecting Pao-t'ou and Yü-lin.[176]

Furthermore, sedentary Chinese could settle in those places where river water made irrigation possible. Farming could be carried on in such areas, and projects to develop irrigation go back to Han times. In Ninghsia, for example, the southwestern corner, there were already four major canal systems by the start of the Ming. By the end of the Ming two more canals had been added, and some 574,600 *mou* (80,444 acres) of farmland were watered by 1,107 *li* (about 369 miles) of canals. The Ch'ing would add four more. The *Ho-t'ao* area in the north was only rarely held by the Chinese, however, and after the Han the development of irrigation there proceeded more slowly. But in the later Ch'ing dynasty, as immigration from the

63

overpopulated provinces of China proper began to pick up, much work was done. An array of north–south canals, still in use, transformed the area.[177]

In Ming times, climate in the northwest was also probably more favorable than it is today. The areas just south of the Ordos desert, where walls were eventually built, were moister and they could support some agriculture. Owen Lattimore argues that the climate has changed over the last several hundred years, and that larger populations lived in the region in the past than do today, and recent work on the history of climate has confirmed this.[178] This fact makes sense of names, such as Yü-lin, which means "elm-wood," for a place that in Ch'ing times appears to have been forested, although today it is menaced by encroaching sand-dunes.

When debate about the Ordos erupted in the Ming dynasty, scholars turned immediately to precedents. These were numerous, because Chinese involvement in the area had a long history. This showed both how important the territory could be to China, and also how difficult it was for China to hold it. The Hsien-yün nomads mentioned in Chapter 2 probably came from the Ordos (or *Shuo-fang*), and the expedition of General Nan Chung may have gone there. The importance of the territory was beginning to be understood even before the unification of China. In the Warring States period, much of the area had formed part of the kingdom of Chao. The campaigns of King Wu-ling, whom we have already met as a champion of nomadic warfare, had as one of their purposes the exploitation of the Ordos area as a base against the rival state of Ch'in centered in the Wei valley. Driving nomads from the territory, the king pushed a corridor along the Yin-shan and the Ordos loop, consolidating Yün-chung and Chiu-yüan by 314 B.C., and building a wall west as far as Kao-ch'üeh before 298 B.C.[179] At the end of the third century Ch'in Shih-huang conquered, as we have seen, both Chao and the territory of the river loop, though after his death the Hsiung-nu reoccupied their former territory.[180] Both the Ch'in and Han capitals lay south of the Ordos (as that of the Ming did not) and were thus particularly vulnerable.

In 177 B.C., in the Han dynasty, we find the Hsiung-nu settled in the Ordos, and in the winter of 167/6 B.C. they launched a great raid from that base, which threatened Ch'ang-an, the Former Han capital.[181] Not surprisingly, the Ordos was one of the first objectives when Wu-ti (r. 140–87 B.C.) reversed the policy for *ho-ch'in*. A series of military campaigns was launched that pushed the Han frontiers beyond the Yellow River loop, as certain officials had been advocating in the first of the Ordos recovery debates that continued to the Ming.

One of these officials had been Chu-fu Yen (d. 126 B.C.), a poor scholar who, under the patronage of general Wei Ch'ing, became influential at the court of Wu-ti. He

[. . .] spoke strongly in favor of occupying the region of [Shuo-fang] in the north. It was a very fertile area, bounded by the Yellow River on the north, he argued, and had been fortified by Meng T'ien during the Ch'in and used as a base for driving out the Hsiung-nu. If it were occupied once more, it would help to reduce the transportation of supplies and soldiers from the interior of the empire, broaden the territory of China, and serve as a foundation for wiping out the barbarians.

This proposal was not immediately accepted. Chu-fu Yen's rival at court, Kung-sun Hung argued that the Ch'in example showed why the Han should not adopt the same policy. History showed that there were huge costs and risks associated with the seemingly attractive strategic goal:

[. . .] Although the Ch'in constantly kept a force of three hundred thousand men in the area to fortify the northern border along the Yellow River, they were never able to accomplish anything, and finally had to abandon the project.

Indeed, all of Wu-ti's high ministers opposed the proposal.[182] Even Chu-fu Yen himself had initially opposed the idea of such a campaign; his adoption of the policy was probably motivated by political opportunism. But the Han did succeed in establishing a base in the northwest, some seven years after Chu-fu Yen's death. In 119 B.C. his erstwhile patron, Wei Ch'ing, led the campaign that occupied it again.

Once secured, the Ordos could become a Chinese base in a way that the more distant nomadic bases of the Tarim and Orkhon never could. Thus, having stirred up hostilities with the Hsiung-nu by attempting unilateral changes in their diplomatic status, Wang Mang (r. A.D. 9–23) began preparations in A.D. 10–11, for a 300,000 man punitive expedition against the Hsiung-nu. It was to be launched from the Ordos, though it never set out, and was strongly opposed by some at court, among them Wang's general, Yen Yu.[183] And the Ordos was important too in the contention for power that followed the death of Wang Mang. Its location gave great power to the local authorities who emerged in the region: Wei Ao in eastern Kansu, Li Hsing and Sui Yü at Wu-yüan, and T'ien Li at Shuo-fang. They came to be aligned with Lu Fang, the Hsiung-nu backed candidate for the throne, whose capital was at Chiu-yüan, a little to the east of present-day Wu-yüan, in *Ho-t'ao*. This location was difficult to attack from China proper, and the Latter Han emperor, Kuang-wu (r. 25–56), attempted simply to contain him, eventually defeating him not on the battlefield, but rather when his lieutenant Sui Yü defected.[184]

In the mid first century A.D., however, the Latter Han gradually withdrew their garrisons from the northwest, and nomads were once again able to reoccupy the territory.[185] In the fifth century the territory was the base of the Hsiung-nu Hsia kingdom (A.D. 407–31), composed of nomads who rejected the sinifying policies of the Northern Wei. This nomad state was ruled by Ho-lien Po-po, a military man who had been made commander for pacifying the north and garrisoning Shuo-fang by Yao Hsing of the later Ch'in (A.D. 384–97). He established a capital which was called T'ung-wan, and his official Ch'ih-kan A-li built a wall around it. The ruins of this city may still be seen at Pai-ch'eng, on the north bank of the Hung-liu river, just south of the Ordos desert margin in Shensi. A poem celebrated its strategic location, "backing on a famous mountain/fronting on a mighty torrent."[186] At the time the site was apparently an open, grassy steppe, ideal for the center of power of a nomad empire. However today its ruins are "surrounded by a waste of sand."[187] This state was absorbed by the Northern Wei in A.D. 431.

After the split of the Northern Wei, the Ordos passed to the Northern Chou, and then the Sui, who created a unified Chinese empire in A.D. 589. But the Turks, whose power was growing, soon occupied the Ordos, and the Sui, unable to resist, resorted to building fortified lines along the southern edge, where the Ming would do the same almost nine hundred years later.[188]

The expansive T'ang dynasty (619–906), swept forward by its new style light cavalry, planted a strong presence in the Ordos. Their garrison at Feng-chou, near modern Lang-shan, commanded the north–south route over the Yin-shan mountains north of the Yellow River loop, as well as the fertile pastures that lay between the river loop and the mountains. When the garrison came under attack in 682–3, the court was not sure how to react. The T'ang presence in the area was designed more for administering groups of nomads who had adhered to the T'ang than for fighting, so when the court heard that hostile nomads had surrounded Feng-chou, they decided to abandon it. The commander, T'ang Hsiu-ching, however, objected to this policy, adducing historical precedents and thus initiating a debate over policy, which foreshadowed the Ming debate. But at the time there was little that the T'ang could do. The reign of the Empress Wu (A.D. 684–704) found the court on the strategic defensive, withdrawing exposed positions and seeking to strengthen the smaller perimeter that remained. When in 706 T'ang forces were defeated at Ming-sha (near Ning-hsia), the T'ang strategic position in the northwest seemed about to collapse.

But the territory of Feng-chou was successfully recovered in 708 by General Chang Jen-yüan (d. 714), and three forts, the *san shou-hsiang-ch'eng*, were established: one about 81 *li* (approximately 27 miles) north of Feng-chou, one about 10 *li* (about 3 miles) northwest of Sheng-chou (on the north bank of the modern Min-sheng canal), and the third in between. All were locations of great strategic importance, commanding the Yin-shan, the river loop, the fertile pastures, and the passes, and their consolidation gave the T'ang a great strategic advantage. As the history remarked, "from this time forth, the Turks were unable to cross the mountains to nomadize, and Shuo-fang was no longer troubled by bandit raids."[189]

From A.D. 982 to 1227 the Ordos was part of the Tangut Ta Hsia kingdom, a part-settled, part-nomadic state that successfully resisted repeated Chinese attacks, thus demonstrating the potential economic strength and cohesiveness of the area. The author of the official history of that kingdom's eastern neighbor, the Chin, notes that:

[The land of the Ta Hsia] was suitable for the three plantings; excellent grass and water made fine pasture for livestock. Precisely for this reason, Liang-chou was the best [place] in the realm for rearing livestock. The earth is firm and fertile, the water clear and cold, the environment vast and desolate, the people's ways [are] fiercely stubborn, reverent of valor, emphatic in honoring agreements, and valiant in battle. Since Han and T'ang times water conservancy has made possible the accumulation of grain to feed border troops ... so although their territory was small, they were able to achieve prosperity and strength by virtue of the character of the land.

Likewise the historian of the Sung, whose domain lay to the southeast wrote:

The area of the Hsia extended over 20,000 *li* [6,666 miles] [...] the land was fertile for the planting of the five grains and especially suited to rice and wheat. In the Kan[-chou] and Liang[-chou] area the rivers were used for irrigation; in the area of Hsing-chou and Ling-chou they had the old canals of T'ang-lai and Han-yüan, all drawing [water] from the Yellow River. Therefore, with the benefits of irrigation there was no worry about drought or flood during the year.[190]

With such economic advantages, the Ta Hsia could support a strong army, and though threatened by both the Liao and the Sung, it resisted all attackers until the Yüan. Chinggis succeeded in destroying it only in 1227, and so devastated the area that it never supported an independent state again. In the Ming it became an unconquered base for nomads; and in the Ch'ing (which did exercise official control over it), a refuge for Muslim rebels. Nor had it lost its strategic significance even in the mid twentieth century: for about a decade after 1935 it was part of the Chinese Communists' Shen–Kan–Ning base area.[191]

The pre-Ming portion of this history was well known to scholars in the fifteenth and sixteenth centuries, when debate about that dynasty's policy toward the Ordos really got underway. Examples from Nan Chung to

T'ang Hsiu-ching were adduced to demonstrate the merit of Ordos recovery proposals. But ironically, the period whose policy was most relevant to Ming concerns was scarcely discussed at all. This was the Yüan. During the century before the Ming founding, a Mongol dynasty with its capital at Peking had faced a strategic situation not unlike that which later confronted the Ming. Like the Ming, the Yüan found it easier to control the farmlands of China than the steppes of the north. Like the Ming as well, it faced disagreement about policy toward the north. But unlike the Ming, the Yüan ultimately succeeded in using the resources of China to pacify Mongolia, and thus to cement together a realm that encompassed both.

It may seem surprising that the Yüan should have faced a threat from steppe nomads. It might be thought that, as an Inner Asian dynasty, the Yüan would have had little difficulty in dealing with the steppe. But in fact, the Yüan faced a series of challenges from rebellious Mongols. Their success in putting down those threats, using essentially the same resources that would be available to the Ming, is instructive.

The nomadic threat to the Yüan came first from dissident Mongols such as Arigh Böke and Khaidu who refused to recognize Khubilai's succession as Great Khan and who disapproved of his policies. Later it came from those who disapproved in general of the increasingly Chinese character of the Yüan court, Haishan and Khoshila, for instance. The Yüan dealt with these challenges by employing a sophisticated combination of military and economic sanctions, which displayed a real understanding of the strategic geography of the steppe and the uses of Chinese resources.

The steppe-based challenge to Khubilai arose upon the death of the Great Khan Möngke in 1258, at a time when Mongol armies were still conquering southern China. The Great Khan's younger brother, Arigh Böke, who controlled Karakorum and the Mongolian heartland, convened a council of princes, or *khuraltai*, and was elected his successor. Khubilai, however, who was supervising the campaign in China, convened a *khuraltai* of his own at the city of Shang-tu, which he had just founded as the northern capital of the Yüan state, outside the Chü-yung-kuan pass. This assembly named Khubilai as Great Khan. The struggle between the two claimants "involved basically a fight for the control of the sedentary production regions, and showed beyond a shadow of a doubt that neither contestant could support himself and his military forces solely on the resources of the steppes."[192]

The strategy Khubilai adopted to meet this threat manifested an understanding of the steppe triangle mentioned above. He defeated Arigh Böke's forces in the area of the former Ta Hsia kingdom, that is to say the Ordos, and closed off as well the Uighur capital of Beshbaliq to the west, near modern Urumchi and vital to control of the Tarim basin. These two areas were sources of sedentary goods for the steppe, and with the flow of supplies to Arigh Böke's capital at Karakorum cut off, Khubilai's rival had little choice but to fall back to the distant Yenisei in Siberia as an economic base.

In the meantime, Khubilai mobilized the resources he was denying to his rival. He assembled horses and troops at Shang-tu. 100,000 *tan* (about 6,650 tons) of grain was collected from the irrigated area around Ning-hsia, and shipped northeastward along the Yellow river to Khubilai's troops on the steppe margin by means of specially built boats. In 1261 Arigh Böke and his forces once again attempted to seize north China, campaigning 1,300 miles from their base. Defeated at the battle of Simultu in November of 1261, Arigh Böke turned to the western Tarim basin, but it was too far from China proper, and too poor, to serve as a base, and in 1264 he surrendered. With this, Khubilai's Yüan state obtained control of Karakorum, and of the economic region surrounding it.[193]

The war with Arigh Böke made abundantly clear the great strategic significance of the steppe border zone, and particularly the Ordos. In its wake Khubilai moved to develop the resources there. As we have mentioned, the Ta Hsia had been utterly devastated by Khubilai's grandfather, Chinggis, and what had been the Tangut capital Chung-hsing was renamed Ning-hsia, "pacification of Hsia."[194] But faced with the need for an economic base in the steppe margin, Khubilai now sought to undo the damage his grandfather had done.

The city of Ning-hsia had possessed an extensive system of irrigation canals since Han times, and in 1264 Khubilai sent Chinese engineers to survey them. Work was begun on restoration of the more than 800-mile-long system which, it was estimated, could irrigate some 90,000 *ch'ing*, or about 2,246 square miles, of farmland. Mongol princes were enfeoffed in the region; and an attempt was made to restore the population. Some 40,000 to 50,000 Tangut households were rounded up and resettled, the government providing them with oxen and tools. Local Mongols and Uighurs were set to work farming, and Chinese peasants were also sent in. To facilitate grain transport along the river toward the east, a series of ten river relay stations, called *shui-chan*, was established, leading to Tung-sheng, a garrison on the steppe margin just to the east of the Yellow River loop.[195]

Before long Khubilai faced a second threat from the steppe. In 1268 or 1269, Mongols unhappy with Khubilai's policies met at the Talas river, and formed a confederation that recognized Khaidu, grandson of Ögödei, as Great Khan. Khubilai again prosecuted a campaign which attempted to use economic means to succeed: blockade of the adversary, and good supplies for one's own forces. But it was a long and difficult struggle. A major and costly thrust westward, which involved placing garrisons beyond the Kansu corridor, and in modern Sinkiang, roughly Han Wu-ti's strategy, proved less effective than had been anticipated, and in 1288 the Yüan withdrew from Central Asia. Attention was then turned to Mongolia, which shared a long border with China, and was thus easier to supply and to control. Khubilai developed a series of garrisons along the steppe frontier, extending from Etsina in the far west, to Ying-ch'ang in the east. By making use of this line of strategic positions, the Great Khan was able to bring the wealth of China to bear on the steppe. This factor, and the Yüan's ability to win allies, finally tipped the scales.[196] The war ended only in 1303, two years after Khaidu's death, and almost nine years after Khubilai's.

The war had shown that the Yüan dynasty in China commanded sufficient resources to manage and control Mongolia. The price, however was the shifting of resources from China proper to the steppe, as Professor Dardess has shown.[197] Under Yüan auspices, administration like that used in China proper was gradually extended to Mongolia itself, until in 1307 it was incorporated into the Yüan empire as a province.[198] Briefer struggles, but following similar patterns, took place in subsequent reigns: the wars with Haishan, Khoshila, and with the secessionists of 1328.[199]

The Yüan example demonstrated how border problems might have been settled by the Ming. But it proved extremely difficult for the Ming to follow. The Yüan had opted for a mixture of warfare, diplomatic maneuvering, and economic suasion, applied with great care, to deal with its adversaries. The Ming, however, were less good at coordinating policy, and were reluctant to subsidize the steppe as the Yüan had. Furthermore, in the Ming the whole question of border policy became politicized. Indeed, the "Ordos recovery" debate came to resemble nothing so much as the debate in France after the First World War, when permanent occupation of the Rhineland appeared possible, and certain figures, notably Maréchal Foch, argued in its favor. But like the French, the Chinese eventually recognized that conquering and holding the territory was simply too risky and expensive to be sound policy, and abandoned the idea of doing so. That, however, meant giving up a natural frontier.

Where states lack natural frontiers, they have often attempted to create artificial ones. After the loss of Varus's legions, the Romans settled for the original Rhine frontier, but they began to strengthen it by constructing the so-called *limes*, a system of roads, forts, and barriers.[200] The French, of course, similarly left the Rhineland, and constructed the Maginot Line to create a barrier where nature had neglected to place one – what at least one author has called "The Great Wall of France."[201] And the Chinese of the Ming rejected proposals to mount an expedition into the Ordos, and instead fortified the frontier thus left strategically vulnerable. In all three cases, the building of the fortifications themselves was only the last stage in a complex process.

This process involved political and diplomatic, as well as technical, issues. For both post World War I France and Ming China had the possibility of making a compromise peace and thus obviating the need for vast defenses. France could have revised the Versailles settlement, and Ming China could have opened trade and diplomatic relations with the Mongols. Neither solution would have been complete, of course, but both would have reduced the burden ultimately placed on the military. The reasons that neither took up such alternatives are murky, and they include both genuine fears about security and political calculations about the unpopularity of appeasement. In the French case, it was largely the imperatives of the political process which ruled out compromise peace and produced the decisions in favor of defensive policy.[202] A basic argument of the next few chapters is that this was true of the Ming case as well.

5

Security without walls: early Ming strategy and its collapse

The basic divisions that would create the sixteenth-century debates in the Ming were present in latent form from the moment that the Ming dynasty came to power in 1368. Although the later debate would focus on the issue of the Ordos, ultimately it was about a far larger issue to which early Ming rulers had provided no clear answer. This was the question of what the new dynasty's character was to be. Was the Ming to be essentially a Chinese version of the Yüan, or was it to be something new?

Territorially, it would have been natural for the new regime to have seen itself as heir to the Yüan, whose realm had extended from the deep south of China to the Mongolian steppe, and beyond Karakorum, some four hundred miles north of Peking. But politically and culturally, it was harder for the Ming to inherit the Yüan mantle. The Yüan had been a nomadic empire: would an ethnically Chinese government be capable of reconstructing very much of it? History provided little guidance. Not since the T'ang had a Chinese dynasty controlled both the south and Peking – but the T'ang had been a rather unusual blend of Inner Asian and Han Chinese elements, and highly cosmopolitan and flexible in its policies. "Chineseness," at least as we recognize it today, is characteristic not so much of the T'ang as of its successor the Sung – a dynasty which had been culturally brilliant but which proved a poor empire builder. The Sung eventually lost even the portion of the north it controlled initially, and reached its highest cultural flowering after its court had fled from the Inner Asian threat and taken shelter at Hangchow, in the deep south. The Chinese past provided no single political and cultural blueprint appropriate for the Ming. It would have to find for itself some balance between the cosmopolitanism of the T'ang and the inward-looking Chinese culturalism of the Sung, and deciding where to draw a northern border would involve making some fundamental decisions about that balance.

As we have mentioned, however, the very existence of this issue has usually been missed, because most commentators believe that an already-extant Great Wall had defined China for the Ming. Thus one relates how by 1368, Chu Yüan-chang (Emperor Hung-wu, founder of the Ming, r.

1368–98) "had grown strong enough to expel the Mongols from the lands south of the Great Wall," while another, speaking of the situation later on, notes that "Since the last decades of the fourteenth century the Chinese had been busy rebuilding the Great Wall in the form that we know today."[203]

But in 1368 no wall marked what was not yet a border. Nor had the new dynasty decided what its final character would be. From the start it blended steppe and Chinese elements. The structure of government followed the Mongol blueprint in many respects. But culture was a different matter. Though Mongol influences were abundantly evident early in the dynasty, the Chinese culture of the south consolidated itself, grew, and later penetrated much of the society. This process eventually created what today we think of as the "traditional Chinese state," an entity which was, as Joseph Fletcher has pointed out for the Ming, "sinicizing in appearances," while it in fact perpetuated "the substance of the later Chinese empire as [...] found [...] under the Mongols."[204] But it also created a basic conflict that is an important theme of early Ming history: the struggle between what Professor Dreyer calls an intense "sense of continuity with the departed Yüan regime" and a powerful feeling of Chineseness, which he calls "Confucianism."[205] As the Ming dynasty developed, the Chinese culture that had originated in the south gradually came to dominate the new state; concurrently with this process, politics changed as well. As the Yüan receded, the Ming court became less like that of a Mongol khan, and more like that of the faction-ridden Southern Sung. Policy toward the steppe consequently grew less and less effective.

Ming security under the founding emperor

These problems were concealed in the early Ming by what appeared to be the new dynasty's overwhelming military strength. Its founder was a remarkable peasant from Anhwei province who had spent some time as a Buddhist monk, and perhaps as a Yüan soldier, before casting his lot with one of the rebel groups that arose in central China in the mid fourteenth century. The one he chose called for the overthrow of the Yüan and a restoration of the Sung dynasty. Under his leadership it defeated its Chinese rivals, and eventually the Mongols as well. In 1368, as the Hung-wu emperor, this peasant began to rule over the new Ming empire, which included Peking and the north of China proper, from his capital at Nanking, on the Yangtze.

The Hung-wu emperor's base had been in the south, and extending control from the Yangtze valley to the north had not been easy. The emperor's caution had been evident in the way the way he planned his campaign against Peking. Unwilling to risk the kind of decisive defeat that the Mongol armies in the north were still quite capable of inflicting, he avoided a direct march on their capital, and instead sent columns northward on four different routes. His prudence, however, had serious strategic consequences. Instead of destroying the Mongol court, he permitted not only the Yüan emperor, Toghon Temür (r. 1332–70), but also the primary Yüan army, which was led by a Mongolicized Chinese, Kökö Temür, to escape into the steppe. There the Yüan continued to pose a threat. Even after Toghon Temür's death at Ying-ch'ang in 1370, the legitimate Mongol line was continued by his sons Ayushiridara (r. 1370–8) and Toghus Temür (r. 1378–88/89).[206]

Although thousands of Mongols had submitted to the Ming and been incorporated into the new system, the Hung-wu emperor was aware of the threat that the undefeated Mongols in the steppe could pose, and continued to pursue them. His campaigns struck at the traditional Mongol capital Karakorum (or more properly Khara Khorum, though we will use the common Western spelling), a fact which suggests that he may have hoped to take that city, win submission from the remaining nomads, and thereafter to govern the Mongol steppe as part of his empire, just as his Yüan predecessors had. A two-pronged attack in 1370 was highly successful: Li Wen-chung occupied Ying-ch'ang, the settlement on the lake called Dalai Nor (Hu-lun-hu, south of Man-chou-li in modern Heilungkiang province), north of K'ai-p'ing (the Yüan capital of Shang-tu) and Ayushiridara was forced to flee across the Gobi to Karakorum, where he was joined by Kökö Temür, whose army had been destroyed by Hsü Ta in Kansu. In 1372 the emperor sent some of his best generals to attack Karakorum, and to campaign as well in the Kansu corridor, Inner Mongolia and Manchuria. But this time the campaign went badly, and the Hung-wu emperor's forces succeeded only in the Kansu corridor. Near Karakorum, the key objective, Kökö Temür overcame Hsü Ta's forces in June, and the other Ming generals too were defeated or forced to withdraw.[207]

The failure of these steppe-directed campaigns caused a lull in military activity in the 1370s, but not an abandonment of basic objectives. A decade later the Hung-wu emperor went on the offensive in the north again, and greatly weakened the nomads. The Ming general Mu Ying made a successful surprise attack on Mongol forces near Karakorum in 1380, and a year later Hsü Ta scored victories against them as well. Two seemingly decisive victories came in 1387 and 1388: one when Feng Sheng and his colleagues conquered the Mongol leader Naghachu; the other when Lan Yü captured the Mongol crown prince and drove Toghus Temür to flight by an attack on an encampment at Lake Büyür. Toghus Temür was murdered by a relative in the following year, and thereafter the shattered Yüan polity remained weak for a generation.[208]

Campaigning in the steppe continued under the Hung-wu emperor's son, who ruled as the Yung-lo emperor (r. 1403–25). He had overthrown the designated heir, the founding ruler's grandson, the Chien-wen emperor (r. 1399–1402), in a bloody civil war. The new emperor behaved very much like a Mongol khan. His seizure of the throne after his father's death followed the nomadic principle of so-called "tanistry," the struggle among sons for succession, the regular practice in the steppe.[209] And unlike his father, who was content to keep the political center of the empire at Nanking, the Yung-lo emperor was a northerner, who had roots at Peking, the old Yüan capital where his father had enfeoffed him, and which served as his power base for taking the throne. Perhaps not surprisingly, the nomads believed that his mother had been a Mongol and that he was therefore a blood relative.[210]

While by orthodox Confucian canons of succession the Yung-lo emperor was a usurper, he proved an effective ruler. Executing the most outspoken partisans of his dynastic rival, his nephew the Chien-wen emperor, he went on to preside over a reign distinguished by great dynamism in foreign relations. The new emperor pursued and expanded his father's policy of granting titles and privileges to nobles from among the Mongols, and the Jurchen people of modern Manchuria: many so-called "loose rein" or *chi-mi* commanderies were established under the two reigns. Titles, at least, were given to tribal units as far north as the Uda river and the shore of the sea of Okhotsk, in what is modern Siberia.[211]

Among the most important of the many changes the new emperor made in the Ming system was the transfer of the capital from Nanking to Peking, a move which has never been adequately explained. Some authorities see the decision as a sign of the emperor's understanding that "only from North China could the empire be protected against the nomadic and steppe peoples constantly threatening its security. Since Sung times (960–1280) the pull back of the capital to central or south China always meant the abandonment of the north to foreign dominion." Others go further. John Fairbank and Edwin Reischauer write: "Our own view is that the capital of China had to serve as the capital also of the non-Chinese area of Central Asia." The "placement of the capital within forty miles of the Great Wall" is thus explained by its function "within a wider Chinese-plus-non-Chinese political context."[212] The real answer, however, may well be that, like his father, the Yung-lo emperor expected that Yüan Mongolia would eventually become part of Ming China. He therefore placed the capital at Peking because that location was best for managing such a domain. In any case, neither the Yung-lo emperor nor his successor, the Hsüan-te emperor (r. 1426–36) attempted to exclude the steppe. Rather, they both applied steady, offensive pressure on the Mongols.

At this time the steppe was divided between the Oirat and the Eastern Mongols, and in 1409 the new emperor sent an envoy to the latter, who was killed by their chief, Arughtai. This action precipitated the first of the great military campaigns into the steppe, under his personal command, for which the Yung-lo emperor was celebrated. Initially he allied with the Oirat, or Western Mongols, against their rivals, and campaigned as far as the River Onon, an affluent of the Shilka in the northeast part of modern Outer Mongolia. But as he played the game of divide and rule, he became concerned lest his Oirat allies grow too strong, and soon began cultivating Arughtai as a counterweight (though he refused Arughtai's request for recognition as overlord of all foreign "barbarians"). In 1414 he turned against his initial allies, the Oirat, and campaigned deep into the steppe, this time as far as the Tula river. The Oirat leader, Mahmūd, was decisively defeated. This again altered the balance of power, making Arughtai less manageable: in 1422 he overran Hsing-ho, and the emperor went on the attack. In 1422–4 the Yung-lo emperor made three more campaigns in the northeast, without conquering Arughtai, during the last of which he died.[213] His grandson and successor, the Hsüan-te emperor, carried on this martial tradition. In 1428 he led three thousand troops against Mongol raiders in the northeast, and is said to have killed three Mongols with his own bow.[214]

Such active campaigning was the most important ingredient in early Ming security policy. It greatly enhanced the dynasty's *wei* or "awesomeness," and that psychological quantity was what really kept the nomads under control.[215] But the opening decades of the dynasty also saw the development of defensive works within the context of a larger offensive strategy.

The Hung-wu emperor undertook two types of defensive measures. In the steppe he placed a series of detachments that seem directed toward control of Mongolia. These are often called the "eight outer garrisons," and their purpose was really offensive, comparable in intent to the fortifications the Han built in the Kansu corridor, which were designed to support conquest of the western regions. They were, in effect, a foothold on the edge of the nomadic world, from which Ming influence could be directed outward. A second, inner line of forts was more defensive: it was the forerunner of the fixed "Great Wall" that would begin to be constructed a hundred years later. This inner line was the first to be established. But as the Hung-wu emperor's reign progressed, and the Mongols were weakened, he began to develop the outer line as well.

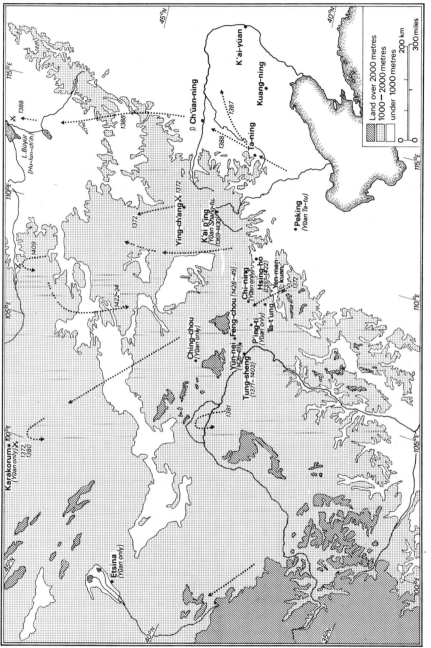

Map 4 Yuan and early Ming frontiers

Land over 2000 metres
1000–2000 metres
under 1000 metres

200 km
300 miles

45°N
40°N

K'ai-yüan

Kuang-ning

Ch'üan-ning

Ta-ning

1387

1388

1388

1372

1372

Ying-chang ×1372

K'ai-p'ing
(Yüan Shang-tu,
1369–1430)

Peking
(Yüan Ta-tu)

Hsing-ho
(1391–1422)

Feng-chou (1426–49)
Chi-ning

Yen-men-
kuan

Ta-t'ung

1372

P'ing-ti
(Yüan only)

Yun-nei
(1402–9)

Ching-chou
(Yüan only)

Tung-sheng
(1371–1403)

1409

1402–24

1381

L. Buyur
(Hu-lun-ch'ih)

×1388

Karakorum
(Yüan only)
1372
1380

×

Etsina
(Yüan only)

115°E
110°E
105°E
100°E

115°E
110°E
105°E
100°E

45°N
40°N
35°N

Thus, in the first year of the dynasty, the *Ming history* records, the Hung-wu emperor sent his general Hsü Ta (1332–85) and others to the north to Shansi and Peking to prepare border defenses, and urged them to put forward suggestions as to how this should be done.[216] Defensive orientation was increased by the setbacks that the Hung-wu emperor's armies encountered in Mongolia and the other border areas in 1372, and in the following year he instructed his generals to stress defensive deployments.[217] As a guide, he adopted the suggestion of his general Hua Yün-lung (1332–74) who called for the establishment of garrisons at more than 130 passes and other strategic points in the immediate Peking area. The plan Hua put forward, however, was not for a linear defense, but rather for a regional one, and the places he mentions are not necessarily on the lines of future walls.

Hua noted that between Yung-p'ing and Chi-chou in the northeast to Wu-hui-ling, not far from Tzu-ching-kuan in the southwest, there were 121 strategically important places, while from Wang-p'ing-k'ou to Kuan-tso-ling, both in the southwest, there were nine, all of which should be garrisoned. From Tzu-ching-kuan to Lu-hua-shan independent battalions or *ch'ien-hu shou-yü-so* should be deployed.[218] Subsequently, forces were placed at Yen-men-kuan and T'ai-ho-ling, as well as other strategic points, totaling seventy three in all. A few years later, in 1376, troops from eleven different guard units were deployed at 196 signal towers at Ku-pei-k'ou, Chü-yung-kuan, Hsi-feng-k'ou and Sung-t'ing-kuan.[219] So, early in his reign, Hung-wu moved to establish defensive positions throughout the Peking region. But he built no wall. Offensive policy still had some life left in it.

It came to the fore with the successful campaigns against the Mongols in the 1380s, which saw the Hung-wu emperor push the Ming presence deeper into the steppe. In the wake of the campaigns came increased deployments, and the completion of the line of eight outer garrisons. By 1398, the year of the Hung-wu emperor's death, the Ming had carved out a substantial foothold in the steppe. The effective frontier began with the garrisons in the northeast, K'ai-yüan, in the far north of Liao-tung, where the Hung-wu emperor had placed troops in 1388, and Kuang-ning where an outpost had been established in 1392,[220] and continued north of the capital, through K'ai-p'ing, garrisoned in 1369, Ta-ning (1387), Ch'üan-ning (1389), Ying-ch'ang (1392), and Hsing-ho (1397).[221] Tung-sheng, in Shansi, strategically located just to the northeast of the Yellow river loop, had been occupied in 1371, was the last and westernmost outpost.[222] It established Ming supervision over the Ordos. Some of these places had been important centers for previous non-Chinese dynasties. Ta-ning, for instance, had been the central capital of the Liao dynasty, known as

Ta-ting-fu. Its location outside of Hsi-feng-k'ou pass gave it great strategic importance. K'ai-p'-ing, another important garrison, maintained until 1430, had been Shang-tu, one of the capitals of the Yüan.[223]

But even this initial Ming frontier line was weak by comparison with that of its Yüan predecessor (see Map 4). In Yüan times, three garrisons had commanded the Yellow River loop; only one, Tung-sheng, did so in the early Ming, though both lines included Hsing-ho, near the western edge of the Peking district, and K'ai-p'ing. In Liao-tung, K'ai-yüan had been garrisoned in Yüan times; Kuang-ning, however was a Ming addition. For the Ming, K'ai-p'ing was the strategic keystone of the defense line, while Tung-sheng served as a link near the river loop, between Liao-tung in the east, and Kansu in the far west. The key garrison of Etsina [Chü-yen or Edsin Gol] in the far west, which had been the Yüan anchor there, was never occupied by the Ming, nor was Karakorum occupied at the start of the dynasty.

But the potential significance of even this limited line of Chinese outposts in nomadic territory was still very great.[224] Its existence demonstrated that, in the early period at least, the Ming seemed to be preparing to continue a somewhat modified Yüan-style policy of active involvement in the steppe, quite unlike the one they would follow a century later. Further evidence of the Hung-wu emperor's ambitions toward the steppe is provided by a plan for a vast military signaling system, that would involve placing beacon towers deep in Mongolia, that he approved in 1397.[225]

The Yung-lo emperor and withdrawal from the steppe margin

Upon his succession, the Yung-lo emperor largely carried on his father's work. Even as he mounted campaigns into the steppe, he strengthened the garrisons at many of the passes through which traffic to and from the nomadic realm passed,[226] and ordered the building of walls of stones to defend certain strategic points, and the strengthening of earth ramparts and ditches elsewhere.[227] During his reign a system of watch and signal towers with associated forts provided with wells and food reserves was developed.[228] Wall-building seems to have had some role during this period, though the first mention of the phrase *ch'ang-ch'eng*, "long wall," in the Ming *Veritable Records* does not appear until the year 1429. This passage reports that heavy rain has caused "long walls" outside of passes in the northeast regions of Shan-hai-kuan, Chi-chou, and Yung-p'ing, to collapse. It would probably be incorrect, however, to think of these walls at passes as constituting either an ancient, or a prototype, "Great Wall."[229]

But nothing the Yung-lo emperor created is anywhere nearly so well remembered among Chinese as something that he destroyed. In the course of his reign, the Yung-lo emperor began a process of rearranging the dynasty's defense line which saw the withdrawal of all but one of the eight outer frontier garrisons that we have mentioned above, and thus, in effect, the abandonment of the strategically-vital foothold in the steppe established by his father. For reasons that are still not altogether clear, the outlying garrisons were withdrawn inland, one after another. The troops at Tung-sheng, key to the Ordos, were redeployed in 1403, and in the same year the Ta-ning garrison was moved back towards Ming territory. At the same time the garrisons were removed from Ying-ch'ang, and Ch'üanning, and some troops withdrawn from K'ai-p'ing. The outpost at Kuangning was abandoned in 1410. These moves destroyed the logic of the defense line; thus, when Hsing-ho was attacked in 1422 it could not be held because of its isolation, and its garrison too was withdrawn. The remaining K'ai-p'ing garrison went in 1430.[230]

This abandonment of the steppe transition zone by the Yung-lo and Hsüan-te emperors would have grave long-term consequences. It effectively destroyed the geographical basis for carrying out a Yüan-style policy toward the steppe. The Ming would no longer have the foothold necessary to control the resources of the steppe margin and to deny them to adversaries. In the whole vital region there would no longer be garrisons to serve for intelligence gathering, for the launching of small punitive forays, or for the distribution of grain and other goods from China proper. Without a garrison at Tung-sheng, the Ordos and the path from it toward the Chinese capital were completely exposed. The ground was prepared for the reversal in the strategic relationship with the steppe that would soon overtake the Ming. The Chinese dynasty would no longer project its power into the steppe from the transition zone. Instead, the nomads would come to occupy the zone, and use it as a base for their own attempts to exert pressure on China. By abandoning the steppe margin the Ming thus not only lost their influence in the nomadic world: they jeopardized their security at home as well.

Historians have been puzzled about why the Ming made such a seemingly foolish decision. At least one of the redeployments appears to have been politically motivated. Ta-ning had been given to a prince early in the Ming, but because he distrusted him during his war for the throne (1399–1402), the Yung-lo emperor removed him, and gave the territory to three Mongol princes, the leaders of the Uriyanghkha tribes, whose loyalty he needed in the succession struggle. But the pattern of withdrawal is far too general for it all to have been the result of an agreement with the Mongols, like the one over Ta-ning. Some have argued that the Yung-lo emperor pulled troops out of the steppe to replenish his garrisons at Peking, which had been depleted by warfare in the south. Or the emperor may have believed that once he had finally conquered the Mongols, the garrisons would not be necessary.

But perhaps the most basic reason for the withdrawal was the difficulty of maintaining the garrisons, and the Chinese unwillingness to spend money to do so, particularly in the increasingly straitened fiscal circumstances of the early fifteenth century. Earlier we quoted Professor Dardess's explanation of how the Yüan channeled Chinese resources into the steppe, and thereby brought it under control. For nomads, used to exploiting the wealth of captured territories, such a pattern was easy to justify. Nomads generally strengthened political cohesion by distributing wealth captured from sedentary peoples. But this was not the Chinese way. Chinese dynasties were by and large unwilling to earmark resources permanently for the steppe. A great campaign might be appealing; regular maintenance of garrisons and economic subsidies was less so. The eight outer garrisons were a drain on resources; they were all, as the *Ming history* tells us Tung-sheng was, "isolated, remote, and thus difficult to hold."[231] To remove them might appear to make good economic sense. But for the Ming, their withdrawal marked the first major turning point away from an effective steppe policy.

Economic causes of Ming military decline

Economic problems did not simply undermine the eight garrisons. They turned out to be the major source of weakness for the early Ming security system as a whole. By the third decade of the fifteenth century, the emperor's reckless spending was beginning to catch up with the dynasty. The Yung-lo emperor's campaigns in the north had been costly, but they were not his only project. He had sent forces into Vietnam, and sponsored the famous voyages of Admiral Cheng Ho. And he spent a great deal constructing and settling his new capital. All of these enterprises were cut back or cancelled in the early fifteenth century.

But profligacy was not the only problem. The Ming system of financing military expenditure had many defects. Although the *Ming history*, which speaks of Han and T'ang precedents, does not acknowledge the fact, the Ming built its military system chiefly on Yüan models, and took over much of the personnel of the Mongol army. But they sought to support their armies differently. While the Yüan had been willing to extract resources from throughout China to support their military establishment, and to send resources into the steppe if necessary, the Ming sought to make their version of the Yüan military self-supporting. They introduced a number of institutions, drawn from earlier Chinese experience, to do this. And when they turned out not to work, the whole structure of Ming defense, as established at the dynastic founding, began to collapse.

Initially, the new dynasty quite literally took over the military establishment of its Yüan predecessor: in 1357 some 500,000 former Yüan soldiers had been enrolled in the future Ming army, and in the year the dynasty was established, the new emperor proclaimed that of the defeated forces, "the young and strong ones should remain permanently as soldiers." In his fourth year, the Hung-wu emperor sent an official north to enroll some 140,000 more households of former Yüan soldiers in his army. Many of these troops, of course, were ethnic Chinese. But nomads formed the "three thousand camp," one of the "Three Great Camps," or *san ta ying*, that constituted the central military institutions at the capital. According to the *Ming history*, "when three thousand surrendered men from outside the borders were obtained, there was established a camp, divided into five departments," which attended the emperor's household and that of the heir-apparent.[232]

The structures of Ming military units also followed Yüan models. The guard units, so-called *wei* and *so* were little more than the Yüan *wan-hu-so* and *ch'ien-hu-so* modified in size and stationed over a larger geographical area than previously. The initial command structure also followed the Yüan system of *yüan-shuai-fu*. And the secret-service forces of the Ming were at the start simply modifications of the *kesig*, or personal guard of the Yüan emperor.[233] Replacement of forces was supposed to be assured by making the provision of soldiers the obligation of specific military households, the *chün-hu*. This, and ancillary systems of recruitment, drew upon Yüan experience.[234]

By 1392, an estimated 1.2 million men were on active service for the Ming, and some 1.7 to 2 million military households had been enrolled.[235] Most of the men on active duty were stationed in the 493 guards scattered throughout the country. At the start of the dynasty, perhaps 200,000 men were on duty in the capital.[236] In the north, by the beginning of the fifteenth century, some 107 guards had been established, with a listed complement of 531,000 men.[237]

To supply this vast establishment, however, the Ming did not follow Yüan precedent. Instead, they were guided by a set of idealized policies, rooted in the Chinese statecraft tradition. Among these was the system of *t'un-t'ien* ["military farms"], which had been traditionally proposed as a way of achieving security without the risks of frequent offensives, or the costs of supplying border garrisons from the center. The idea was to settle soldiers permanently along the frontiers, where, in times of peace, they would farm under the supervision of their officers, and in their spare time practise military skills. In wartime they could be mobilized to fight. It was used during the Han by general Chao Ch'ung-kuo, whose example was repeatedly cited in later times.[238] Its apparent success then led writers about defense repeatedly to endorse it.

The system promised to provide a self-supporting yet effective army: indeed the Hung-wu emperor, who implemented it more widely than any other ruler in Chinese history, boasted that he had supported an army of one million men without using so much as one kernel of peasant-produced grain.[239] The final organization of the system was carried out by the Yung-lo emperor, who established the regulations and norms that governed the numbers of soldiers assigned to military farms and the system of collecting and distributing grain. Farms in exposed areas were grouped near small forts, where men and animals could take shelter in case of raids.[240]

Other aspects of military supply were handled similarly. Service households were established to manufacture various necessities; while horses were purchased or traded from the nomads, as well as raised privately and in government-run horse farms.[241] The government monopoly on salt was used to provide an incentive to merchants to ship grain to the border, and even to grow it there, by giving them certificates that could be exchanged inland for the valuable commodity.[242]

Taken together, these institutions, were supposed to create an independent and indefinitely self-supporting military establishment. It, in turn, would form a component in a general structure of harmonious and self-equilibrating rule. Unfortunately, it quickly became clear that the system did not produce enough horses, grain, or recruits, to meet the dynasty's needs. Military farming simply did not work. The borderlands were marginal agriculturally, and even efficient farmers (which soldiers generally were not) had trouble making ends meet. Soldiers fled the harsh conditions; officers tended after a generation or less to become, in effect, landlords, with their former troops as their tenants. By the sixteenth century most of the soldiers on the frontier were in fact mercenaries paid in silver, and horses were scarce.

This decline has been carefully documented by economic and social historians, who have often found in it the basic causes of the Ming's increasing problems in managing the steppe. The decline was particularly damaging because under the Ming system resources once assigned to specific uses at the beginning of the dynasty could not be re-allocated. By the sixteenth century the court had in effect to pay for defense twice: once through the system just described, which continued to consume and tie down resources long after it had ceased to produce any military power, and then once again through the improvised system, upon which security actually depended. But it would be wrong to blame Ming military failure on economic and social causes alone, without looking as well at failures of strategy, which had both intellectual and political causes.

Strategic reasons for the decline of Ming security

The fundamental issue in Ming security policy was the approach to the Mongols. The Yüan experience suggested that a comprehensive policy was required: it would not be enough for the Ming simply to intervene in the steppe from time to time. Instead, it should seek to maintain economic and political equilibrium there. The first goal would require trade, and at times of disaster, subsidies. The second would demand either close diplomatic ties with selected Mongols, or the imposition on all of them of a Peking-centered political structure. Something like this, after all, was what the nomads were accustomed to. Over the centuries in which China had been divided between north and south, with the north usually linked to the steppe, and even more during the Mongol hegemony, a web of economic, political, and cultural connections had knitted much of Inner Asia to the northern part of China proper. This process had reached its climax under the Yüan, when Mongol power in Inner Asia had stimulated a tremendous upsurge in commerce and travel. The caravan trade had revived, and merchants, ideas, and inventions spread easily across Eurasia.[243] Now the Ming were threatening to break up this world, by establishing a frontier somewhere south even of the eight garrisons. The effect of such an action might be profoundly destabilizing, for the new boundary would cut right through the network of economic connections and interdependencies which had linked north China to the nomadic world for hundreds of years.

The problem would have been ameliorated had the new dynasty been willing to permit the nomads extensive trade. But even at the start the new dynasty was not willing to allow this: it attempted, instead, to organize its economic relationship with the steppe according to the Chinese conception of "tribute."

This system, mentioned above, was a structure of fictive kinship through which non-Chinese rulers accepted a position of ritual subordination to the Chinese emperor. This relationship was expressed through periodic missions, in which the tributary or his envoys would present goods and perform required rituals, in return for Chinese patronage and gifts. Tributaries might call for Chinese help if attacked, while the exchange of tribute and gifts amounted to a form of trade. Some modern scholars have argued that this system and belief in it pretty well defined pre-modern international relations in East Asia, in a Sino-centric way. Others, more recently, have challenged this view.[244] Here let us note only that the concrete details of the tribute system as most scholars describe it are drawn from the practice of the Ch'ing: that is, from the Manchu dynasty that, even before it conquered the Ming, had extended its control over most of the steppe from which threats to the Ming came, and which had thus solved the basic problems of steppe management by military means. With military hegemony, the Ch'ing rulers could prescribe the nature and ritual of tribute. But of course it was warfare or its threat, and not the tribute ritual, which kept the Ch'ing's neighbors in line.

The Ming situation was quite different. The Ming never conquered Mongolia, and thus never created a military and political framework in which they could insist on tribute. The Ch'ing used tribute to dress up a relationship of military subordination. The Ming, to the extent it could, tried to use tribute relations as a tool to compensate for its lack of such military power. For tribute to work under such conditions, it would have to be far more genuinely reciprocal than in a case where one side imposed it by force. Those aspects of it which seemed to suggest a real Chinese claim to superiority would have to be muted if the nomads were to accept it.

This task was made easier by the fact that the nomads had their own rationalization of the "tribute" system, one which gave them a high status in a way that mirrored what the Chinese saw in the system. Thus the Mongols believed that because they had helped the Yung-lo emperor to take the throne, as a result they were "entitled to the goods derived from tribute presentation." Mongol chronicles, according to Father Serruys, may be "poor witnesses to the exact nature of the events, but they clearly reflect a tradition among the Mongols that return gifts for their tribute were a tribute to them, non-payment of which was apt to trigger instant retaliation."[245] Such a system could work well only as long as both parties agreed to see what they chose to in it, and not to push their opposing interpretations to the test. This the Ming proved increasingly unwilling to do, and rather than simply let "tribute" be the rubric for trade, reformers of various kinds would repeatedly try to squeeze the whole steppe–settled interaction into the choking confines of ritual statutes.

This political problem was made worse by the way questions dealing with foreign policy were worked out at the Ming court. After the first two reigns, its political structures began to foster a virtually unchecked proliferation of factions. This problem was apparent even in the early period: it had been the founding emperor himself who had unwisely created the seed-bed from which the chronic and damaging political controversies of the later Ming emerged. Toward the end of his reign he had become very suspicious of his high officials, both civil and military. He purged and executed his Prime Minister, Hu Wei-yung (d. 1380), who was suspected of conniving with the Mongols to the north. And he began to kill his leading generals. Both the civil government and the military hierarchies were fragmented, so that the former became a series of departments, such as the six boards, but lacked a head and coordinator, while the latter was split into five groups of commands, with no commander-in-chief. Such a structure guaranteed that uncoordinated and contending interests would develop. Furthermore, decisions about relations with the nomads within the tribute system came under the formal jurisdiction of the ministry of rites, while military matters were handled by the ministry of war. These divisions virtually ensured that political competition and uncoordinated policies would undermine Ming power. For the system to work at all, strong rulers, like the Hung-wu and Yung-lo emperors, were absolutely necessary.

Certainly strong disagreements about frontier policy were evident from very early in the dynasty. Conflict between advocates of offensive and defensive policy, for example, broke out during the reign of the Yung-lo emperor, roughly the first quarter of the fifteenth century. It was a good example of the already growing conflict between approaches to the steppe inherited from the Mongols, and those learned from the canonical texts of Chinese history. During the Yüan, some officials, unhappy with the way Khubilai's General Bayan was using nomadic tactics that permitted the enemy to make deep raids, had followed a more Chinese approach and argued for "the contrary idea of permanent border defense, a strategy which explicitly demanded such anti-nomadic supporting activities as the establishment of military-agricultural colonies, the organization of grain supply routes, and the construction of walled fortresses."[246] In the second part of 1421, as the emperor began preparations for his third great campaign into the steppe, several of his ministers advanced similar criticisms of his plans. One of these was Hsia Yüan-chi (1366–1430), who was imprisoned; another, Fang Pin (minister of war, served 1409–21) committed suicide.[247] The anti-war constituency grew stronger after the Yung-lo emperor's death in 1424. Hsia argued against continuation of the occupation of Vietnam, and it was ended in the Hsüan-te period (1426–36) so that resources could be concentrated on the northern frontier.[248]

Nevertheless, the early Ming was relatively strong. A combination of military forces on the border, and memory among the nomads of the military exploits of the Hung-wu and Yung-lo emperors, provided a certain security for the Ming until the middle of the fifteenth century. Then, however, a series of events unfolded that destroyed the system as it had existed, and created a need for new policies to fill the vacuum.

The collapse of the early Ming security system

The early Ming military system collapsed in 1449, when a Ming court that no longer remembered much about how to fight the Mongols sent an army into the steppe to confront a Mongol who dreamed of restoring the Yüan. The situation arose because the early Ming emperors, while managing to keep the inhabitants of the steppe divided and on the defensive, had failed to unite and control the steppe under their own auspices as the Yüan had. We have argued above that steppe confederations develop in response to the creation of settled states. If that is so, then it was only a question of time before the Ming would face a unified and hostile steppe. When this new steppe power inflicted a crushing defeat on a large-scale Chinese punitive expedition, the security system of the early emperors was shattered. The battle at which this happened, T'u-mu, took its name from a postal relay station some sixty or so miles northwest of Peking, and perhaps twenty five miles outside of the important pass at Chü-yung-kuan, where 'The Great Wall" visited by tourists of today would be built in its aftermath.

By the mid fifteenth century, the steppe beyond this pass was once again being unified. Unfortunately, this unification was not being carried out by the Ming, or even by nomadic leaders amenable to Ming influence. The Yung-lo emperor's campaigns had weakened the Eastern Mongols, and as a result the Oirat became more powerful. Under the leadership of Toghan (d. 1439/40) the Oirat sponsored Toghto-bukha to be Khan, against A-t'ai, the candidate of the Eastern Mongol leader Arughtai'. In 1434 Arughtai was killed in the battle of Mu-na-shan, fought in the northeastern Ordos area, near modern Wu-yüan.[249] The Eastern Mongol remnant fled to Etsina, where, too late, they received Chinese support designed to help balance the Oirat.[250] With the Eastern Mongols destroyed, the way was clear for a single Mongol hegemon.

This turned out to be Esen (d. 1455), son of Toghon, and the first of a series of Mongol leaders in the heroic mold who began restoring the unity, power, and prestige of the steppe peoples as the Ming developed. Their purpose was to change the terms of their relationship with the Chinese state: they wanted closer diplomatic relations and easier trade, and when these proved difficult to obtain, they threatened to conquer China as their ancestors had done. In a little more than a decade before the battle at T'u-mu, Esen had made himself hegemon of an area which stretched from modern Sinkiang to Korea.[251] But because he was not a descendant of Chinggis, Esen could not hope to become the legitimate khan. Instead, he married his daughter to Toghto-bukha, the young khan, and initially satisfied himself with power rather than status.

87

The Oirat tribe had been enrolled as a Ming tributary early in the dynasty.[252] Trading missions from the Mongols were permitted to visit the capital several times a year, though the number of their members and the routes they could take were strictly controlled. But for a variety of reasons, such arrangements were far from satisfactory for the Mongols. The volume of trade was not sufficient, and many aspects of the diplomatic relationship proved offensive. Furthermore, the Ming proved unwilling to play the role of (perhaps unwilling) active patron and subsidizer which the Mongol nomads expected from whoever controlled north China.[253]

But while the Mongols found such limited relations with the Ming inadequate, some Chinese found them excessive. Even formal tribute was more of a concession than many were willing to make. Drawing their ideas from the Chinese xenophobic tradition that was much elaborated in the Southern Sung, they tended to dislike and look down on nomads for both cultural and moral reasons. Fearing the political role they might once again play, such Chinese wished to end all trade. Esen, who demanded greater access to Chinese goods and markets, and who was furthermore clearly ambitious for power in the steppe, and perhaps in China as well, was just the kind of nomad leader they dreaded, and felt must be stopped at all costs.

How should the Ming deal with such a threat? An ideal policy would probably have sought to use economic means to weaken Esen and strengthen the hands of those who, like his son-in-law the Khan, wanted a more peaceful relationship with the Chinese. If warfare was nevertheless unavoidable, the Ming would want to field a well trained army capable of defeating the nomads. But by the middle of the fifteenth century neither of these approaches was as feasible as during the dynasty's early period. The dynasty had given up its foothold in the steppe. In place of the willingness to employ diplomatic and economic means for dealing with the steppe which both the Hung-wu and Yung-lo emperors had manifested to some extent, a narrowly sinocentric and isolationist approach was beginning to emerge. And the Chinese army was no longer what it had been under the Yung-lo emperor. Manpower was declining, and the skills of riding and archery were being forgotten. Finally, the political situation at court was beginning to impede the making of workable policy.

The Cheng-t'ung emperor (r. 1435–49) was only twenty-one when Esen challenged the Ming, and though theoretically an autocrat, he could not help but be influenced in conflicting directions by his friends among the eunuch palace staff who had brought him up, and by the imposing officials of the outer court. His natural inclination was toward a "punitive expedition," and this was in accordance both with precepts of the classics, and the practice of his forebears, the first three Ming emperors. But as with

Hsia Yüan-chi under the Yung-lo emperor, the civil bureaucracy recognized the risks an offensive campaign would entail.

The crisis was precipitated by a dispute over tribute relations. Before Esen came to power, Oirat tribute missions had numbered fewer than a hundred men. Esen, however, sent far more: 2,302 in 1442, 1,867 in 1444 and over 2,000 in the winter of 1448/9. To house and feed all these Mongols, not to mention provide them all with gifts in return, was no small burden on the Ming court. In 1448 the Oirats falsely stated that their embassy numbered over 3,000 apparently in order to obtain more goods. When Wang Chen, a eunuch who had particular influence at court, learned of this, he retaliated by reducing to twenty percent the gifts they were to receive. Other disagreements followed, and Esen began to organize an attack.[254]

In 1449 he proposed to raise a great army and attack the Ming. His son-in-law, the khan Toghto-bukha disapproved. "We are indebted to the Great Ming for both clothing and food," he is quoted as saying. "How can you be so ungrateful as to make such a plan?" Esen, however, would not listen to Toghto-bukha, saying "If the Khan will not make the attack, then I will do it myself." He evidently prevailed, and the campaign got underway, with the Khan, commanding one army, moving eastward to attack Liao-tung, while Esen led a main force toward Ta-tung.[255]

As reports of Esen's activities reached the court, officials led by the minister of war, K'uang Yeh, spoke out strongly against undertaking an attack. "The Six Armies must not be lightly employed," they said. Two days later the Minister of Personnel led a large group of officials submitting a joint memorial arguing that the emperor was overreacting, that defensive measures should prove adequate, and that with food and water supplies inadequate, a campaign would be very dangerous. "Armies are instruments of violence; warfare is a dangerous business. The sages of antiquity undertook war with cautious respect, not daring to do so carelessly. The Son of Heaven, although the most exalted of men, would not go personally into those dangers. We officials, although the most stupid of men, nonetheless say that this must not occur."

But the young emperor had listened more to his personal entourage, led by Wang Chen. Wang was a eunuch as well as the emperor's tutor. He knew very little about Mongols, but understood well how to strengthen his own position at court, and those of his relatives, by abetting the emperor in his dreams of triumphant conquest. To the remonstrances of his officials the young emperor replied, "These words of you Ministers all convey well your loyalty and patriotism. But the caitiff bandits offend against heaven and dishonor our favor to them. They have already violated our borders; they have murdered and plundered our military and civilian population there. The border garrison commanders have repeatedly asked for armies to come to their aid. We have no choice but to lead a great army in person to exterminate them."[256]

From beginning to end this decision proved disastrous. Preparations were in the hands of the palace staff, who were more concerned that the emperor, on his return, should pass through Wang Chen's native village, than with strategies needed to fight Esen. Indeed, the dangers quickly became apparent. The day before the army was set to depart, word came of a defeat near Yang-ho in which two senior field commanders and all their troops had been killed. As the emperor's palanquin passed on the way to the field, a supervising secretary threw himself down in front, stopping it, and pleaded, "Your Majesty may make light of your imperial person, but what of the dynasty, what of the state?" On the fourth day the army, said to be half-a-million strong, passed through Chü-yung-kuan and into the area of Mongol activity. Storms and heavy rain boded ill. On the eighth day the court astronomers reported that continuing the campaign would be "against all signs," and on the thirteenth day the sight of the Yang-ho battlefield, strewn with thousands of unburied Chinese corpses, terrified everyone. Finally, after sixteen days, Wang Chen decided to call off the expedition.

But an ambush awaited the army on its way home. After camping at T'u-mu, the Ming forces moved out on 1 September 1449. Though this day was the Mid-Autumn Festival, "normally a happy time of family reunion and feasting," the Ming army had been without water for two days, and was suffering intensely. Furthermore, it was now aware that it had been surrounded by Esen's forces. The emperor ordered the drafting of peace terms. But Wang Chen directed that the army should move forward, and it moved about a mile. "On observing this action, the enemy now attacks in full force from all sides. The Chinese army breaks, gives ground in great disorder, and becomes a mob. The Mongols shout: 'Throw down your arms and armor and be spared.' Ignoring their officers, the Chinese soldiers go wild, strip off their garments, and run towards the Mongol cavalry, only to be cut to pieces."[257] The emperor's guards attempted to protect him, but most were killed. The emperor himself was unharmed. He had sat down on the battlefield, in the midst of a hail of arrows, where a no doubt astonished Mongol prince later discovered him, and took him to Esen's camp.

The Ming emperor was now a prisoner of the Mongols. That intangible prestige the early Ming emperors had accumulated through their military exploits, their *wei* or "awesomeness," was dissipated. The balance of power between the Chinese and the nomads had shifted dramatically, and Ming now faced strategic dilemmas that its founders had never imagined.[258]

6

Toward a new strategy:
the Ordos crisis and
the first walls

The defeat at T'u-mu was a disaster for the Ming. The dynasty's military prestige was shattered at a stroke. During the initial period of panic at the capital when news of the defeat and of the emperor's capture was first received, it looked as if its very rule might totter. There was talk of leaving Peking and fleeing south, as the Sung had done some three hundred years earlier. But Esen failed to press home his advantage, and in Peking the new Minister of War, Yü Ch'ien (K'uang Yeh had perished during the campaign) took charge and stopped the panic. The captive emperor's younger brother was elevated to the throne as the new ruler, the Ching-t'ai emperor (r. 1450–9); while the captive was declared "Grand Senior Emperor"; in effect kicked upstairs and out of the picture. Defenses were reorganized and strengthened.

But even though immediate disaster was averted, the strategic position of the Ming had been gravely affected by T'u-mu. The dynasty had been put on the defensive: permanently, as it turned out. The possibility that the Ming might eventually succeed to the Yüan's position as hegemon of the steppe, which still had been plausible even a few years before, now seemed out of the question. The number of the Ming's points of similarity to its Mongol predecessor was diminishing, and its strategic predicament came to resemble more and more that of earlier, ethnically Chinese dynasties, which had tried vainly to cope with nomadic threats.

What was more, the loss of one emperor and the installation of a new one created an anomalous political situation that greatly complicated policy-choice. Because the elevation of a new emperor could be justified only by the exigencies of a military crisis, an incentive was created for his supporters to maintain the state of emergency by keeping military tensions high. They wanted to avoid the return of the former emperor as the result of a compromise with the Mongols, because such a development would threaten the positions of the new emperor's partisans. Therefore they naturally adopted a hard line towards the nomads, and initially refused to trade or negotiate with them. This approach, in turn, made the nomads' position difficult, and left them no alternative but to raid.

The politically-induced hardening of the Ming attitude toward the nomads coincided with a grave deterioration in the dynasty's military position on the border. Most of what remained of the Ming presence in the steppe transition-zone had now been entirely lost. After T'u-mu, the Mongols had quickly overrun many Ming positions. In 1450 an official in the west was reprimanded for having abandoned without approval and moved away from the border the populations of Chia-chou, Sui-chou, Yen-fu and Ch'ing-fu, all important places in Shensi that formed a crescent to the east and south of the Yellow River loop. The court feared that the nomads would occupy the abandoned forts, and use them as bases. The minister of war called for an enquiry, and operations to recapture the positions were ordered for the following spring.[259] Elsewhere, in Hsüan-fu, eight other forts were overrun, including Tu-shih-k'ou, the northernmost point on the capital defense line.[260]

But most seriously of all, after T'u-mu groups of Mongols began, for the first time since the founding of the Ming, regularly to nomadize and even to settle, in the strategic Ordos. The Tung-sheng garrison, the early Ming outpost in the region, had been withdrawn by the Yung-lo emperor, in 1403. Now, as the nomads moved into the territory, the full consequences of that action began to become clear. As the problem was recognized in the century that followed, what to do about the Ordos became the basic issue in Chinese military debate.

Essentially, there were two choices. One would be to send an expeditionary force into the region, and establish strong military outposts there. It would then be possible to exercise a high degree of control over the nomads in their own territories: the steppe and steppe transition zone. Such a forward military posture would furthermore render major defensive works unnecessary. Alternatively, the Ming could concede the Ordos to the Mongols, in which case the possibility of exerting much control over the steppe would be lost, and the Ming's best hope would become a defensive and accommodative policy. Political debate over the issue, and attempts to exploit it for political ends, are among the most important motifs in Ming military history of the late fifteenth and the sixteenth centuries. The decision to build the first major Ming walls was the outcome of one such debate.

During the period of uncertainty following the defeat, Mongol indecisiveness greatly assisted the Chinese. After T'u-mu and the capture of the emperor Cheng-t'ung, Esen hesitated over his next step. Though in the flush of early success he had talked about restoring the Yüan dynasty, his original goal had probably been to capture Ta-t'ung and Hsüan-fu, the two most important garrisons controlling access to the capital from the east. So in early September the Oirats brought the captured emperor before the gates of Hsüan-fu, but were greeted by gunfire and turned away. At Ta-t'ung the commander of the city met the emperor, and delivered a ransom to the Oirat, but kept the city itself closed. The Mongols withdrew, taking their prisoner with them.[261]

The Mongols were trying to use the authority of the captured emperor to make the Chinese do what they wanted. But the Ming responded by stressing its character as a nation, and devaluing the captured emperor by replacing him. When, in October, Esen and his army broke through Chinese lines at Tzu-ching-kuan, and reached Peking, they were told that "'It is the altars of the Earth and of Grain [that is, the dynasty and the nation] that are of great importance, while the ruler [as an individual] is unimportant.'" Furthermore, aware of the problems that the former emperor's return would create, the Chinese were unwilling to bargain for him. No conditions would be granted for the captive's return. After making several unsuccessful attacks, Esen withdrew five days later.[262]

In the steppe, Esen proved equally inept, and the coalition he had created began to fall apart. His failure either to take control of Peking and put a puppet emperor on the throne, or lacking that, to win some Chinese territory, or at very least, to extract vast ransoms from the Chinese, with which to reward his allies, seemed to indicate to them that he was no longer the man of destiny. The Khan, Toghto-bukha, his nominal superior, wished to return to his previous relationship with the Chinese, and sent an envoy to the Ming court.

This disagreement led Esen to proclaim himself Khan in 1453, and to go to war with Toghto-bukha, who was killed. In 1455, though, Esen himself perished, and his son and followers fled north to the Orkhon. In the south, a son of Toghto-bukha became Khan under the patronage of Bolai, chief of the Ta-tan tribe which had defeated the Oirat and which now became the hegemonic power in the steppe.[263]

The strife which then developed among the nomads greatly worsened the situation on the Chinese frontier. The Mongols had previously tended to stay in the north. But now, needing resources with which to wage their internecine struggles, they began to draw nearer to the Chinese border, and in particular to the Ordos. The logic of the steppe triangle described in Chapter 2 began to tell. Esen's defeated forces occupied the northern part of the Mongol homeland (they would emerge again in the Ch'ing period as the Dzungars), and in the far west the rise of the Moghul state of Turfan in the 1450s had closed the Tarim oases. To support his forces, therefore, Bolai had no alternative but to turn south for food and water. He began from time to time to move his herds and followers into the Ordos and the grasslands of the Kökönor region, in modern Ch'ing-hai.[264]

During the Mongolian civil war that ensued, fighting frequently erupted in the Ordos, and from time to time spilled into China proper. Bolai was no more secure than Esen had been: in 1466 he was assassinated by his associate Ma'alikhai. In 1471 Ma'alikhai was killed by Bäg Arslan, another Mongol who, having established himself in the Ordos proclaimed the brother of Toghto-bukha to be Khan. As they prosecuted their own civil wars, the Mongols made frequent demands for trade with the Ming. When these were turned down, as they almost always were, the nomads raided and plundered.[265]

As we have mentioned, by putting a new emperor on the throne the Chinese had effectively devalued the one the Oirat had captured. But they also created a very difficult political situation which, as its consequences were played out, worsened the relationship between the Chinese and the Mongols. The political exigencies of the moment meant that one could not question the legitimacy of the new emperor, yet rather well-developed Chinese political theories made it impossible, on the other hand, to deny that the former ruler was in some sense still a fully legitimate sovereign as well. These abstract issues linked up with the personal interests of various people at court.

Some of the captive emperor's officials kept positions at court under the new emperor, albeit with their influence diminished. But if the former emperor were to be re-enthroned they stood to gain a lot. Not so those who had come to high positions as a result of the crisis, most importantly Yü Ch'ien and the new emperor himself. For this second group the return of the elder brother was something to be avoided at all costs. It would be better if he could somehow be forgotten.

So when the emperor's return was finally negotiated, in September of 1450, he arrived to be greeted by only two or three officials, and was then locked away in the Nan-ch'eng palace in the southeast corner of the Forbidden City. The new emperor clearly planned to stay in power, and to make his own son, rather than his brother's, the heir.

This situation led to a deterioration in tribute relations with the Oirat. Although they continued to send missions, even during the period of the former emperor's captivity, their habit of sending, along with their regular tribute, a separate gift for their former captive, was a reminder of his presence, and thus a source of embarrassment to his successor. The response of partisans of the new emperor was to refuse to send Chinese envoys in return, even though this meant risking war by offending the Mongols. Not everyone felt this was sound policy, however: a number of officials began to feel that the Minister of War, Yü Ch'ien, was purposely keeping military tensions high, in order to keep his own position.[266]

During this period northern border defenses were substantially strengthened, because both of the genuine weakness of the Ming, revealed by the T'u-mu defeat, and of the interest of the dominant party at court in maintaining a sense of military tension. The fortifications at about fifty important passes, among then Tzu-ching-kuan, guarding the route Esen had taken to the capital were ordered improved, and in addition border embankments and ditches were ordered raised and deepened. Where ramparts had deteriorated, they were to be restored.[267] Work was begun in 1450 at several locations, among them Ning-wu pass.[268] And a censor was sent to take charge of constructing new fortifications at the most important pass of all, Chü-yung-kuan, work which was completed in 1455.[269] The work undertaken in this period marked a major shift toward defensive construction.

The court situation, however, was dramatically changed in 1457, when a group of supporters of the former emperor broke down the gate of the palace where he was held captive, and restored him to the throne. In the course of the *coup d'état* Yü Ch'ien and several of his collaborators were killed, and the Ching-t'ai emperor either died of illness, or was murdered, shortly thereafter. But by this time the border situation had deteriorated considerably, and nowhere more so than in the Ordos, upon which attention now focused.

The Ming court could not agree about how to treat the Mongols who had succeeded Esen, and who were increasingly based in the Ordos. A certain amount of trade and tribute was permitted, but not enough to end raiding. Bolai (fl. 1451–65) leader of the Ta-tan, sought to establish a relationship with the Ming. In 1455 he attempted to send an embassy, but was refused. In 1457, however, he sent five hundred men with gifts of horses and camels, while beginning in about 1458, he began to attack regularly.[270] Mongol groups associated with Ma'alikhai entered the Ordos region seeking water and pasturage in 1461, and were also permitted some tribute missions, in the course of which they often raided settlements within China. In June of 1462 Bolai sent a delegation of three hundred, which the emperor objected was too large, and in December of 1463, more than one thousand.[271] The Ming had no consistent policy of response.

The most influential figure at the palace was probably Li Hsien, the senior Grand Secretary (1408–67, cs. 1433). Early in his career he had sent a memorial warning the emperor about the danger posed by the ten thousand or so Mongols who lived in the Ming capital, while in 1449 he had gone with the army to T'u-mu, but escaped. He proved politically adept, managing both to acquire a position of power at the court of the new emperor, and not to lose his influence when the older brother was restored in 1457. Indeed, as his potential rivals fell from power, he emerged in the later part of the T'ien-shun emperor's reign (1457–64) as the senior figure at court.[272]

Nevertheless, he understood that a simplistic hard-line policy would not solve the Ming's problems. He recognized the economic needs of the nomads. In 1459 he wrote that "the [Mongols] are a calamity for China only because they desperately need clothes and food."[273] Four years later he urged that exchange be permitted: Bolai, the Mongol leader "sends men to present the tribute [...] only because he desires goods and profit; if we give them he will be happy; if we reject him he will be resentful, and no doubt he will raid the borders."[274]

During the decade that followed, the nomadic presence in the Ordos gradually became the center of concern. Some specific information about the territory in question, and its history, was provided in April of 1466 when a bureau director of the ministry of war, Yang Chü, reported to the emperor a conversation with a veteran company commander, Chu Chang, then over seventy years old, who had known the area in his youth. The veteran spoke of its broad fields, rich soil and abundant salt lakes. According to the memorialist, in the Cheng-t'ung period (1436–50) two different military officials had urged the construction of forts and signal towers along the frontier, but neither proposal had been carried out. The border in the area was not defined clearly and was certainly vulnerable: it was only a year or so before that border markers had been placed there.[275] However, if forts and signal towers were built now, it would be possible to defend the area, and permit the development of agriculture. That in turn could provide a local food supply for soldiers defending the area, as had been done in earlier dynasties, such as the Han and the T'ang.[276] Without such measures, transfers of troops to the region, which had already been carried out, could have little effect.[277]

Such a reoccupation would require a military campaign. In July of 1466, Li Hsien proposed such a policy. Beginning with the famous words of Chia I's memorial about the Hsiung-nu, Li noted that the nomads were no more numerous than the inhabitants of a single Chinese district.[278] He pointed out that Ming laxity had permitted Mongol tribes to take control of the strategically important *Ho-t'ao*, and urged that a major campaign be prepared for the following spring, with horsemen to be transferred from other defense districts (from as far away as Hsüan-fu in the east), and that provisions, war carts, horses, etc. be prepared along the Shensi border.

The emperor approved of the idea. Yang Hsin, who had previously served in Shensi, was recalled from his current duty at Ta-t'ung, and placed in command of the enterprise. He remained at court, though, and over the winter the nomads raided several times, even as they struggled among themselves.[279] No offensive materialized, and the following year saw Chu Yung defending the borders as Ma'alikhai presented tribute.[280]

In June of 1468 a supervising secretary, Ch'eng Wan-li suggested that a force of 20,000 men should be sent to the northern border to conquer the Mongols. He proposed a novel approach: the Ming army should divide into mobile detachments of 3,000 men each, which would scour the grasslands until they learned in which of the scattered grazing units the Mongol leaders were staying. These would then be attacked, the leaders killed, and the border problem thus solved. The emperor liked the suggestion, but nothing was actually done.[281]

Instead, inconclusive fighting simmered for the next two years.[282] In April of 1470, the ministry of war discussed the problem of the nomads, and the various possible strategies: attack, measures to divide the Mongol forces, or defense.[283] In May the minister of war, Pai Kuei (1419–75, cs. 1442) asked for suggestions about how to deal with the nomads.[284] The Prince of Hsiang, Chu Ch'ung-ch'iu, offered to lead an attack, but was turned down by the emperor.[285] In March of the following year Chu Yung recommended that either offense or defense be chosen as a basic policy, and the decision was made for the time being to take the defensive, owing to the lack of horses and provisions of the Chinese side.[286]

These proposals envisioned something like the campaigns of the Han, recorded in the dynastic histories, and would have required that tens of thousands of troops be sent from the capital or other areas to the edge of the Ordos. But at the time, the Ming garrisoned the northwest frontier for only part of the year: troops were sent there for active campaigning in the spring, when the nomad's horses were still weak from lack of food over the winter. By autumn, when the nomads' horses were fattened from summer grazing, and when the harvests of the Chinese were a tempting target, the Ming adopted a defensive stance. Such forces might have been adequate to deal with the kind of occasional threat faced by the early Ming, when the nomads generally stayed far to the north. But the Ming troops were inadequate to cope with the situation now that the Mongols had settled in the Ordos, nor could the troops alone undertake large-scale campaigns. A major policy decision was needed.

In 1472 the court faced the issue. The preceding winter had seen raids all along the border from Ning-hsia to Ta-t'ung by the nomads based in the Ordos. In January a local commander, Ch'ien Liang, had been badly defeated; over six hundred of his troops had been killed'[287] In March Pai Kuei submitted a memorial prompted by the incident and suggesting measures to improve Chinese military strength in the northwest.[288] This he followed shortly by a memorial setting out in detail his recommendation for a major expedition to "recover" the Ordos, which he argued was the only

97

long-term solution to the border problem. He believed such a campaign could solve the problem for once and for all, "achieving permanent peace by means of one major effort": *i lao yung i*.

Pai proposed that the expedition should get underway in the second month of the next year, after two months of preparation. Initially fifty thousand troops would be sent to the border, along with half a year's supply of grain. The first detachment of troops would prepare fortifications and bases, and would be joined subsequently by one hundred thousand more men. This force would be commanded by a viceroy, and would sweep the nomads out of the Yellow River loop and establish a self-sustaining Ming presence there.[289]

Pai Kuei served as minister of war from 1467 to 1475. His grandfather is said to have been a battalion commander in the Yüan army, and Pai himself had much military experience. He had campaigned with Chu Yung to secure the Liao-tung borders in 1443. He probably got some of his ideas about how to deal with the Ordos from that service. The first real wall system of the Ming appears to have been begun in Liao-tung, during the time he was there. To protect Han settlers in the peninsula, two stretches of rampart were constructed near K'ai-yüan, one to the west in 1442, and the other to the east in 1447. They appear originally to have been built "by erecting two parallel rows of stakes and then filling the middle with [earth]." Later the Ch'ing would build its famous "Willow Palisade" or *liu-t'iao-pien*, which was repeatedly repaired and expanded, in the same region but not along the same route.[290] In 1449 Pai had gone with the army to T'u-mu, returning to the capital after the defeat, where he was put to work training troops. Later he served in the southwest, in the Ming wars against the Miao tribesmen of Kuei-chou; also in Shensi. In 1462 he and another official had been dispatched to Ku-yüan in the northwest, where he reported defeating Bolai. By the time he made his recommendations, he was a full minister, and had achieved a position of considerable authority within the capital.[291]

In May of 1472 a court meeting approved of an offensive, though not exactly the one that Pai had proposed. Although Pai wished to await discussions with two officials who had just returned from the borders, two other officials, the minister of personnel Yao K'uei (1414–73, cs. 1442) and the Marquis of Hui-ch'ang, Sun Chi-tsung, considered that the danger from the nomads was too pressing. Troops on the borders – 80,000 they said – were sufficient; the problem was lack of a unified command. Accordingly in June Chao Fu (d. 1486) was appointed the *p'ing-lu chiang-chün* ["general who pacifies the barbarians"], with Wang Yüeh (1426–99, cs. 1441), of whom we shall hear more, assisting him, and given instructions to inflict a major defeat on the nomads.[292]

A number of measures were taken to implement the policy. Chao took as personal assistants seven officers from the capital guards, as well as one thousand Mongol soldiers and five hundred firearms specialists from the capital. His forces would be supplemented by new local militias. An officer was placed in overall charge of finance, and other officials were put in charge of supply at the local level.

But it was difficult to hide the ineffectiveness of this policy. The nomads continued to raid, and Chao Fu and Wang Yüeh were accused of being unwilling to attack.[293] "The generals and officers charged with pacifying the west have not yet achieved anything," the ministry of war concluded, and sent a censor to investigate. In the meanwhile, proposals were made for a major expedition in the following year.[294]

At the end of October of 1472 Wang Yüeh and Chao Fu reported that they faced difficulties. For their plan of attack to succeed, they would need more troops: at least 150,000, far more than the 20,000 they currently commanded, and building up such a force would require the transfer of forces from the capital and from other parts of the empire. Supplying such an army in the impoverished northwest would be at least as much of a problem as getting it there in the first place. The generals suggested that instead of mounting an expedition, the court should withdraw Chinese settlers from the flat and relatively indefensible land of the north into the more mountainous area south of the steppe margin, where cavalry was more easily stopped, and where farming would be less exposed to nomadic attacks.[295]

 Such arguments still did not, however, win over the court. Pai Kuei replied that the commanders had over eighty thousand troops, and yet had reported no victories. Perhaps they were overcautious; it seemed that a single nomadic horseman was enough to frighten away several thousand Ming troops. As for the suggestion of withdrawing to the hilly country, that avoided the general problem of how to deal with the Mongols. They were a major problem, and would have to be confronted. The commanders were ordered to submit new plans.[296]

To this Chao Fu and Wang Yüeh responded by stressing again the weaknesses of the Ming position. The army was small, and supplies were lacking. Both Shensi and Shansi were drought-stricken; people were fleeing; and with the early onset of winter, deaths from cold would be added to those from starvation. Anyone who continued to advocate a military expedition under such circumstances was either badly misinformed, or else so carried away by the theories of ancient writers on strategy as to have lost all touch with reality. It would be best for the two commanders to return to the capital and confer. Chao Fu was replaced. But his successor had no greater luck, and nomadic occupation of the Ordos continued.[297]

Another approach to the whole problem, however, was possible, that of static defense, and it had been gaining strength as the ineffectiveness of the planned offensives grew clear. When in March of 1471 Chu Yung asked for a decision on offensive or defensive strategy, the court had approached the issue cautiously. They were worried that grain was scarce in the northwest, and horses for an offensive campaign were lacking; therefore they were inclined to instruct commanders to concentrate on the defensive.[298] At that time three officials had furthermore been sent to inspect the borders: Yeh Sheng (1420–74, cs. 1445) the right vice-minister of rites; Yü Tzu-chün (1429–89) and Wang Yüeh. Their reports from the field, and recommendations when they returned, supported the building of a border wall, and the erection of forts and signal towers.[299]

The strongest champion of wall-building was Yü Tzu-chün. He was an important and influential figure, both in politics and military affairs, and his career casts some light on the way policy was made in the Ming. Born in Szechwan in 1429, he received his *chin-shih* degree in 1451. After initial service in Fukien, in 1460 he was made magistrate of Hsi-an (Sian), where he worked six years in all. Hsi-an is in southern Shensi province in the Wei river valley. Since ancient times, geographers and strategists have recognized the vulnerability of this area to attack from the Ordos to the north. During Yü's incumbency as magistrate, relations between the nomads and the settled peoples were good, with trade being carried out at periodic markets. But when Yü was briefly transferred away from the area, to Chekiang, one of his biographers tells us, the populace became concerned. Without his policy guidance, incidents with the Mongols increased. In February of 1471 the court decided to re-appoint Yü to the region, as grand coordinator (*hsün-fu*) with the rank of right vice censor in chief.

In Yü-lin, the settlement on the southeastern edge of the Ordos desert that he made his headquarters, Yü undertook many worthwhile activities. Even today the area is remote: in Ming times it was utterly isolated, with a poor, uneducated, and ethnically mixed population. Yü established a school and adoped bright students as his own disciples. He obtained seeds from other places, and taught the local people to farm, a detail which seems to indicate a largely pastoral economy. He promoted self defense: metal weapons were manufactured for the first time during his incumbency. But he considered that the problem of security would really only be solved when a wall was built to protect the settlement and neighboring farmlands, and the larger towns of Shensi to the south. This assessment of the larger security picture led Yü to submit, in August of 1471, a memorial in which he recommended that such a wall, about thirty feet high, should be constructed between Yen-sui and Ch'ing-yang.[300]

Yü's proposal however, ran directly against the approach to the problem that we have seen was being taken at court. Walls had a bad reputation historically: the last dynasty to have built one in this area was the Sui, one of the short-lived regimes that, like the Ch'in, had done a lot of wall-building. Walls were also expensive. Rounding up local labor to build them, still the usual practice at this time, interfered with the peoples' livelihoods, and stirred resentment. Furthermore, wall-building was neither a comprehensive nor a permanent strategy. Would it not make far better sense to grasp the nettle and take the Ordos? And even if money could be found for a wall, the solution would only last for the relatively brief period before it was eroded away. The minister of war, Pai Kuei, and other senior officials argued that Yü's plan would be too expensive and burdensome, and called for further study.[301]

Rather than wishing to defend the southern edge of the Ordos, the court still wanted to occupy the whole area. Referring to proposals of a year earlier to build embankments at the places where rivers provided access, the court showed familiarity with the military problem and the possible ways of approaching it. But they feared the costs of passive defense. The people of Shensi were few and difficult to tax. They would flee if exactions were too great. Futhermore, earthen walls would erode quickly, and thus could not be considered a permanent solution to the problem. The emperor in particular noted how important it was to consider the welfare of the people.[302]

But the offensive policy, sound as it may have been in strategic principle, was unrealistic in practice, as many officials realized. The Mongols were very strong. In the Ordos they had a fine base, with both water and pasture. The Ming, by contrast, had virtually no capacity to transport an army even to the southern margin of the Ordos, let alone support it once there. A Ming army would not necessarily prove victorious in any case. The Mongols could draw them deeper and deeper into the desert and steppe, refusing to give battle, the treatment Arughtai had meted out to the Yung-lo emperor. Or they might lay some horrible ambush, and destroy the whole force. There was, in other words, plenty of reason for caution, and over the next few months officials who favored it began to speak out quietly.

Yeh Sheng was one of these: a veteran of the T'u-mu crisis and former supervisor of military supply in the Shansi area, he had already been sent, as mentioned above, to inspect the northern frontiers, and had spoken up in favor of defense. At the time of T'u-mu he had played an important role in strengthening defense: after 1451 he had served in the Hsüan-fu area, northwest of Peking, where he had helped to re-establish the eight lost forts. In the process he had acquired an unusual degree of first-hand knowledge of border affairs.[303] The reports Yeh sent from his tour of inspection undertaken in 1471 were also not encouraging. Soldiers, he said, were few. In Shensi and in Hsüan-fu he had found only 8,000 troops, even including locally raised militia (*min-chuang*). After meeting with Wang Yüeh in Yen-sui just south of the Ordos, he reported that even if military dependents there were included, that still made only 12,000 troops. They were supposed to defend a border about 1,500 *li* (or 500 miles) long that was fortified not by some ruined "Great Wall" but rather by only twenty mud forts (*pao*). To make up for such weaknesses, the Ming made a practice of sending troops to vulnerable border areas for temporary duty during the fall raiding season. In the early years of the dynasty this had been adequate, for hostilities were not extensive. But now the roughly 15,000 troops a year that were rotated to the Ordos border from Ta-t'ung, Hsüan-fu and Shansi were only a fraction of what was required.[304]

An expedition to conquer the Yellow River loop area could be carried out, Yeh wrote, but it would have to be vast; he estimated that between one hundred and two hundred thousand soldiers would be needed, as well as another hundred thousand coolies for transport work. He urged that "at the present time there are no able generals; military preparedness along the border has long been without substance; and the transportation of supplies would be laborious and expensive." He concluded that "the clearing of the Yellow River loop and the restoration of Tung-sheng are not to be lightly considered." Rather, he advocated defensive work, the "strengthening of walls and clearing of fields" (*chien-pi ch'ing-yeh*) and other measures.[305] On 24 May 1472 Yeh was recalled to the capital to participate in the court meeting to discuss policy already described. As we have seen above, however, that meeting continued to favor the offensive.[306]

The meeting in 1472 did show, though, that influential officials were beginning to have second thoughts about the whole offensive approach to border problems. The burden of military expenditure on the population was so well known as to be a cliché of Chinese statecraft. For centuries wise rulers had built security not through military operations, but by fostering the welfare of the people – or so it was thought.

Conditions were desperately poor in the border areas, as they are even today, and one can think of the officials who planned great offensives or great walls as Ming equivalents of modern economic planners, in air-conditioned buildings in the capital of some third world country, cooking up utterly unrealistic development schemes. In the autumn of 1472 one official had condemned the throne for burdening the people of the frontier area. Shansi, Honan, and Shensi, he pointed out, had suffered from a year of drought, yet special taxes were already being levied to pay for military operations. The peasants, he feared, would be driven to banditry. The office of scrutiny for the ministry of punishments noted that taxes were being collected a year ahead in some areas, and the people were being impressed for transport work. These special levies were leading people to flee.[307] This sort of news was profoundly disturbing. Opinions, including the emperor's began to change.[308]

Yü continued to press his case. On 20 December 1472 he submitted a memorial outlining the situation on the border, and again making the case for wall-building. He argued first against offensive strategy. Since 1469, when raiding had become a serious problem, troops had repeatedly been dispatched to the borders, where there were now perhaps 80,000 men and 75,000 horses. If further campaigns were to be carried out in the following year, Yü argued that the cost would become unsupportable, and might lead to catastrophe for the border population. He proposed instead that 50,000 people from Shansi be relieved of other tax obligations and put to work to take advantage of the period in the spring and summer when, because the nomads' horses had not yet recovered from the privations of winter, no attacks were likely. During that period, something like a wall should be constructed, not by building layer upon layer of brick or stone, but rather by cutting away the rather solid loess soil of the region so as to form a barrier. While in two months it might not be possible to finish the work entirely, the number of routes that the nomads could follow in attacking could certainly be reduced. Relieved of the danger of constant attack, the people south of the frontier would then be able to rest, and their economy would revive. Building on such restored strength, it would be possible to consider a large attack to the north. The emperor was impressed, and noted that wall-building was a long term strategy. Perhaps reflecting Yü's influence, there was also talk of restoring peaceful tribute relations.[309]

When the commanders concerned met to discuss policy, the consensus that emerged also favored Yü Tzu-chün. On 12 January 1473, the border commander Chao Fu memorialized that he had recently consulted, as he had been instructed to do, with Wang Yüeh, Yü Tzu-chün, Ma Wen-sheng, and others, to discuss the policies of attack and defense. The policy of attack had envisioned a force of 150,000 men advancing over a period of two months; it was estimated such an expedition would cost at least 450,000 *tan* (about 29,925 tons) of grain, and require 110,000 porters besides the troops. In addition to being expensive, making a deep penetration of the Mongol territory would be quite risky. The project of building a wall and fortified points was by contrast not so expensive and relatively long term. Fifty thousand men were requested.[310]

At that point, a good opportunity for wall construction was created by an offensive victory. Wang Yüeh (1426-99) was one of the Ming's finest generals. Like many other military figures, he did not come from a

Fig. 3 Wang Yüeh (1426–99), proponent and practitioner of an offensive strategy, was one of the last Chinese generals able to fight like a nomad. He built one of the first significant Ming border walls, and one of his victories over the Mongols provided the breathing space during which Yü Tzu-chün's important wall south of the Ordos was constructed. (From *Li-yang Wang Hsiang-Min Kung-chi* (1st ed. Soochow 1530), reprinted Taipei 1970 as vol. 13 of *Ming-jen wen-chi ts'ung-k'an*.)

hereditary military family, but was rather by training a scholar, and passed the *chin-shih* examination in 1451. Yet he won early renown for his stature, strength, and mastery of archery on horseback, and spent most of his career commanding troops. His specialty was the surprise attack deep into enemy territory, usually directed not against the Mongol soldiers, but rather against their families and dependents who would be left in camp during times of campaign, often near some body of water.

Wang had been placed in charge of the area from Yü-lin to Ning-hsia in 1473. He received a report that some Mongol followers of Bäg Arslan had embarked on a raid south of Ning-hsia, leaving their tents and dependents at the Red Salt Lake (*Hung-yen-ch'ih*), a place about one hundred twenty miles west of Yü-lin, just inside the desert margin. Essentially the Ming had two ways of defeating the Mongols. One was somehow to drive them against a body of water, such as a river or large lake, which would cut off their retreat, thus depriving them of their advantage of mobility, and permit the Chinese to slaughter them. This was the approach used by Lan Yü in 1388, when he destroyed the Mongols at lake Büyür.[311] The other was to attack, not their able-bodied warriors, but their encampments, which contained their women, children, old people, property, and herds. Such tactics might seem both cowardly and cruel, but they made military sense: nomads had no fixed towns or property which could be ravaged, and therefore one had to attack the population itself, and the herds upon which it depended.[312] In this important battle, a little of each probably contributed to Ming success.

Wang set out with forty-six hundred horsemen, and rode day and night. They surprised the enemy, or rather the enemy's guard, and presumably women and children, and killed several hundred. They set afire the tents, and led off thousands of camels, horses, cattle, sheep, etc. When the main Mongol army heard of this catastrophe, they began to hurry back, but fell into an ambush prepared by the Ming forces. These setbacks led the Mongols to retreat to the northwest, and leave the border relatively quiet for several years.[313]

This victory provided the opportunity for the undertaking of Yü's project, which was completed in 1474. Along with a shorter wall, built to the west by Wang Yüeh in the same year, and forming part of the same system, it was the first major wall built by the Ming. Wang's wall was some 387 *li* (129 miles) long, and extended from modern Heng-ch'eng in Ling-wu county to Hua-ma-ch'ih.[314] According to Yü's report of 4 August, his was much longer: it was 1,700 *li* (566 miles) long, extending from Ch'ing-shui-ying in northeastern Shensi to Hua-ma-ch'ih in northwestern Ning-hsia. A total of more than eight hundred strong points, sentry posts, beacon-fire towers, etc., were established along its length, and it took over forty thousand men several months to complete, at a cost of over one million silver taels. It was intended to be a barrier against the nomads, as well as a shelter for military farms that were the source of over sixty thousand *tan* [3,990 tons] of grain per year.[315]

Yü's work endured, and the system of defense was elaborated (see Map 5). The line that Yü had built was called the "great border" (*ta-pien*). In the reign of the Hung-chih emperor (1488–1505) Ch'in Hung (1426–1505, cs. 1451) built the "secondary border" (*erh-pien*) nearby. Yang I-ch'ing (1454–1530, cs. 1472) built a "new border line" (*hsin-ch'eng*) and repairs and enlargements were also subsequently made by Wang Ch'iung (1459–1532, cs. 1484), T'ang Lung (1477–1546, cs. 1508), Liu T'ien-ho (1479–1545, cs. 1508), and Yang Shou-li (1484–1555, cs. 1511). By the middle of the sixteenth century the system had become very extensive, with two defense lines, numerous signal towers, and detachments of soldiers deployed along the line.[316] Wang's wall eroded, and was also repaired, in 1531 and 1537.[317]

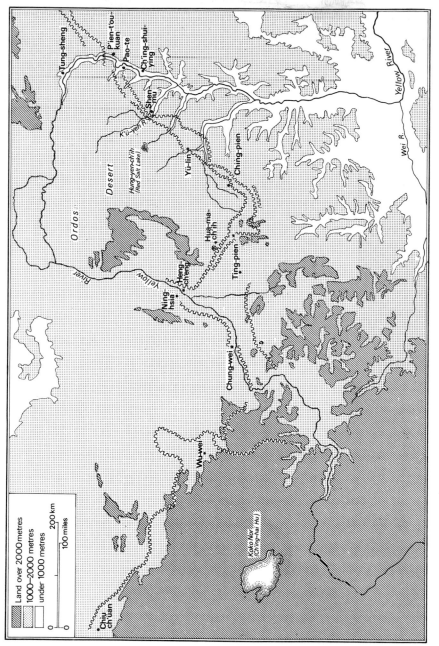

Map 5 The Yellow River loop and the Ordos

The system appears to have passed its first major test in 1482. A large group of Mongol raiders was trapped within and against the fortifications, and, unable to escape, suffered a severe defeat at the hands of Hsü Ning and other generals. This was seen by the people of the border areas as a vindication of Yü Tzu-chün's strategy.[318]

7

Politics and military policy at the turn of the sixteenth century

Although Yü Tzu-chün's wall proved rather successful, and its construction was followed, over the next century, by the building of more walls to the east which with it eventually became "The Great Wall," at the time of its completion it was viewed as little more than a strategic stop-gap. The basic issues of Ming defense policy had not been resolved then, although over the decades that followed, it became clear that changes in the situation both in China and in the steppe were making them more pressing than ever.

The most important change came among the nomads. In the steppe to the north, where previously the Mongols had been divided, a series of strong new leaders emerged, who created confederations encompassing most of the tribes. In addition, a new problem arose in Central Asia. To the west, the area beyond the Kansu corridor, most importantly Hami, came under the rule of the new state of Turfan.

The situation was potentially dangerous: the Ming ran the risk of overextension if it tried to meet threats on both its northern and western borders. But it also offered possibilities. If China were willing to undertake the diplomatic steps, and commit the resources required, the relationship with the steppe might be managed. A division between powers in Mongolia and the Tarim basin even offered room for maneuver. If one power was won over to the Chinese side, then it could be used to offset the other. It was precisely by engaging in such operations, we should recall, that the Yüan court of Khubilai had eventually succeeded in controlling the vast border region they called Ling-pei.

The early Ming rulers had shown some interest, and even ability in such an approach. But after the middle of the fifteenth century, and in the sixteenth century in particular, this had changed. China was no longer ruled by decisive men like the Hung-wu and Yung-lo emperors, who had held sway from 1368 to 1425. Rather, the Sons of Heaven tended to be palace-reared products, often coming to the throne while still very young, and having no knowledge or experience of life beyond the Forbidden City. Though despotic in their exercise of power, they lacked vision and consistency, and were preoccupied with the affairs of the court and the capital. Often they fell under the influence of powerful civil officials, eunuchs, or palace ladies. Without a strong executive the Ming system functioned poorly. The Hung-wu emperor, suspicious of his prime minister and generals, had in 1380 abolished the positions at the head of both the civil and military hierarchies, and this meant that the emperor had to serve as his own prime minister and commander-in-chief. When emperors were not capable of doing this, as in the sixteenth century, policy-making was certain to be contested by a number of different officials, none of whom enjoyed any clear precedence.

These structural problems were compounded by a general rise in political factionalism. Some of this reflected simply the clash of personal ambitions in a situation where no clear paths of advancement existed. To get ahead one had to improvise, clearing new routes to the top for oneself and forestalling competitors. But it had deeper roots as well. By the turn of the sixteenth century the center of intellectual and economic power of the Ming had shifted toward the south. Prosperity and intellectual revival there led to the reassertion of ways of thought that stressed the differences between the "civilized" and the "barbarian," and to the eclipse of residual Yüan pragmatism and cosmopolitanism. Northerners and southerners increasingly found themselves in rivalry for court positions. Both intellectually and in the realm of political style, the tension between the syncretic Yüan legacy and the more purely Chinese traditions of the south began to be resolved in favor of the latter. In the Chia-ching period of the mid sixteenth century, arguments over the succession further divided the intelligentsia and the bureaucracy. Basic constitutional uncertainty and chronic factional rivalry penetrated every aspect of policy-making in that court. The military and strategic issues that had already been defined intellectually in the debates of the 1470s took on political coloration in the sixteenth century. Political disputes began to affect decisions about military questions to an unprecedented degree.

Such developments had a particularly deleterious influence on border policy. Advocacy of attack on the nomads, and rejection of their requests for trade or diplomatic relations, repeatedly proved to be a good way to win celebrity and attract imperial favor. Therefore persons whose hold on power at court was insecure – eunuchs or grand secretaries threatened by rivals – often concluded informal alliances with sympathetic military figures to promote such policies. This uncompromising approach also appealed to a broad constituency among the educated classes where philosophical ideas that rejected as demeaning any Chinese dealings with "barbarians" were increasingly widespread.

The problem was that such policies were utterly divorced from reality, and unworkable in practice. Many Chinese of the period sincerely believed in the idealized patterns of foreign relations decribed in the books from which they had been educated. But there were also enough officials who had first-hand experience of dealing with the nomads, knew that attempts at conquest were futile and risky, and saw that only by a combination of measures, including tolerance of trade, could the border situation be managed and stabilized. Officials of this second sort had, somehow, to block the policies the first group advocated, and, if possible, implement their own. But this was a politically difficult task. The intellectual constituency advocating compromise was small and not particularly vociferous. It could talk about costs and risks, and attempt to draw on the pacifistic tradition of some Chinese philosophy. But usually it could do no more than frustrate hard-line policies, usually by linking them to unrelated issues. Positive compromise was even more difficult. It could be approved only by brute political force: for example by a strong official, confident of imperial backing, and able simply to override all opposition. Even then, victories by the compromisers were likely to be short-lived. It was very much in the interest of the first, more hard-line ideological group to abort any potentially successful compromise, for to solve the problems on the border and actually achieve peace would greatly strengthen the position of the official who brought it off. The best way to abort the compromise was to devalue the achievement by arguing that too much had been given away, that the peace was a humiliation for China, and its author a traitor. And this was relatively easy: it could be done simply by using emotive rhetoric, as we will explain in Chapter 10.

Such a political pattern might be expected to lead to long-term deadlock over policy, occasionally broken by exceptional persons or circumstances. That is exactly what happened in the later Ming period. For more than half a century after Yü Tzu-chün's wall had been completed, no single military strategy was adopted or implemented. A series of Ming courts essentially temporized in the face of an unprecedentedly serious Mongol threat. The eventual turn toward extensive wall-building probably reflected the fact that all contenders could agree on it, despite its doubtful military merits.

Until the end of the fifteenth century, the Ming had never faced a challenge from a unified steppe. The campaigns of the Hung-wu and Yung-lo emperors had disrupted and divided the nomads. Esen, the victor at T'u-mu, had been unable to maintain his pre-eminence in the steppe for long, in spite of his victory. His Oirat tribe were defeated by the rival Eastern Mongols, whose leadership, however, proved no more stable. The late fifteenth century had seen a series of short-lived leaders: Bolai until 1466 when he was assassinated; Ma'alikhai until he in turn died at the hands of Bäg Arslan; and then Ismāʿīl, who having killed Bäg Arslan was in turn briefly his successor.[319]

But in the 1480s there emerged a leader who proved far more successful than any of his short-lived predecessors. This was Batu Möngke, a descendant of Chinggis, who in 1488 proclaimed himself Dayan-khan: Khan, that is, of the Yüan, a title which announced both his legitimate descent from the Yüan rulers, and his destiny to unify the Mongols.[320]

Batu Möngke did not succeed in imposing order in the steppe immediately. He fought a long war with a rival called Ibrahim, who was possibly a descendent of Esen. This conflict much worsened the Ming situation by taking warfare to the region beyond the Kansu corridor, until then reasonably secure. In 1509 Batu Möngke had driven Ibrahim from his original base near Chang-chia-k'ou to modern Sinkiang and Ch'ing-hai, from which his forces raided the whole western Ming frontier, from Szechwan in the south to Ning-hsia in the north. Called by the Chinese "sea bandits" (*hai-k'ou*), after the lake in their region that is called Kökönor in Mongolian and Ch'ing-hai in Chinese, Ibrahim's forces remained a problem until one of Batu's grandsons finally defeated him in 1533.[321] Between 1508 and 1510 Batu Möngke conquered the Ordos, and in 1512 he appointed his second son, Barsubolod to be *jinong* (from the Chinese *ch'in-wang*) or viceroy over the region, a title his son Günbilig-mergen (1505–42/3) in turn inherited.

Had the Chinese rulers of the time possessed an understanding of the dynamics of the steppe comparable to that of the Yüan rulers, or even of their own founding emperors, they might have improved their own military situation by making use of the rivalries among these nomads, and perhaps supported Batu Möngke to some extent. Not that a complete peace would have been possible: rather, the nomadic threat could have been reduced in scale by economic and diplomatic means, so that what remained might have been militarily manageable.

Restoring trade relations to what they had been at the beginning of the fifteenth century would have been an important step. During the whole period under discussion the Mongols were willing to accept tributary status, the Ming ritual requirement for trade. In the Hung-chih period (1488–1506) tribute missions were once again permitted, and subsequent Chinese commentators saw this as one of the reasons for an associated drop in the level of hostilities. But after 1500 regular tribute from most of the Mongols had ceased, and hostility had taken its place.[322] As a result, Batu Möngke was forced to attack China in order to obtain the goods he could not get by trade, but which were necessary to him, both for the prosecution of his war against Ibrahim, and for his building of a steppe confederacy.

What was worse, Batu Möngke understood what the Ming had forgotten: the strategic importance of the steppe transition zone. So in addition to creating powerful nomadic armies, he began to establish fixed outposts along the Ming frontier. In Yüan times Khubilai had built a line of forts in the steppe transition zone from which to control his rivals in Mongolia, and the Hung-wu emperor's eight garrisons had a similar purpose. In 1514 Batu Möngke established a sort of mirror image of these deployments: a line of several tens of permanent camps from which he could project influence inward, harrying the borders of Hsüan-hua and Ta-t'ung, the two most important defense areas between the Ordos and the Ming defense capital.[323]

From the 1520s onward, the title of Khan passed to Batu Möngke's grandson Bodi-alagh. But his two other grandsons, Günbilig-mergen, and his younger brother, the Altan khan, posed the real threat to the Ming. Known to the Chinese as *Chi-nang* and *An-ta*, respectively, these two made their base in the Yellow River bend.[324] Not permitted to trade with the Ming, the powerful Mongols had no choice but to obtain Chinese wealth by force. And this fact led the Chinese, inevitably, to consider how to improve their defenses.

Among those in China who expounded the defensive approach to dealing with the nomads during this period was Ch'iu Chün, (1420–95, cs. 1454) a brilliant and wide-ranging scholar and official from Hai-nan Island.[325] In 1487 he presented to the throne his encyclopedia of statecraft, the *Ta-hsüeh yen-i pu*, or "Supplement to the Extended Meaning of the *Ta-hsüeh*", an attempt to provide practical and empirical documentation to supplement the theory of statecraft presented in the basic Confucian text, the *Ta-hsüeh*, and in Chen Te-hsiu's (1178–1235) speculative exposition of it, the *Ta-hsüeh yen-i*, or "Extended Meaning of the *Ta-hsüeh*". Ch'iu was an admirer of Yü Tzu-chün, of whom he wrote a biography. His encyclopedia furthermore contained a long section on the history, geography, and strategic situation of the Ordos, which went far beyond anything earlier in the Chinese historical canon.[326]

Although Ch'iu more than anyone else pointed out the crucial importance of the Ordos, he did not propose to solve the problem by a military campaign. Rather he favored gradual measures, including the strengthening of defenses and the local economy. Ch'iu's work clearly stimulated active debate on the issue. As Tamura Jitsuzō points out, although proposals for Ordos recovery had antedated Ch'iu's work, only after he put forth his views on the matter did it come to be hotly argued at the Ming court.[327]

Certainly Ch'iu Chün had little doubt about the merits of Yü's defensive strategy. The history of the Sung dynasty was usually a source of

Fig. 4 Ch'iu Chün (1420–95), the scholar-administrator, whose exposition in his *Ta-hsüeh yen-i pu* (1487) articulated new approaches to border problems. He was one of the first Ming figures to point out the key strategic importance of the Ordos. His biography of Yü Tzu-chün endorsed wall-building. (From *Ch'iung-t'ai shih wen hui-kao*, preface dated 1661, reprinted in *Ch'iu Wen-chuang kung ts'ung-shu*, Taipei, 1972).

precedents for hard-liners, who lamented the many compromises it had made with its northern neighbors. But Ch'iu took as his example the Sung's wars with the Tangut Ta Hsia in the Ordos region, which had led to tremendous losses, numbered in the hundreds of thousands on the Chinese side.[328] Naturally many at the Sung court had wanted to conquer the Ta Hsia, much as some Ming politicians wanted to "recover" the old Ta Hsia realm in the Ordos, now in Mongol hands. But other Sung politicians had called for a more long-term and less immediately militant policy. Two were particularly celebrated, Fan Chung-yen (989–1052) and Han Ch'i (1008–1075). They had developed both defenses and economic strength along the border, and it was to them that Ch'iu Chün compared Yü Tzu-chün.[329]

The parallel brought out the fundamental importance of economic relations in each case. Management of the friction between the two countries during the reign of the Tangut ruler Li Yüan-hao (1032–48) had depended upon trade relations. In the negotiations between the two states, increases in the gifts presented by the Sung to the Ta Hsia ruler were used to offset his concessions on some fundamentally intractable problems of ritual status.[330]

To those who thought as Ch'iu Chün did, a model for future policy was offered by Yü's wall combined with such economic measures. In the 1480s it was proposed that more of the frontier should be similarly fortified. But the proposal never succeeded: Offensive strategies still had powerful political and military attractions.

Yü's wall had made it harder for the Mongols in the Ordos to raid into southern Shensi and Shansi, but had done little to protect the capital. Between the wall's eastern terminus, not far from the Yellow River, and Peking itself, lay what in the later Ming came to be the most heavily fortified stretch of frontier, but which at this time still lay relatively open. Yü himself now proposed building walls to strengthen this area as well.

The gap between the Ordos and the capital was a favorite corridor for nomadic raiders. The chief garrisons were at Hsüan-fu, on the Yang river some eighty-five miles west of the Forbidden City, the palace in the center of Peking, and at Ta-t'ung, on the Yü, a tributary of the Sang-kan river. These two cities controlled the passage from the Yellow river loop to the pass at Chü-yung-kuan, the most direct route to the capital.

The Northern Wei, a dynasty based in this area which had incorporated both nomadic and settled populations, placed its first capital, P'ing-ch'eng, near modern Ta-t'ung, and constructed border defenses to protect it on the north. The Northern Ch'i had also built walls to defend the area. Ta-t'ung had received its present name from another Inner Asian dynasty, the Liao, which in 1044 made it their western capital. Modern Ta-t'ung, an industrial city, is still something of a border town: near it the railway line to Ulan Bator and then to the Trans-Siberian abruptly turns toward the steppe. After the Yung-lo emperor withdrew his forces from Hsing-ho to the north, Ta-t'ung was left as the most important of the Ming border garrisons. But in holding it, the Ming had to face the same geographically-imposed problems that had confronted previous tenants. The land north of the city is flat, virtually "a southward projection of the Mongolian plateau."[331] When the nomads moved in, no natural barriers impeded their progress.[332]

Early in the Ming, probably by the first decades of the fifteenth century, an attempt had been made to solve this problem by building earth ramparts. Two rather short east–west walls were constructed to cut the route south along the valley of the Yü river. The more southerly of these, the *erh pien* or "secondary border," lay some ninety *li* (30 miles) to the north of the city. Another ninety *li* beyond the first was the *ta pien* or "great border." The early fortifications in the area were simple, no more than earthworks, and literary sources tell us that by the sixteenth century they had long since decayed.[333]

Fig. 5a,b This adobe wall was built by the Ming north of Ning-hsia, between the Ho-lan mountains and the Yellow River. It demonstrates that even in the Ming, the only dynasty regularly to build walls of stone, traditional methods of earth construction were still commonly used. (Photo: Robert E. Wallace, US Geological Survey.)

While he served as Minister of Revenue in 1484, Yü Tzu-chün proposed that war chariots be designed to carry ten soldiers each, specifically for use against nomadic attacks in this area; but despite the emperor's approval, the vehicles were "far from perfect, and the plan had to be temporarily abandoned."[334] Shortly thereafter Yü himself was placed in charge of military affairs in Hsüan-fu and Ta-t'ung.

Yü's first step was, on his appointment to the ministry, to undertake a tour of inspection of the frontier. After forty days traveling in the Ta-t'ung, Shansi, and Hsüan-fu defense areas, he submitted a report to the emperor that described how both peasants and garrison soldiers lived in grinding poverty, and fortifications were deficient. There were only 170 signal towers in the whole region. To secure it, Yü proposed a wall that would be an extension of the one he had already constructed in northern Shensi. "Your servitor," he wrote, "has already built one such [wall] in Yen-sui; pray take that as a model and apply it to Hsüan-fu, Ta-t'ung, and P'ien-t'ou-kuan." The wall would run from Ssu-hai-yeh, near the capital, to the Yellow River, a distance of more than 1,300 *li* (433 miles). In addition to the wall, 440 more signal towers, each about three *chang* (36 feet) high should be built. 86,000 men would be needed to work for several months to complete the project. It was approved, and work was ordered to begin in the fourth month of 1485.[335]

Had Yü's wall been built, it would have interrupted access from the steppe to the capital from the west and north. But Yü's second wall-building project did not prove as successful as his first. He found himself on the wrong side in court politics.

The most powerful figure at the late Ch'eng-hua court was a eunuch, a member of the Yao people, from Kwangsi, called Wang Chih (fl. 1476–81). Eunuchs often served in Chinese courts, particularly as dynasties became weaker. In the early Ming they were theoretically outlawed, but even at the time of T'u-mu we can already see them playing critical roles in court affairs. Wang had risen from obscurity by securing command of the so-called *hsi-ch'ang* or Western depot, a eunuch-run office that played a role analogous to the modern secret police. But after protests from civil officials led to the temporary closing of the depot, Wang began to seek power within the regular bureaucracy. He exerted his influence to secure the dismissal of officials unfavorable to him, and to obtain important commands for his collaborators.

The *Ming history* tells us that Wang Chih, taking advantage of the trust of the Ch'eng-hua emperor (r. 1465–88), "wished to establish his position by achieving merit on a border compaign." The merit means two things: in general, of course, it means the prestige gained by a successful military campaign, but it also refers to the traditional Chinese practice of conferring tangible awards – money, titles, preferred and often hereditary positions for one's family members – on those who distinguished themselves militarily. Two commanders, Wang Yüeh and Chu Yung cooperated with him, and in 1480 they undertook a campaign.[336]

We remember Wang Yüeh (1426–99) as the general who masterminded the attack on a Mongol encampment at Red Salt Lake in October of 1473 that permitted Yü's wall in Shensi to be built. In 1480 Wang, with Wang Chih, carried out a successful raid on a Mongol encampment at Wei-ning-hai-tzu, a lake just outside the Ming frontier in modern Inner Mongolia. It led to his appointment as earl of Wei-ning, and to rewards – hereditary positions in the elite secret-police unit, the embroidered-uniform guard – for the son of the general and for the foster son of the eunuch Wang Chih.[337] Wang Yüeh was a gifted general: his successes improved the dynasty's security, though they did not contribute much to a long-term solution of border problems. His collaboration with Wang Chih, however, showed the possibilities for cooperation between those willing to risk high stakes for military victory on the borders, and those willing to do the same to obtain power at court.

In contrast to Wang, Yü Tzu-chün was a cautious man, who disliked offensive warfare and regularly opposed it. When he was minister of war (1477–81), he had conspired with Liu Ta-hsia to conceal files concerning the Vietnam campaign of 1407 from the Ch'eng-hua emperor, in order to prevent him from undertaking another one.[338] Trying to avoid provoking the tribal peoples of the border regions, he had called for the punishment of Ch'en Yüeh, another military collaborator of Wang Chih, for murdering nomads who were simply attempting to present tribute. He opposed Ch'en Yüeh's proposal for a punitive campaign against the Jurchen settlement in Chien-chou (Liao-tung) because of minor incidents, and disapproved the proposal made by Ch'en Yen, governor of Kwei-chow, that a large army should be raised to crush the Miao people. He called for the impeachment of Chao Fu, one of the commanders of the offensive campaigns in the northwest.[339]

Not surprisingly, given their policy disagreements, Wang Chih had tried to oust Yü. In 1481, he had almost succeeded, but Yü had been saved by the need to leave court to mourn his mother. Yü reciprocated the hostility: like any sound Confucian he was a sworn enemy of the eunuchs at court. He would have known the classic passage in the *History of the Latter Han* in which it was explained that eunuchs were "defective human beings" who, "with agile minds and glib tongues, used clever displays to confound the truth," thus deluding "witless and young rulers" until "faithful and worthy men were outwitted, and the altars of earth and grain were demolished and became ruins."[340] In 1484 Yü had even submitted a memorial urging that eunuchs be brought under control, and put back to their original duty of minding the household affairs of the palace itself. As Ch'iu Chün observed in his biography of Yü, given the power of eunuchs at court at the time, these were not prudent sentiments to express.[341]

The wall-building project provided an opening for Yü's adversaries, among them a eunuch whom he had impeached. Yü did not supervise work on the new wall project himself, as he had on the earlier, but rather delegated it, and when a supervising secretary of the ministry of works was sent to inspect, he reported that the construction was costing too much, and arousing dissatisfaction among the people. Political opposition fixed on this, and the work was halted. Shortly thereafter, in November of 1485, Yü Tzu-chün retired. More than fifty years passed before major wall building was again undertaken. Political struggle had led to policy stalemate.[342]

Politics and military affairs continued to be entangled in the next two reigns, those of the Hung-chih emperor (r. 1488–1506), and of the Cheng-te emperor (r.1506–22). The second of these was called "The Martial Emperor" because of his personal love of offensive campaigns. Wang Chih eventually fell from power at the Ch'eng-hua court, and Wang Yüeh was banished, both in the early 1480s. But in 1487, at the start of the next reign, Wang Yüeh was pardoned, and made commander at Kansu in the far west. In 1498, at the age of seventy-one, he led a force of light troops beyond the Ho-lan mountains north of Ning-hsia, took the Mongols by surprise, and scored an impressive victory.[343] He wanted to push on further, and recover the old Ming tributary state of Hami in the Tarim basin as well.[344] But even a commander as skilled as Wang could not singlehandedly restore the kind of prestige the Ming had once enjoyed. He died in 1499, and subsequent campaigns by Ch'en Jui and Chu Hui against the Mongols did nothing but call attention to Ming weakness and military imcompetence.[345]

The issue kept coming back to the fate of the Ordos. In 1501 Mongols based there attacked Hua-ma-ch'ih, a fortress along Yü Tzu-chün's defense line, and then defeated another Ming army near Ku-yüan. A new commander was sent to the region, Ch'in Hung (1426–1505, cs. 1451), who had served in Shensi and Hsüan-fu during the last quarter of the fifteenth century. His command area, called officially Shensi three borders, included the districts of Yü-lin, Ning-hsia, and Ku-yüan.[346] Ch'in Hung hurried to Ku-yüan and to the battlefield nearby where he carried out funeral rites and buried the remains of the Ming soldiers. At the same time he began reforms, impeaching officials, restoring discipline, and attempting to revive the system of military farming. In the three years that he was in charge, he appears greatly to have increased the extent of defenses in the region, though details are lacking. He repaired and extended Yü's wall, and is said to have built more than 14,000 watch towers and 6,400 *li* (2,133 miles) of embankments and ditches in areas which had previously been undefended.[347] Like Yü Tzu-chün, Ch'in apparently sought to establish a defensive quarantine line south of the Ordos.

But such defensive policies were not to the taste of the new Cheng-te emperor, (r. 1506–22) who succeeded to the throne in June of 1506.[348] In that year several groups of tens of thousands of nomads broke the embankments at Ku-yüan and made an attack. In the wake of it, all the leading officials began once again to discuss the importance of recovering the Ordos.[349] The emperor probably sympathized with them. But on the advice of Liu Ta-hsia (1437–1516, cs. 1464), he appointed to the northwest area Yang I-ch'ing (1454–1530, cs. 1472), not a dashing cavalry general, but rather a scholar who had spent most of his career dealing with military matters.[350]

Yang's analysis of the strategic situation made the Ming dilemma clear. Yü Tzu-chün's wall, he noted, had provided twenty years of security, but now the defenses were decaying and the situation was deteriorating. The root of the problem was the nomadic occupation of the Ordos, and the best strategy would be to recover Tung-sheng, the garrison northeast of the river loop that Yung-lo had abandoned, and create a border that would follow the river enclosing the Ordos, and extend from Ta-t'ung in the east to Ning-hsia in the west. But Yang recognized that was impossible for the moment. The troops and supplies needed could never be assembled at the isolated Ming garrisons south of the desert, and the risk of defeat had to be considered. Therefore the most secure strategy for the time being was defensive, and in particular wall-building. Yang outlined an ambitious plan to add to and extend Yü's work, and some money was appropriated for it.[351] We can imagine that Liu Ta-hsia, who had a reputation as a man cautious about offensive warfare, would have approved of this sound analysis. But Liu Ta-hsia, like his protégés, including Yang himself, fell afoul of Liu Chin, a powerful palace eunuch. The new emperor had been brought up and educated by eunuchs, and trusted them. Yang, who was associated with Liu Chin's rivals, was forced out of office in April of 1507, along with others concerned with border defense. Only forty *li* (13 miles) of the wall Yang had set out to construct were finished.[352]

Yang returned to office after Liu Chin's fall, in which he played an important role. But by that time military affairs had become increasingly the prerogative of the emperor alone, who was fascinated by warfare, and liked to think of himself as the Chinese answer to Batu Möngke. He favored Mongol dress, and spent much of his time living and traveling in border areas. In October of 1517 he took part in a battle near Ying-chou, a garrison city about forty miles south of Ta-t'ung, in which a large Mongol force was actually defeated. But though he loved to fight, Cheng-te really had no coherent policy: his actions in that sphere were, like his personal life, capricious and confused. All his enthusiasm for battle did not change the overall strategic situation, nor did he match his personal martial sympathies with support for the kind of institutional reconstruction that would have been required to secure the border. The basic policy questions that had been clear since T'u-mu continued to be unresolved, and were more hotly debated in the reign that followed than ever before.

The next reign, that of the Chia-ching emperor (r. 1522–67), was particularly faction-ridden, owing chiefly to his irregular accession. When the Cheng-te emperor (1506–22) had died without an heir, the chief grand secretary, Yang T'ing-ho (1459–1529) had arranged for the succession to pass to his cousin, and proposed that, for ritual purposes, he be treated as the adopted son of his predecessor. This Chia-ching emperor was only a boy when he became monarch, and one of Yang's purposes was probably to put someone tractable on to the throne. But as it turned out the new ruler was unwilling to accept the ritual status that Yang T'ing-ho had proposed. The scholars who had arranged the succession adduced historical evidence to bolster their position, but when it became clear that the new emperor was unhappy with such a status, other scholars came forward with support for his viewpoint. The issue may seem inconsequential today, but that is only because we no longer judge political legitimacy by descent. In Ming times it was crucial. As had happened already twice, in the Yung-lo period (1403–25) and after T'u-mu, Chinese theories of government and practical demands were difficult to reconcile. But the emperor was the emperor. Yang was forced to retire, and power passed to the faction which had supported the emperor in this bitter debate, which was known as the "Great Ritual Controversy."[353] Once the vulnerability of the top power-holders had been demonstrated by Yang T'ing-ho's fall, and once the emperor had realized that it was important for him to avoid being captured by any single grand secretary or faction, and therefore to shift his support unpredictably, a struggle for control at court developed which was never resolved.

Military policy became an important battlefield for this sort of factional struggle. The emperor was aware of the problems on the border, and he deeply hated the Mongols. A southerner, he had no intuitive understanding of border matters, and along with some of the other actors in the military drama, he believed it utterly humiliating and wrong for a Chinese emperor to have anything to do with nomads. He even went so far as commanding that the character *i*, which means "barbarian," should always be written as small as possible.[354]

Such attitudes on the part of the emperor, and many of the best educated members of society, posed an insoluble problem. To make peace with the Mongols would require some dealing with them: trade and tribute would have to be restored at least to what they had been at the start of the dynasty. If that was not done, the Ming would certainly face a prolonged period of military disaster. The nomads, now unified, would raid, and nothing the Ming did, whether it was raise huge armies or build vast walls, would stop them. A vicious circle would develop. The worse the raiding, the greater the call for such measures, and hence the greater the fiscal and social burden on the court. But since such measures did not address the basic problem, they would bring a solution no nearer. A number of Ming officials, among them some of the emperor's close advisors, understood this problem, but found it impossible, for political reasons, to deal with it effectively. A strong prime minister or commander-in-chief might have been able to force through measures to restore trade relations. But in a highly factionalized court, where no single minister held paramount authority, even to advocate such a course would be to invite damaging attacks from rivals who would accuse him of being too soft on barbarians.

In the 1540s at the court of the Chia-ching emperor, the same disagreement about policy that we have already seen between Pai Kuei and Yü Tzu-chün in the 1470s, was reproduced by grand secretaries Hsia Yen (1482–1548) and Yen Sung (1480–1565) respectively. Hsia, a rather orthodox Confucian, was the sponsor of an Ordos expedition proposal put forward by Tseng Hsien (1499–1548), a field commander, while Yen Sung, well-educated like Hsia, but far more willing to compromise, and then and thereafter the most powerful court official, opposed it, though with subtlety. The difference in the mid-sixteenth-century case was the far higher political stakes and consequences. A misstep by Hsia Yen in the policy duel was used to eliminate him from the grand secretariat, and eventually led to his execution.

8

The second debate
over the Ordos

The Ordos debates of the mid sixteenth century were as important a
turning point in the history of Ming military policy as the battle of T'u-mu
had been a hundred years earlier. Then, however, the Ming had been faced
by Esen, who in short order proved himself incapable of pressing home the
advantages won in battle; then, too, a strong figure, Yü Ch'ien, had taken
charge at the Ming court and stabilized a dangerous situation. In the
sixteenth century, during the reign of the Chia-ching emperor (1522–67),
by contrast, grave consequences flowed from chronic factionalism at court
as the dynasty faced the Altan khan, the most effective Mongol leader since
the fall of the Yüan.

By the early 1540s the Altan khan (1507–82) had restored unity to the
steppe, which had been divided by tribal war after Batu Möngke's death in
about 1532. Reconstructing a steppe confederation necessarily involved
access to Chinese resources, and these the Altan khan initially attempted to
obtain by peaceful means. In 1541 and 1542 his requests for trading
privileges stirred up extensive argument in the Ming court. When they
were refused, the Khan raided instead, beginning a "sequence of requests,
refusal, and raid" which recurred for nearly thirty years.[355]

But by the sixteenth century, more than simple Mongol raids threatened
the Ming. The nomads were settling down along the border in a strategically ominous way. The Altan khan, for example founded a city – today's
Hu-ho-hao-t'e (Huhehot), the capital of the Inner Mongolian Autonomous Region – to the west of the Ming capital, sited so as to exert a
strategic threat to Ta-t'ung and Hsüan-fu. Called Köke khota or "blue
city" (*Pan-sheng* in Chinese, from the Mongolian *bayishing* or "house") and
lying in the steppe transition zone northeast of the Ordos, it had a
commanding position in relation to the strategic corridor from northern
Shensi to the capital. It controlled Ta-t'ung rather as one chess piece can
check another.

The Altan khan's new settlement was in the tradition of border cities
founded by nomads at earlier times when they were organizing themselves
to establish hegemony or rulership over a settled neighbor. Karakorum, for

instance, in its heyday had boasted a cosmopolitan population, even including craftsmen from Europe. The population of the Altan khan's new city included many Chinese, mostly members of the outlawed White Lotus sect of Buddhism who had fled there, and who served the Altan khan as advisers and guides. Its architecture suggested that, like many Inner Asian leaders before him, the Altan khan was creating a mixed administrative center for a mixed empire. The Mongol leader's palace was modeled on that of the Ming. Above its second gate hung the inscription; *wei-chen hua-i* or "overawe Chinese and barbarians," and certain features of the settlement, such as "Altan's new town" and "Altan's new tower" were probably built by Chinese. With its city wall and official buildings inside, and irrigated fields surrounding it, Pan-sheng showed that the Altan khan knew how to make the most of the strategic advantages conferred by a foothold in the steppe transition zone, while the Chinese refugees living there apparently urged him on, and certainly taught him much about Ming warfare.[356]

The growth of this permanent Mongol strategic presence posed problems for the Ming. The long-standing debate about policy toward the Mongols continued, focusing on trade and tribute, and tending to pit border officials, who favored both, against palace officials and the emperor himself, who opposed them. Trade with the Mongols had been cut off in about 1500, and its restoration was one of the chief points of contention.[357] Thus in 1532, a year of famine in the north, the Mongols requested permission to present tribute, in accordance with the Ch'eng-hua and Hung-chih precedents. But the emperor was displeased, and ordered that active measures be taken to resist. The supreme commander of Shensi and the three borders, T'ang Lung (1477–1546, cs. 1508), nevertheless disagreed, noting that, like Esen almost a century before, the Mongols had concentrated a force of 100,000 in the Ordos area, and that the best strategy would be to permit tribute in order to lower tension.[358]

When the Altan khan requested permission to trade in 1541, Shih Tao (1484–1553, cs. 1517), who had been appointed grand coordinator of Ta-t'ung in 1536, expressed a similar view. He pointed out that trouble on the borders had become grave with the breaking off of tribute relations fifty years before, and argued that immense benefit could be achieved by re-opening the relationship. But the court countered by saying that the Mongols wished to make the Chinese relax their defense efforts, and that such a scheme would best be frustrated by refusing trade. The request was turned down, and a price was put on the Altan khan's head.[359]

In the 1540s the Altan khan repeatedly sent envoys to the borders to request trade, persisting even after several of them were killed by the

Chinese. His father had enjoyed trade and tribute privileges, and he could not understand why that status should not be passed on. Though with the borders closed to the Mongols, he had no choice but to raid, he still did not give up his attempt to reach a diplomatic agreement.[360] In both 1541 and 1542 he sent the son of a Chinese prisoner, Shih T'ien-chüeh, as an envoy. An argument developed at court about how to respond, with Yang Po, then an official in the ministry of war, and Yang Shou-ch'ien, both in favor of dealing with the emissary. But opinion at court went the other way: the envoy was beheaded, and Shih Tao was punished.[361]

Henry Serruys translates much of Yang Shou-ch'ien's memorial, the *Ch'iu-kung chi* or "Record of the Request to Present Tribute" (1542) which explains the incident and the arguments.[362] Yang Shou'ch'ien probably learned a good deal about military affairs from his father, a *chin-shih* of the year 1493, who served as grand coordinator in both Ta-t'ung and Ning-hsia, where, the *Ming history* tells us, he was very popular with the border people. Yang Shou-ch'ien himself passed the *chin-shih* in 1529, and served in Shansi and Yen-sui, where his promotion of military farming greatly pleased the court.[363]

Yang's memorial betrays some of the puzzlement and frustration that border officials must have felt with the way the Altan khan's requests were being handled. Officials were afraid to speak out in favor of any reasonable policy:

Up to now nobody understands the evil of our unreasonably provoking the fierce Barbarians into oppressing [the people of the border regions] in countless ways. The governor [of the military district of Ta-t'ung], Shih Tao, was severely punished for entertaining intercourse with foreign barbarians. Although he was set free without being executed, those in responsible positions are afraid.[364]

But if advocacy of the position was risky politically, the arguments for trade nevertheless continued to make sense.

One was that the Ming maintained trade and tribute relations with other peoples: in Liao-tung with the Jurchen, at Hsi-feng-k'ou with the Mongols of the three commanderies of the Uriyanghkha, and in Kansu with traders from Central Asia. Did it make sense to refuse such treatment to the Altan khan? Of course there were all kinds of objections. Agreement to trade could be compared to the unpopular peace treaties the Sung dynasty had made with its northern neighbors. Or it could be argued that the nomads would spy or otherwise cause trouble if they were permitted to enter the empire.[365] Against this it was argued that far from being a risk, to permit tribute relations was perhaps the only way of gaining the breathing-space needed to strengthen defenses. During the reign of the Ch'eng-hua emperor in the late fifteenth century, renewal of relations with the Mongols had been carried out because the Ming feared that they did not have time to prepare defenses. The same argument was now applied to the need to strengthen defenses along the line where Yü Tzu-chün had suggested that another wall should be built. "If [now] we take advantage of the respite [presented by peaceful tribute relations] to complete construction of border walls at Hsüan-fu, Ta-t'ung, and Hua-ma-ch'ih; construct many large fortified villages inside [those territories]; [and] call upon the people to cultivate [this land area] completely so that grain becomes cheap" would it not be possible to guarantee security?[366]

One of the most persuasive advocates of making peace with the Mongols was Weng Wan-ta (1498–1552), who from 1544 served as military commander of the region just west of the capital, and who built extensive walls there. He supported a policy that sought to manage the Mongols by a mixture of economic, diplomatic, and military measures. Weng was from Chieh-yang county in Kwangtung province, and passed the *chin-shih* examination in 1526, after which he served for a time as provincial magistrate in Wu-chou in Kwangsi. But his rise to high office began only at the time of the Vietnam campaign in the years 1537–40. Then too the issues of offensive and defensive policies arose. Weng favored economic and diplomatic means over military, and preferred walls to expeditionary forces. In spite of this he enjoyed great favor with the emperor. But the emperor would not accept Weng's prescriptions for dealing with the Mongols. Thus when in 1546 the Altan khan had renewed his requests, and Weng urged that peace be made, the emperor refused. The *Ming history* notes that the emperor relied on Weng Wan-ta very much, and granted whatever he requested, with the only exception being his recommendations about the Altan khan.[367]

These broad arguments over strategy acquired a clear political focus in the late 1540s, when the most important of all the Ordos debates erupted. The debate began when Tseng Hsien, the commander of the Shensi three borders defense area, proposed a massive offensive to drive the nomads from the Ordos, to be followed by permanent fortification of a new Ming defense line along the loop of the Yellow river. Although Tseng's plans were far more detailed than any that had come before, their essence differed not at all from the calls for Ordos recovery that had been made beginning in the mid fifteenth century, as we have already recounted. What made Tseng's proposals more important than those of his predecessors was not their substance, but rather their political fate. Tseng was, by all accounts, a talented and devoted official, and grand secretary Hsia Yen, detecting a political opportunity, attempted to use his strategic proposals to secure his own position at court. Eventually Hsia staked his reputation on the policy, only to be brought down by his rival Yen Sung, who opposed it.

In his late forties when he made the proposals, Tseng Hsien was a competent and ambitious military commander. Though born into a military family, he had been classically educated. His second official assignment, undertaken five years after he qualified as a *chin-shih* in 1529 took him to Liao-tung as inspector general with the rank of censor, where in 1535 he successfully put down a military mutiny, using greater toughness than his predecessors.[368] As he rose in the bureaucracy, he became increasingly concerned with the problem of nomadic raids. Having served in Shantung since 1541, he was transferred to be grand coordinator of Shansi, and thus a subordinate of Weng Wan-ta, in 1544. He did well. On 23 February 1546 the *Shih lu* entry states:

The emperor observed that over the last year the nomads had not attacked Hsüan-fu, Ta-t'ung, or Shansi, and that the border defense there had been successful. The grand coordinator of Shansi, the censor-in-chief Tseng Hsien, had long served on the borders and his meritorious achievements were outstanding. He was elevated to the rank of vice minister of war.[369]

Three months later, on 8 May 1546, Tseng was appointed supreme commander of the three border districts of Yü-lin, Ning-hsia, and Ku-yüan.[370]

In his new post Tseng immediately undertook active measures. He got rid of subordinates he believed to be incompetent: about a month after his appointment, on 10 June 1546, agents of the *chin-i wei*, or "Embroidered-uniform Guard" (the palace eunuch police organization), arrested four high-ranking officials in Tseng's area, while three others were demoted or had their salaries cut. He moved to gain control of more troops and resources, and went on the offensive, killing many Mongol women and children in one battle, at Ma-liang shen.[371] He strengthened defense as well. The nomads harassed the local people, frightening them so that they "did not dare to go out and gather wood," and Tseng, following time-honored precepts of Chinese statecraft, organized counter-attacks, and built up the network of local forts, measures which led, apparently, to limited withdrawal by the nomads.[372]

But Tseng was not satisfied with these accomplishments, and began to consider how the problem of the northwest frontier might be permanently solved. He suggested two approaches: first, renewal of fortification, and second, a series of campaigns to establish a Ming presence in the Yellow river loop. He made these proposals for the first time in two memorials submitted on 8 January 1547.[373]

The soundness of the proposals Tseng made in 1547 was open to question. But our sources agree that grand secretary Hsia Yen was very pleased when he heard of them through a kinsman, Su Kang. Sponsorship of them potentially offered him a chance to establish unchallenged ascendancy at court. As we shall see, Hsia Yen's position was not yet secure. A decade earlier he had used advocacy of a hard line in the debate over Vietnam to strengthen himself. Now there was the prospect of organizing a military campaign, with all the patronage and control of resources that would entail. And finally, if his plan should succeed, Hsia could become famous forever, by "making an accomplishment of the kind that is seen only rarely in history" (*pu shih chih kung*). By ridding the Ming, once and for all, of the menace of the nomads to the northwest, he would make his position both at court and in history secure. Of course all would be for naught if the expedition Hsia sponsored should fail. But Hsia had great confidence in Tseng, whom he was sure could succeed. He memorialized to the emperor that he had "no servant more loyal than Tseng."[374]

Tseng proposed striking at the root of the border problem, and made his case in traditional terms. Like Li Hsien a century earlier, he quoted Chia I's famous memorial criticizing the *ho-ch'in* system. In the past, he pointed out, the nomads were regulated by means of ritual, and when the Chinese court was virtuously administered, then distant peoples submitted. Tseng argued that recently the nomads had resisted such moral influence and taken to raiding the northern frontier, so that a paradoxical situation had arisen in which nomads no more numerous than the inhabitants of a single large Ming prefecture were able to strike fear into the hearts of far larger numbers of Chinese. This had been possible, according to Tseng, because the Chinese had abandoned the strategically important Ordos area, and the nomads had occupied it.

Their dens and nests there are now firmly established. To drive them out will be difficult. But I fear the consequences [of their presence in the River loop] will daily grow more serious. Therefore, there is no better policy for dealing with them than recovery of the Ordos area. Not to approve this plan, but rather out of fear to choose the inferior policy of taking defensive measures only, may be compared to attempting to stop water from boiling without knowing enough to remove the firewood; it will not stop catastrophes along the border.

Tseng's memorial detailed an eight point plan of action. Evoking the strong and decisive emperors of the past, it envisioned an attack by 300,000 or more men, combining land and water operations. Echoing Kao Lü, Tseng urged that the Chinese should take advantage of their military strengths, which by Ming times included their knowledge of firearms. The campaign would cost more than 2,000,000 *tan* (133,000 tons) of grain, and about 3,000 *liang* (3,900 ounces) of silver. When it had been completed,

Tseng advocated that an extensive program of fortification should be undertaken. But this campaign was not to be initiated without careful planning. The Chinese could choose their time of action. For the nomads the best fighting time was in the fall, when their horses were well fed after a summer's grazing. But for the Chinese, it was the spring, when the nomads and their mounts were underfed, while the Chinese, with their superior resources, could nevertheless muster strength. If commanders were carefully chosen; if fodder and provisions were sufficient; and if discipline were strictly enforced; then success would be possible.[375]

Almost as soon as they were made, these proposals became entwined in the long-standing rivalry of the two most influential grand secretaries of the time. Hsia Yen and Yen Sung are both well-known figures in Chinese history. Hsia is usually thought of as an intelligent and principled man whose lack of political savvy led to his demise. His rival, Yen Sung, is by contrast considered one of the great villains of Chinese history, an extraordinarily corrupt man who, with his son, brought disaster to sixteenth-century Ming China. Recently such judgments have been challenged, notably by Professor Kwan-wai So, who has undertaken a reappraisal of Yen Sung.[376] Foreign policy provides some confirmation of Professor So's reassessment, for it would appear that there Hsia Yen did positive damage, while Yen Sung, though not putting any positive measures into effect, did forestall some potentially disastrous initiatives. Both men, however, seem to have been most concerned not with the content of policy so much as with their own positions at court.

Technically speaking, Hsia Yen and Yen Sung were fellow provincials.[377] Yen was born into an artisan family in 1480 at Fen-i in Yüan-chou county of Kiangsi province, while Hsia was born in Peking, but to a military family registered at Kuei-ch'i in Kuang-hsin prefecture, some two hundred miles to the east in Kiangsi. Yen won his *chin-shih* degree in 1505 at the age of 25, while his fellow provincial Hsia succeeded only on his third try, winning the degree in 1517 at the age of 35. Yen, however, suffered from poor health, and spent ten years at home before returning to government. Hsia's rise to high office was faster than Yen's. He became grand secretary in 1537, vacating the post of minister of rites to which Yen was named subsequently, possibly through Hsia's influence.[378] But if Hsia was hoping thereby to recruit Yen as a follower, he was to be disappointed. Instead, by the early 1540s the two men were rivals for paramount influence in government.

In August of 1542 Hsia Yen was dismissed from the office of grand secretary, and in September of the same year, Yen Sung succeeded him. It did not take long, however, for the emperor to realize that Yen Sung alone threatened to become too powerful, and therefore to bring in someone to counterbalance him. So in October of 1545, Hsia was summoned back, and in January of the following year he again became chief grand secretary.[379] Hsia's position was thus, as we have mentioned, insecure.

On his return Hsia was almost certainly concerned to consolidate his position to avoid another fall. He had a number of courses of action open to him. The emperor was fond of Taoism; Hsia had already shown skill in composing the blue-paper prayers that were a part of Taoist ritual, and for this he was greatly in the emperor's favor.[380] However, Yen Sung was also similarly skilled. Hsia apparently decided not to compete with Yen Sung by trying to use Taoism as his path to the top, but rather to carve out a role for himself as a champion of the values of those literati who abhorred Taoism. This stance, however, led to friction with the emperor. Hsia declined, for example, "a [Taoist-style] hair-dress with fragrant-leaf design [. . .] and a pair of leather shoes with silk layers to wear" which the emperor had given his ministers.[381] If Taoism was not the best path for Hsia, however, military policy might yet hold possiblities. Such, briefly, was the political background for the debate over Tseng's proposals, which Hsia enthusiastically backed.

When Tseng's memorial was received, the ministry of war, then headed by Ch'en Ching, had been asked to respond. The ministry's recommendations were cautious. Certainly they had no quarrel with his motives; the moral justification for the campaign was sound (*ch'i ming shen cheng*) and Tseng's personal determination exemplary (*ch'i chih shen jui*). However, Tseng had made two sets of proposals, one for fortification and one for a military expedition. Of these, the second was particularly difficult, risky, and expensive. The Ministry noted that Yang I-ch'ing had also expressed a wish to "recover" the river loop, but had been more realistic about its cost. He had known that the Ming empire of his time, some forty years earlier, was not equal to the task, so he had called instead for more effective fortification. Relieving the local people of excessive military expenditures while making them secure from raids would permit a gradual recovery (perhaps over ten years) of the border economy. That in turn was an indispensable prerequisite for carrying out any plan envisioning an occupation of the river loop area. The difficulty of finding sources of finance for military operations, whether from the capital treasury, from the sale of salt certificates, or from the sale of official ranks, was well known. The ministry concluded by noting that a broad consensus favored improving fortifications, slowly rebuilding the empire's strength, rather as Yang I-ch'ing had suggested, and only then attempting the sort of military campaign Tseng had in mind. The border commanders were also skeptical.[382]

But the emperor, perhaps reflecting Hsia's influence, was not inclined to follow the cautious counsels of the ministry of war. Like the Cheng-t'ung emperor at the time of T'u-mu, he was fascinated by an active policy. He noted that the occupation by nomads of the Ordos area was a crisis which had already existed for a long time, and which was a matter of great personal concern to him. None of his officials had previously advocated a military campaign to occupy the region, and now Tseng did, demonstrating "great understanding of the situation." He instructed Tseng and the various officials involved to meet and develop a more detailed plan. And he instructed that 200,000 *liang* (260,000 ounces) of silver be appropriated for him.[383]

With the emperor's clear support for Tseng's plans, Hsia's hope of bolstering his precarious influence at court looked well set to succeed. He and the other advocates of offensive policy however, managed to undermine themselves by inept handling of court politics. As more or less orthodox Confucians, they were reluctant to deal with eunuchs, or imperial favorites, or with those they believed to be corrupt. They preferred to depend upon the emperor's willingness to make such people toe the policy line. This approach did not win them popularity. Rather, during the very months when their prospects seemed rosiest, they created, by their own actions, a grouping of adversaries that would eventually bring them down. A number of influential persons moved into opposition to Hsia and Tseng, and into alliance with Yen Sung. Among these were Ch'iu Luan, Lu Ping, and Tsui Yüan.

Ch'iu Luan (1505–52) was perhaps the most important. He had deep roots in the northwest, and had been appointed grand defender (*chen-shou*) of Kansu in February of 1544.[384] Born at Chen-yüan near Ning-hsia, he was the grandson of Ch'iu Yüeh (1465–1521), a soldier who had been ennobled as a reward for his part in putting down the 1510 rebellion of Chu Chih-fan, a fourth-generation descendant of the Ming founder.[385] Ch'iu understood the situation in the northwest, but his compromising approach did not suit Tseng, who sought his removal.

Less than a year after Tseng Hsien had assumed his post, he urged punishment for Ch'iu and for Yang Po, the grand coordinator of Kansu, for inadequate resistance to an attack on Yung-ch'ang (near Wu-wei in modern Kansu) on 22 January 1547. The emperor agreed to punish lesser officials, but perhaps following Yen Sung's advice, waived penalties for Ch'iu and Yang. In July Ch'iu refused Tseng's order to transfer three thousand troops to Lan-chou, saying that to do so would leave him with inadequate forces. Yang Po concurred over the action, and the emperor ordered only mild punishment.[386]

When a supervising secretary (*chi-shih-chung*) of the office of scrutiny of the ministry of war, reopened the case, the minister of war, Ch'en Ching, found that Ch'iu had been adequately punished, and urged only that supreme commanders be reminded to give orders openmindedly, while governors and grand defenders be warned against resisting orders and then turning to the court for support.[387]

In the summer of 1547 the policy conflict grew more heated. Tseng reported to the capital that he and some of his colleagues had begun making preparations for the campaign. Local funds were initially used to prepare weapons and supplies, and construction of defensive works was begun on 7 April 1547. However, because the officials who were supposed to approve the policy had not responded, though the deadline for doing so had passed, Tseng was obliged to halt work on June 12.

Despite his court backing, Tseng's plans were clearly not popular. Given the loose organization of any Ming military project, non-cooperation could lead to a standstill. Whether for reasons of personal interest, or because of reservations about policy, many officials were withholding support.

The emperor referred Tseng's complaint to the ministry of war. It recommended that he reiterate his instructions and set a December deadline for the receipt of opinions, and that after that time, in the absence of a consensus, he himself should set the strategy.[388]

Tseng was also taking risks. He had started preparing weapons and walls before final authorization had been received, and sought the chance to fight as well. His victory, mentioned above, in the summer of 1546 had been preceded by a defeat which he had concealed. Furthermore, Tseng was stirring up anger among the desperately poor border population by pressing them into labor service, and by requisitioning metal cooking pots and farm implements to be cast into weapons.[389] Reports of popular dissatisfaction worried the court, and at the end of the summer, an earthquake provided the portent that permitted Tseng's opponents to move.

For Tseng and Hsia, however, the immediate problem was lack of support from the ministry of war. Here summer brought them some success. On 20 July a strong supporter of Tseng, Wang Chin, was made grand defender of Ning-hsia, and on 21 September Wang I-ch'i was made minister.[390]

But while the summer of 1547 saw Hsia eliminate several obstacles to his plans, in its course he also alienated two important imperial favorites. One was Ts'ui Yüan (1478–1549), a son-in-law of the Ch'eng-hua emperor (r. 1465–88), who had earlier been helpful to Hsia in offsetting the influence of Kuo Hsün (1475–1542) against him. This was an important debt, for Kuo was not only the descendant of one of the Ming founder's closest collaborators; he had also had played a pivotal role in the Chia-ching emperor's victory in the Great Ritual Controversy. The other new enemy was Lu Ping, whose mother may have been a wet-nurse to the future emperor, and who had been a friend since childhood and become a particular favorite after he saved the emperor's life in a fire in 1539. He had risen to control the Embroidered Uniform Guard, and to be a vice commissioner of the five military commissions.

On 23 November both Ts'ui and Lu were impeached by an investigating censor Ch'en Ch'i-hsüeh (1514–1593, cs. 1544), who accused them of a number of crimes, including corrupt dealings in salt. Hsia Yen urged the emperor to condemn these favorites, but he would not. One source reports that Lu Ping, hearing of the charge, hurried to bribe Hsia Yen. At Hsia's residence he knelt for a long time, till Hsia Yen, taking no real notice of him, haughtily forgave and dismissed him. The annalist T'an Ch'ien observes this treatment so angered Lu that "as a result, with Yen Sung, he sought a way to bring down Hsia Yen, but Hsia Yen was unaware of this."[391]

Indeed, neither Hsia Yen nor Tseng Hsien realized the degree to which resentment against them was increasing. All they saw were their successes: commanders replaced, a new minister of war, an emperor who appeared solidly on their side. So early in 1548, the proposal for Ordos recovery was made again, in far more detail that two years before. On 10 January 1548 Tseng, with some of his subordinates, submitted an exhaustive memorial, including eight maps and diagrams, again advocating the military campaign. The memorial was designed to rebut those who were criticizing Tseng's idea, and its heart consisted of eighteen points, each a detailed proposal, with accompanying matter concerning arguments for and against. The introduction to the memorial reiterates a good deal of what had gone before, and contains text of arguments in support of Tseng's position by other officials. This was the definitive proposal, and the maximum effort of those supporting a military campaign to recover the Ordos.[392]

The submission of the new, detailed proposals also coincided with the closing of the net around Ch'iu Luan, who was removed from office on 14 January and arrested by a secret police officer some ten days later. By this time Ch'iu was under a good deal of fire. Tseng had repeatedly complained to the emperor against him. His crimes were too many to enumerate: he was corrupt, soliciting bribes and embezzling military stores; he used soldiers for his own purposes; he falsely reported a major victory, etc. Not surprisingly, affairs in Kansu were in a sorry state. The regional inspector (*hsüan-an*) of Kansu agreed, and censured Ch'iu on six points of dealing badly with nomads. Yang Po, now opposing Ch'iu, submitted thirty

Table 1.   *Cost of Ordos recovery as estimated by Tseng Hsien*

Item	Cost in *liang* [=1.3 ounces] of silver
grain ration for 60,000 men over fifty days' campaign	54,000
pickled vegetables for same	30,000
grain ration for 60,000 horses over fifty days' campaign	63,000
hay ration for same	600
grain and fodder for 25,000 extra horses, oxen, and camels	51,250
extra salary and travel expenses for 2,000 Shantung pikemen	13,000
salaries for additional officers required	5,000
Subtotal	216,850
money for rewards	100,000
Grand total	316,850

Source: HMCSWP 15:411–12
Note: Tseng starts with quantities in kind, and then converts to silver. This step has been omitted in the interest of simplicity. He also appears to have added incorrectly, and arrived at 276,250 *liang*.

accusations. But in prison Ch'iu did not forget his grievances against the advocates of the Ordos expedition. Rather, he too lent his assistance to the emerging faction opposing Hsia and Tseng.[393]

These changes in the political balance at court eventually doomed Tseng's proposals. Before we examine just how that happened, however, let us recall that a real policy issue was at stake in the argument, and that practical as well as political considerations affected the outcome. Tseng Hsien had maintained that the campaign he proposed was affordable. Yet the immediate ground upon which it was resisted, both by officials on the border and at court, was that it would be too expensive. This was Yen Sung's argument. And an examination of the figures suggests that it had merit.

Tseng Hsien's estimate of the cost of a year's campaign in the Yellow River loop area is presented in Table 1. The amount arrived at is not forbiddingly large; as Tseng points out, in recent years the outside troops (*k'o-ping*) assigned to Hsüan-fu, Ta-t'ung, and Shansi had received funds from the capital (*ching-yün*) of 1,450,000 taels (1,885,000 ounces of silver). Certainly these funds, and others already assigned, ought to have been sufficient to pay for the three-year campaign that was envisioned. And if those funds should not be sufficient, there was always salt revenue.

But a closer look at Tseng's figures suggests that they were gross underestimates of the true costs of the campaign. Early in his memorial, Tseng pointed out the sorry state of defense in the northwest: there were in fact only 60,000 soldiers fit for service. Clearly he could not plan to use all of these in his campaign, for to do that would denude all defensive installations. So we must assume that some portion of the troops would have to be newly raised. If they were to be mercenaries, then they would have to be paid in silver, above and beyond their rations. Tseng, however, has allowed only for rations. But even leaving aside the question of pay for mercenaries, we must assume that any troops above and beyond those already in the area (i.e. the 60,000) would have to be maintained year round. Any horses, oxen, or camels that were similarly new would also have to be maintained year round. If we assume that all the soldiers and horses are new, and that the cost of keeping them year round is the same as that on campaign, then the actual per year cost of Tseng's force would be 1,252,755 taels, or about 1,628,581 ounces of silver.[394]

Furthermore, the expenses Tseng has listed are not complete. He has not allowed for clothing for the troops, or even for simple weapons, not to mention all the firearms that he wants. An even more serious miscalculation would appear to be his failure to allow for transportation costs. In calculating his prices in silver, Tseng ignores the fact that he will not be supplying his troops with silver when on campaign, but rather in kind, there being no places to buy grain, hay or pickled vegetables in the Ordos desert. If we assume that his sixty thousand soldiers will be riding sixty thousand horses, and that their supplies will be carried by other beasts, then using other figures, one can calculate that the total of 135,000 *tan* (8,977 tons) of grain needed for the men and cavalry horses would require, for example, 67,500 camels to carry it.[395] He lists as well 3,000,000 *shu* (bundles) of hay as necessary: how that could possibly be transported is hard to imagine. So simply by adjusting a few of Tseng's figures realistically, we find that the cost of his projected campaign easily reaches something of the order of 3,750,000 taels (4,875,000 ounces of silver) over the three years during which he plans to campaign.

This is an impressive figure, and yet even it does not reflect the most fundamental error in Tseng's whole system of computing costs. For Tseng has presented only the operating expenses for his campaign. The capital costs, or start-up costs, are nowhere included. A large proportion of the horses and other beasts of burden, for example, will have to be purchased, or else shifted from somewhere else, which amounts to the same thing. The men, even if we assume they are conscripted, will have to be given clothing, weapons, etc. 85,000 horses and other animals are bound to be extremely expensive. Furthermore, the campaign is only one half of Tseng's strategy. Once the nomads have been forced to withdraw from the Ordos area, he wants to build a wall there. That will be very expensive (Yü Tzu-chün's wall to the south had cost over 1,000,000 taels) and furthermore would involve transport over long distances, and the conscription of large numbers of workers. Tseng's proposals would, in fact, have been extraordinarily, even crushingly, expensive for the Ming. So, from a practical point of view, there was solid basis for skepticism about them.

Such practical reasons led a number of influential figures with firsthand knowledge of the border situation to join the opposition to Tseng and Hsia. They felt no political animus, but rejected the policy proposals on their merits. Weng Wan-ta, for example, disagreed deeply with Hsia Yen and his associates over the desirability of tribute relations with the nomads, believing that nomadic requests for trade were just and should be honored; and he thought to resist by force of arms, especially given the state of defenses in Chia-ching times, was futile. He criticized the proposals for taking the Ordos. The river loop, he argued, was an ancient part of China. However,

Before Hung-chih times [1488–1506] we would yearly clear out the area. Thereafter we permitted the nomads to come and go, and to remain, and raise their cattle there. Now it may be likened to their household, and now that it has been established for a long time, though we may wish to recover it at a stroke, that will not be easy.

Nor, Weng pointed out, were the Chinese forces at all familiar with the land, with its strategic points, its pathways, its sources of water and forage. The Ming horses would be tired after three days' campaign, while the nomads could easily assemble forces at a shout.

And Weng raised more disturbing problems as well. The entire expeditionary force might be lost. And how would the area be held after the conquest? He stressed that attack always favored the nomads, while defense was the Ming's strength. His arguments too echoed those made a thousand years earlier by Kao Lü in his memorial, "In Favor of Long Walls": the nomads were best at riding and attack, while the Chinese strength was defense.[396] Referring to the renegade Chinese Wang San, who had been defeated near Ta-t'ung in 1547 only with great difficulty, Weng pointed out that an attack on the distant Ho-t'ao area could not possibly be so successful, for it would involve penetrating deeply into nomadic territory.[397]

Another strong critic of Tseng's proposals was T'ang Shun-chih.[398] T'ang was of distinguished lineage: his ancestors for six generations were all civil service degree holders or recipients of imperial honors. T'ang himself served in government for only six years, though: thereafter he retired, and devoted his attention to philosophy, mathematics, and belles-lettres. But he retained connections at court: in later years he was associated with Yen Sung.

In a letter to Tseng Hsien, probably written in 1548, he outlined his criticism of the Ordos recovery plan. The letter is respectful in tone: it refers to Tseng's early achievements on the border, and only then turns to the Ordos recovery proposal. The idea was not new, T'ang notes: in earlier times men who were concerned with the welfare of the nation had considered it as well. But they had been cautious: unwilling to attempt the attack at a time when the nomads were in actual occupation of the contested territory. Today the enterprise remains risky. It can only be undertaken with full knowledge of the economic and military strengths and weaknesses of the dynasty, and with a clear and well-thought-out plan for what is to be done after the expedition has succeeded. But success is not very likely. For an attack to work, good intelligence is essential. Yet the border with the Ordos has long been closed, and in a hundred years not a single Chinese has been there. Information now available is based on what one or two surrendered Mongols have said. Such poor information could lead to disaster.

Furthermore, it is unlikely that a single battle will be sufficient to drive the nomads from the Ordos. Even if it were possible, how could the two thousand *li* (666 miles) of new border that would thus be created ever be held? Until it was fortified, the scattered Chinese forces would be vulnerable. But to fortify would be an enormous task, and would require denuding other areas of soldiers and workers, and thus exposing them to attack. Controlling and administering the new area might well prove more difficult than capturing it in the first place. There would undoubtedly be logistical problems. Furthermore, while it was true that the nomadic horses were really fit only in the fall, the Chinese also had seasonal problems. Firearms – they would, of course, have been flintlocks and perhaps small cannon – might be difficult to operate in certain kinds of weather. And what if the Mongols should learn of the Ming plan of attack and concentrate their forces? Their hundred thousand cavalry would be more than a match for any Ming expedition. T'ang's letter was a polite and reasoned argument against Tseng's proposals, and one with which it would be hard for a prudent man to disagree.[399]

Yet another critic of the proposals was Yang Po (1509–1574, cs. 1529). A native of Shansi, Yang served in the Hsi-an area, and later in the ministry of war. In 1539–40 he made a tour of the entire length of the northern border with the grand secretary Chai Luan, and was an early advocate of improved relations with the Altan khan. Like Weng Wan-ta he served with Mao Po-wen in the Vietnam campaign, and in 1546 was assigned to Kansu. He was quite successful there, and received promotions in 1549. He returned home shortly after the death of his mother, and thus, because of the prolonged period of mourning that ritual demanded, took no part in the controversy aroused by the Altan khan's raid in 1550. Upon his return he continued to rise in the governmental hierarchy, and to serve on the frontier, where he played a major role in the fortification of Ku-pei-k'ou and Liao-tung. In 1555 he rose to be minister of war, and it was with that rank that he assumed the post of supreme commander of Hsüan-fu and Ta-t'ung, where he rebuilt much of the defense line begun by his predecessor Weng Wan-ta. Yang had been associated with Ch'iu Luan when he worked in Kansu, and at one point he had supported Tseng Hsien's impeachment of him. Ch'iu, resenting this, had later tried to block Yang's promotions. But despite this personal animus, the two men agreed that the Ordos recovery proposals were unworkable.[400]

The final decision against Ordos recovery appears to have been determined, however, by a mixture of political and military arguments, ultimately brought to bear on the interpretation of an omen. On 10 February 1548 Ts'ui Yüan and Yen Sung met at Yen's house to plot Hsia's downfall. Their alliance had begun in the previous year when Hsia, forgetting how much he had helped him in the past, had acquiesced in Ts'ui's impeachment. Now four men guarded Yen Sung's home, and during the meeting no one was allowed in or out. A bargain was clearly struck. In the weeks that followed, Ts'ui, who was influential at the palace (and whose son-in-law, Hsieh Lan, was one of Tseng's subordinates) spread rumors that Tseng had been misappropriating tens of thousands of taels that should have gone for military supplies, and had been using them to bribe people to support his plans.[401]

Five nights later came the court meeting that led to the abandonment of Hsia's and Tseng's project. At that meeting, on 15 February 1548, the emperor for the first time revealed deep misgivings about the project, and spoke contemptuously of Tseng (see below). The expression of such an attitude clearly shocked Hsia Yen, who immediately dropped his sponsorship of the project, and turned his full attention to limiting damage to his position and that of his protégés. What had led the emperor to change his mind?

Imperial acceptance of the charge that Tseng had been passing out bribes would account for his changed estimate of his character. But the military decision may have another explanation. In August of the previous year there had been a severe volcanic eruption in Shensi, at just the time that Tseng was arousing murmurs of discontent by his exactions of supplies and labor to prepare for the campaign. This was singularly inauspicious, for the character *peng*, used to refer to the collapse of a mountain in the earthquake, is also used for the death of an emperor. On 11 February the emperor mentioned the earthquake to Yen Sung, and instructed that divinations be carried out. These forecast disaster. It appears that the emperor's advisers were able to tie all these strands together by reference to a Han precedent, and so lead the emperor to change his mind.[402]

At the court meeting at which he revealed his change of mind the emperor asked whether the proposed campaign was justified. The phrase he used, *ch'u shih kuo yu ming fou* (is the dispatching of an army justified?) fits into a pattern of argumentation over war and peace that has a long history. It is in particular reminiscent of the words used by the Han official Wei Hsiang (d. 59 B.C.) to oppose a similar plan for a military campaign. Like the Ming emperor, Wei had asked what the justification for the proposed campaign would be. Having done so, he quoted a line from the *Tao te ching* that implicitly condemned offensive policy: "after a great war comes the year of adversity."[403]

The Chia-ching emperor was a well-read man, and it is plausible that he might have recalled the *Han shu* passage describing the incident himself. If not, Yen Sung might have brought it to his attention in connection with the "adversity" that the divinations about the earthquake foresaw. Both men probably would have recalled that two verses before the phrase quoted from the *Tao te ching* is another passage that argues against the use of force: "those who aid the ruler with Tao do not use military force to conquer the world."[404]

Other aspects of the parallel are also worth attention. One is that the signs of unrest resulting from Tseng's actions led to a fear of rebellion by border residents. Wei Hsiang had alluded to a similar danger in the Han by quoting Confucius's injunction against the plan of Chi-sun of Lu to attack the small state of Chüan-yü: "I am afraid that the sorrows of the Chi-sun family will not be on account of Chüan-yü, but will be found within the screen of his own court" (i.e. discontent at home was a greater danger than aggression from abroad).[405] Another is that while the Taoist elements in the precedent would have special appeal to the emperor, to argue from Wei Hsiang and from Confucius was to argue on Hsia's own ground, and thus to make his reply difficult.

We have no proof that this well-known parallel figured at all in the discussion. But it is hard to imagine even if it did not, that the lines of argument were not quite similar, invoking the anti-military strands of both Taoism and Confucianism against the military expedition that one faction at court was promoting.[406]

With the emperor's change of mind the final phase of the drama began. At the court meeting mentioned above, the emperor had asked for a thorough reexamination of the whole issue. The nomadic occupation of Ho-t'ao, he stated, was a matter of long standing, and if the Ming today should attempt to conquer the area, he wondered whether the justification would be sufficient. He further wondered whether the resources of the Ming empire, both men and supplies, were adequate. And he had harsh words for Tseng Hsien. His person was not worth speaking of (*i Hsien ho tsu yen*). What concerned the emperor was not court personalities, but rather the welfare of his subjects. An ill-considered campaign in northern Shensi might be so unsuccessful, or so burdensome, as to lead to the deaths of thousands of innocent people.

The campaign was cancelled, and a process of political recrimination got underway towards a bloody climax. As soon as the emperor's negative decision was known, Hsia Yen began to try to limit damage to himself, while Yen Sung apparently worked subtly to ensure that his adversary's defeat would in fact be total. Hsia's prospects seemed favorable at first: the emperor directed his wrath at Tseng Hsien, who was arrested immediately, while he allowed Hsia to retire without losing his rank, ordering only that he be investigated. But the link between Tseng's case and Hsia's could not be broken. While still in prison, Ch'iu Luan, whom Tseng had removed from his command, began to settle scores by delivering an indictment accusing Tseng of crimes ranging from stirring up trouble on the border to concealing defeats, to bribing and maintaining that he had furthermore paid bribes to Hsia Yen through a relative, in order to promote his Ordos recovery proposals. As a result of these charges, Tseng was executed on 25 April 1548, while Ch'iu Luan, rehabilitated, was released from prison less than a month later. When Hsia heard of Tseng's execution he is said to have fainted, realizing that his own fate was probably sealed. His intuition was not wrong: he too was beheaded, on 31 October 1548.[407]

In retrospect, this political drama has come to overshadow almost completely the substance of the debate and indeed to color the way the merits of the policy positions are seen even today. Hsia Yen and Tseng Hsien have become minor Chinese patriotic heroes, while Yen Sung is known to this day as a major villain. The factions they defined, and the positions they exemplified, however, had an importance for the rest of the Ming dynasty that involved far more than personalities. The court struggle that put an end to the Ordos debate brought one specific episode of political competition to a conclusion. But it solved none of the policy problems that had precipitated it. The Mongols were still strong and threatening. Yet division about policy was so deep at court and within society that no action to cope with them seemed possible. At a time of real danger, the Ming government was politically paralyzed.

9

The heyday of
wall-building

Unwilling to trade with the Mongols, and unable to defeat them militarily, by the middle of the sixteenth century the Ming had no policy choice left but the final one mentioned in Chapter 2: namely, to attempt to exclude the nomads by building walls. We have already seen how this approach had begun to be applied in the fifteenth century. But it was fully adopted only in the sixteenth, when most of the Ming wall system was built. This chapter will sketch the pattern of development during that century. First it will survey the border as a whole, a task that can be accomplished only incompletely, owing to the lack of archaeological work, but which can show how Ming efforts shifted to follow the Mongol threat. Then it will examine in detail the one section of the border for which we do have good information: namely, the area of Hsüan-fu and Ta-t'ung, west of the capital, where during the sixteenth century Weng Wan-ta carried out extensive wall-building, one component of a comprehensive plan he developed to solve Ming military problems by shifting its approach fundamentally. Finally, it will say something about the more important wall-building projects right up to the dynasty's fall.

By the end of the sixteenth century, the border defense system whose remains are visible today had been created. But significantly, contemporaries did not speak of it as a "Great Wall." In Ming documents the frontier defenses are usually called the *chiu pien-chen*, or "nine border garrisons." This phrase refers not to a mode of construction, but to places: to the key defense points, the locations where the largest detachments of the Ming army were deployed. From east to west one enumeration gives these as Liao-tung, in modern Manchuria; Chi-chou, northeast of Peking; Hsüan-fu, northwest of the capital; Ta-t'ung, in northern Shansi; Shansi or T'ai-yüan, further west; Yen-sui or Yü-lin, south of the Ordos; Ku-yüan closer to central Shensi; Ning-hsia, at the entrance to the corridor westward; and Kan-su, near its western end.[408]

The evolution of this system was complex, and even in its final form it lacked neatness. Thus, traditional lists of the garrisons differ slightly, and the "number nine is apparently rather arbitrary and probably chosen for its cosmological meaning."[409]

As the deployment of garrison forces grew more elaborate in the sixteenth century, methods of fortifying became more sophisticated as well. Early Ming ramparts and city walls, even the wall Yü Tzu-chün built south of the Ordos, had been constructed of pounded earth, and work on them had usually been carried out by local people, called up for a season of *corvée*, as had been done for millennia. But such works did not last; by the 1520s Yü's wall had eroded away.[410]

To create a more permanent frontier, some of the new construction was carried out in brick and stone. This change made wall-building far more demanding: work that one man had done in a month when earth was the building material, might now require 100 men to do in stone.[411] Beyond this fact very little is known about the building of the Ming "Great Wall." Here and there crews have left tablets with their names and dates: these were apparently designed to permit responsibility for any poor work to be assigned. At Chia-yü-kuan, for example, one tablet records work done in 1540.[412] But it is not hard to hypothesize the other developments that would necessarily follow from such basic changes in building technique. Since peasant labor would no longer be satisfactory for such work, skilled masons, who would have had to be paid, must have been recruited. A considerable network of brick-kilns, quarries, and transportation routes must have been developed. All of this would have required that resources previously obtained locally in kind would now have to be provided for by the capital, by means of allocations of silver. The overall effect on Ming state and society of this change in modes of border defense is a topic that awaits comprehensive investigation. But its origins in the changing military situation are fairly clear.

The sequence of the border sectors where sixteenth-century wall-building took place reflected the shifting Mongol threat. In general, wall-building began in the west and moved east. Yü Tzu-chün's wall, built in the far west in the 1470s, was the Ming response to the migration of nomads into the Yellow River loop. To the extent that Yü's wall was effective, it naturally redirected nomadic attacks eastward, so that by the early 1500s the Mongols had moved their attack route to the Ta-t'ung and Hsüan-fu area west of the capital, where so far no walls had been built. When walls were built in this sector, as this chapter will describe, the nomadic attack route shifted yet again, to the northeast and east. This was the sector where most of the wall-building activity in the last part of the Ming was carried out. In addition to these three primary segments, lesser wall-lines were maintained in the Kansu corridor in the west, and in Liaotung to the east.

An impression of how this general process took place may be obtained by making a brief survey of the Ming defense line, and in particular by looking at the three most important forts along it. These are Chia-yü-kuan in the far west, Chü-yung-kuan not far from Peking, and Shan-hai-kuan at the eastern end of the wall, only ten miles or so from the sea. These three forts are also the most commonly visited sites on the Wall, and over the last thirty years they have been extensively restored. For most people it is the memory of one of them that fixes the image of "The Great Wall." Although the sites were fortified early in the dynasty, in their present forms they all appear to be essentially sixteenth-century works.

The westernmost of these forts marked the Ming's boundary at the end of the Kansu corridor, that narrow route between mountains to the south and deserts to the north that has been followed by caravans between China and Central Asia since ancient times, and that today is the route of the railroad that links Lanchow in Kansu to Urumchi in Sinkiang. As the train on that line leaves Chiu-ch'üan, passengers can clearly see a fort with high walls and two impressive three-storey gate towers, whose multiple roofs and curling eaves dominate the surrounding plain. This is Chia-yü-kuan. No fortress, it should be noted, stood here at the beginning of the Ming. Yü-men-kuan, the famous Jade or Jasper Gate built by the Han near the end of the second century B.C., and much alluded to in literature, lay at a point about two hundred miles to the west, and had by Ming times long since fallen into ruins – these would be discovered and described by Sir Aurel Stein in 1906. The Ming fort was established in 1372 by General Feng Sheng, who settled troops on the present site, probably chosen because of a fresh-water spring, and who built a relatively simple earth-walled enclosure. We hear little about this garrison until more than a century later, in 1495, when the western gate tower was added, to be followed by the eastern in 1506–7.[413]

In 1539, as security in the west deteriorated, the minister Chai Luan (1477–1546, cs. 1505) made an inspection of the borders and recommended much rebuilding at Chia-yü-kuan. As a result the fortress walls were nearly doubled in height, to their present nine or more meters, with new courses of brick simply being added on top of the original pounded earth wall.[414] Other changes were made as well. For more than 160 years the fortress had stood alone guarding the valley. Minister Chai urged that long walls should be constructed to improve security in the area. Three lengths of such wall may now be traced near the fortress. Two were built between 1539 and 1541: the "western long wall," some 30 *li* (10 miles) long, and the "eastern long wall," some 73 *li* (24 miles) long. The third was not built until 1573: the "northern long wall", which extends some 30 *li* (10 miles) to near Chiu-ch'üan, and connects to other border walls.[415] While the walls of the fortress itself are substantial, with ramps for horses leading to the parapet, the long walls in the vicinity are much smaller, and today difficult to trace in places.

East of Chia-yü-kuan low and discontinuous walls run in stretches along the Kansu corridor. The explorer Langdon Warner, who traveled there on his way to the cave temples at Tun-huang, spoke of following the wall for several days. It was "but a scant fifteen feet high, and impressed one only by reason of the fact that it had got there at all from the sea coast." He judged it "probably not of the greatest antiquity ... by the still visible trench from which the clay to build it had been dug."[416] Near the city of Wu-wei the wall divides, with a northern stretch running through Chung-wei to Ning-hsia, while a southern section passes through Lanchow and continues northeast to Ting-pien. Neither the route, nor the origins, of this so-called "Tibetan loop" are exactly known.[417]

West of the Yellow River a number of walls were built, beginning in the late fifteenth century, and repaired or extended in the sixteenth century. At San-kuan-k'ou, west of modern Yin-ch'üan city (Ning-hsia), the Hsi-kuan-men wall, built in 1531, and some 80 *li* (27 miles) long, is still visible.[418]

To the east of the Kansu corridor lies the Ordos frontier that we have already discussed. Today relatively continuous remnants of the rammed earth Ming ramparts apparently extend from the neighborhood of Yü-lin northeastward to a point just west of Shen-mu on the K'u-yeh river.[419] From Shen-mu to the point of the Yellow River where it flows southward out of the Ordos loop, many forts and towers remain, but no continuous wall.[420]

The Yellow river forms the boundary between the provinces of Shensi and Shansi, and on its eastern bank begins the next important defense zone. During the sixteenth century two primary defense lines were constructed there, as will be explained below, one to the north and the other to the south, enclosing the garrison cities of Hsüan-fu and Ta-t'ung in a lozenge of walls. Maps suggest that these walls may once have converged close to Peking, at Ssu-hai-yeh, a small settlement in the Chün-tu mountains northeast of the greatest of the Ming fortresses, Chü-yung-kuan.

Chü-yung-kuan is the place where most people visit "The Great Wall." Less than forty miles northwest of the Forbidden City (and within the limits of modern Peking municipality), it guards the most convenient pass through the mountains that lie between the capital and the river valleys and steppe beyond. The strategic significance of this pass has been known since ancient times. *Huai-nan-tzu* (ca. 130 B.C.) lists Chü-yung among the nine points under heaven.[421] In the nineteenth century the words *t'ien hsien* or "natural strongpoint" were carved on a rock overlooking the pass.[422]

Fig. 6a The Great Wall was never an important theme in traditional Chinese painting. What Wang Fu (1362–1416) depicts here in one of his *Eight Scenes of Peking*, is not a wall, but rather the Yün-t'ai ("Cloud Terrace"), a beautifully decorated ceremonial arch built by the Yüan dynasty in 1345 just south of where the Ming would later build the very impressive defensive walls commonly visited today. (Collection of the Peking Historical Museum.)

Fig. 6b The Yün-t'ai as it appears today. (Photo: Peking Slide Studio.)

The Han may have defended the pass, and the Northern Ch'i fortified the area in A.D. 554,[423] while the Chin held up the Mongols here, and the Yüan established military farms.[424] Yüan emperors passed through Chü-yung-kuan on their way to and from the northern capital at Shang-tu and the last of them, Shun-ti (r. 1333–67), ordered the construction of a religious monument along the route. This is the exquisite Yün-t'ai, a ceremonial arch decorated with bas-relief Buddhist images and designed to bring good fortune to all who pass under it. Within the arch is carved a famous set of religious inscriptions. In Sanskrit, Tangut, Uighur Turkish, Tibetan, Mongolian, and Chinese, they suggest the cosmopolitan character of the traffic that once passed through. One of the earliest Chinese railways (built 1905–9) climbed over this pass and connected the capital to Kalgan (or Chang-chia-k'ou),where the caravan route to Urga (now Ulan Bator) and Siberia branches off from the main route west.

But the fortifications that have made Chü-yung-kuan China's premier tourist attraction were built by the Ming. In 1368 the general Hsü Ta established a garrison in the pass and built fortifications, though our sources contradict one another about both their nature and their location.[425] Most likely they were at the northern end, where new stone walls were apparently built on the foundation of an ancient gate, and repaired in 1404 and 1424. Although fortified early, it was only after the resounding defeat of the Ming army at T'u-mu in 1449 that the pass became a first line of defense. In the wake of that battle a censor was sent to take charge of constructing fortifications, and in 1455 this work was completed. The new fortifications were to the south of Hsü Ta's original garrison, perhaps near the Yün-t'ai, and they were grouped around a new gate, above which an inscribed plaque was placed.[426] More repairs were carried out in 1481, and in the sixteenth century there was much new building, which included the walls visited today. Archaeological evidence dates some of the construction on the Pa-ta-ling ridge, north of the pass proper, to 1539 and 1582.[427]

The sixteenth century also witnessed the building of the impressive and well preserved Ming walls between the capital and the sea. East of Peking, between mountains to the north and the south, there lies a strategic coastal strip through which runs the road to Manchuria and Korea. At the Manchurian border, where the strip narrows, the Ming built the great fortress complex of Shan-hai-kuan, famous for its large arched gate on which is inscribed "First Pass Under Heaven," *t'ien-hsia ti i kuan*. Between that fort and the capital stretch walls and ranks of signal towers: a fortified line broken by two major and a score of minor passes. The road to the Ch'ing summer capital Jehol (Ch'eng-te) passes through one of these, Ku-pei-k'ou, while the Luan river flows south at the second major pass, Hsi-feng-k'ou, located midway between Peking and the sea. Although defenses in this area were established already early in the Ming, they did not reach their full development until the second half of the sixteenth century, when warfare in Korea, and the developing threat of the Manchus made this frontier critical.

Shan-hai-kuan, literally "Mountain-sea barrier," is some two hundred and sixty miles east of Peking, and not far from the site of an ancient gate, called Yü-kuan. The present site was apparently first fortified in the Northern Ch'i dynasty. A guard was established at the site in 1381, and the first fort begun in 1382. A hundred years later, between 1488 and 1505, walls were built at 170 strategic places between the pass and Chü-yung-kuan, but as was the case at Chia-yü-kuan and Chü-yung-kuan, the impressive surviving fortifications did not take shape until the military crisis of the sixteenth century. According to one Chinese scholar, long walls were begun at the time that the original fort was constructed, but these were apparently relatively limited in extent. It was only after nearly two centuries had elapsed that the Ming once again began serious work at the pass and its environs. Various secondary forts and other components of the defensive complex were built in 1565 and 1584, while the increasing importance of Shan-hai-kuan was marked by its separation from the Chi-chou commandery, and establishment as an independent command in 1571. A stretch of long wall that runs from the fortress to the sea, some ten kilometers to the south, was constructed in its present form by Ch'i Chi-kuang, who served as commander of Chi-chou from 1569 to 1583. Work on the fortifications was still not complete at the time of the Manchu conquest.[428]

As interest in the Great Wall has increased in recent years, the Chinese authorities have begun to restore and open up some other important sections of Ming fortifications. One of these, not far from Chü-yung-kuan, about twenty kilometers north of the Ming tombs, is the set of parallel walls near Huang-hua-chen, built between 1528 and 1619.[429] Another is the Chin-shan-ling, ten kilometers east of Ku-pei-k'ou, and built after 1570 by Ch'i Chi-kuang and T'an Lun, who will be discussed in detail below.[430] New photographs of Ku-pei-k'ou have also been published recently, as have descriptions of some of the less well-known passes, such as Tzu-ching-kuan, Yen-men-kuan, and Niang-tzu-kuan.[431]

We do not yet possess enough information to make a full study of the development of the system of which the stretches of frontier and important forts just mentioned form parts. But recent Chinese archaeological work on the Hsüan-Ta defense area, just west of the capital, and so-called after its two major cities, Hsüan-fu and Ta-t'ung, has made it possible to look in some detail at one very important example of the general sixteenth-century

Fig. 7 The mid and late Ming period saw an unprecedented amount of fortification building. The section of wall shown here, with its watch towers and crenellations, forms part of the important eastern stretch leading through mountainous country to the Gulf of Pohai. (From a Republican (1929) revision of the Lin-yü county gazetter, the *Lin-yü hsien chih*.)

pattern of fortification construction. A valuable survey recently under-taken in Shansi province provides the first comprehensive description of the ruins of the defense lines in the Ta-t'ung area.[432]

Development in the Hsüan-Ta area shows how the deteriorating mili-tary situation after 1449 led to a series of changes both in administration and in methods of fortification. In the early years of the dynasty, the scattered encampments near the border had been under the command of military personnel alone, and lacked any overall strategic supervision. But by the fifteenth century, the new situation on the border led to an attempt to treat defense more comprehensively, both by linking up forts into a system, and by bringing local officers into a more comprehensive command structure. In 1436, for example, a censor was sent from the capital to Hsüan-fu and Ta-t'ung, and after the T'u-mu defeat a *hsün-fu* ("grand coordinator") had been posted there. Even during the last quarter of the fifteenth and the beginning of the sixteenth centuries, however, such officials were only occasionally sent, in times of emergency. But in 1513 a single officer was placed in command of the area, and he was given the title *tsung-tu* ("supreme commander") in the early 1520s.[433] Weng Wan-ta, whom we have already met, was appointed to this office in 1544.

The command encompassed three defense areas: Hsüan-fu, Ta-t'ung, and Shansi, with the passes south of it. Detachments of guards under Ta-t'ung's command formed a defensive arc from Yang-ho in the northeast to the Ordos in the northwest; and the defense area controlled as well the territory south of the inner frontier, between the Shansi defense area to the west, and that of Hsüan-fu on the east. South and west of Ta-t'ung was the Shansi defense area, named after Shansi *chen*, a garrison just south of the Ning-wu pass, and not to be confused with the entire province of Shansi (the defense area included only the more northern part). The Ning-wu pass, and that at Yen-men further east, were the chief strategic points in this area. The long western frontier with Shensi was vulnerable to nomads crossing the river, while along the eastern border lay the passes controlling access to the capital from the southeast.

We have already mentioned the early Ming defense lines in the Ta-t'ung area, the *ta-pien* and the *erh-pien*, and how they had decayed. By the sixteenth century, the territory north of Ta-t'ung where the two defense lines had once run was no longer in Chinese hands, and again controlled by the nomads.[434] And nomadic raiding routes that had shifted to run through this area, after fortification of the southern edge of the Ordos desert made that part of the frontier militarily challenging.

Morale and loyalty, of both officers and men, were always serious problems, even in this most important section of frontier. Mutinies among the troops occurred several times. The countryside around Ta-t'ung is dry and unproductive. In Ming times military service on the border was generally grim, and conditions at Ta-t'ung were no exception. Those soldiers whose duties were not hereditary were often prisoners exiled for life. Diet was poor, officers cruel, and lonely hours manning watchtowers in the snows of winter frequently led to frostbite or worse.[435] Fighting the Mongols was generally a hopeless task, and officers and men preferred to avoid hostilities, and to profit instead by trading and other relations with the nomads. For the central government, simple disciplinary control of the garrisons was very difficult, a problem often made worse by attempts at reform.

A major mutiny broke out at Ta-t'ung in 1524, when the new emperor approved a proposal to strengthen its defenses. The grand coordinator Chang Wen-chin (cs. 1499) proposed that five forts (*pao*) should be built on the inner of the two old defense lines. The forts – Hung-ssu, Chen-ho, Chen-ch'üan, Chen-pien, and Chen-lu – would guard the approaches to the city from the northeast, and extend the Ming presence back into the area from which it had long been withdrawn.[436] The local garrison did not appreciate the plan. In 1524 mutineers killed Chang Wen-chin, and the construction of the five *pao* was deferred. Another mutiny erupted in 1533, and not until 1539 was the work completed.[437] In the period that followed, the Ta-t'ung defenses began to be thickened, and walls constructed.[438] In 1544, for example, Chai P'eng, Weng's predecessor as commander, reported to the court about walls he had built.[439]

The walls that were built in the 1540s appear to have been new work. One stretch has been examined by modern archaeologists, who conclude that its uniform composition (it is made of multiple layers of pounded earth, each some eighteen to twenty millimeters thick) proves it to be entirely a Ming work.[440]

In addition to walls, other fortifications were constructed. The largest were forts, called *ch'eng* or *pao*. Between them were smaller towers, called *tun-t'ai*, about one *li* (1/3 mile or about 1,760 feet) apart in more distant areas, half a *li* (1/6 mile or 880 feet) nearer to important points. Smaller still were hundreds of small signal-beacon platforms, *feng-huo-t'ai*, which were not necessarily near walls, but which rather radiated out from central points such as Ta-t'ung, or provided a signal-path connecting one command point to another. Garrisons of men and horses in the *ch'eng* and *pao* were substantial, ranging from several hundred to several thousand, while the *tun-t'ai* by and large had small crews, at most several dozen men, and often fewer than ten.[441]

The way that all these different structures functioned in the Ming defense system is not well understood. Certainly even the smaller towers, the *tun-t'ai*, could serve as forts or strong points. On occasion the Mongols attacked them, scaling them with grappling hooks, or using smoke to drive the garrisons out. From the larger forts – the *ch'eng* and the *pao* – mounted troops could be sent out on raids into Mongol territory, or to relieve other sections of the frontier. In the sixteenth century, firearms, which terrified the nomads and were thus very effective, began to be mounted in some towers.[442]

The important purpose of the towers, however, was not combat but signalling. Nomadic forces were very mobile and easy to concentrate, which gave the Mongols a great advantage. They could always choose the site of battle. No matter how many troops the Ming might commit to the north, they had to defend a very long perimeter, and could never match the forces the nomads might assemble at a single point. Since Han times Chinese had sought to compensate for this disadvantage by developing sophisticated beacon systems which, using fire by night and smoke by day, could rapidly relay information for use in mobilization and deployment. In T'ang times the standard required that a signal cover 2,000 *li* (666 miles) in a single day and night.[443] Ming signal-systems were probably similar, but we know little about them. They are known to have used cannon-fire in addition to fire and smoke. The hundreds of ruined signal towers that can still be seen along the old frontier are witness to their importance.

Most of the towers, which were eventually very numerous, were built late in the dynasty. By 1587 there were 788 *tun-t'ai* and 89 *ti-t'ai* (probably similar to the former, though perhaps designed for combat) in the Ta-t'ung area.[444] A list of seventy-two large forts, *ch'eng* and *pao* in the same area shows that only fifteen of these had been built (and only of earth at that) by 1425. By 1534, more than a century later, only five more had been added. The rest were built later, most in the decades from about 1540 to 1570, still of earth. Only toward the end of the century when the density of fortifications had increased, did the border in this area begin to look the way we intuitively visualize it, with many walls and towers. Just how different it looked before the sixteenth century can be realized if we note how infrequently brick and stone were used in fortification before the very late period. Of the forts we have listed, only three had been cased in brick before 1571: all the rest remained earth. Today thirteen fortresses survive in the vicinity of Ta-t'ung: some of their locations are shown on Map 6.[445] How forts were first built in earth, and then much later bricked, is shown in Table 2.

The architect who developed the conception for much of this defense system was Weng Wan-ta. When he took command of this defense region, generally considered the most important of all, his task was more than simply the tactical one of defending Ta-t'ung and other points. He had to consider broad questions of military policy. To understand what he

Table 2.   *Construction of forts in Ta-t'ung area*

Year	Built in earth	Earth fort bricked
Pre-Ming	1	–
1368	1	–
1370	1	–
1372	1	1
1374	1	1
1375	1	–
1384	3	–
1398	3	–
1405	1	–
1409	2	1
1438	1	–
1459	1	–
1459	1	–
1462	–	
1481	1	–
1485	1	–
1500	1	–
1535	1	–
1539	5	–
1540	1	–
1543	4	–
1544	8	–
1545	4	–
1546	8	–
1548	2	–
1558	7	–
1559	2	–
1560	1	–
1561	1	–
1562	1	–
1565	2	–
1566	1	–
1569	1	–
1572	–	17
1573	1	15
1574	–	11
1575	–	1
1578	–	1
1580	–	1
1581	2	1
1582	–	3
1583	–	1
1584	–	1
1585	–	1
1586	–	2
1587	–	1
1591	–	2
1595	–	1
1596	–	2
1600	–	2
1601	–	2
1605	–	1
1609	–	1

Source: Ch'en Cheng-hsiang, "Ch'ang-ch'eng," 168–71

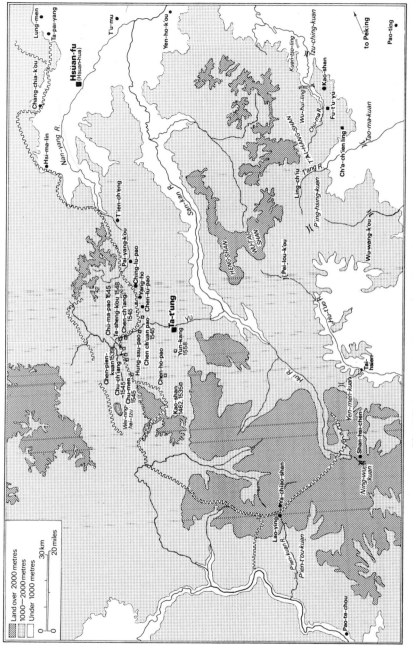

Map 6 Defenses in the Ta-t'ung and Hsüan-fu areas

accomplished, one must look strategically at the entire stretch of the northern border that lies between the Ordos and the capital.

The commander presented the basic thinking which had guided his work in the area with which he had been entrusted in a memorial submitted in 1547. It explained his general strategy, which was to shift the capital defense line to the north, and place a permanent garrison along it. Early deployments had established two major defense lines between the Mongol territories and the capital: the so-called "outer frontier" (*wai-pien*) and the "secondary frontier" (*tz'u-pien*). Between the two lay Ta-t'ung, and then east of it, Hsüan-fu. Weng explained that to get to the capital, an enemy had to pass through each of the frontiers in turn. To attack Shansi *chen*, for instance, which was just south of Ning-wu pass in the secondary frontier, raiders would first have to get past Ta-t'ung and the defenses to the north of it. Likewise, to attack Tzu-ching pass, southwest of the capital and also part of the secondary frontier, they would have to get through Hsüan-fu and the primary defenses.[446]

But until Weng's arrival, the secondary frontier had been for all practical purposes the capital's main line of defense. Raiders had no difficulty penetrating the outer frontier and reaching the area southwest of Peking, where large numbers of troops were deployed to stop them at the inner passes. Weng had acted on the assumption that the capital's security could be improved if walls were built in the north across the commonest attack routes, garrisons shifted there, and the outer border thus made the primary line of defense. Weng hoped to station troops there permanently, rather than dispatching them only in the autumn when the danger of attack was at its greatest. Such strengthening of the outer defenses would reduce raids into the interior; while if the nomads should break through, they could still be stopped in the zone between the outer and inner frontiers. Only if both failed would it be necessary to rely on the inner passes. The pattern Weng proposed was followed, and from the 1540s the mass of Ming forces in Hsüan-fu and Ta-t'ung began to be shifted northward.

When Weng wrote in 1547, the strengthening the defenses of Ta-t'ung and Hsüan-fu by building border walls was already seventy or eighty percent completed; indeed, he observed, with a few more months of work it would be possible to finish a continuous boundary a thousand *li* (333 miles) long separating, as he put it, the *hua* and the *i* – that is to say, the Chinese and the barbarians.[447]

Although Weng was the first to act on it, his analysis followed an already established approach. In 1545 the minister of War, T'ang Lung, had compared the capital and its environs to a dwelling place: the garrisons at Hsüan-fu and Ta-t'ung were like a fence (*fan-li*), the passes at Tzu-ching, Chü-yung and other places were like the doors (*men-hu*), while the capital

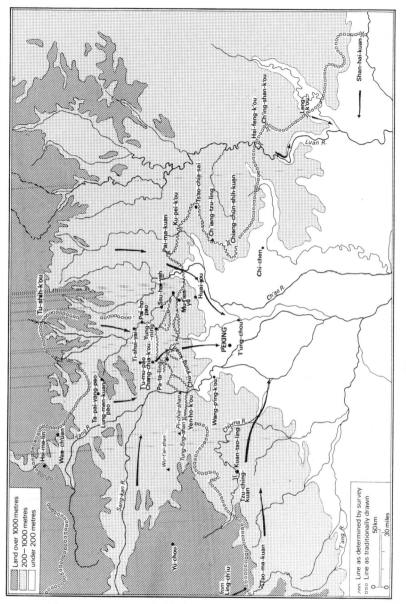

Key (top left):

Land over 1000 metres
200–1000 metres
under 200 metres

Scale (bottom left):

Line as determined by survey
Line as traditionally drawn

50km
0
0   30 miles

Labels on map:

Shan-hai-kuan
T'ieng-k'ou
Ch'ing-shan-k'ou
Hsi-feng-k'ou
Luan R.
Chang-chün-shih-kuan
Ch'ang-tzu-ling
Ts'ao-chia-sai
Ku-pei-k'ou
Chi-chen
Pai-ma-kuan
Ch'ao R.
Ssu-ma-yeh
Mu-tien-yü
Huai-jou
Tu-shih-k'ou
Pa-ho
Yung-ning
Pao
PEKING
T'ung-chou
Ti-shui-yai
Tu-mu-pao
Chang-chia-k'ou
Pa-ta-ling
Hsi-ma-lin
Waa-ch'üan
Ta-pai-yang-pao
Lung-men-kuan-pao
Yang R.
Sang-kan R.
Wu-ra-shan
P'u-chia-shan
Tung-feng-shan
Yen-ho-k'ou
Chü-yung-kuan
Wang-p'ing-k'ou
Ch'i-ma R.
Kuan-tso-ling
Yü-chou
Tzu-ching-kuan
from Ling-ch'iu
Tao-ma-kuan
T'ang R.

Map 7 Inner defenses of the capital

itself, Shun-t'ien, and Pao-ting to the southwest, just inside the inner passes, were like the *shih*, or inner chambers.[448]

In his memorial, Weng described these frontiers in detail, dividing each into three sections. The first section of the outer frontier began in the west. From the edge of the Yellow River at Pao-te chou, the frontier ran northwest to Lao-ying, some 254 *li* (85 miles). The second stretch began nearby, at Ya-chiao shan, and ran to Yang-ho some 647 *li* (216 miles). Finally, the last and longest section ran 1,023 *li* (341 miles) from Yang-ho to Yung-ning and Ssu-hai-yeh, just to the north of the capital, and northeast of the pass at Chü-yung-kuan.

The secondary frontier was less continuous than the first. It began at Lao-ying, the same place as the second stretch of the outer frontier, but then turned south and east, running some 800 *li* (267 miles) past Ning-wu, Yen-men, and Pei-lou to P'ing-hsing. The second portion began at Pao-ting southwest of the capital and made an arc toward the northwest, then turned northeastward to a point west of the capital. It ran over some 1,070 *li* (357 miles), passing through Lung-ch'üan, Tao-ma-kuan, Tzu-ching-kuan, Wu-wang-k'ou, Ch'a-chien-ling, and Fu-t'u-yü, and ending at Yen-ho-k'ou. The last section began at the capital itself and formed a short arc, north to south, just to the west of it. From Shun-t'ien it ran through Kao-yai and Pai-yang-k'ou to Chü-yung-kuan, about 180 *li* (60 miles).

The outer border was relatively near to the Mongols, and the strongpoints were on its outer side. The inner border by contrast ran mostly through mountainous terrain, and its strongpoints were on its inner edge. The most difficult of the areas to defend was Ta-t'ung, followed by Hsüan-fu, and then by P'ien-t'ou-kuan and Lao-ying in Shansi. The northern defense circuit of Ta-t'ung was the most difficult to defend within it, while the western circuit of Hsüan-fu was the most difficult in that defense area. In the far west, at P'ien-t'ou-kuan and Lao-ying, rivers formed the natural defense. The most important passes in the inner defense line were at Tzu-ching, Ning-wu, and Yen-men; less exposed were Chü-yung, Tao-ma, Lung-ch'üan, and P'ing-hsing.

The frontiers Weng described are shown on Map 7. Essentially, raiders who penetrated the outer defenses north of Ta-t'ung had two choices. They could approach the capital directly, from the northwest along the San-kan river valley. Or they could attack from the southwest across the passes at Tao-ma-kuan, Tzu-ching-kuan, and other points on the inner frontier, which provided an exit from the highlands into the North China plain.

Weng carried out wall-building along these frontiers from the very beginning of his service as supreme commander. He reported the completion of 500 *li* (167 miles) of walls in the Shansi defense area and the passes that led from it to the province of Shansi proper early in 1546, and of fortification designed to strengthen territory to the east, nearer to the capital, in August of 1546.[449] In the area of T'ien-ch'eng, Yang-ho, and K'ai-shan-k'ou in the eastern circuit of Ta-t'ung, he had constructed 138 *li* (46 miles) of border walls, as well as seven forts and 154 signal towers, while near Hsi-yang-ho, Hsi-ma-lin, and Chang-chia-k'ou-pao in the western circuit of Hsüan-fu, he had erected 64 *li* (21 miles) of border walls and ten towers (called *ti-t'ai*). Natural strongpoints had been strengthened along 50 *li* (17 miles) of terrain. Reviewing the work, the emperor noted that in Hsüan-fu and Ta-t'ung defense areas, the fortifications had long been defective, and the nomads able to move with impunity. Many recommendations for repair and construction had been made, but nothing had been done. Now more than 200 *li* (67 miles) of wall had been built, and at less than the estimated cost. Both Weng and his collaborator Chou Shang-wen were promoted.[450]

Meanwhile, work had continued on other walls in the area. In the ninth month of 1546 20,000 *liang* (about 26,000 ounces) of silver were appropriated to supply the troops working on walls in Ta-t'ung.[451] In the same month Chou Shang-wen reported work on walls from Hsi Yang-ho to Ya-chiao shan. When the wall was completed, it was over 400 *li* (133 miles) long, and had associated with it more than 1,000 towers.[452]

In the sixth month of 1548, when the completion of walls in Hsüan-fu, Ta-t'ung, and Shansi was reported, Weng Wan-ta was promoted; his son was made a student at the National Academy; and his subordinates received salary increases.[453]

With this work, Weng and his collaborators laid the foundations for the most important sector of the Ming defense system, one that appears to have been steadily augmented thereafter. At its height the system encompassed about 850 kilometers (528 miles) of wall, some of it double, triple, or even quadruple, arranged in three sections: the "river wall" (*ho-pien*) which ran along the Yellow River's edge from near P'ien-t'ou-kuan about 70 kilometers (43 miles) south; then the "outer border" (*wai-pien*) which ran east from near P'ien-t'ou-kuan along the modern Inner Mongolian frontier to the present Hopei border, some 380 kilometers (236 miles); and finally the "inner border" (*nei-pien*) which ran southeast from near P'ien-t'ou-kuan to P'ing-hsing-kuan, some 400 kilometers (249 miles) away. Today only parts of these fortifications remain: some in stone, some earth, and some discernible only in traces if at all.[454]

But just as Yü Tzu-chün's work had solved problems in one sector of the frontier while creating new ones elsewhere, Weng's strengthening of the Hsüan-Ta sector shifted the Mongol pressure to the west and east. In the west, Shensi came under renewed threat from nomads attacking from the Yellow river loop. And to the east both Chi and Liao were exposed. Weng was aware of the problem: he was troubled by the way that the lack of defenses at Hsi-feng-k'ou, Ku-pei-k'ou, and other passes to the northeast threatened the flank of Hsüan-fu.[455] The nomads were not slow to make the obvious adjustments in their tactics. In the seventh month of 1548 a raid was reported on Ssu-hai-yeh and Ta-pai-yang. These were points considerably to the east of the previous nomadic attack-route: Ssu-hai-yeh is a little west of north of the capital, where the outer and secondary frontiers come close together. Weng's solution, proposed in 1549, was yet more walls.[456]

In Han and T'ang times, he pointed out, when the capital had been at Hsi-an, dynasties had been particularly concerned with the northwest: P'ien-kuan and Shuo-fang. The Ming was different, concerned with Yu and Chi-chou in the northeast. This was because of the location of the Ming capital at Peking. Furthermore, in the past the Ming had been chiefly concerned with Shansi. Now they were concerned with the rear of the capital: with Lung-ch'ing, Yung-ning, and other places just west of north. The reason was simple: nomads were like water. When they encountered obstacles they looked for other places to get through, and Lung-ch'ing and Yung-ning in Hsüan-fu were just such places. This was because fortification had been carried out mostly in the western circuit of Hsüan-fu, that nearest to Shansi. The northern and eastern circuits had not been fortified, because it was too expensive, and defences had seemed less urgently needed than in the west. The terrain, for one thing, was very difficult. However, Weng pointed out, the tribes in the area would discover how to get through the frontier, and raiding would then pick up. As a result, while the west and the center circuits of Hsüan-fu were now strong enough to hold, in the eastern circuit, from Ssu-hai-yeh west to Yung-ning, and the northern circuit, from Ti-shui-yai or Tu-shih-k'ou south to Lung-men-ch'eng, a distance of about 700 *li* (233 miles) was open.

Weng recommended that the defenses in this area be connected to those of the Chi-chou defense area further east. A link between the eastern circuit of Hsüan-fu and the first signal towers in Chi-chou, which adjoined it, would make a big difference. From that point toward the sea, past Ssu-hai-yeh and Yung-ning, old fortifications should be restored; new walls built where the terrain required it; and deployments made to take advantage of terrain. The project would require at least 70,000 men, would take 152 days, and cost some 436,600 *liang* (567,580 ounces) of silver.[457]

The plan was approved, and the ministry of war appropriated 70,000 *liang* (91,000 ounces) of silver, a shortfall which, like the others were common in this period, probably reflected the general weakening of Ming finances. However, Weng did not long remain in a position to supervise the project. In the fifth month of 1549 he was made minister of war, but remained in that office only briefly, returning to Kwangtung at the death of his father.

Weng had presided over the beginning of a defensive building program unprecedented in Chinese history. But Weng had never believed that walls alone, even the walls he built, could solve the Ming's problems. He strongly advocated trade and diplomatic relations with the nomads as the only viable long-term policy. Events of the next few years would show how right he was. But such policies proved impossible to adopt. As the Ordos controversy showed, political rivalry at the Ming court crippled its ability to make consistent foreign policy. Unfortunately, this political paralysis coincided with renewed Mongol activity.

While the court searched for a policy, the Altan khan exerted relentless pressure on the Ming from his secure footholds in the border zone, and took advantage of the gaps in the Ming defenses. In June of 1548 his forces had attacked Hsüan-fu and defeated the imperial army; in October they penetrated as far as Huai-lai. In March of 1549, the Khan again attacked Hsüan-fu, driving away the imperial army, though his own forces were bested in several encounters as the Ming blocked his retreat. During this raid the Mongols shot an arrow into Weng Wan-ta's camp to which was attached a note stating that if trade were not allowed, they would attack Peking that autumn.

When that attack came, it demonstrated both the tactical effectiveness and the strategic uselessness of the double fortified line Weng Wan-ta had built west of the capital. That line held: the Mongols were unable to penetrate it. But to reach the capital they needed only to ride north, head toward the sea, and then strike south again, through the relatively unfortified area to the northeast of Peking. In 1550 Altan demonstrated just how this could be done.

The Khan made his camp at Wei-ning-hai-tzu, just outside the Ming frontier, west of Hsing-ho in modern Inner Mongolia, and about seventy or eighty kilometers north of Ta-t'ung. By March of 1550 a drought had lasted for over 150 days, and the hungry Mongols were reported by spies to be gathering for a major attack. On 29 June 1550 Altan penetrated broken wall at Tun-k'ou, and destroyed the forces that tried to stop him in the Ta-t'ung area. Later he joined up with forces coming from the Ordos, and formed an army of 100,000. From their new camp at Tuan-t'ou-shan the nomads threatened Hsüan-fu. Ch'iu Luan, who was in command at Ta-t'ung, bribed the nomads not to attack that city, and they could not penetrate Hsüan-fu. Weng's defense line seemed to have held. But that line did not cover the whole border: the northeast was relatively open, and to reach the capital the Mongols needed only to shift to that less well defended route. .

Moving to attack Chi-chen to the northeast, the nomad army made a northerly loop past Chang-chia-k'ou and Tu-shih-k'ou, and in late September followed the Chao-ho valley south to Ku-pei-k'ou. There they broke through the Ming defense lines by sending cavalry detachments to cross the border by minor roads and through breaks in the walls, and defeated the Chi-chen forces. Two days later the nomads were camped at T'ung-chou, east of the Peking suburbs which they looted and burned for three days and three nights before withdrawing. A vanguard of seven hundred men came to the walls of the capital itself: the An-ting gate.[458]

From the parapets of the Peking city wall, a court official could watch the nomads ravaging the surrounding countryside, and wonder grimly whether a particular column of smoke was rising above his own burning estate. Eunuchs who held property to the northwest complained that the army was being held back. It was a sight to concentrate the mind, but it was not a situation the Ming could do much about. They were plainly outclassed militarily, and the reaction at court was bitter recrimination and argument about policy. The issue raised was the same one that arose in connection with the Ordos campaign proposals – whether to compromise with the Mongols on diplomatic and economic issues. As we shall see in the next chapter, under the pressure of this crisis, the court did briefly agree to such measures, but reverted to its previous hard line as soon as the immediate Mongol threat had disappeared. Without compromise, warfare continued, and with it wall-building on an unprecedented scale.

The remainder of the sixteenth and the beginning of the seventeenth centuries – roughly the reigns of the Chia-ching (d. 1567), Lung-ch'ing (r. 1567–73), and Wan-li (r.1573–1620) emperors – saw the climax of Ming wall building. Indeed, until recently, some ordinary Chinese appear to have thought of "The Great Wall" as having been largely built during the third of these reigns, for there is sometimes confusion between the phrase meaning "wall ten thousand *li* long," and that meaning "Wan-li reign-period wall," since the two differ only slightly in pronounciation.[459] Taken together, these three reigns in the mid sixteenth century certainly mark the heyday of wall-building.

From the 1550s on, work on walls continued all along the border. The Altan khan's raid had shown the weakness of the northeastern frontier, and in 1551 work was undertaken at Shan-hai-kuan, and in Chi-chou, the defense area to the east of the capital.[460] The capital itself received a new outer wall in May of 1553.[461] And work continued in the area to the west of the capital. The stretch of wall built by Weng Wan-ta in the eastern circuit of Ta-t'ung is repeatedly mentioned. In 1553 repairs were proposed.[462] A request for the construction and repair of signal towers in the southern

Ta-t'ung defense area was submitted in the spring of 1556.[463] Money was appropriated for work in Hsüan-fu.[464] Work on signal-towers and small forts in Shansi was reported finished in January of 1557.[465] In 1558 a report on the Ta-t'ung wall stated that sections of it had tumbled down, and called for the construction of more signal-towers as a matter of priority.[466] More work at Chi-chou was done in 1558.[467]

From 1567 to 1573, the reign of the Lung-ch'ing emperor, debate continued regarding the best policy to be followed on the northern border, but without resolving the policy impasse.[468] Extensive fortification work was carried out, both during that period and the decades that followed, into the seventeenth century. Shan-hai-kuan was strengthened in 1565.[469] At Ku-pei-k'ou, a key position far to the north and east, there was also work. A massive fortified complex, with 158 beacon-towers, was discovered near here in 1980, and has been dated to the late 1560s or early 1570s.[470] But perhaps the most important work came on the northeastern frontier.

In April of 1568, T'an Lun (1520–77, cs. 1544) had been appointed senior vice minister of war, and supreme commander of the defense areas of Chi and Liao. Chi-chou was the defense area extending from the eastern edge of Hsüan-fu to Shan-hai-kuan, while Liao-tung controlled the Ming perimeter in southern Manchuria. The northern border of Chi-chou was formed by a mountain range from east to west; south of this was a coastal plain. Border ramparts had been constructed earlier (when is not clear), but at the time T'an was appointed, fortifications in the area were still very weak.

In the third month of 1569 T'an submitted a memorial pointing out that the border between Shan-hai-kuan in the east and Chen-pien-ch'eng, northeast of Ta-t'ung in Shansi, was 2,400 *li* (800 miles) long, and difficult to defend. It would be well to choose the most important points, and plan for their reinforcement in time of emergency. The border should be divided into twelve circuits, and 3,000 signal-towers built. Every year 1,000 could be built, at a cost of about fifty *chin* (65 ounces) of silver each. They would be three *chang* (30 feet) high, and twelve *chang* (120 feet) in circumference, and each would hold fifty soldiers. When there was no attack, the troops assigned to protect the walls and the towers would stay in the towers and keep a lookout. When there was an emergency, the wall defenders would guard their assigned portions, while the tower garrisons would attack the mass of nomads. The cost would be about 50,000 *liang* (65,000 ounces) of silver in all.[471]

T'an was assisted by another of the outstanding military figures of the sixteenth century, Ch'i Chi-kuang (1528–1588), who had come to the capital from the southeast in 1567, and who was transferred to the

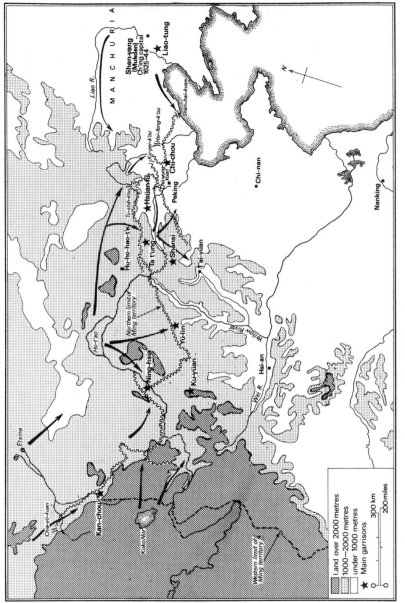

Map 8 The late Ming defense line

northeast the following year. Ch'i undertook, among other projects, the construction of towers along the border ramparts.

Since the 1560s, we are told in Ch'i's biography, although border ramparts (*yüan*) had been repaired, no signal-towers had been constructed. When Ch'i inspected the frontier, he sent a memorial recommending their construction. In summary, he said,

the Chi-chen border rampart extends for 2,000 *li* [666 miles]. If there is one weak point, and then one hundred strong points, the whole is weak. In recent years it has been annually repaired and annually destroyed. This is futile and unprofitable. I request that towers be built over the rampart to watch the four directions. A tower should be five *chang* [50 feet] high [...] and have three storeys. Each tower should hold one hundred men, with their armor, weapons, and food.[472]

Ch'i proposed that construction battalions should be created, each of which was to complete seventy towers a year.[473] This program proved too ambitious. Ch'i had wanted 3,000 towers in all; but the government authorized only 1,200, and construction took more than ten years from the time the proposal was made.[474] The towers were designed to house thirty to fifty men with their equipment; and most of the construction materials were produced by the labor-force itself. The silver provided by the capital was a relatively small amount.[475]

In 1573 the repair of the walls of the northern circuit of Hsüan-fu was ordered. These walls had originally been built by Weng Wan-ta, and in recent years they had been partially demolished by nomads. The job of repairing them would take three years, and require over 190,000 men, as well as about 180 *liang* (234 ounces) of silver per *li*, in addition to other expenses.[476]

At about the same time, another important figure in the border policy of the period, Wang Ch'ung-ku (1515–89, cs. 1541), submitted a memorial regarding the defense of Ta-t'ung. Wang had served in the northwest, in Ning-hsia and the Shensi three borders commandery, until he was transferred to Hsüan-Ta in 1570, where he would serve until 1573. Repairs to the Ta-t'ung defenses would take five years, and the total cost would be about 375,000 *liang* (487,500 ounces) of silver. The walls were weak, Wang wrote, and the beacon-towers were situated far outside them, in isolation. When the enemy attacked, the defenders could do nothing. Wang recommended that the Chi-chou system should be imitated. A strong tower should be built every *li* or so, inside the border, perhaps with walls between them. This would permit effective resistance.[477] Wang had apparently also recommended that the walls on the eastern circuit of the Shansi defense area should be strengthened. In April of 1574, 16,033 *liang* (20,839 ounces) of silver were appropriated.[478]

In April of 1576 Yang Chao and Wang I-o proposed further changes in the defenses of Chi-chou and Ch'ang-chou. Taking as their guide the maxim that if it were possible for even a single horse to get through then security could not be guaranteed, they recommended the repair of border walls: some 700 *li* (233 miles) in Chi-chou, and more than 90 in Ch'ang-chou. They had only 40,000 troops that could be used for this work, which was long term. It would require eight years in Ch'ang-chou and thirteen in Chi-chou. The cost, they estimated, would be a bare minimum of 18 *liang* (23.5 ounces) of silver per *chang* (10 feet) of wall, and five *liang* (6.5 ounces) of silver per tower. That would work out to 3,240 *liang* (4,212 ounces) of silver per *li* or 2,559,600 *liang* (3,327,480 ounces) of silver for the whole 790 *li* (263 miles) not including towers. If we allow one tower per *li*, then we must add 3,950 *liang* (5,135 ounces) of silver, bringing the total to 2,563,500 *liang* (3,332,615 ounces) of silver. The ministry advanced only 42,000 *liang*, or 54,600 ounces of silver.[479] Such building and repair continued, with few interruptions, until the end of the dynasty, and indeed was still going on in 1644 when the Manchus entered Peking and overthrew the Ming.

Thus the Ming created a fortified defense line of unprecedented scale and sophistication, which sought to secure the empire against threats along all possible routes (see Map 8). Like the Maginot Line, it was brilliantly conceived and executed, at least on the tactical level; like it as well it was based on strategic miscalculations: it ignored, for instance, the ease with which the Mongols could find ways through or around it. The Altan khan avoided the Wall and reached Peking in 1550 as easily as the Germans, following von Manstein's plans, would bypass the Maginot line and take Paris in 1940. The problem with both French and Chinese approaches to defense was that they were dominated, on the strategic level, by internal political disputes. Wall-building was undertaken only after other options, both more aggressive and more compromising, were discarded. In particular, the governments of each of the two countries proved unwilling, for internal political reasons, to show much flexibility in dealing with their potential adversaries, preferring to attempt simply to exclude them, and these considerations, rather than specifically military calculations, gave fundamental shape to their strategies. The consequences, in both cases, were not trivial.

PART III

The significances of wall-building

Construction work was still proceeding on Ming walls when the dynasty fell, and those walls, like the Maginot Line, turned out to be of little use when the real threat appeared. In the Ming case, the threat came from the Manchu state, initially a typical frontier polity, which grew up like others we have examined, on the margins of China: in the Manchu case, in the northeast territory beyond the Shan-hai-kuan gate. But in 1644, with the assistance of some high-ranking Chinese defectors, the Manchus (who by then had a well-organized state) entered China proper. They captured Peking, and in June established there the new Ch'ing dynasty, which would endure until 1912.

Had the Ming taken an active interest in steppe politics, they might have been able to control this Manchu threat before it grew too strong, by using trade and diplomacy to bind its leadership to the Ming, for example, while simultaneously seeking to develop some Mongol military counterweight to it.[480] But the political problems that earlier beset policy toward the Mongols afflicted that toward the Manchus as well, and it is no exaggeration to say that the same sorts of political squabbles we have already seen contributing to the ineffective policy of wall-building, helped bring about, in the seventeenth century, the catastrophe of foreign conquest that the wall was designed to prevent.

The Manchu conquest changed China in many ways, some of which bear directly on our story. It deprived the Wall whose story we have been telling of most of its original significance. No longer did it mark a military or even a national boundary: the Manchus held the territory on both sides of it. The Mongols and other steppe peoples no longer posed a threat to China proper, because the Manchus controlled them politically, organized them, and settled them in fixed territories. And whatever abstract philosophical significance the Wall may once have had as a boundary between "barbarism" and "civilization" was also necessarily expunged, for with a non-Chinese ruling house in Peking, those categories themselves were banished from official political discourse. Ch'ing China, the immediate ancestor of the modern state, was not a nation, but rather a vast multi-ethnic empire twice the size of the Ming state, which derived its unity from the fact that it was ruled by a single house. For as long as that situation endured, the "Great Wall" would have little significance, either physically, or as a symbol.

The end of the Ming, however, should not mark the end of the story of the Great Wall. Although they disappeared for a while in the Ch'ing, the cohesiveness of whose Manchu elite was reinforced by kinship ties, the patterns of factional politics that contributed to the Wall's building in the Ming reappeared later, though in different connections. At the same time, foreigners began to think of the Wall as embodying a uniquely Chinese approach to foreign relations. After the fall of the Ch'ing, moreover, the Wall began to acquire a role that it had never had before, as a focus of Chinese national identity and pride. Thus, after the Wall had lost all its original importance as a military barrier or a boundary, it acquired new and enduring significances, which the two chapters of Part III will examine. The first of them will ask whether the story of wall-building in fact contains (as is so widely believed) some deep truth or general lesson about China's approach to the rest of the world. And the second will attempt to explain how the Ming Great Wall, suitably mythologized, became, in effect, modern China's national symbol.

The first of these questions involves political patterns. When its full consequences, including the Manchu conquest, are considered, it becomes clear that the significance of the Ming's political weakness is not confined to the role that we have already assigned in leading to the building of the Great Wall. The complex of weak rule and idealized rhetoric, and the great difficulty of compromise that such a political configuration produced, was one of the prime factors causing the ultimate fall of the Ming dynasty. As such it is worth examining analytically, with an eye to finding patterns that may be applicable to other periods, and this is what Chapter 10 attempts. After outlining how the political process undermined security in the Ming, it suggests that the Ming events fit into a larger pattern of Chinese politics and foreign policy, visible both in the past, and also, in modified form, today. Understanding of this pattern, it argues, is the key to making sense of many of the ebbs and flows of Chinese foreign policy, and in particular to its periodic bouts of wall-building, whether real or figurative.

Such an understanding, however, is far from the popular idea of the Great Wall of China, and its significance, with which this book began. In the early Ch'ing, the Ming Great Wall was understandably considered (if at all) by most Chinese to be an embodiment of futility and failure, much as the French continue to view their Maginot Line. But there is little trace of that appraisal today. In the case of the Chinese Wall, a rather striking change has taken place: the Great Wall has been transformed, over the last century or so, into China's unofficial national symbol. It is the focus of pride and patriotism at home, and the object of awe and respect abroad. Chapter 11 will trace this remarkable metamorphosis, and attempt to explain how and why it occurred.

The political process which led to the building of the Wall, and the cultural one which transformed it into a national symbol, are of course quite distinct. But they have certain elements in common. Walls physically delimit areas, while words, ideas, and myths mentally delimit cultures, and to some extent, political systems. By the seventeenth century the Ming had created for itself both a military frontier and a national boundary marked by a Great Wall. That Ming wall no longer marks China's boundaries, but in its mythic form it still has an identity-providing role. Like the physical wall, the mythical wall is the product of the ongoing process of Chinese state and national definition. The first wall is the product of politics, the second of culture. Chapters 10 and 11 will explore the processes that created them both, and their interconnections.

10
The Great Wall and foreign policy: the problem of compromise

Weng Wan-ta envisioned the wall system he helped to create as but one component in a comprehensive solution to the problem of the nomads, a solution that would also include diplomatic and economic relations with them and thus become accommodating, rather than exclusive. But these latter aspects of Weng's policy were not accepted by the Ming court at the time, and they are not commonly associated with Chinese walls today. For most writers, the "Great Wall" is a monument evoking what they think of as a perennial and culturally-rooted Chinese desire to distinguish the civilized from the barbarous, and to exclude the latter, and therefore constitutes for them a concrete expression of China's unchanging foreign policy. Mark Mancall, for instance, states that the Wall "demarcated the entire Chinese culture from an ecological, social, and cultural region of foreignness. Behind the Great Wall, the processes of Chinese history could work themselves out."[481] Wolfgang Bauer makes it "the symbol of a land turned in on itself, one which had closed off even the last frontier which had been left by nature."[482]

Our narration, however, should have cast some doubt on this notion of a single wall embodying a single policy. The themes we have pursued in connection with it have been more those of ideological and policy disagreement, and decision-making stalemate. Wall-building, we have argued, was only one of the options available to the Chinese, and others, including offensive military action and diplomatic and economic accommodation, were both promising and widely popular at times. In the Ming, as we have seen, wall-building was nobody's first choice: it was adopted only as other proposals were vetoed.

So one is struck, when looking at the Chinese past, not by the existence of a steady and enduring foreign policy (perhaps summed up by the Great Wall), but rather by the absence of any such policy. Political contention, disagreement, and policy stalemate are the pattern for long periods, and their effects on decisions, rather than the influence of a culturally determined approach, are the real explanations for many developments. This is certainly true of wall-building. Far from being the barriers that allow the "processes of Chinese history" to work themselves out undisturbed, the walls turn out to have been, themselves, products of those historical processes.

We have paid particular attention to the linkage between internal and external politics in the Ming. During the Ming, external policy made little sense measured against its ostensible goals of bringing peace and stability to the borders. From the point of view of the Mongols, the Ming was actually responsible for creating much hostility. The extreme reluctance of the Ming to establish or honor any kind of diplomatic relationship, or to permit trade at anything like the level that both nomads and border-dwelling Chinese desired, not to mention the killing of nomadic envoys and waging of military campaigns in which women and children were a major target, appeared to be hostile acts which left the nomads little choice but to use force to obtain what they needed from China. This pattern has led Lattimore to argue that "[the Great Wall frontier] [...] was not necessitated by the aggression of the nomads against China. That aggression came later, as a consequence of the demarcation of the frontier."[483] And certainly one must recognize the substantial contribution that irrational Chinese policy played in exacerbating the hostility that would have accompanied any relationship between Chinese and nomads. Chinese policy was largely responsible for the warfare that in turn made wall-building or similar measures necessary. Nor was this situation limited only to the Ming. Parallel cases may be found in the Han, Sung, and other earlier dynasties, while analogous situations crop up later as well, in the response to the West in the nineteenth and twentieth centuries, and even today.

The basic problem, in the Ming as at other times, was an inability to compromise, even over decades during which a high military cost was being paid for inflexibility. To the extent that the Wall is itself a product of that inability, it sums up rather well one major continuity in Chinese foreign policy. The failure to reconcile pragmatic and idealized visions of the world, and the tendency to inject morality into political controversies, are two of that policy's most enduring characteristics. Such tendencies are of course found in other countries, but they seem particularly conspicuous in the Chinese case. We will argue that their origins have more to do with politics than with culture.

Both the conflict of pragmatic and idealized visions, and the moralization of politics, are factors clearly important in the Ordos controversy that we have examined. Although the ultimate decision in that case rejected the idealized alternative and was thus, in our terms, rational, that was not how it was seen at the time, or even how it is usually seen today. Even while the protagonists were living, many Chinese saw the rivalry between Hsia Yen and Yen Sung, which gave political charge to the policy disagreement, as an example of the opposition between an orthodox and righteous approach to rule, and a corrupt and self-serving one. This perception was reinforced by the executions of Tseng and Hsia, which transformed them into patriotic martyrs, and then enshrined them in the written tradition.

The *Ming history*, for example, places Yen Sung's biography in the section devoted to "treacherous ministers," while Tseng Hsien's proposals, and Hsia Yen's support for them, are, by contrast, treated uncritically.[484] The account of the Ordos debate in the standard historical compendium *Ming-shih chi-shih pen-mo* (1658) also takes such a tack, as does the only modern article on the subject.[485] The issue has been further confused by artistic treatment: in the popular mind, images of Hsia Yen and Yen Sung are as likely to come from imaginative literature as from historical writing, for example from the opera *Ming-feng chi*, attributed to Wang Shih-chen (1509–59, cs. 1526). Even modern Communist writers have not escaped from the traditional categories: the preface to an edition of the opera published in China in 1959, though couched in Marxist vocabulary, nevertheless notes that it portrays:

[...] the struggle of two kinds of power. One is reactionary, represented by the traitorous minister Yen Sung and his gang of lackeys [...] and the other, represented by Hsia Yen, is patriotic, humane, and righteous.[486]

Such a moralistic approach, it should be noted, scarcely treats the foreign component of foreign policy at all. While it may make sense – indeed, even be justified – in terms of the rights and wrongs of domestic politics, widespread adoption of such an approach in the foreign sphere greatly complicates policy-making. Embedded in the written tradition, and well known to educated Chinese, culturally and artistically inculcated ideas about what China is, and what constitutes a decent policy and what is treachery, can define goals unrealistically and lead the state into impossible quests and costly predicaments.

But there is also a strong pragmatic current in the Chinese tradition, one which, furthered by a strong government, can lead to highly effective diplomacy. The influence of the idealistic strand (which is often thought of as more genuinely "Chinese") turns out to be decisive only at certain times, notably those when no powerful emperor or executive is in command, and China has relied on cultural consensus to maintain cohesion and make policy. Then unrealistic ideas of what is right can become politically potent, if only as weapons for criticism and veto. When that happens, the kinds of compromises required by any realistic border or foreign policy become well-nigh impossible politically.

The sixteenth century of the Ming is a particularly good example of how domestic politics can create an inability to compromise. Most of the century saw weak and ineffective emperors, and faction-ridden bureaucracy. During the period the dynasty faced a series of related foreign-policy problems: not only the intractable warfare on the northern frontier that we have already described, but also the question of whether to intervene in Vietnam, and chronic disorder along the southeast sea-coast. This last had been caused by the prohibition of maritime trade, a policy which gave rise to "piracy" as surely as its inland equivalent, the virtual elimination of trade with the steppe, caused nomadic raiding. Debate over what to do about the problems simmered at court, with the uncompromising position maintaining the upper hand until the last quarter of the sixteenth century. Then the political situation changed, and compromise solutions were enforced to both sets of problems. Taken as a whole, Chinese foreign policy during the decades from the 1550s to the 1580s when wall-building was at its height, provides, not coincidentally, a fine case-study in the problems of compromise.

Hsia Yen and Tseng Hsien played a role in this debate, albeit posthumously. Though destroyed in the political struggle, they acquired after death a sort of countervailing cultural power, in a way not unfamiliar in Chinese politics. Even while their enemies were triumphant at court, they were entered by broader circles of the literati public into the ranks of martyrs representing honest government and uncompromising policy against the barbarians, and the influence of their examples, thus defined, in turn made further compromises with the nomads more difficult. The immediate political battle may have been won by the pragmatists, but the long-term and highly important battle for historical approval was won by the Ordos "recovery" advocates. This meant that even by the 1550s, the wrong lessons were being learned from the whole debate. This led to mishandling not only of the Mongol problem, but also, and even more seriously, to failure to cope with the Manchus. Instead of pondering the actual nature of the nomadic threat, and considering how, realistically, it might be dealt with, Chinese intellectuals increasingly saw the issues of the Ordos debate and the related arguments that followed, in domestic terms, as clashes between corrupt and treacherous officials on the one hand, and upright and resolute ones on the other, and neglected their practical foreign dimensions almost completely.

The tension between foreign policy needs and domestic politics became clear again as early as 1550 when, as we have seen above, the Altan khan carried out a great raid on Peking. In autumn of that year the Khan had led his forces around the Ming fortifications, and brought them under the very walls of the capital. Once more debate about policy toward the nomads heated up. Some at court believed that trade and diplomacy could have averted the crisis, while others saw the raid as a sad confirmation of the need to "recover" the Ordos. If only Hsia Yen and Tseng Hsien had been permitted to carry out their pre-emptive strike against the nomads, rather than being undone by court maneuvering and treachery, all would have been well. The two factions were pretty well stalemated politically. But with Mongols burning the suburbs, one could not simply ignore the situation. Gradually, the views of those who had opposed the Ordos recovery proposals and favored compromise, came to the fore.

On 26 September 1550, Ch'iu Luan wrote a letter in which he argued that all of the trouble on the frontier went back to the single fact the Mongols needed goods that only China could supply. He pointed out that trade fairs already existed for other nomads. What sense, he asked, did it make to refuse such trade to the Altan khan who, if he were permitted to sell horses and buy the goods he needed, would be willing to make peace with the Ming?[487]

Any decision to accommodate the Mongols, however, would require imperial sanction. On 2 October the emperor held an audience, the first in more than ten years. Among topics of discussion was a letter from the Altan khan, brought to the court by a Chinese official, who had been captured by the Mongols and was now released. The letter asked for permission to present tribute, in accordance with standard Ming procedures. The court officials were noncommittal. Yen Sung, however, seemed flexible. The powerful grand secretary outraged his colleague Hsü Chieh, the minister of rites, who was theoretically in charge of all matters pertaining to "tribute" by observing, accurately enough, that the Mongols were simply raiding out of hunger, and that this was nothing to get upset about.

Scapegoats were found for the success of the Khan's raid. The minister of war, who had kept the army back on the advice of Yen Sung (who said that a defeat near the capital could not be concealed), and another high official, were ordered executed; others were arrested. Such actions suggested a hard-line stance. But an understanding that compromise might be in order was manifested by the decision to recall Weng Wan-ta from his home in Kwangtung.[488]

In the meantime, Ch'iu Luan, just out of prison, was given great authority. Yen Sung, who had sided with Ch'iu Luan during the debate over the Ordos, and who was probably grateful for the evidence Ch'iu had presented that led to Hsia Yen's execution, arranged for him now to be appointed commander of all the troops and training camps in the capital

area. 60,000 troops were recalled from the frontier, as preparations got
underway for a campaign against the Mongols.[489]

The court tried to avoid the politically contentious issue of trade with the
nomads by simply getting rid of the Altan khan through a pretext. The
court refused the Altan khan's letter, on the pretext that because it was not
written in Mongol, its authenticity could not be established, and followed
Hsü Chieh's suggestion that the nomad be told to return to Mongolia, and
then submit his requests to the governor of Hsüan-fu, which would bring
satisfaction. The ruse bought some time for military preparations. But
when the Khan did as they told him, and his second petition arrived at the
capital, the court began to realize that the question could not be avoided
indefinitely.

More discussion followed. Su Yu, who had replaced Weng Wan-ta,
argued strongly in favor of granting tribute status, and opening markets
along the borders where Mongols and Chinese would be able to trade.
Initially this would be done for one year; then, if it brought peace, the
question of whether to continue the policy would be examined. Finally, on
9 April 1551, a decision was made to open border markets. With this
breakthrough, peace was achieved.[490]

The emperor's personal presence in the court discussion had probably
been necessary to break the policy deadlock. But even so, the terms of the
settlement with the Altan khan were controversial, and almost as soon as it
had been made, it began to be revised, until it was abandoned. Some of the
opposition was simply ill-informed. Thus when Shih Tao urged that the
poorer Mongols be permitted to trade their cattle for millet and beans, a
reasonable enough request, the court turned it down – noting that the
Mongols did not eat these products (untrue), and that they therefore must
be intended for Chinese runaways who lived among the Mongols (people
who far from needing foodstuffs from China were in fact producing grain on
their own in Mongolia!).[491] But that was not the point. The stronger issue
was a feeling that by treating with the Altan khan, the Ming court was
violating the moral norms which underlay the state. We have seen that the
Chia-ching emperor (r. 1522–67) was basically opposed to compromise,
and that without a strong emperor to sanction unambiguously such a
violation, no bureaucrat who valued his office was going to advocate it. So
not surprisingly, new deliberations were held. The number of trading fairs
to be permitted was initially reduced from four to two.[492] By 6 September
the government had reversed itself entirely, and Shih Tao, who had been in
charge of the policy, had fallen. Even to mention the possibility of trade
relations with the Mongols was thenceforth forbidden.[493]

The Altan khan did submit tribute once in the year of the settlement, the only year in the next twenty in which he did not attack, and even after the policy was abandoned, he did not abandon his hope of establishing relations with the Ming. In 1553 the Altan khan and his son sent six envoys to present tribute of horses and to request markets. All six were arrested. Four died in captivity, and two others were only released twenty years later when peace was finally made.[494] In the summer of 1559 the Altan khan proposed a settlement to the governor general of Shensi, but the approach led to nothing.[495] The consequence of the failure of compromise after 1550 was no less than the military disasters that ensued over the next three decades.

The difficulty the court had in compromising with the Mongols was part of a general pattern during the mid sixteenth century: it arose as well in connection with Vietnam policy, and with the so-called "Japanese Pirates" on the coast.

The Vietnam campaign of the years 1537–40 foreshadowed many of the issues that would later arise on the northern frontier, particularly the questions of offensive and defensive policies. During the campaign, Weng Wan-ta, whose role in the north we have just described, reached high office for the first time, and took a major role in the debate. The former rulers of Vietnam, who had been tributaries of the Ming, had been overthrown, and the new rulers sent a mission to Peking to request investiture. The question at the Chinese court was whether or not to send a military expedition to Vietnam to overthrow these "usurpers," a question not unlike that at stake in the Ordos debate. A number of officials expressed doubt about the wisdom of the campaign, but the war party, led by the minister of rites Hsia Yen, was dominant. Weng Wan-ta, however opposed it. He had been surveillance vice commissioner (*fu-shih*) specially charged with preparation for the campaign, and he advised Mao Po-wen, the commander, that the best strategy was to bring about the submission of the Vietnamese by intimidation, perhaps, but not by direct application of force. The successful use of his approach greatly increased his reputation.[496]

A similar set of issues arose in connection with the problem of the so-called "Japanese Pirates." There had always been some disorder on the coast, but the problem was greatly worsened by a prohibition on maritime trade in the coastal provinces of southeast China which was introduced at Hsia Yen's suggestion in 1523. It was similar to the prohibitions on trade with the Mongols, and the Japanese "pirates" were in fact smugglers, many of them Chinese, not Japanese. Smuggling led to violence; when merchants on land could not pay for goods they accepted, or when debts were left unpaid, raiding took place. The raiders were very well armed and beyond the capacity of the Ming to control. As the situation degenerated in the mid sixteenth century, Yen Sung and Hsia Yen disagreed over policies towards the "pirates," just as they did over *Ho-t'ao* "recovery." Hsia Yen appears to have supported the hard-line policy adopted against piracy by Chu Wan (1494–1550), while Chao Wen-hua (d. 1557), who was blamed for laxity in the anti-pirate campaign, was a Yen Sung protégé.[497] The key to a solution was obviously the lifting of the interdict, which Chao had recommended, and which Yen Sung appears to have favored as well.[498] But Hsia favored strictness, and his appointees fought hard for discipline on the coast, though with little success.

As is true for the Ordos debate, historians have been kinder to Hsia and his followers than to Yen Sung's appointees, whom they paint as corrupt and ineffective. But in fact, these officials developed a strategy that finally worked: trade, under regulation, and improved military readiness, though they had to wait for the lifting of the interdict, which came only after the death of the Chia-ching emperor, in 1567.[499] The issue of the pirates served almost as a dress rehearsal for the eventual policy of compromise and pacification of the northern frontier, to be examined below. Policies, skills, even personnel, were transferred from one frontier to the other. But until the basic foreign policy of exclusion and isolation was shifted, the military hard line of the Ming brought only trouble, on the coast as much as in the north.

How are we to explain such long resistance to compromise? Surely the issue cannot have been simply a little trade at Ta-t'ung or Fu-chou: it must have been something more. Broadly speaking, the mid-Ming seems to have witnessed a reassertion of the tradition of idealized foreign (and domestic) policy, whose origins we have already mentioned in Chapter 2. It was promoted by the rising class of largely southern literati who, by the sixteenth century, were gaining influence as the Ming court grew weaker. To oversimplify, the court defined China dynastically, and saw politics in kinship terms. The literati, by contrast, saw China culturally, and understood politics as an aspect of morality. The viewpoints of these groups were almost irreconcilable.

The kind of inflexibility in foreign policy advocated by many influential Ming literati had an impressive pedigree. In the Han, Chia I and others had made names for themselves by protesting against the "humiliations" imposed by the *ho-ch'in* system, described in Chapter 2. Their policy took no notice of the realities of the non-Chinese world: these were viewed as irrelevant. They based their case not on empirical information about what was feasible, or would or would not bring peace, but rather on convictions, drawn from the newly-ascendent Confucian theories, about what the larger world ought to be like, and how an ideal Chinese state should deal with this imaginary world.

The approach had reached an apogee in the Sung, with the glorification of Yüeh Fei, and Yang Chi-sheng (1516–55), who was perhaps the most famous critic of compromise policy in the Ming, fits right into this tradition. He was famous for his outspoken attacks on Yen Sung, and although he had no particular knowledge of frontier affairs, in 1551 he castigated Yen's soft line toward the Mongols following the Altan khan's raid in a celebrated moral attack that came right out of Sung polemics.

Yang's memorial drew upon many traditional elements. It began with conventional assertions that the nomads, or "barbarians," had violated the way of Heaven, a transgression which it fell naturally to the Chinese emperor to punish. But, it continued, the emperor had never followed through on his original intention to launch a punitive expedition into the north, but instead listened to the pacifistic urgings of some of his courtiers. Like Chia I in the Han, and his successors thereafter, Yang found such seeming immorality and cowardice an outrage. Like his predecessors as well, Yang wrote in a way that suggested he took the actual military power of the nomads not at all seriously – they were "dogs and sheep" whom it ought to be possible to "exterminate." Those among the Chinese who advocated peace were therefore suspect. They made practical arguments regarding the need to buy time, the advantage of obtaining horses from the nomads, and the possibility of reaching a long-term compromise. Yang dismisses all such ideas as logically or empirically flawed, and raises questions about the loyalty of those who make them. He suggests, for example, that the commanders at Hsüan-fu and Ta-t'ung frequently co-operated with the nomads.[500]

Yang's target, Yen Sung, soon exiled him. After further brushes with the palace security agencies, Yang was eventually condemned to death. For his execution, at the age of thirty-nine, he composed a poem that is still well known.[501] Like the others we have mentioned, Yang became a patriotic martyr, remembered right down to the present. On 25 June 1937, a bare fortnight before the Japanese attack at the Marco Polo Bridge which started the main phase of the Second World War in China, a memorial service was conducted in his honor in Peking.[502]

Other societies have their patriotic heroes, of course, but in Chinese culture their position is nevertheless striking. Though the risks associated with the measures they advocate are often widely recognized, they continue to be widely honored. Foreign policy success, however, has usually been achieved only in the teeth of their opposition, by adopting approaches that they condemn. The dynasty having (arguably) the most successful foreign policy was probably the T'ang, and as we have seen, the emperor T'ai-tsung prided himself on treating the *hua* and *i* equally, exactly the

approach to which Yang Chi-sheng and others like him objected most
vigorously.

The distinction to which the T'ang emperor referred was one which, as
we have seen in Chapter 2, ultimately had its roots in a view of the nature
of the Chinese polity. It was an aspect of a definition of China that was
fundamentally cultural, and that spread with learning whenever the
society became wealthy enough to support a class of literati.

The cultural definition of China conflicted in fundamental ways with
the definitions of the state that were imposed by ruling houses. A ruler
such as T'ang T'ai-tsung did not derive his sense of legitimacy from his
membership in a culture which had defining rules: it came from his
personal and clan position. The same was true of the Mongols, of course,
and even of the early Ming rulers. The lack of national or cultural feeling
among the ruling class of that dynasty's early period was noted with
surprise by Ch'ien Mu in 1964, for example.[503] With such cosmopolitanism, however, went a certain flexibility in approach to foreign policy.
T'ang, Yüan, and early Ming ideas of dynastic loyalty had only an
attenuated cultural component, and therefore could accommodate non-
Chinese relatively easily. T'ang China had residents of many nationalities,
as did Yüan, while in the early Ming Mongols comprised a substantial
proportion of the population in the capital and served in large numbers in
the military, without causing too much concern. As long as they were loyal
to the ruling house, that virtue was sufficient. And as long as such a
concept of politics could be enforced, foreign issues could be handled with
considerable flexibility.

But the sense of common culture as a definition of China also has a long
history. Such a feeling was already evident in the Shang and Chou, well
before a powerful ruling house had created a truly unified state in China.
When centralized rule was imposed by the Ch'in, both its institutions and
rationales rested uneasily on this earlier cultural foundation. At times
when dynastic rule was felt to be too strong or oppressive, the idea of a
moral basis for China's unity could provide a basis of judgment for the
court's critics. When dynastic rule was weak, it could also provide a basis
for social cohesion. Indeed, ideology has usually come to the fore at such
times of weakness, not only in the Ming, but in the Warring States period,
the later Han, and the later Sung, not to mention the twentieth century.
The coexistence of cultural with dynastic definitions of China is probably
one of the fundamental contributors to that state's remarkably long
heritage of unity. But the cultural definition, with its hard specifications of
what does and does not belong, is far less accommodating and inclusive
than the principle of loyalty to a ruling house. Like the later nationalisms
of Europe, Chinese culturalism in the form we are describing necessarily

involved exclusive definitions that in turn made conflicts extremely difficult to resolve.

How this happened can be seen in ideas about boundaries. To a dynast, whatever he controls is his territory. But to one concerned with culture, distinctions, often with transcendental sanction, may prove necessary. We have already mentioned the Chinese idea that "Nature," or *T'ien* ("Heaven") – rather than a particular ruler – had drawn China's boundaries. It is similar to the idea, espoused by the generation of the French revolution, that while ruling houses were human, nations were part of the natural order. "The Abbé Grégoire in 1792 consulted 'the archives of Nature' in order to prove that Savoy was really a part of France; in 1793 Danton went further: 'The frontiers of France,' he said, 'are indicated by Nature. We will attain them in all their four points: the Atlantic Ocean, the Rhine, the Alps, and the Pyrenees.'"[504] Widespread acceptance of such ideas can greatly facilitate national integration, while making external accommodation more difficult. Furthermore, as the European case also amply demonstrates, widespread acceptance of uncompromisable, "nationalistic" ideas can fundamentally change the nature of politics.

Just how this process occurs is not entirely clear, and it is in any case far beyond the scope of this essay. But it seems to have something to do with the sort of shift in definitions mentioned in the paragraph above, away from the human and arbitrary, to the ostensibly natural or even divine. Its consequences are clear enough. Acceptance of objective definitions of nation independent of dynasty can substantially strengthen the literate, culture-creating people who produce such ideas, while weakening the dynasts themselves. The truth of nature is far harder to shift than the policy of man, and widespread belief in it provides a weapon for the educated against the merely powerful. Such a change in belief clearly lay behind the rise in power of nationalist movements in nineteenth- and twentieth-century Europe. China in the period we are discussing is unquestionably pre-nationalist, but there is still a certain parallelism between the political role of a Yang Chi-sheng, and that of a later European, or even Chinese, nationalist, using words to oppose armies, bureaucracies, and even dynasties. The existence of a yardstick of idealized virtue independent of the *raison d'état* of the ruling house, makes it possible for literate people to argue politics with rulers. And at times of dynastic weakness, those who make objections based on such a standard can, periodically, exercise what is in effect, an ideological veto over policies considered immoral according to their understanding – which those of accommodation were almost by definition. The use of this veto at such times is a basic and enduring feature of Chinese politics.

The predicament of the Ming in the mid sixteenth century was to a large extent the product of the effective use of vetoes by competing factions which, however, lacked the power to push through any positive policy. The opponents of Ordos recovery, as we have seen, managed to veto that proposal by an appeal to practicality, as well as by political manipulations which included playing on the emperor's fears through use of portents. But the positive policy of accommodation which would have been a sound alternative to the risky Ordos campaign was also subject to veto, by the morally upright and orthodox members of the court, and indirectly by literati opinion at large. Nor was the war of vetoes in the mid sixteenth century entirely disinterested. We have already shown how factions lined up for and against Ordos policy, and sought to promote their own interests as much as the dynasty's. This complex political game which turns on such use of a veto, is scarcely unique to China of the 1550s. Rather, it is one of the fundamental patterns of Chinese politics, and one that emerges in particular when higher authority is weak.

A number of students, most notably Andrew Nathan, have described the pattern in the modern period. Use of the veto, according to Nathan, is one of the maneuvers used to maintain factional equilibrium: It can help to maintain balance among contending forces, by preventing any one from growing too strong. As Nathan had noted in his study of the 1920s, in a situation in which power is divided, a competitor will have as its "most important and usually most immediate concern, to protect its power base while opposing accretions of power by a rival faction."[505] We have already explained how Tseng Hsien and Hsia Yen's plan to "recover" the Ordos, if it had been successful, would have made them far stronger than any of their rivals, and how their rivals therefore managed to quash the plan. To make a successful peace with the nomads and be recognized for that achievement, would in an analogous way strengthen whoever did it. Therefore it will be in the interest of rivals to prevent such an achievement, and thus keep open at least the possibility that they will be able to win later.[506]

Accommodation is not difficult to prevent, particularly in a system having the sorts of hard definitions we have just mentioned. One effective way is to devalue peace: to transform compromise into sell-out. Here the essential maneuver is to discredit those in power by using intellectual pressure to increase foreign-policy demands to the point at which any settlement is impossible, because none will measure up to abstract criteria of success: to make the ideal the enemy of the merely practicable, if necessary by redefining the ideal.

In such situations, in other words, an incentive exists for certain players to redefine the very cultural values that are used as the yardsticks for success. Thus, if one wants to paint one's opponents as traitors, one's task is made easier if one can narrow the definition of patriotism. The tremendous refinement and redefinition of many of the fundamental categories of Chinese philosophy and ethics that took place during the very period we are describing played an important role in making possible the sort of political maneuvering described above. Parallel phenomena are similarly found in earlier periods.

Arguably, such a process of redefinition of reference terms in order to frustrate rivals and strengthen one's own position lay behind the advocacy of new understandings of the Chinese state that emerged in the second century B.C. These originated ultimately in the adoption of Confucianism as a state orthodoxy, and made it almost impossible for the Han dynasty to continue or restore the *ho-ch'in* system. It is probably visible as well in the Sung, when a hardening of the political line toward the north coincided with a more general recasting of Confucianism once again, a process which had clear consequences for foreign policy.

In Ming times, we find an analogous process of redefinition taking place in the sixteenth century, usually in the south, as philosophy flourished once again in private academies where literati would gather and argue about both abstract issues of metaphysics and immediate matters of state. The rate of new foundations of such so-called *shu-yüan* increased in the sixteenth century: it had been roughly one per year in the first Ming century; from the 1520s to the 1560s it was about eight, while by the 1570s it had reached ten.[507] Ill-will developed between the southern literati and many at court: Yen Sung, for example, "was said to hate all the philosophical speculation of the day"[508] and may have sponsored the attack on the academies carried forward in 1538 which led to their prohibition.[509]

In foreign policy, the academies were centers of the revival of the written Chinese tradition, which was so different from the unwritten pragmatic norms of dynastic rule that had been practiced in the Yüan. Although they had never recorded their methods, the Mongols understood well how to manage the nomadic–settled relationship, and how to administer a multi-ethnic empire. The Chinese written tradition, by contrast, was less flexible. Tolerance of "barbarians" was a violation of morality, as were many of the other techniques used by effective rulers. Even rulers – the Yung-lo emperor, for instance – could come in for criticism, as could officials who fell short of the demands of idealized political morality. At a time when there was no strong executive, the stalemate between court and literati groups having quite different ways of thinking about China and the problems that faced her, could utterly paralyze policy and decision-making – as it did in the middle years of the sixteenth century.

In the Ming case, the costly stalemate over policy toward the Mongols was finally broken only when a strong central authority was restored. This was done by one of the most important figures in the late Ming, the grand secretary Chang Chü-cheng (1525–1582, cs. 1547). Chang came to power with the Lung-ch'ing emperor. The new emperor, twenty-nine years old when his father died, was "by no means well indoctrinated in statecraft or prepared properly to take up the reins of government. By nature, further-more, he was neither strong nor ambitious, had no interest in national affairs, and sought pleasure only."[510] Chang Chü-cheng, however, had clear ideas about government. He had been one of the new emperor's teachers, and in 1567 he was made a grand secretary. He quickly became influential, and maintained his position throughout the reign. He further-more served as tutor to the Wan-li emperor (r. 1573–1620) who came to the throne when he was only nine years old. Chang was therefore able to maintain his influence through all of one reign and the first decade of another, until his death in 1582.

Chang had a coherent approach to border problems. He understood the necessity of making a peace, even a temporary one, with the Mongols, in order to relieve the pressure on Ming defenses, and he wanted then to reform many aspects of the border-defense system. While ruling out offensive warfare, he was in favor of taking advantage of the respite a peace would offer in order to make future defense more secure by strengthening and rebuilding walls and watch-towers. He wanted to put the logistic supply for border units on a sound basis by attempting to restore the system of military farming that the dynastic founder had favored. But most important, alone among grand secretaries of the sixteenth century, Chang had the political power to enforce his will, and take unpopular steps without fear.

Chang's power was personal. It was based above all on his close relationship to two emperors, supplemented by carefully-cultivated friend-ships with eunuchs whose informal influence in the palace was very great, men such as Feng Pao (fl. 1530–82). Such an approach was eminently practical, and probably grew out of Chang's knowledge of how earlier Ming courts had in fact operated. This approach to holding power made Chang far more secure as a chief grand secretary than any of his predecessors had been, and thus able to break through some of the policy disagreements that had plagued earlier courts. He was able, for instance, to override objections to his foreign policy made by the literati whose philosophical speculations provided support for the non-compromising position. He is said to have "so hated the kind of philosophical discussion fashionable in the academies that to speak of it made him gnash his teeth"; and in 1579 he closed the academies.[511]

As his defense specialists, Chang made use of several talented men who had acquired their first experience in fighting the "Japanese Pirates," a case where the coordination of military, economic, and political means had all been essential to the solution. Kwan-wai So has summarized some of the contributing factors in that case. The pirate problem was basically solved in the 1550s through a number of related measures. The assignment of able officials to the southeast, men such as Ch'i Chi-kuang and others who trained troops was important, as was the introduction of firearms, so that the Ming forces no longer feared the firearms of the pirates. Signaling was greatly improved and city walls were built. There was also an increase in cooperation among the provinces. But none of these would have worked, So argues, had it not been for a change in Ming trading policy. The Portuguese established a presence in Macao, and in 1554 reached an agreement with Chinese authorities that permitted trade and required a payment of a twenty percent customs duty. Once the trading position was made legal it was in the interest of the traders to ally with the authorities to preserve it. All these factors together shifted the balance.[512]

What we see here is the immediate precedent for the policy Chang Chü-cheng adopted on the northern border two decades later.[513] T'an Lun, Wang Ch'ung-ku, and Ch'i Chi-kuang, all of whom had served in the anti-pirate campaigns, played important roles on the northern border. But to change what was now a well established, if futile, policy there would not be easy: it was achieved only by very deft political utilization of an extraordinary opportunity.

This came in 1570 when the Altan khan's grandson, Bagha-achi, came over to China after a quarrel with his grandfather. Wang Ch'ung-ku (1515–89, cs. 1541) insisted on treating him very well and used the occasion of his capture, and discussion at court over what to do about him, to press not simply for a one-off agreement, in which some of the Chinese who had fled to the Altan khan might be returned when the Mongol hostage was handed over, but rather for a settlement that would permit regular trade.

After early service against the pirates, and in Shansi, Wang Ch'ung-ku had been appointed grand coordinator of Ning-hsia in 1564. An expert commander, he learned the geography of the border well, personally accompanied his troops, and encouraged defections among the nomads, even while from time to time leading offensives against them. In the winter of 1567 he was made supreme commander of Shensi. There he ordered the compilation of maps, which he distributed to his commanders. But the terrible situation in the Hsüan-fu and Ta-t'ung area led to his transfer to that defense area in 1570. From their base at Köke-khota, the Mongols and their Chinese followers could raid easily along the whole frontier of the capital region. Local commanders were ineffective, and often killed nomads who were trying to submit, in order falsely to claim the rewards given for heads taken in battle. The Chinese knew nothing of the situation among the nomads, while the Mongols knew every move the Chinese made. Wang's adminstration changed this, and soon Mongols and renegade Chinese alike were serving him as intelligence gatherers.[514]

When the Altan khan's grandson fled, Wang recognized that the dynasty had a rare opportunity to alter its policies, and achieve peace. Wang urged that the Altan khan be made a prince (*wang*) and be given a seal, with his nobility receiving lesser titles in the Ming military hierarchy. Earlier precedents for trade, from the Hung-chih (1488–1505) period, would be revived, and in addition subsidies would be paid to the Altan khan. The Altan khan's grandson would be returned, and the Altan khan himself would hand over to the Ming various Chinese who had fled and taken refuge with him.[515]

The proposal did not initially appeal to the monarch. However Chang Chü-cheng and Kao Kung, the grand secretaries, finally persuaded him that it was acceptable. The court met to discuss the policy, and to vote. At a meeting of higher officials, twenty-two accepted it, seventeen rejected it, and five had qualified opinions. The minister of war proposed a slightly different version. On 2 April 1571, it was agreed that Wang's original eight-point proposal be adopted with only minor changes. On 13 June 1571 a solemn meeting was held just outside the Ta-t'ung borders at which the Altan khan and his followers swore allegiance to the Ming, promised to respect its borders, and the Mongol princes received their new ranks in the Ming hierarchy. The Altan khan turned southward and performed the necessary ritual, and received the imperial decree.[516] Altan's city (today's Hu-ho-hao-t'e), which had burned in 1559 and been rebuilt, then received in 1575 the name it retained through much of the twentieth century, Kuei-hua *ch'eng* or "city returning to civilization."[517]

The peace policy proved extraordinarily successful, as is evident from a variety of sources. In 1577 the expenses for armies in Hsüan-fu, Ta-t'ung and Shansi were reported to be only 20–30% of what they had been before peace was made, while in 1583 the armies were far better supplied than before. Subsidies to the Mongols amounted to only a tenth of what defense had previously cost. Farming and harvesting along the border, previously disrupted, returned to normal.[518] By 1584 the situation was so improved as to prompt a warning from the ministry of war that the sense of peace and prosperity must not become a pretext for relaxing precautions. In 1590 grand secretary Shen Shih-hsing stated that for twenty years no military action had been necessary anywhere on the whole frontier from Hsüan-fu, just west of the capital, to Kansu on the empire's western border.[519]

Having achieved peace, Chang sought not to jeopardize it. His approach to military matters was in most respects conventional. He linked the external security of the state to the health of its internal governance, stressed the importance of avoiding both war and invasion by the maintenance of preparedness and a deterrent capacity, and favored strong defenses.[520] But unlike his immediate predecessor, Hsü Chieh, and others, he believed that trade with the nomads was essential: to divide them, to corrupt them, to bring them into a regular relationship that would make them more manageable while providing the Ming economic opportunity and time to strengthen further border defenses.[521] To avoid warfare, he kept his own subordinates under control: both T'an Lun and Ch'i Chi-kuang, for example, chafed at the bit in the northeast, and proposed mounting offensive operations against the nomads. Chang, however, ruled out that idea.[522]

Rather than launch campaigns, Chang took his cue from the long tradition favoring maintenance of strength by military farming, and turned his attention to reforming that system. He personally demanded that governor-generals increase their farm production, and a high rate of return, of perhaps 1.4 million *tan* of grain (93,100 tons) and 180,000 taels (234,000 ounces) of silver for the fourteen border units is shown in the *Ta Ming hui tien* for the years 1578–79.[523] But as Ray Huang points out, Chang did not attempt to change the system, and perhaps substitute an entirely professional army, paid in silver, for what was clearly the outmoded arrangement made at the beginning of the dynasty. Rather, he simply managed to squeeze more out of the system as it existed, which meant that when he died there was silver in the treasuries and, by the 1580s, the total cultivated area of military farms was probably not less than 600,000 *ch'ing*, or roughly 15,000 square miles.[524]

What was striking in Chang Chü-cheng, then, was not his originality. He was not the author of new and imaginative policies. Rather, he was simply the politician with the sense to see what had to be done, and the authority to do it. His role in making peace with the Altan khan essentially demonstrates this. The successful conclusion of peace, and the subsequent fall in military expenditure, with no corresponding increase in security problems, shows that there was a better alternative to the way the Ming had been dealing with the nomads. And the way Chang achieved his success, by using his personal power to break factional deadlock, confirms what has been argued about the inherent weakness of the Ming political system.

As long as Chang lived, the defense and foreign policies that he had championed could be maintained. But they had relied for support on his extraordinary power: once that was gone the old quarrels surfaced again. He had not been able to remake institutions; only to control them from a personal power-base.

After Chang's death, peace gradually broke down, and the conflict that had earlier existed between the proponents of compromise and the hard-liners reasserted itself, leading to a re-politicization of border policy that proved fatal to the dynasty. The late sixteenth century saw the future rulers of the Ch'ing (1644–1912), the tribal Manchu people begin to build up a state of their own in the northeast, and the beginning of the seventeenth saw them throw off their tributary status and begin to threaten the Ming. Unfortunately, the intellectual inheritors of the anti-Mongol militants of the mid-sixteenth-century period were unwilling to accept realistic policies. Chang's accommodative policies did not survive long.

After his death, the grand secretary who had done more to restore Ming security than anyone else in over a hundred years, was almost immediately disgraced. And although most criticism concentrated on his behavior at court, failure to observe mourning, alleged love of luxury, etc., he also received some blame for his military policies. He was faulted for being a compromiser, who failed to attain the sort of "victory" for which Tseng Hsien and Yang Chi-sheng had argued. Indeed, as Chang was being criticized, these men were received posthumous honors. Tseng Hsien was rehabilitated shortly after 1567, granted the posthumous title Hsiang-min, and rank of minister of war. After 1573 "a petition was presented requesting the erection of a shrine in Shensi in Tseng's honor," while in 1587 his memorials on Ordos recovery were republished, with a laudatory preface, in a move that was probably connected with ongoing criticism of Chang.[525]

Policies like Chang's would probably have worked far better in dealing with the new threat of the Manchus than did those which drew on the uncompromising tradition. In the event, however, policy toward the Manchus was beset by many of the same problems that had earlier plagued that toward the Mongols. The Manchus had taken control from the Ming of the territory east of Shan-hai-kuan, and there were those at court that wanted to take it back. Some, like Hsiung T'ing-pi (d. 1625), believed that a solid defense was the best that could be hoped for, and that recovery of Liao-tung was out of the question; others, like Wang Hua-chen (d. 1632), proposed offensives, which led to costly defeats. In the early seventeenth century, when they began to argue, as before, over what policy to adopt toward this new threat, old patterns reappeared. A modern student suggests that if only the Ming had stuck to a policy of strong defense coupled with diplomatic accommodation, the fall of the dynasty need not have occurred. But no such accommodation was reached, and in 1644, at a time of domestic rebellion in China, the Manchus, brought in by a Ming general, established the last dynasty, the Ch'ing. And just as in the case of

Mongol policy, blame for failure must fall to a large degree on the intrigues that lay behind poor Ming policy decisions.[526] This time, however, the price was the dynasty itself. Looking for the causes of the fall of the Ming, the Ch'ing literatus Chao I (1727–1814):

blamed the scholars for their empty talk. He claimed that in the early days the Manchus had no intention of conquering China; had the Ch'ung-chen emperor [r. 1628–45] made peace with them, he could have concentrated all his army on suppressing the rebels instead of fighting both. Chao tried to show that on several occasions the emperor had the intention of making peace with the Manchus, but because of the opposition of scholars who knew very little about the seriousness of the situation, the monarch gave up his original attempt.[527]

Such a realistic opinion is rather unusual in historical writing on the subject.

The Ch'ing conquest was of course a major watershed in Chinese history. In 1644, when the Manchus passed through Shan-hai-kuan on their way to Peking, they had already assembled an empire which included most of Mongolia and Manchuria, the territories north and east of the Ming Great Wall, and the sources of many of the Ming's most serious security problems. To this they added what the Ming had held, as well, eventually, as Sinkiang, Taiwan, Tibet, etc. creating ultimately an empire that was twice the size of its Ming predecessor. In this new polity, the Ming wall had no strategic function, though it did until the nineteenth century mark a line north of which Chinese were not to pass. But it no longer had the roles of military and national boundary that it held in the Ming.

More than that, the Wall lost, at least overtly, the symbolic role it had enjoyed in the Ming as a dividing line between "barbarism" and "civilization." The Ch'ing polity was run by Manchus, who, by Ming standards, were foreigners. Their empire lacked the sort of cultural definition that had been increasingly important as the Ming developed. It was simply the patrimony of the Manchu royal house, containing several distinct cultures, each of which was dealt with separately. Much of Ch'ing cultural policy in the Chinese part of the empire was furthermore designed to weaken the embryonic culturalism already evident in the Ming, by suppressing the whole tradition of argument about what constituted *hua* and *i*.

Not surprisingly, then, the Ming Great Wall, which was after all an unmistakable structure and no longer just the folk-memory of earlier times, fit only uneasily into the Ch'ing world, in which the military challenges to which it was a response had disappeared, while the cultural attitudes that it also embodied were forbidden. And for much of the Ch'ing, as we shall see in the final chapter, no one paid much attention to it. As long as the Ch'ing rulers were decisive, and their empire was militarily strong, they could impose their cosmopolitan policies throughout the empire without regard for the secret disapproval of a few anti-Manchu Ming loyalists among the literati.

But when, in the nineteenth century, the quality of Ch'ing rule declined, and the technologically superior European powers began to inflict damaging defeats, Ming- (or perhaps we should say "Chinese-") style politics began to reassert itself. Cultural definitions of the polity began to compete with the dynastic, as they had in the late Ming, but even more vigorously, for the Manchu rulers were foreign. By the late nineteenth century the court was once again embroiled in arguments between hard-liners and compromisers whose outlines were familiar to anyone who knew Ming history. At root, these debates concerned, once again, what China was. The Wall, of course, could play no direct role in them for the new unit which all took as defining was not the Ming polity bordered by the fortified frontier, but rather the Ch'ing empire which extended far beyond it. But the Wall could serve as an expression of the need to define and protect "Chineseness," and gradually came to be incorporated in that part of the debate which drew upon a new stream of ideas from abroad, to form the modern political amalgam of Chinese nationalism. Its definitions, in turn, continue to plague practical politicians to the present day.

Although the Ming arguments concerned specifics of policy toward the nomads, their real stakes were far higher, which is why they continue to be relevant. At root they were about how culturally exclusive China must be in order to remain Chinese; about the nature and range of the authority of the Chinese ruler; about where – and whether – to draw a line between the steppe and China proper. They were, in other words, arguments in which fundamentally different images of the polity collided. In them, the T'ang idea of an empire straddling rice-paddies and steppe confronted the Southern Sung vision of a culturally uniform China; the early Ming sense of continuity with the cosmopolitan Yüan conflicted with the reassertion, in mid dynasty, of a narrower and culturally more limited vision. These were arguments at the very most basic level of state-building: at the level of blueprints, as it were, even before foundations are laid.

It is important to note this fact, because it is usually obscured by a belief that the fundamental questions of what China was and how far her territory extended had been answered, at least until modern times, by the drawing, at the dawn of her history, of a single "Great Wall frontier." But in fact the problem facing successive dynasties has not been conquering "China," or recovering it, or even ruling it. The first problem has always been defining it, and that is as true today as it ever was. That process of cultural definition has always been highly controversial and it has never been completely resolved: indeed, the Ch'ing experience complicated it by introducing large numbers of people of distinct cultures into what has become modern Chinese territory. In the past its issues have served as reference points in factional competition in court after court, while the importance and bitterness of those competitions has made the basic cultural issues more acute. In the period immediately following the end of the Ch'ing, the issue, which became an aspect of the new "nationalism," played a central role in political competition. And the process continues in the present. Whether we look simply at the patterns of politics within the Peoples's Republic of China, or whether we adopt a more comprehensive view and encompass the various ideas of Chineseness that are found in the competing cultural and political entities that constitute the Chinese world today, we find that, just as in the past, although exactly what China is remains an almost impossible question to answer, nevertheless accusations of lack of loyalty or patriotism in respect to this ill-defined entity remain among the most highly-charged and damaging in politics.

These facts can perhaps suggest a few modifications in the way we look at Chinese international relations. Today the Great Wall is often invoked as a symbol of Chinese foreign policy, and is thought of as summing up somehow a single and enduring attitude toward the outside world. The belief is that because this attitude was culturally based, even culturally determined, it somehow transcended politics. Isolation from the outside world, the assertion of superiority, the idea of China as the "Middle Kingdom" – all are aspects of Chineseness that the Wall sums up. But our account so far has shown that far from being the product of deep cultural orientations the Wall, at least, is the product of particular ideas and circumstances, and that these in no way constitute an exhaustive or even a unique definition of Chineseness.

The real history of the Wall discloses that rather than seeing Chinese foreign policy as more or less consistent and culturally determined, we should see it as the product of the clash of several competing ideas of Chineseness. Some of the ideas are more practically feasible than others, and in the case of the Wall, the ultimate explanation is found in the way that the adoption of an impractical policy was forced by the victory of one particular set of cultural definitions.[528]

Such concerns remain fundamental in modern Chinese foreign policy. In his study of China's diplomacy after the death of Mao Tse-tung in 1976, for instance, Michael Yahuda draws a clear distinction between what he calls the "strategic" and "societal" dimensions of policy.[529] The particular importance of such domestic factors as ideology and national self-definition has also been recognized for the imperial period. Many scholars of Chinese diplomacy have called attention to the formative importance of the hierarchical ideas of the tribute system.[530] And examinations of the period following the end of the last dynasty in 1912 nearly always emphasize the importance of nationalism in the period before 1949, and of the doctrines of communism and Maoism in the period after.[531]

But in analyzing foreign policy outcomes, most authors do not accord much importance to such domestic factors. Rather the changing external environment has been taken as primary, and China's foreign policy is generally assessed as having responded to it, pragmatically and successfully by and large, even though that foreign policy may have been couched in terms which have been both politically-charged and intimately linked to the domestic situation. Thus the tribute system is often judged to have worked well in ordering the Inner Asian and maritime frontiers. Its failure came only when an inappropriate attempt was made to apply it to relations with western nations. And despite the extraordinary role of Maoist doctrines in the internal politics of China of the last thirty years, many authors would agree with Yahuda's conclusion that in the end they were less important than national interests: that "if there is a consistency underlying China's foreign policy it is to be found in the geopolitical thought which had guided it, rather than in the didactic principles consistently invoked by its officials."[532]

Yet while it is true that China has shown a capacity to do what has to be done in spite of all sorts of ideological or political hindrances, the extent to which her foreign policy is customarily analyzed in "strategic" rather than "societal" terms is nevertheless troubling. Few authors have placed domestic considerations first in their foreign-policy analyses, and fewer still have been willing to identify missed opportunities or failures that originated domestically. In the modern period one notable exception is Kuang-sheng Liao, who has both applied the concepts of linkage between the domestic and foreign spheres in his analyses of contemporary policy making, and clearly stated that the dominance of internal factors at times has exacted large costs. He argues that antiforeignism, for instance, has greatly hindered China's modern development.[533]

Study of the history of Chinese frontier-policy from before unification through the Ming and even beyond suggests a conclusion parallel to Professor Liao's. Again and again policy on the border has been internally constrained, or even driven, and this fact has had real costs. Rather than being the results of the sorts of deep ecological and socio-economic forces that writers such as Lattimore have proposed as explanations, it appears many Chinese decisions about border policy have been determined by internal political struggles of the type we have described, taking place both on the concrete level of factional struggle, and on the more abstract plane of politically-useful philosophical redefinition of such concepts as loyalty patriotism, and the nation.

To draw such a conclusion from the study of the Wall may seem paradoxical. For the "Great Wall," after all, is often presented as a symbol of cultural consensus, the logical fulfillment of a Chinese world view. But it should be clear that the fateful decisions that led to the "Great Wall" were not the product of a way of thinking shared by all Chinese and strange to most others. Rather, like similar decisions elsewhere, those about the Maginot Line for example, they were political, and reflected political struggles at court, taking place in a cultural context. The way they have been analyzed here will provide, it is hoped, a suggestion of a profitable future direction for scholarship of Chinese foreign relations. It is true that the Chinese tradition has much to say about way the world should be ordered, and how such ordering should be brought about. But the level of generality that can find a coherent Chinese "world view" is useless when it comes to analyzing actual policy-choices. For the real history of the Great Wall shows that whatever shared framework there may have been did not give Chinese approaching foreign policy a set of definitions or options that transcended politics. Far from it. Like their equivalents in other societies, the culturally derived elements of the Chinese approach to foreign policy defined an area of conflict.

In the struggle that took place in that area, a Chinese "world view" was not necessarily something that united the contenders: it could easily become a focus of disagreement, and even, on occasion, a weapon. To see the Great Wall clearly is to recognize it not as a product of cultural consensus, but rather as one of political dissension.

11

The Wall acquires
new meanings

It may be true that seen clearly, the Great Wall is best understood as a product of the kinds of strategic and political controversies that we have described so far. But we began with the fact the the Great Wall is not often so clearly seen. It is known to us not directly, but interpreted, through a screen of legend and preconception: what we have called, in the Introduction, the historical myth of the Great Wall. The story of this myth is in many ways just as important and significant as the interpretation we have sought to substitute for it, and in closing it is perhaps appropriate to examine the origins, development, and influence of the myth of the Great Wall of China itself.

The task has far more than purely antiquarian interest. Its origins and growth tell us much about both China and the West. To understand it fully we must explore historiography, legend, and the passage of cultural influences between Europe and the Orient. Ultimately it will lead us to basic questions of modern Chinese national identity. This is because the modern Great Wall myth appears to be above all a product of contemporary China's self-definition. We have seen how a process of national redefinition from the Yüan to the Ming dynasties formed the background for the decisions that led to the creation of the Ming defense system. A similar tranformation of China from the end of the Ming up to the present led to the creation of the modern Great Wall myth.

Examining the myth will show that it originated in China, but that it began to assume something like the form it has today only after it reached Europe, apparently in the late sixteenth century. There it was incorporated into a partly real, partly fantastic view of China whose development had more to do with European intellectual currents of the time than with any genuine information about Asia. When, however, in the twentieth century, China began to discard the institutions and the culture that had served as her national definition in earlier ages, this largely Western notion of the Great Wall of China was reintroduced, quite unconsciously it appears, in the role of national symbol.

The earliest antecedents of the modern myth are found in the Chinese tradition regarding the ancient walls we examined in Chapter 1, and particularly the wall of Ch'in Shih-huang. Though that wall disappeared in fact, it lived on in histories and the popular imagination. For historians of the successor Han dynasty, Ch'in walls exemplified the futility of Ch'in Shih-huang's military policies and his tyranny toward the people, while among the people, the memory of forced labor and death on the frontier led to the development of a tradition of legend and song. Both, in their own ways, agreed on the significance of the Wall: it symbolized the failure of Ch'in rule, and the way the emperor had failed to grasp the importance of virtue in supporting rule, but had instead relied on force.

Two of the writers we have already met reveal such a primarily moral approach to the question of wall building. Ssu-ma Ch'ien's (145-?87 B.C.) account of the building of the Ch'in wall in the *Shih chi* is, as we have seen, rather sketchy, but he is careful to draw the moral from the suicide of the first Ch'in emperor's close collaborator, Meng T'ien. When Shih-huang died, his heir ordered Meng to kill himself, ostensibly to expiate an unspecified crime, though in fact the purpose was to remove a powerful and threatening figure from the political scene. In his text, Ssu-ma Ch'ien reproduces what is probably an earlier version of the story:

Meng T'ien heaved a great sigh and said: 'What crime have I before heaven? I die without fault!' After a long time he added: 'Indeed I have a crime for which to die. Beginning at Lin-t'ao, and extending to Liao-tung, I have made ramparts and ditches over more than ten thousand *li*, and in this distance it is impossible that I have not cut through the veins of the earth. This is my crime. He then swallowed poison and so committed suicide.[534]

Talk about the "veins of the earth" reflects the influence, growing at the time, of Chinese theories of *feng-shui* or geomancy. But while Ssu-ma Ch'ien quotes Meng he does not fully accept what he says. For him the general's crime is something far less mysterious. In his summary at the end of the general's biography he asserts that Meng met death "because he conscripted forced labor and did nothing to 'alleviate the distress of the common people, support the aged, care for the orphaned, or busy himself with restoring harmony among the masses.'" "'Is it not fitting that he [...] should meet death for this?'" he asks. "What did his crime have to do with the veins of the earth?"[535]

A similar commentary is found in the "Faults of Ch'in," by Chia I. According to Chia, the Ch'in emperor had misunderstood the basis of successful rule. He

believed in his heart that with the strength of his capital within the Pass and his walls of metal extending a thousand miles, he had established a rule that would be enjoyed by his descendants for ten thousand generations.[536]

But as the collapse of his dynasty shortly after his death demonstrated, force alone could never take the place of virtue. These examples entered the Confucian canon, and thereafter the Wall of Ch'in became, for the literati, an unambiguously negative symbol. It stood for despotism, cruelty, and ultimately, political failure. Not surprisingly, the heirs of Chia would object, as we have seen, to fortifications and promote offensive policies instead.

This elite tradition was not the only Chinese memory of the events, however. A folk tradition developed as well and, like the elite view, it has remained influential right down to the present. The Chinese peasantry seem not to have forgotten the forced dispatch of hundreds of thousands of their number to the north to war with the Hsiung-nu, settle in their territory, and build barriers along its margins. Out of their memory, folk-songs and folk-tales developed, and in 48 B.C., Chia Chüan-chih stated that "Songs of the Long Wall have never ceased up to now."[537] We even possess four lines which probably originated in such a song. They warn parents:

> If a son is born, mind you don't raise him!
> If a girl is born, feed her dried meat.
> Don't you just see below the Long Wall
> Dead men's skeletons prop each other up.[538]

Such songs were valued by the Han government for the insight they gave into popular feeling, and gave rise to a genre of mock ballad, called *yüeh-fu*, that the literati often used as a vehicle for moral criticism. Ch'in Shih-huang's wall was among standard themes.

A number of such *yüeh-fu* poems, written to the title "Watering Horses at the Long Wall Hole," were composed during the Latter Han. One, by Ch'en Lin (d. A.D. 217) runs as follows:[539]

> I water my horse at a Long Wall hole,
> The water's chill hurts my horse's bones.
> I go and tell the Long Wall officer,
> 'Mind you don't keep us T'aiyüan men for good!'
> '*Corvée* has a set time to run!
> Swing your sledge! lend your voice!'
> 'We men would rather die fighting!
> Why be bored to death building the Long Wall?'
>
> The Long Wall how it winds and winds,
> Winds and winds three thousand leagues.
> Border towns full of strong young men,
> Homesteads full of widowed wives.

I write a letter to my wife at home:
'Better remarry, don't stay on at my home.
Better to serve new in-laws.
From time to time think of your old husband.'
Her reply reached the border:

'What you came up with is so silly!
You are in the thick of disaster –
How could I stay in another man's house?'

'If a son is born, mind you don't raise him!
If a girl is born, feed her dried meat.
Don't you see just below the Long Wall
Dead men's skeletons prop each other up?'

'With bound hair I went to serve you,
My aching heart sealed with care.
I know full well your border grief –
How can your wife survive for long?'

Other popular traditions of the Wall appear to have included a popular legend that told of a race of "hairy men," whose ancestors had escaped conscription under Ch'in Shih-huang, and whose skin had turned white from living in the thickly-forested mountains for many years. These "hairy men" would ask anyone they met whether the Wall was finished, and whether Ch'in Shih-huang was still alive. An unfavorable answer would cause them to flee. A "hairy girl cave" on Huashan mountain in southern Shensi is said to have been the hideout of a female wall-builder who survived there eating roots and growing white hair all over her body for eight hundred years before becoming a divinity.[540]

But the fullest expression of the popular tradition is found in one of the oldest and most popular folk-tales in the entire Chinese repertory: the story of Meng Chiang-nü. It tells of a woman whose husband has been sent to the wall-construction site in the far north. In winter, worried about his welfare, she sets out to take him warm clothes, only to learn on her arrival that she is too late: her husband has already perished. Overcome, Meng Chiang-nü kneels down and sobs. Her grief, however, mysteriously causes the wall to break open, and reveal her husband's bones. These she takes back to his native place for a proper burial.

This tale is alive in the folk tradition today: temples to Meng Chiang-nü are not uncommon, and a recent emigrant from China tells how, during the Cultural Revolution, peasants in Hunan gathered from miles around to hear a blind singer chant the story at a funeral.[541]

The Meng Chiang-nü legend was also one of the first to be studied by China's founding generation of modern folklorists, led by Ku Chieh-kang

孟姜女故事

明嘉靖間西清堂刻本新刊諸家選極五寶訓解啓蒙故事

Fig. 8a A Chia-ching period illustration from a Ming version of the Meng Chiang-nü legend.

Fig. 8b Meng Chiang-nü as the demure model of Chinese femininity as seen by the recent modern West in Genevieve Wimsatt's *Lady of the Long Wall* (New York, 1934).

Fig. 8c Meng Chiang-nü presented in a more popular style in Wang Shu-hui
and Chang Hen-shui, *Meng Chiang-nü* (Peking, 1957).

(1893–1980), and what he and his students discovered about its origins provide an illuminating perspective on the Great Wall myth.[542] No wall of any kind is mentioned in the earliest antecedent of the Meng Chiang-nü story, which is found in the *Tso-chuan*. The story is simply of the virtuous wife of Ch'i Liang, who insists that ritual proprieties be strictly observed when she receives condolences for the death of her husband in war.[543] To this spare outline the *Lieh-nü chuan*, edited by Liu Hsiang (79–8 B.C.), adds a second part, in which a city wall appears:

Ch'i Liang's wife had no children, nor any relatives whatsoever. Since she had no place to turn to, she wailed over the corpse of her husband at the foot of the city-wall. The sincerity of her grief was such that none of the passers-by was not moved to tears. Ten days later, the wall toppled down.[544]

The wall of Ch'in Shih-huang joins the tale only in the versions that begin to be written down in the T'ang. During the "period of disunion" which preceded that dynasty, warfare had been endemic, and as we have seen, some states turned to wall-building for protection. Thousands of men were sent away to work on these walls: many perished, and their widows became so numerous that the states took to assigning them husbands from among prisoners or other wall-builders.[545] Most scholars now agree that the folk-memory of the horrors of this period breathed new life into the legend of Ch'in Shih-huang, and blended it with the story of the virtuous widow Ch'i Liang, to create a version of the Meng Chiang-nü legend having all the elements found in it today.

The same themes of suffering that are found in the Meng Chiang-nü legend also became stereotyped themes of Chinese poetry.[546] T'ang poets, Li Po (705–62) for instance, evoked the loneliness of soldiers sent to the north to fight the Hsiung-nu, or to the west, beyond Yü-men-kuan, the "Jade Gate" of the Han, in westernmost Kansu. Such poems are full of conventional allusions: to the bones of soldiers and wall-builders, the former bleached on the desert floor, the latter buried inside the wall; to the lack of water in the desert; to the menace of the nomads; to the aching loneliness of the garrison soldiers.

But what is most striking about even literary references to walls in the period between the end of the Ch'in and the mid-Ming, when major wall-building got underway, is not their abundance, but rather their relative scarcity. Although the Wall is treated, it is not a major theme, even in poems about service along the border. One is driven to wonder just what sort of an idea of border walls Chinese of this period had.[547] Just how vague it may have been is suggested by the fact that, as already mentioned, the phrase that translates the modern concept of "Great Wall" into modern Chinese, *wan-li ch'ang-ch'eng* occurs only rarely in premodern Chinese literature. Indeed, Morohashi's great dictionary devotes two pages to it, without citing a single exact occurrence. The closest is the remark of T'an Tao-chi (d. 435), a military hero of the Chin and Liu Sung dynasties, upon learning of his disgrace: "So you would destroy your Great Wall [*wan-li chih ch'ang-ch'eng*]!"[548] It can be found, of course, in the super-inscribed poems of the paintings of Peking scenery by the early Ming painter Wang Fu, mentioned in the Introduction.[549] But the contrast with the present ubiquity of references to the Wall is striking.

Furthermore, in all of these traditional references, the real concern had been with questions of morality and character, while the Wall itself serves a supporting role, as setting. In the fifteenth century, however, as the Ming dynasty began to build far more elaborate walls than had ever been known before, the legends acquired new concreteness. The Ming court, well aware of the bad reputation of Ch'in walls, took care to distinguish its fortifications from theirs. As we have noted, they used a new phrase for their work: *pien-ch'iang* or border walls, instead of *ch'ang-ch'eng*, or long walls, the earlier term.[550]

But none of this prevented the Ming walls from beginning to mix into the folk tradition: the new walls provided an impressively concrete setting for the legends, while the legends contributed a spurious genealogy for the walls. On the official level, critics of Ming policy used the Ch'in analogy to make their points. The literatus Li Meng-yang (1473–1529), who had served on the desert frontier at Yü-lin, just at the time the Ming were building their first walls there, painted a grim picture of life on the border.[551] And in the early Ch'ing, Wan Ssu-t'ung (1638–1702), a Ming loyalist, satirized the futility of sixteenth-century wall-building in the mock folk ballads of his *New Yüeh-fu*. The title evokes the original *Yüeh-fu*, and Wan's poems are in popular style, doggerel rather than allusive classical language. Their message is clear: by ridiculing their wall-building policies Wan makes the Ming emperors no better than the reviled tyrant Ch'in Shih-huang, and compares their reigns unfavorably to the Han and T'ang dynasties, which had both faced nomads on their northwestern frontiers, but instead of building walls, sent troops into the Ordos, driven out the nomads, and established permanent garrisons. But not all writers treated the Wall with contempt. Chao I (1727–1814), for example, praised the First Emperor for having secured China's boundaries.[552]

Among the people, the Meng Chiang-nü legend seems to have provided orientations as early as Ming times. The travel diary of Ch'oe Pu (1454–1504), a Korean official who was shipwrecked on the China coast in the fifteenth century contains an account of his return to his own country via the pass at Shan-hai-kuan. There he was told that portions of fortifications he saw had been built by the Ch'in (whose border had in fact been well to the north), and was even shown the *wang-fu-lou* or "husband-lookout tower" where Meng Chiang-nü had once stood.[553] The temple to Meng Chiang-nü at Shan-hai-kuan whose origins are sometimes placed in the Sung, and which still exists, appears to be of Ming date, constructed or reconstructed in 1594.[554]

Such scattered evidence suggests that while legends about it existed before the modern period, ideas about the "Great Wall" in those times were nowhere near so important a feature of Chinese culture as they are today, and furthermore that when it was discussed, it was given a quite different symbolic value. In both high and popular culture, the story of Ch'in Shih-huang was told and retold. It might be simple or elaborate but its message was usually the same: the Wall was the work of a tyrant, and it had no military utility. Only rarely in the corpus of traditional literature about the border and border fortifications does one find anything positive.

Futhermore, our evidence suggests that until recently both educated and ordinary Chinese had a rather different understanding of just what "the Wall" was than they do today. Wan Ssu-t'ung and other writers clearly grasped that the Ming walls were new and had not been built by the Ch'in. They made the connection between the two by analogy: to criticize the latter was implicitly to condemn the former. In the early part of this century peasants living near Ming ruins seem also not to have confused them with Ch'in work. Thus when the explorer Frederick Clapp and his colleagues reached Shen-mu, in Shensi, on the route of Yü Tzu-chün's wall, "the natives said: 'This is *not* the Great Wall; this is the 'First Frontier Wall,' built only four hundred years ago; the 'Great Wall' is farther north."[555] Even today the "Great Wall" is not known to every Chinese. We learn in a description of the current patriotic campaign to rebuild the wall, for instance, that "in some outlying mountain districts people only knew the wall as *laobian* (old frontier) and were unaware of its history."[556] Of course, *bian*, or *pien* in Wade-Giles, was the Ming's term for the walls they built.[557] This peasant usage is most likely unchanged since the Ming, and rather than showing ignorance, it probably manifests an original under-standing of walls that has been displaced elsewhere by the myth. The origins of the myth are not entirely clear. But it appears to have entered modern Chinese consciousness not directly from any indigenous tradition, but rather via a detour, which took it first to Europe.

Even before the first sea-borne Europeans reached China in the six-teenth century, westerners had some vague conception of a wall in the middle of Asia. There was the tale of the tribes of Gog and Magog, mentioned in the Bible, and a long-established legend in the Middle East as well as the West which told how Alexander the Great had enclosed them behind a wall.[558] Rashīid ad-Dīn (1250–1318) repeatedly refers to this *sedd*

Iskender, "Wall of Alexander," in connection with his descriptions of the outer barriers built by the Chin dynasty (1115–1234).[559] The same tradition probably accounts for the experience of ibn-Batuta (1304–77), the Arab traveler, who visited China in about 1347. He asked about the "Rampart, or Great Wall of Gog and Magog," and was told that it was sixty days' journey away, in a territory occupied by wandering tribes who "ate such people as they could catch."[560] These tribes were probably the celebrated *anthropophagi*, whom Ammianus Marcellinus (330?–395?) located not far from the land of the Seres, which he had described as surrounded by *celsorum aggerum summitates*, a phrase which has been read as "summits of lofty walls," and glossed as "doubtless including the famous Chinese wall," though in fact it apparently means simply mountains.[561] Later these legends would be linked to the Chinese wall, but they appear not to have predisposed the initial European reception of information from China. At the start, at least, that knowledge arrived in Europe in much the same form that it was known in Asia.

The earliest European accounts of the Chinese wall are modest and empirical compared to what would follow. In 1559 Gaspar da Cruz (ca. 1520–70) reported "a Wall of an hundred leagues in length. And some will affirme to bee more than a hundred leagues." Benedict Goes (Bento de Goes, 1562–1607), writing in 1604, made it two hundred miles long. Matteo Ricci (1552–1610), by far our best source, mentions the Wall only once in his diary, saying that "to the north the country is defended [...] by precipitous hills, which are joined into an unbroken line of defense with a tremendous wall four hundred five miles long."[562] A garbled account of Tamerlane's expedition against Ming China, based on Arabic, also describes a wall "fortie leagues long" that was guarded by "between fiftie and three score thousand men." These last figures were so low as to lead the compiler Samuel Purchas (1577–1626) to wonder whether "Perhaps this was not the ancient wall of which the Chinois write," though in fact they correspond well to the actual situation during the Yung-lo period (1398–1405).[563]

These sources also mirror the Chinese understanding, mentioned above, of wall-building as a supplement to or enhancement of nature. Goes observed that much of the Wall was "naturall of rockes or hils," while Bishop Juan Gonzalez de Mendoza (1550–1620), who made its length five hundred leagues, added "that foure hundred leagues, of the saide wall is naturall of it selfe, so that they be high and mightie rockes verie nigh together; but the other hundred leagues is comprehended the spaced or distance that is betwixt the rockes, the which [the emperor] caused to be made by mens handes of verie strong worke of stone."[564] Gaspar da Cruz likewise believed that the Wall was not continuous, and drew a parallel with similar defense works in south Persia: there were "some mountains or hills intermixt between; for a Persian lord affirmed to me that the like works were in some parts of Persia, intermixt with some hills or mountains."[565]

Such a conception is reflected as well in the early maps of Abraham Ortelius (1527–98), and those that drew upon them. His *Theatrum Orbis Terrarum* was first published in 1570. The description of China in the English edition of 1606 states that "on the North, it hath the *Tartars* [. . .] from whom it is defended and severed partly by an artificall wall, made by the hand and labour of man, partly by a naturall mountaine which runneth for many hundred miles." The map itself shows a double range of mountains very clearly, but no discernible wall.[566] The fortification, however, is supplied strikingly in one of the charts that followed, engraved by John Speed in 1626. It shows the Wall as a rather prominent but discontinuous work, which fills the gaps between mountains, while the accompanying text translates Ortelius's Latin, and explains that it shows:

A wall of 400 league, betwixt the bankes of ᵞe hill, built of ye King of China against ye breaking in of ye Tartars on this side.[567]

Kindling European interest also led scholars to look for references to the Chinese Wall in earlier literature. Jacobus Golius (1596–1667) perused the Arabic sources, extracting what he takes to be an early reference, included in his *De regno Catayo additamentum*:

The city of Zamkhāzī was occupied. The land of Zamkhāzī is the land of the Khitā and voyagers assert that the wall surrounding their lands and cultivated areas and all of their abodes is 23 days journey in length from west to east.

Possibly from Nasīr al-Dīn al-Tūsī (1201–74), the passage was later quoted by Father Athanasius Kircher.[568]

Another early source was provided by Russian travelers. Ivan Petlin's deposition of 1619 tells how his embassy followed the Wall for ten days, while the slightly later account by the Dane E. Isbrants Ides, of the Russian mission which he accompanied to Peking in 1692, does not spare praise of "the *Chinese* wall, round which [their official escort] told us, a Man could not travel in three years time," which he describes as "four Fathoms high, and of such thickness that eight persons may ride upon it a-breast." Both Russian reports use new words to refer to the structure: Petlin calls it the Chinese *krym*, while Ides make it the *tsagan krim*. In both cases the Russian transliterates the Mongolian: *sagan* means "white," while "kerem" is the Mongolian version of a common Turkish root which means "wall" or "fortified city." Today the Russians use another phrase, *velikaia kitaiskaia stena*, which appears to have been introduced from western Europe.[569]

The new terminology reflected the way that the European image of the Chinese wall was beginning to change by the middle decades of the seventeenth century. By then the Ming wall system was complete, and what traveler would not have been impressed by the fortress at Shan-hai-kuan, on the Manchurian frontier, or by Chü-yung-kuan, the gateway to the capital, or Ku-pei-k'ou, on the route from Peking to what, after 1644, became the Manchu summer capital, Jehol?

The new idea of the Wall comes through clearly in the account given by the Jesuit Martino Martini (1614–61), whose *Atlas Sinensis* appeared in 1665. Martini claimed to be an eyewitness, and described the Wall as built entirely of stone, and quite continuous: it was interrupted only at one point by some mountain peaks and at a few others by rivers. Like his contemporaries, Martini ran into trouble because he generalized about a whole frontier, thousands of miles long, on the basis of some atypical stretches of wall in the capital region. Furthermore, like other early authors who had looked into the Chinese records, Martini erroneously identified the walls existing in the seventeenth century with the vanished wall of Ch'in Shih-huang, and thus exaggerated their age as well as their size.[570] An account of a Dutch visit in 1655 was published in 1669, and it estimated the Wall's length at 300 leagues (or 900 miles) while describing it as "everywhere alike; it is about Thirty Cubits, or forty five foot high, and some fifteen Cubits broad."[571]

A greater impact was probably made by the *China Illustrata* of Father Athanasius Kircher (1602–80). This presented vivid images of the Wall: one plate showed a section with a three-storeyed, rather European looking tower, a water-gate, and an elephant with attendants. In the frontispiece was a map, from which the Wall virtually leaps out.[572] By the turn of the century, the modest early accounts of the Wall were being displaced by others yet grander still, like that of Ferdinand Verbiest (1623–88) who affirmed that "the seven wonders of the world put together are not comparable to this work; and all that Fame hath published concerning it among the *Europeans*, comes far short of what I myself have seen."[573]

Europe of the eighteenth century provided fertile soil for myths about China generally, and by the end of the century the idea of the Chinese Wall, thus described, had completed its conquest of the Western imagination. William W. Appleton has described the situation in England, where:

During the seventeenth and eighteenth centuries a mythical China had been created. Largely a synthetic product, the China that Stuart and Augustan Englishmen visualized was seen refracted through Jesuit eyes; it was associated with the artistry of Chippendale, the wit of Goldsmith, and the deistic worship of Confucius. Few were the British voyagers who brought back firsthand accounts, and fewer still were the genuine Sinologists.[574]

206

In France, too the idea of an oriental monarchy of great age and formidable cultural achievements, ruled by a mandarinate, also exercised a powerful influence on the *philosophes*, and they, in turn, did much to fix and popularize such a conception of China.[575]

Voltaire (1694–1774), for example, treated the Wall repeatedly, though he was never able to make up his mind as to exactly what the real point about it was. In the *Essai sur les mœurs*, he admitted that in fact the Wall had been useless against China's enemies, but nevertheless "described it in detail as a great feat of engineering 'superior to the pyramids of Egypt by its utility as by its immensity.'" In the *Dictionnaire philosophique*, the Egyptian pyramids are "merely childish and useless heaps" in comparison with the Wall, which is "a great work." In the *Fragments sur l'histoire*, "in which anti-clerical deism is paramount, he disparaged accounts of ancient constructions by the Jews, comparing them to the Great Wall, 'one of the monuments which does most honor to the human spirit.'" But in his *lettres chinoises*, he reverses his previous valuation, terming the Wall a work "'as vain as immense, and moreover unfortunate in having seemed at first useful, since it had not been able to defend the Empire.'" And in the article, "Anciens et Modernes" in the *Dictionnaire philosophique*, "Voltaire denounced the wall as a monument to fear as the pyramids were a monument to fear and superstition."[576]

The description which Voltaire gave in his *Essai sur les mœurs* was quoted almost verbatim by Louis, Chevalier de Jaucourt (1704–80), the gentleman-scholar with a medical degree from Leiden, who wrote the entry about the Wall for Diderot's (1713–1784) *Encyclopédie*. It describes the Wall as a monument greater in immensity than the pyramids of Egypt, five hundred leagues long, and built in 139 B.C.[577]

Among the sources for the ideas for the *philosophes* was probably the work of Du Halde, published in 1737, to which was appended maps derived from the surveys made by three Jesuit fathers for the Ch'ing emperor K'ang-hsi. It provided a seemingly authoritative description:

Two hundred and fifteen years before the Coming of Christ this prodigious Work was built, by order of the First Emperor of the Family of *Tsin*, to defend three great Provinces against the Irruptions of the *Tartars*.

The account of the Wall's construction was also very specific, telling how the emperor:

As soon as he had determin'd on this grand Design, he drew a third Part of the labouring men out of every Province, and in order to lay the Foundations of it on the Sea-Coast, he commanded several vessels loaded with Iron to be sunk [...] as likewise large stones, upon which the Work was caused to be erected, with so much

Nicety and Exactness, that if the Workmen left the least Chasm discoverable between the stones, it was at the forfeit of their Lives.[578]

These paragraphs gather together some of the many varying details that had been accumulating in earlier European accounts, accounts whose filiation is still by no means clear. Both Martino Martini and Athanasius Kircher tell the story about the sinking of the ships,[579] while the passage about the workmen being executed for leaving gaps between bricks, also mentioned by earlier writers, can be traced back to an identifiable Chinese source: the story of the construction of the wall around T'ung-wan-ch'eng, the capital of Ho-lien Po-po's Hsiung-nu Hsia kingdom in 413 A.D. (see Chapter 3 above). In charge of the work was Ch'ih-kan A-li, who "caused the workers to bake bricks to make the city wall. [He used to test the bricks] and if an awl would bore a hole as much as an inch deep, he would have the worker [responsible] killed and buried inside the wall."[580]

In the British Isles, the publication in 1763 of John Bell's (1691–1780) description of his visit to China in 1719–22 contributed to a vogue for things Chinese that was apparently the object of Dr. Johnson's (1709–84) sarcasm a few years later. In April of 1778 he playfully urged Boswell (1740–95) to visit "the wall of China," for by doing so he would "do what would be of importance in raising your children to eminence. There would be a lustre reflected upon them from your spirit and curiosity. They would be at all times regarded as the children of a man who had gone to view the wall of China."[581] Though Boswell never made the trip, a mission led by Lord Macartney (1737–1806) did pass Ku-pei-k'ou on the way to see the emperor Ch'ien-lung in 1793–4. Their careful reports and observations appeared to confirm the most extravagant account.

The British group made good use of their time at the Wall. The medical officer Dr. Hugh Gillan (?–1798) carried out experiments to determine the origin of the blueish color of the brick (iron, he decided), while John Barrow (1764–1848), later to found the Royal Geographical Society, made the calculations mentioned in the Introduction. The amount of stone in the Wall, he determined, was equivalent to "all the dwelling houses of England and Scotland" and would suffice to construct two smaller walls around the earth at the equator.[582] As for Macartney himself, probably no one has summed up the contemporary European view of the significance of the Wall better than he did:

At the remote period of [the Wall's] building China must have been not only a very powerful empire, but a very wise and virtuous nation, or at least to have had such foresight and regard for posterity as to establish at once what was then thought a perpetual security for them against future invasion, choosing to load herself with an enormous expense of immediate labour and treasure rather than leave succeeding generations to a precarious dependence on contingent resources. She must also have had uncommon vigilance and discernment so as to profit by every current event and to seize the proper moment of tranquility for executing so extensive and difficult an enterprise.[583]

But probably more influential than anything written by members of the Macartney mission were the illustrations prepared by Lieutenant Henry William Parish. His draftsmanlike elevations and cross sections, which filled one plate in the folio subsequently published, provided a (spurious) sense of scientific certainty about the Wall, while his romanticized view of it snaking over the hills provided a model that was widely copied in the century that followed.

Parish's work was certainly the source for the plate showing the Wall in the influential set of volumes, *China, in a series of views* by Thomas Allom and G.N. Wright, which appeared just after the Opium War.[584] That war had opened up China to a trickle of visitors, and in the second half of the nineteenth century popular travel accounts began to contribute to the elaboration and propagation of the myth. Trips to "The Wall" – by which was usually meant either the "Old Dragon's Head," which is accessible by sea, or the Chü-yung-kuan pass – became increasingly frequent.[585] The flavor of late-nineteenth-century ideas about the Wall is unmistakable in the *Voyage Autour du Monde*, of Ludovic Hébert, marquis de Beauvoir (1846–1929), who wrote:

It is a supremely wonderful sight! To think that these walls, built in apparently inaccessible places, as though to balance the Milky Way in the sky, a walled way over the mountain tops, are the work of men, makes it seem like a dream [...] This fantastic serpent of stone, its battlements devoid of cannons, its loopholes empty of rifles [...] will be stored in my mind like a magic vision [...] If one stops to think after admiring such a magnificent view, how easy it is to see in it the work of a people of overgrown children led by despots.[586]

Not everyone, of course, was willing to accept such accounts. Doubts about the Chinese wall had been widespread in the seventeenth century, when they appear to have prompted the writing in 1694 of the first dissertation on the topic. This was by one Jonas Locnaeus, who was particularly troubled by the lack, in the Chinese tradition, of definitive descriptions of it. After a careful survey of the western literature on the subject (his only source), he lamented that:

Whereas the Chinese are praised on account of their extreme diligence in recording matters done among them, concerning the time of the construction of such a famous work there is no agreement whatsoever among historians.[587]

Fig. 9a H. W. Parish's and, a little later, Thomas Allom's romantically inspired views of the wall created a much imitated genre. From George L. Staunton, *An Authentic Account* . . . (London, 1797).

Fig. 9b This scene, from Thomas Allom and G. N. Wrigt, *China, in a series of views* . . . (London and Paris, 1843) is clearly modeled on Parish.

In addition to complaining about the defects of Chinese records, Locnaeus reviewed what little was known about the Wall, and in a reasonably skeptical way. Although he concluded that the wall was a "wonder of the world," he had at least been puzzled, and his work demonstrates how uncertain and fluid were notions of the Wall at the time he wrote. Such doubts, however, appear to have been swept away by the authority of the *philosophes*.

Not until the nineteenth century did the next wave of skeptics appear, In 1841 Charles William Wall touched upon the topic in his *Examination of the Ancient Orthography of the Jews*, carefully reviewing the evidence available from both western and Arabic sources, and concluding that it did not sustain the idea of a barrier built in antiquity and surviving to the present. Rather unfairly, considering the true origin of the Great Wall myth, he called it "a rich specimen of Chinese imposture."[588] In 1881 appeared an important scholarly essay by Dr. O.E. von Möllendorff, a German diplomat, which challenged the myth on the basis of Chinese sources.[589] And a little later two French articles of similar import stirred up a minor controversy. The first of these, by l'Abbé Larrieu, a former director of the Catholic mission at Hsüan-hua, attacked in particular Martino Martini's account, and argued that the Wall, "as commonly described, does not exist and has never existed."[590] Father Larrieu's comments were sound from a scholarly point of view, and widely noted. They were answered indignantly by some Protestant missionaries: the Reverend J.H. Roberts of Kalgan (Chang-chia-k'ou, near which stand wall ruins) wrote that "This wall is no more a myth than are the Pyramids of Egypt or the Bunker Hill Monument."[591] But another article, published in 1891 by a medical doctor who had worked at the French legation in Peking, provided further support for Larrieu.[592]

Such hard-headed empirical arguments got nowhere. By this time the Great Wall of China as imagined in the West was acquiring a life of its own. It even began to feed back into scholarship, where (without anyone ever checking its credentials) it was incorporated into general historical theories. Gradually it acquired a role in the fall of Rome with the suggestion that the Wall's construction cut off the Hsiung-nu who had until then preyed on China, forcing them into a migration that ended when, as the Huns, they sacked the great Western capital.[593] Karl Marx (1818–83) had the Wall stand for the whole stagnant (as he thought) Chinese social and economic system. In one memorable passage, he even envisions a post-revolutionary future for it. Writing in the *Neue Rheinische Zeitung*, he alludes to the way that China had been "swamped with cheap British and American machine-made goods," and the consequent collapse of Chinese handicraft industry, which might in turn cause revolution. Then,

Fig. 10 Considered by many to be Robert "Believe-It-or-Not!" Ripley's masterpiece, this panel, published in May 1932, reflects the role as patriotic symbol that the Great Wall assumed in wartime China. (Photo: c. 1932 Ripley International, Inc. Registered Trademark of Ripley International, Inc.)

When our European reactionaries, on their next flight through Asia, will have finally reached the Chinese Wall, the gates that lead to the seat of primeval reaction and conservatism – who knows, perhaps they will read the following inscription on the Wall: *République Chinoise: Liberté, Égalité, Fraternité!*[596]

By the end of the nineteenth century facts were clearly becoming irrelevant to accounts of the Wall: it was the concept itself, well founded or not, that engaged the imagination. And the concept became ever more inflated, until it finally broke loose from the last empirical tethers. In 1893 the *Century Illustrated Monthly Magazine* described the Great Wall as "the only work of man of sufficient magnitude to arrest attention in a hasty survey of the earth's surface." By the first decade of the twentieth century this glimmer of a claim had matured into the fascinating assertion that the Great Wall was visible from the moon, or in another version, Mars.[595] Its rapid and widespread acceptance demonstrated how thoroughly Europeans and Americans had transformed the Ming fortifications originally scorned by Chinese literati. They had become more than a wonder of the world; more even than a work of which Chinese and humankind more broadly might be proud. Those walls had become a monument that would attract the notice even of the inhabitants of other planets; the structure that Robert Ripley (1894–1949) called in 1932 (in his best-ever *Believe it or Not!*), "The mightiest work of man."[596]

A long time passed, however, before the Chinese began to match such enthusiasm. In 1793, George Staunton (1737–1801) had noted how while Macartney, Barrow, and Parish busied themselves with their observations of the Wall, the Chinese looked on the fortification "with perfect indifference; and few of the mandarines who accompanied the Embassy seemed to pay the least attention to it."[597] Indeed, as the western misconception of the Wall began to percolate into China, apparently around the turn of the twentieth century, serious Chinese scholars felt obliged to try to stamp it out. Thus Chang Hsiang-wen (1867–1933), geographer, historian, and major figure at Fu-jen University, published in 1918 an article reminding readers that the present Wall was of Ming date, and emphasizing that it must not be confused with earlier works.[598] A few years later Liang Ch'i-ch'ao (1873-1928), the brilliant disciple of K'ang Yu-wei (1858-1927), and a leader in the movement for constitutional monarchy, took mistaken belief about the Wall as a prime example of historical misinterpretation in his *Chung-kuo li-shih yen-chiu-fa*, a treatise on method.[599]

But in the same year that Chang wrote his critical article, the "Father of Modern China," Sun Yat-sen (1886–1925), spoke somewhat differently. Sun was a republican, politically opposed to K'ang and Liang, and his conception of the Wall was as grand as any *philosophe*'s. In the *Sun Wen hsüeh-shuo* he describes it as the greatest of all engineering feats in China. And although he concedes that Ch'in Shih-huang was a despot, Sun nevertheless argues that the Wall attributed to him preserved the Chinese race. Without it, China would have been conquered by nomads as early as the Han, and would never have been able to expand to absorb the southern Chinese (from among whom Sun came). But thanks to the Wall, Chinese civilization was able to develop in peace until it was strong enough to assimilate even such conquerors as the Yüan and the Ch'ing.[600]

Sun clearly had not been keeping up with scholarship. But he had instinctive sense of what his country needed, and that, above all, was a modern sense of identity: some blend of cultural, racial, and national sentiments that could take the place of loyalty to the Manchu dynasty, to whose abdication on 12 February 1912 Sun had contributed so much. Gradually the informal adoption of the Wall as national symbol would fill some of this need, albeit incompletely and imperfectly.

When Sun wrote, China was at a political low ebb: the republic was in disarray, yet the road back was blocked as well – two monarchical attempts (1916 and 1917) had just failed. In a few months, the all-consuming iconoclasm of the May Fourth movement would erupt, to make even more difficult, by its wholesale attack on the Chinese past, the construction of any new focus for loyalty. The departure of the Ch'ing had created a vacuum at the heart of Chinese civilization which to this day has not been filled: neither veneration of the person of the president, nor the five-barred flag or its successors, nor even the cults of Sun Yat-sen and Mao, have really taken root in modern China. And for a state that, more than many others, had depended upon the uniformity and power of the symbolic and cultural orders to maintain its cohesion, this has been a profoundly destabilizing evolution. The transmutation of the Great Wall into a positive and a national symbol, which Sun Yat-sen quite innocently began, was at root a response to it.

But it has been a slow and incomplete process. Even today, the Wall remains an ambivalent symbol, as it was for Lu Hsün (Chou Shu-jen 1881–1936), whose masochistic contempt for Chinese culture was, in a paradoxical way, deep patriotism and recognized as such. In 1925 he published a fragment about it: the Wall, he wrote, had cost many lives to construct, and he personally felt surrounded and enclosed by it. It was composed, he further observes, of "both old and new bricks." Thus it stood for the traditional Chinese culture that some of his contemporaries were attempting to save and restore. Yet it had majesty and strength: it was the "Mighty and accursed Great Wall."[601]

It took war to transform such love and hate into a more uncomplicated nationalism. The Japanese occupation of Manchuria in 1931–2 focused the world's attention on China and her will to resist: Ripley's cartoon, mentioned above, appeared a few weeks after the Shanghai ceasefire, and imagery of the Wall became popular in China too, particularly on the political left. The Communists in the mid thirties were reluctant to embrace the flag and other symbols of the Republic of China: at the same time, stress on their Soviet connections was politically inadvisable. Such considerations perhaps account for the interest they began to take in the Wall. In 1935, the year they fled to Yenan, their leader Mao Tse-tung (1893–1976) wrote a poem in which the Wall played a role. Near the end of the "Long March," surveying Mt. Liu-p'an, between Kansu and Ning-hsia, the last high mountain the Red Army had to cross before its destination, Mao exulted:

> We've scored a march of twenty thousand *li*.
> We shall the Great Wall reach,
> Or no true soldiers be!

In this poem, the Wall seems to stand "for the frontier of resistance against the Japanese invaders," but in another famous poem, "Snow," written in February of 1936, the symbolism changes. Now it becomes a symbol of the magnificence and ancient heritage of China:

> Either side of the Great Wall
> One blinding vastness
> [...]
> To touch this pure white with a blush of rose –
> O, enchantment past compare!

Nor was Mao Tse-tung the only Communist leader to write about the Wall: Ch'en Yi (1901–72), Yeh Chien-ying (1898–1986), and Chu Teh (1886–1976), among others, have also contributed to the genre.[602]

The association of the Wall with resistance to Japan is even clearer in the song, "March of the Volunteers," composed by Nieh Erh (1911–35) with lyrics by T'ien Han (1898–1968), and first heard in the 1935 film "Children of the Storm." This calls upon all "who will not be slaves/to take our own flesh and blood, to build a new Great Wall!" It "enjoyed continued popularity in China, particularly in left-wing and Communist circles" (from which both composer and lyricist came) and in 1949 it "was adopted as the official national anthem of the People's Republic of China."[603]

By and large, however, the Wall had little role in the iconography of Republican China. It was repeatedly damaged in the first half of the twentieth century. In 1900, foreign forces quelling the Boxer uprising destroyed part of the Chen-hai-lou tower at the sea on the eastern end of the Wall,[604] while sections of wall at Shan-hai-kuan were caught in fighting between Chi-hli and Feng-t'ien forces in 1922, and again during Chang Tso-lin's withdrawal to his Manchurian base in the second Feng-t'ien–Chih-li War of 1924. Even today scars from the battles are visible.[605] No one, however, seems to have been much concerned: in those days the Wall had not yet become the goal of patriotic Chinese pilgrims.

In 1952, however, the new Communist government began restoration of certain badly-damaged sections: pictures in *China Reconstructs* show the Wall covered with scaffolding.[606] Articles appeared periodically in the Chinese press treating it, and the few tourists who managed to obtain the coveted Chinese visa were almost certain to visit it. But in the first years of the People's Republic, the Wall was not yet on center stage.

This was because the ancient Wall was an imperfect symbol for the "New China." The People's Republic was, after all, engaged in constructing a society of an entirely unprecedented type, and like the U.S.S.R. in its early years, it sought to create its own symbols. Most of the early ones attempted to capture the idea of modernization; later, these would be superseded by the Maoist personality cult. The Wall seems to have been most important at times when such alternate sets of national symbols, and the ideologies that gave them power, had either not yet taken root (as in the 1950s), or were being discarded (as at the present time), and when the government therefore made national rather than political appeals.

Thus such attention to the Wall as a national symbol as was evident in the early 1950s (which matched the then generally appreciative attitude to much of the Chinese past) did not last long. It was overtaken first by the anti-rightist campaign of 1957 (an attack on the very non-Communist intelligentsia to which purely national symbols were designed to appeal) and then by the Great Leap Forward, a utopian frenzy that eventually left several tens of millions dead, and much of the face of China deeply altered.

The Leap transformed the center of Peking, for example. In the capital, a relatively small and harmoniously-proportioned square had for centuries provided an approach to the Gate of Heavenly Peace, the symbolic center of the Chinese cultural world. But during the summer of 1958, acres of Ming and Ch'ing structures were demolished to make way for the construction of what were called the architectural "miracles" of the Leap. In less than a decade, these became paramount symbols of national identity. Liang Heng tells us in his memoir of the Cultural Revolution that when (aged thirteen) he arrived in the capital in summer of 1967, as Red Guard rallies and Mao-worship pressed toward their climax, the "miracles" were what he wanted to see above all: "everything that was legend – the Great Hall of the People, the Monument of the Heroes of the People, the Historical Museum."[607] The "newly born things," all of nine years old at the time, temporarily had displaced the real past in the shared consciousness of many Chinese.

Nor was the "real past" simply ignored during the Great Proletarian Cultural Revolution: as had been recounted a thousand times, it was expunged. Beginning in 1966, priceless rare books were systematically burned, ancient bronzes melted for scrap, and people with learning tortured and killed. The Great Wall did not escape either. During the Cultural Revolution hundreds of kilometers were destroyed, sometimes with dynamite and quarrying machinery, and the material used for road, reservoir, and building construction. Peasants took stone from the Wall to build houses for themselves and shelters for their livestock.[608] But even as the physical Wall was being pulverized to build People's China, some of the moral traditions associated with it in the old culture were gaining new life.

Such tendencies had been evident as early as the Hundred Flowers campaign, when one "rightist" had criticized the Communist technique of control through mass movements. "Since 1952," he was reported to have stated, "campaign has succeeded campaign, each one leaving behind a Great Wall in its wake, a wall which estranges one man from another." A similar example is the poem written in 1971 by Huang Xiang, "Confessions of the Great Wall," in which the Wall stands for "the web of controls that, at the time the poem was written, inhibited every Chinese, making him or her belong to a 'unit;' confining him or her to one place, denying the freedom to travel to the next county, let alone to a neighboring country. It was the repression that cut Chinese off from each other's thoughts and feelings, the censorship that cut them off from what was happening in other lands."[609]

Such criticism became more focused in the mid 1970s. This was the time when the cult of Mao began to assume a new form: perhaps because of fear that after his death someone might compare the Chairman to Ch'in Shih-huang, a campaign was started to rehabilitate and extol that first emperor and arch-villain of the Confucians. Ch'in Shih-huang was presented ever more favorably (the ballyhoo associated with the discovery of the *terra-cotta* army near his tomb in 1974 was part of this), and Mao Tse-tung transformed more and more explicitly into his modern reincarnation. But as the Communist equivalents of the old court historiographers attemped to restore the ancient despot's reputation, one of his traditional adversaries began to stir back to life, as far as we can tell without any official assistance. This was none other than Meng Chiang-nü.

The story of Lady Meng had become known in the West in the nineteenth century, and by the twentieth become subject of several publications, notably of a beautiful volume, published in an edition of only 480, that presented her as exotic and quintessentially feminine. Meanwhile, in China of the twenties and thirties, her story was being exhaustively studied by vaguely populist and nationalistic folklorists. Some of them found the lady who (in various versions of the story) married a man across class lines, traveled alone to the far north, and rebuked the emperor, a prototypical new Chinese woman.[610] But in the 1970s, in her new life, Lady Meng became something even more: she was transformed into a counter-revolutionary.

To criticize Mao, it was enough simply to speak of Meng Chiang-nü. And as Mao basked in an official cult of the glory of Ch'in Shih-huang, she became the target of a campaign of criticism that extended down into the primary schools, where small children who probably had learned the traditional story at home were set essays to write denouncing her. One article in the *People's Daily* put a political gloss on what had been discovered about the tale's development. It enquired, "What is the origin of 'the wailing of Meng Chiang-nü at the Great Wall?'" It answered that while Ch'in Shih-huang's centralization and wall-building "accorded with the interests of the people," nevertheless:

the reactionaries of past ages who favored the restoration of the old order always resorted to any means to denunciate Ch'in Shih-huang as the greatest criminal of all time for the purpose of opposing reform and progress. By describing the wailing of Ch'i Liang's wife at the city wall as Meng Chiang-nü wailing at the Great Wall, the disciples of Confucius and Mencius were deliberately attributing an evil deed to Ch'in Shih-huang.

Few Chinese would have been at all confused as to the real meaning of such an article, and if they had been, a simplified version also circulated. For criticising Ch'in Shih-huang (read Mao), Ch'i Liang's wife, the paragon of virtue and chastity, was labeled a "Great Poisonous Weed."[611]

Such examples show how, in certain contexts, the Wall can be a negative symbol even in today's China, and at both elite and popular levels. But most of the time this continuation of the two traditions that we saw in existence already in the Han, is overshadowed by a new role for the Wall. In the last few decades, it has become one of the few genuinely-felt national symbols. It is the theme of any number of *ai-kuo ko-ch'ü*, or "patriotic songs." After 1949 it emerged as a popular theme for Chinese painters. Some were serious professional artists, among them Feng Shih-lu (1915–) who began doing folk-style woodcuts at Yenan in the 1930s, turned to "traditional" Chinese painting after 1949, and painted a Wall scene in 1954; and Ch'ien Sung-yen (1898–), always a specialist in landscape, whose works today fetch thousands of dollars.[612] But other representations of the Wall, as any visitor immediately notices, are clearly by local craftsmen filling up space in new hotels and restaurants. The visit to the Wall is worth an essay in itself: there is the journey up the narrow and wild mountain pass, the contagious enthusiasm of tour leaders (one told the author that the Wall is "the greatest thing in the world"), the approach past dozens of shops selling Great Wall souvenirs, and finally the structure itself, with its misleading historical signs, and throngs of Chinese and visitors waiting to be photographed against it. Many depart proudly clutching certificates attesting to their presence at the "only manmade structure visible from the moon."

The Wall of Lu Hsün and Huang Xiang may be still the traditional Wall of the Chinese literati, of Chia I and Wan Ssu-t'ung. But the Wall at the center of this flourishing patriotic cult is unquestionably the Wall of the *philosophes*.

What does it mean? Most Chinese are proud of the Wall because they believe that it is something, perhaps the only thing, left from their ancient civilization, that is truly world class. They revel in its size, and are delighted at the reverent awe with which most foreigners approach it. They also appear to value it for its authenticity: at a time when other symbols are discredited, distrusted, or simply not felt, the Wall has always seemed real and legitimate. That in fact is probably why the Communist government has paid so much attention to it, despite its many negative associations.

But some students of Chinese culture may be tempted to greater boldness in their analysis of the Wall as a symbol. China was traditionally a culture; now it is being transformed into a nation. These two conceptions are apparent in two different gifts made to the United Nations by rival Chinese governments. The Republic of China, whose capital since 1949 has been at Taipei, held the China seat until 1971, when it was expelled, and replaced by the People's Republic. Taipei's gift to the world body was a marble tablet on which was inscribed the celebrated passage from the *Book of Rites*, much favored by Sun Yat-sen, which describes the idealized universal "age of Grand Unity" of ancient times:

When the Great Way was practiced, the world was shared by all alike. The worthy and the able were promoted to office and men practiced good faith and lived in affection. Therefore they did not regard as parents only their own parents, or as sons only their own sons. The aged found a fitting close to their lives, the robust their proper employment; the young were provided with an upbringing and the widow and widower, the orphaned and the sick, with proper care. Men had their tasks and women their hearths. They hated to see goods lying about in waste, yet they did not hoard them for themselves; they disliked the thought that their energies were not fully used, yet they used them not for private ends. Therefore all evil plotting was prevented and thieves and rebels did not arise, so that people could leave their outer gates unbolted. This was the age of Grand Unity.[613]

Fig. 11 Repair and reconstruction work being carried out on ruined stretches of Wall in accordance with Deng Xiaoping's 1984 dictum: "Let us love our China and restore our Great Wall!" (*China Reconstructs* 34, 3 March 1985.)

221

This passage is utterly lacking in cultural specificity: it is a vision of universal harmony based on personal, and not national, virtue. The tablet bearing it was removed in 1974, and replaced with the gift of the People's Republic. In contrast with the Confucian text, this summoned up no universal vision: now hanging in the North Lounge of the United Nations headquarters in New York, it was a spectacular tapestry, 32 feet by 16 and weighing 600 pounds, which portrayed the Great Wall of China. It was intended to evoke, as then Deputy Foreign Minister Ch'iao Kuan-hua put it, without further explanation, "the new outlook and new style of the new China."[614]

When Ch'iao spoke, Mao Tse-tung was still alive. But two years after this gift was made, the Great Helmsman died, leaving, in a small way, the same kind of vacuum that had confronted Sun Yat-sen and the others in the years immediately following the end of the empire. Mao's person had been the focus of loyalty for much of the history of the People's Republic, and an attempt was made to have his corpse continue in this role, rather as Lenin's does in the U.S.S.R. But while Lenin may "live," as the Soviet slogan has it, Mao is irretrievably dead (and poorly embalmed to boot). His statues have come down nearly everywhere, his thoughts have been elevated to high camp, and his followers (Ch'iao Kuan-hua among them) have lost their jobs. Doubts about the truth of Marxism have also become so widespread that officials speak of a *hsin-yang wei-chi*, or "crisis of faith." As recent outpourings of dissent confirm, the People's Republic, and the moral and symbolic order over which it presides, face a very real crisis of legitimacy.

Efforts have been made since Mao's death to deal with this problem by reconsecrating the revolution while downplaying Mao's role in it: the best example of this process is the renewed stress on the Long March, the foundation epic of the People's Republic.[615] But far more important than such very difficult redefinition of a revolutionary tradition and of an ideology to go with it has been the revival, in "New China," of "traditional Chinese culture," both at the popular and elite levels. Like the Chinese Nationalist government before them, the authorities of the People's Republic now wrap themselves in the mantle of "Five Thousand Years of Chinese Culture." Since such an idea of the Chinese past is itself an invention, the Great Wall is perhaps not such a bad symbol for it.

In any case, the image of the Great Wall has become ubiquitous since Mao's death. Consider the lavish musical pageant staged for the thirty-fifth anniversary of the Communist government in 1984. Called "Song of the Chinese Revolution" it takes place, as it were, in the shadow of the Wall. In the prelude – "The Morning Song of the Motherland" – "rays of sunlight penetrate the mist to reveal a hundred dancers performing at dawn before a projected scene of the Great Wall surrounded by green hills."[616] In Act V the

Fig. 12 Richard Nixon on his ceremonial visit to the Wall in 1972 (Photo: UPI/Bettmann News.)

Fig. 13 A typical stretch of Ming-dynasty wall, as found in the vicinity of the Chinese capital. Ming walls were distinguished by their use of stone, crenellations, and watch towers (Photo: author.)

theme returns: "[a] coloratura soprano sings the well-known song 'Spring-time for Science' and with stirring rhythm a group of male dancers evoke the Great Wall of Iron built by the People's Liberation Army."[617]

But the most vivid illustration of the Wall's new role as symbol of contemporary China is the current campaign to restore it, mentioned in the Introduction. The campaign involves surveying the Wall, rebuilding damaged stretches in the capital region, pushing forward with academic research on the topic, and improving the work of preservation. It is full of ironies. Many ordinary people have donated what they can to it, clearly feeling that the Wall is something authentically Chinese, of which they can be proud even at a time when most aspects of Chineseness are in flux. One touching account, "Her Tribute," found in a collection of genuine journalistic reportage on contemporary China, depicts a school teacher in her fifties, clearly no stranger to the "crisis of faith" who explains she

was a Catholic, a theist; later I believed in communism, but still as a theist, not believing in the cause of communism, but deifying our leader. The "cultural revolution" shook me. I went back to being a Catholic; not openly of course, but to find something I could trust in.

She feels little loyalty to her school (at a reunion she contributed ten yüan), and while she knows "pandas are a 'national treasure' linked with ecology," she admits "I don't like them." Later the narrator has her rediscover a cautious faith in communism, but her most endearing trait is a simple and honest patriotism. When her husband dies, she takes the 500 yüan (U.S. $134 at the current official rate) he had earned from writing, and donates it to rebuilding the Wall.[618]

Such feeling for the Wall has had active manifestations too. A number of Chinese have attempted to walk the entire length of it. One of these, Liu Yutian, completed the trek on 5 April 1986, and received glowing coverage in the Chinese media.[619] Liu was not a professional explorer: a railway worker in Sinkiang, he developed his plan from a mixture of love of country and curiosity, the former, at least, a feeling shared by many who helped him along the route – students in Lanchow, for instance, who "carried Liu in their midst, jubilantly throwing him up in the air and shouting, 'Rejuvenate China!' "[620]

All of these Wall-centered activities seem quite natural to most participants: the cult of the Wall had the authenticity of the dragon dance, and little of the orchestration and manipulation found, for example, in the Maoist mass rallies. But the meaning of the Wall image itself remains unclear. Is it a proud symbol of a proud nation? Richard Nixon seemed in little doubt in February of 1972 when he proclaimed: "This is a Great Wall and it had to be built by a great people."[621] By doing so, he demonstrated the Wall's newly acquired role in China's foreign relations: the visit to it, virtually obligatory for any state visitor, is the functional equivalent of the imperial audience of earlier times, the occasion when by admiring this world-wonder, he pays homage, not anymore to the Chinese emperor, but to the Chinese people and their country. But what does the Wall mean within China? We have seen that there it has continued to serve as an image of oppression and despotic rule even while being made the center of a patriotic cult.[622] The confusion is unlikely ever to disappear completely: the ambiguities have deep roots, and are intertwined through the whole fabric of China's ever-changing image of itself. Particularly in the iconoclastic twentieth century, the confusion of roles and meanings associated with the Wall reflects the confusion at the heart of the modern Chinese sense of self, which cannot easily be resolved. But the image of the Wall seems bound to endure: whether seen positively or negatively, the Great Wall myth keeps its power. Whatever the future brings, the Great Wall, useless militarily even when it was first built, seems guaranteed to keep its position as a multivalent symbol of Chineseness, and to mirror for the rest of us our fantasies about that society.

Abbreviations used in the notes

Citations of the standard dynastic histories are to the Peking Chung-hua shu-chü edition.

CHC   Cambridge History of China

CCPK   *Chung-kuo ch'ang-ch'eng i-chi tiao-ch'a pao-kao chi*

DMB   *Dictionary of Ming Biography*

FT   Tseng Hsien, *Fu T'ao i*

HS   *Han shu*

HMCPK   *Huang-ming chiu-pien k'ao*

HMCSWP   *Huang-ming ching-shih wen-pien*

KC   T'an Ch'ien, *Kuo ch'üeh*

MMS   Haneda Toru and Tamura Jitsuzō, eds., *Mindai Man-Mō Shiryō*

MS   *Ming shih*

MSL   *Ming-shih lu*

MSCSPM   *Ming-shih chi-shih pen-mo*

MTC   Hsia Hsieh, *Ming t'ung-chien*

SC   *Shih chi*

SMR II   H Serruys, *Sino-Mongolian Relations During the Ming* II The Tribute System and Diplomatic Missions (1400–1600)

SMR III   H Serruys, *Sino-Mongolian Relations During the Ming* III Trade Relations, The Horse Fairs (1400–1600)

SPPY   *Ssu-pu pei-yao*

SPTK   *Ssu-pu ts'ung-kan*

TCTC   *Tzu-chih t'ung-chien*

TMHT   *Ta Ming hui tien*

Notes

1 *China Reconstructs*, 34.3 (March 1985), p. 6.
2 "Ch'ang-ch'eng pao-hu yen-chiu kung-tso tso-t'an-hui ts'e-chi," in *Chung-kuo ch'ang-ch'eng i-chi tiao-ch'a pao-kao chi* hereafter cited as *CCPK* (Peking: Wen-wu, 1981), pp. 3–5.
3 Zhang Zhihua, correspondent for the *Peking Evening News*, quoted in the *New York Times*, 24 July 1984, p. A4.
4 William Morris, ed., *The American Heritage Dictionary of the English Language* (New York and other cities: American Heritage Publishing Co., and Houghton Mifflin Co., 1969), 577.
5 Cheng Dalin, *The Great Wall of China* (Hong Kong: South China Morning Post, Ltd. and New China News, Ltd., 1984).
6 William McNeill, *The Rise of the West* (Chicago: University of Chicago Press, 1963), pp. 306–7.
7 The author has a slide of this sign.
8 *New York Times*, 24 February 1972, p. 17. For a typical guidebook description, see: New World Press and Radio Peking, eds., *Sixty Scenic Wonders in China* (Peking: New World, 1980), pp. 1–4.
9 Jacques Gernet, for example, in his "Foreword" to Luo Zewen (Lo Che-wen), Dai Wenbao, Dick Wilson, Jean-Pierre Drege and Herbert Delahaye, *The Great Wall of China* (New York: McGraw-Hill, 1981), p. 6.
10 K. A. Wittfogel, *Oriental Despotism* (New Haven: Yale University Press, 1957), p. 37.
11 Owen Lattimore, "Origins of the Great Wall of China: A Frontier Concept in Theory and Practice," in *Studies in Frontier History: Collected Papers 1928–1958* (London: Oxford University Press, 1962), p. 98.
12 Frederic Wakeman, *The Fall of Imperial China* (New York: The Free Press, 1975), 71.
13 Richard L. Edmonds, "The Willow Palisade," *Annals of the Association of American Geographers* 69 (December 1979), p. 618 n. 100, citing "Zaiavlenie Pravitel'stva S.S.S.R," *Pravda* 14 June 1969, pp. 1–2; translated in *The Current Digest of the Soviet Press*, 21.4 (1969), p. 10.
14 See Frederick J. Teggart, *Rome and China: A Study of Correlations in Historical Events* (Berkeley: University of California Press, 1939), n. 22, pp. 232–3, for a valuable list of references to this idea.
15 *Science and Civilization in China* (Cambridge: Cambridge University Press, 1954–) IV.3 (1975), p. 47 note f.
16 Among the more important general works are: Wang Kuo-liang, *Chung-kuo ch'ang-ch'eng yen-ko k'ao* (Shanghai: Shang-wu, 1931); Shou P'eng-fei, *Li-tai ch'ang-ch'eng k'ao* (1941); "Ch'ang-ch'eng tsai kuo-shih-shang ti ti-wei" in *Kuo-li T'ai-wan Ta-hsüeh shih-chou-nien hsiao-ch'ing chuan-k'an* (Taipei, 1956), pp. 45–66; and Lo Che-wen, *Ch'ang-ch'eng* (Peking:

Pei-ching ch'u-pan-she, 1982). A recent book of high quality, based on research several decades old is Chang Wei-hua, *Chung-kuo ch'ang-ch'eng chien-chih k'ao (shang pien)* (Peking: Chung-hua, 1979). Two interesting interpretative essays are Chin Ying-hsi, "Tso-wei chün-shih fang-yü-hsien ho wen-hua hui-chü-hsien ti Chung-kuo ku ch'ang-ch'eng," pp. 271–91 in *Ti shih-liu chieh kuo-chi li-shih k'o-hsüeh ta-hui Chung-kuo hsüeh-che lun-wen-chi*. Ed. Chung-kuo shih-hsüeh hui (Peking: Chung-hua, 1985), and Lu Yao-tung, *Lo-ma ch'ang-ch'eng* (Taipei: Shih-pao ch'u-pan-she, 1977). Two Japanese books treat the Wall, both titled *Banri no chōjō*, one by Uemura Seiji (Tokyo: Sōgensha, 1944), and the other by Aoki Tomitarō (Tokyo: Kondō Shuppansha, 1972).

17 See David J. Breeze and Brian Dobson, *Hadrian's Wall* (Harmondsworth: Penguin, 1978), p. 81 and *passim*.

18 Luo Zhe-wen and Liu Wen-yüan, "Ch'ang-ch'eng ti pao-hu, yen-chiu ho li-yung," *Jen-min jih-pao* (overseas edition), 3 April 1986, p. 2, and 4 April, p. 2 (summarized in "Great Wall secrets lure expert sleuths," *China Daily*, April 28, 1986, p. 4); also Yü T'ung-k'uei, "T'an wan-li ch'ang-ch'eng," *Wen-wu ts'an-k'ao tzu-liao* (1956), No. 6, p. 70.

19 The three Jesuit fathers, Bouvet, Régis, and Jartoux, first presented a map of the border defenses to the emperor in 1708, and the original appears to be lost. Speaking of it on page 10 of his *Chine ou Description Historique, Géographique et Littéraire de ce vaste empire, d'après des documents chinois* (Paris: Firmin Didot Frères, 1844), M. G. Pauthier, states that "Le dessin complet de cet ouvrage gigantesque a été levé et envoyé en France par les missionaires, dans le dernier siècle. C'était un dessin sur satin, donnant l'étendue entière et tous les contours de la grande muraille. L'original a disparu, mais une copie doit se trouver dans un des dépôts publics de Paris." The Jesuit map probably did not represent entirely new cartographic work but rather followed one of the maps of the borders prepared for military purposes by the Ch'ing in the late seventeenth century. One such, the so-called "Lateran Map," is preserved in the Vatican. (See M. J. Meijer, "A Map of the Great Wall of China," *Imago Mundi* 13 (1956), 110–15.) Versions of the Jesuit maps were later published in Europe, in J. B. Du Halde's *Description [. . .] de la Chine* (The Hague: H. Scheurleer, 1736) and in J. B. d'Anville's *Atlas* (The Hague: H. Scheurleer, 1737), and appear to have been copied thereafter. See Arnold H. Rowbotham, *Missionary and Mandarin* (Berkeley and Los Angeles: University of California Press, 1942), pp. 267–8.

20 Author's personal information. The atlas is the *Chung-kuo li-shih ti-t'u-chi* (Peking: Chung-hua ti-t'u-hsüeh she, 1975–).

21 Two sets of maps should be mentioned: the U.S. Army Map Service, Series L 500 (which are not available for much of western China), and the Operational Navigation Charts, People's Republic of China, prepared by the Defense Mapping Agency. The errors occur on ONC G-8, where a road is mislabeled as "Great Wall" and where walls that have been examined by American and Chinese geologists are not shown. (A letter from Lt. Col. Robert G. Swanson, of the Defense Mapping Agency to Dr. Alta Walker, U.S. Geological Survey, copy in author's possession, deals with the road, while the missing walls are described in Zhang Buchun, Robert E. Wallace, *et al.*, "Fault Scarps Related to the 1739 Earthquake, and Seismicity of the Yinchuan Graben Ningxia, Huizu Zizhiqu, China," *Bulletin of the Seismological Society of America* 76.5 (October 1986), pp. 1253–87.

22 The most comprehensive survey is found in *Chung-kuo ch'ang-ch'eng i-chi tiao-ch'a pao-kao chi* (Peking: Wen-wu, 1981).

23 Luo Zhewen, "New Survey," *China Reconstructs* 34.3 (March 1985), pp. 8–14.

24 Needham, *op. cit.*, p. 54 note f, quoting Chin Shou-shen, "The Great Wall of China," *China Reconstructs* 11.1 (1962), pp. 20–4.

25 *New York Times,* 25 February 1972, p. 1; *Time,* 99.10 (6 March 1972), p. 15.
26 *Washington Post,* 21 August 1979, p. A4; Orville Schell, "The New Open Door," *New Yorker,* 19 November 1984, p. 86; Compare Schell, *To Get Rich is Glorious: China in the 80's* (New York: Pantheon Books, 1984), p. 112.
27 John Barrow, *Travels in China* (Philadelphia: W. F. M'Laughlin, 1805), p. 224.
28 The literature includes an article by the present author, "The Problem of the Great Wall of China," *Harvard Journal of Asiatic Studies,* 43.2 (1983), pp. 643–63; also Joseph Needham, "Walls and the Wall," in *Science and Civilisation in China,* iv:3 (Cambridge University Press, 1954–), pp. 38–57; O. E. von Möllendorf, "Die Grosse Mauer von China," *Zeitschrift der Deutschen Morgenländischen Gesellschaft,* 35.2 (1881), pp. 75–131, and Édouard Chavannes, "Les plus anciens spécimens de la cartographie Chinoise," *Bulletin de l'École Française d'Extrême-Orient 3* (1903), pp. 214–47. Cheng Dalin's recent book, *The Great Wall of China* (Hong Kong: South China Morning Post, Ltd. and New China News, Ltd., 1984) has good pictures and some useful text, as does Luo Zewen et. al., *The Great Wall* (New York: McGraw-Hill, 1981), and to a lesser degree Yu Chin, comp., *The Great Wall* (Peking: Cultural Relics Publishing House, 1980). William Edgar Geil provides an idiosyncratic account in *The Great Wall of China* (London: John Murray, 1909). Other popular works include L. N. Hayes, *The Great Wall of China* (Shanghai: Kelly and Walsh, 1929); Peter Lum, *The Purple Barrier* (London: Robert Hale, 1960); Robert Silverberg, *The Long Rampart* (Philadelphia: Chilton, 1965); and Jonathan Fryer, *The Great Wall of China* (London: New English Library, 1975). L. S. Vasil'ev's review article, "Velikaia kitaiskaia stena," *Voprosy Istorii* (1971), No. 1, 204–12 leans heavily on Silverberg.
29 Kwang-chih Chang, *Shang Civilization* (New Haven and London: Yale University Press, 1980), p. 273.
30 For general information, see Chang Wei-hua, *op. cit.* also Cheng Chao-tsung, "Ho-pei-sheng Chan-kuo Ch'in Han shih-ch'i ku ch'ang-ch'eng ho ch'eng-chang i-chih," in *CCPK,* pp. 34–9; Ning-hsia Hui-tsu Tzu-chih-ch'ü po-wu-kuan, "Ning-hsia ching-nei Chan-kuo Ch'in Han ch'ang-ch'eng i-chi," in *CCPK,* pp. 45–51, and Shih Nien-hai, "Huang-ho chung-yu Chan-kuo chi Ch'in shih chu ch'ang-ch'eng i-chi ti t'an-so," in *CCPK,* pp. 52–67.
31 See Chang Wei-hua, *op. cit.,* pp. 30–45.
32 See photographs in Cheng Dalin, *op. cit.,* pp. 137–40. Professor David N. Keightley has kindly permitted me to examine his 1965 unpublished paper, "The Long Wall of Ch'i, A Preliminary Study."
33 See Yu Chin, *op. cit.,* n.p.
34 See Cheng Dalin, p. 142; Yu Chin; also Hsiang Ch'un-sung, "Chao-wu-ta meng Yen Ch'in ch'ang-ch'eng i-chih tiao-ch'a pao-kao," in *CCPK,* pp. 6–20, and Pu-ni-a-lin, "Ho-pei-sheng Wei-ch'ang-hsien Yen Ch'in ch'ang-ch'eng tiao-ch'a pao-kao," in *CCPK,* pp. 40–4.
35 See map in Cheng Dalin, p. 138, also Ko Shan-lin and Lu Ssu-hsien, "Yang-shan nan-lu ti Chao ch'ang-ch'eng" in *CCPK,* pp. 21–4.
36 *Shih chi* (Chung-hua shu-chü ed.), 40.2885; Burton Watson, trans., *Records of the Grand Historian of China* (New York: Columbia University Press, 1961) ii, p. 159.
37 Note in particular two beautifully illustrated books: Peter Nancarrow, *Early China and the Wall* (Cambridge: Cambridge University Press, 1978) and Leonard Everett Fisher, *The Great Wall of China* (New York: Macmillan, 1986).
38 "Great Wall donations pay off," *China Daily,* 24 June 1985, p. 1.
39 C. P. Fitzgerald, *China: A Short Cultural History* (London: The Cresset Press, 1935), p. 519.

40 Derk Bodde, "The State and Empire of Ch'in," in *The Cambridge History of China*, ed. Denis Twitchett and Michael Loewe (Cambridge: Cambridge University Press, 1987) Vol. I, p. 62.

41 Owen Lattimore, "Origins of the Great Wall of China: A Frontier Concept in Theory and Practice," in *Studies in Frontier History: Collected papers 1928–1958* (London: Oxford University Press, 1962), p. 115.

42 Bodde, "The State and Empire of Ch'in," p. 63.

43 Cheng Dalin, *op. cit.*, p. 147.

44 *Shih Chi* (hereafter *SC*) 88.2565. Translated by Derk Bodde, in his *Statesman, Patriot, and General in Ancient China: Three Shih Chi Biographies of the Ch'in Dynasty (255–206 B.C.)* (New Haven: American Oriental Society, 1940), p. 54.

45 *SC* 110.2886; Translated by Burton Watson in his *Records of the Grand Historian of China*, II.160.

46 *SC*, 6.252; 110.2886; 88.2565; *Han shu*, 94A.3748.

47 Bodde, "The State and Empire of Ch'in," p. 62.

48 Jonathan Fryer, *The Great Wall of China*, p. 50.

49 See photos in Cheng Dalin, pp. 143–149. Recent archaeological work is summarized in Cheng Te-k'un, "Ch'in-Han Architectural Remains," *Journal of the Institute of Chinese Studies of the Chinese* University of Hong Kong 9 (1978) 2, 503–8. See also Hsiang Ch'un-sung, *op. cit.*, Shih Nien-ha, "O-erh-to-ssu kao-yüan tung-pu Chan-kuo shih-ch'i Ch'in ch'ang-ch'eng i-chi t'an-so chi," in *CCPK*, pp. 68–75; Luo Zhewen, "Lin-t'ao Ch'in ch'ang-ch'eng, Tun-huang Yü-men-kuan, Chiu-ch'üan Chia-yü-kuan k'an-ch'a chien-chi," *Wen-wu* (1964) 6, pp. 47–57; T'ang Hsiao-feng, "Nei Meng-ku hsi-pei-pu Ch'in Han ch'ang-ch'eng tiao-ch'a chi," *Wen-wu* (1977), No. 5, pp. 16–24, describes the Liaoning ruins, while Itō Chūta, *Tōyō kenchiku no kenkyū* (Tokyo: Ryūginsha, 1943) I, 309–10, reports the wall of stones near Chang-chia-k'ou said to be of Ch'in date.

50 In addition to articles already cited, see Jos. L. Mullie, "La Grande Muraille de Yen et de Ts'in," *Central Asiatic Journal* 13.1 (1969), 99–136; Édouard Chavannes, tr. *Les Mémoires historiques de Se-ma Ts'ien* 5v. (Paris: Leroux, 1895–1905), II.167–9; 228–9; Derk Bodde, tr. *Statesman, Patriot, and General in Ancient China*, pp. 54, 61; Derk Bodde, *China's First Unifier: A Study of the Ch'in Dynasty as Seen in the Life of Li Ssu, 280?–208 B.C.* (Leiden: E. J. Brill, 1938 reprint ed., Hong Kong University Press, 1967), pp. 140, 180. In Chinese, see Chang Wei-hua, *Chung-kuo ch'ang-ch'eng chien-chih k'ao (shang pien)* (Peking: Chung-hua, 1979); Huang Lin-shu, *Ch'in-huang ch'ang-ch'eng k'ao* (Hong Kong: Tsao-yang, 1972).

51 Chang Wei-hua, *Chung-kuo ch'ang-ch'eng chien-chih k'ao*, pp. 132–6; see maps facing pp. 108, 118, 128, 136.

52 Huang Lin-shu, *Pien-sai yen-chiu* (Hong Kong: Tsao-yang, 1979). See his map, facing page 30.

53 See Rafe de Crespigny, *Northern Frontier: The Policies and Strategy of the Later Han Emprie* (Canberra: Australian National University, Faculty of East Asian Studies, 1984), p. 29, n. 35. Professor de Crespigny cites Édouard Chavannes, tr. *Les Mémoires historiques de Se-me Ts'ien Vol.* II, p. 168, which divides the two words, and J. J. M. de Groot, tr. *Chinesische Urkunden zur Geschichte Asiens* I: *Die Hunnen der vorchristlichen Zeit* (Berlin and Leipzig: W. de Gruyter & Co., 1921), p. 40.

54 de Crespigny, p. 456, n. 35 to chapter 1.

55 *Chi-fu t'ung-chih* (1910: reprint, Taipei: Hua-wen, 1970), 70.2274–5.

56 In *Ssu-pu pei-yao* (Facsimile ed. Taipei: Chung-hua shu-chü, 1965) vol. c-12, A7a.

57 H. Desmond Martin, *Chingis Khan and His Conquest of North China*, (1950: reprint ed., New York: Octagon, 1977) p. 159. Cf. *Yüan shih* 120.2960.

58 *Ch'iu-chien hsien-sheng ta-ch'üan wen-chi.* In *Ssu-pu ts'ung-k'an ch'u pien so-pen.* (Taipei: Shang-wu, 1967), vol. 74, chüan 80, p. 776.

59 See William Marsden, tr. *Travels of Marco Polo* (London: Printed for the author, 1818), Introduction, pp. xxxvii–xxxix, and pp. 230–4, n. 446. The television scenes have no warrant in the text.

60 George L. Staunton, *An Authentic Account of an Embassy from the King of Great Britain to the Emperor of China* [...] (London: G. Nicol, 1791), pp. 184–5.

61 *Pi tien chu lin shih ch'ü pao chi hsü pien* (Taipei: National Palace Museum, 1971), pp. 381–6 gives the inscriptions on the paintings. Thanks to Julia Marie White, whose "Topographical Painting in Early Ming China: *Eight Scenes of Peking* by Wang Fu" (M.A. Thesis: University of California, Berkeley, 1983) treats the paintings, and who called them to my attention.

62 Michael Loewe, "Han Foreign Relations," in *Cambridge History of China*, Vol. 1, ed. Denis Twitchett and Michael Loewe (Cambridge: Cambridge University Press, 1987), p. 398.

63 See Édouard Chavannes, "Les plus anciens spécimens de la cartographie Chinoise," *Bulletin de l'École Française d'Extrême-Orient* 3 (1903), pp. 214–47, esp. 222, bottom of page, and 221–4.

64 See Walter Fuchs, "The Mongol Atlas of China by Chu Ssu-pen and the Kuang-yü-t'u." *Monumenta Serica Monograph* VIII (Peking: Fu Jen University, 1946).

65 *Liao shih* 32.373.

66 Loewe, "Han Foreign Relations," p. 386; Ying-shih Yü, *Trade and Expansion in Han China: A Study in the Structure of Sino-Barbarian Economic Relations* (Berkeley and Los Angeles: University of California Press,1967), pp. 41–2.

67 Watson, tr. *Records* Vol. II, p. 173; *SC* 110.2902; *HS* 94B.3810.

68 Loewe, "Han Foreign Policy," p. 398; *HS* 94B.3810.

69 The Han created a commandery in Chang-i only in 104 B.C. See Michael Loewe, *Crisis and Conflict in Han China* (London: George Allen and Unwin, 1974), p. 218.

70 Watson, *Records* Vol. I, p. 290.

71 Chang, pp. 133–4; 143; map facing page 137.

72 *CCPK*, p. 9.

73 *TCTC*, 136.4262.

74 M. Aurel Stein, *Ruins of Desert Cathay* (London: Macmillan, 1912), II, p. 63.

75 Itō Chūto, *Tōyō kenchiku no kenkyū* (Tokyo: Ryūginsha, 1943), I, pp. 309–10.

76 *HS* 9.297; 94B.3803–4.

77 Henry Serruys, "Towers in the Northern Frontier Defenses of the Ming," *Ming Studies* 14 (spring 1982), pp. 8–76, p. 24.

78 *T'ung-tien* (Shanghai: Shang-wu, 1936) 200.1086.

79 Chou Mi, *Kuei-hsin tsa-shih*, in *Hsüeh-chin t'ao-yüan* (reprint, Taipei: I-wen, 1965), *hsü-chi*, A.44a–b.

80 Chang Te-hui, *Sai-pei chi-hsing* (1 ch.), in *Huang-ch'ao fan-shu yü-ti ts'ung-shu* (Taipei: Kuang-wen, 1968), p. 1448; Cf. *CCPK*, p. 82.

81 *CCPK*, p. 83.

82 "Ho-pei-sheng Wei-ch'ang-hsien Yen Ch'in Han ch'ang-ch'eng tiao-ch'a pao-kao," in *CCPK*, p. 41.

83 Luo, *The Great Wall*, p. 120.

84 See A. F. P. Hulsewé, *China in Central Asia* (Leiden: Brill, 1979), 74, n. 31.

85 Ku Chieh-kang and Shih Nien-hai, *Chung-kuo chiang-yü yen-ko shih* (Changsha: Shang-wu, 1938), 268; Hung Liang-chi and Wu Yü-chui, *Li-ch'ao shih-an* (Ch'ien-lung edition in Harvard-Yenching Library), 17.14a.

86 See n. 552 below. *Feng-chien*, which today translates the Marxist notion of "feudalism" into Chinese, but which had a somewhat different meaning in ancient times, is another good example of how meanings may change.

87 Quoted by Wang Kuo-liang, his pupil, in his *Chung-kuo ch'ang-ch'eng yen-ko k'ao*, p. 67.

88 Chu Tung-jun, *Chang Chü-cheng ta-chuan* (Wu-han: Hupei Jen-min, 1957), 7. I am indebted to Dr. James Geiss for bringing this passage to my attention.

89 Owen Lattimore, "Origins of the Great Wall of China: A Frontier Concept in Theory and Practice." In *Studies in Frontier History: Collected Papers 1928–1958* (London: Oxford University Press, 1962), pp. 112 and 98.

90 Fang Chao-ying. "The Great Wall of China: Keeping Out or Keeping In?," talk presented at the Australian National University, typescript, n.d.

91 A. M. Khazanov, *Nomads and the outside world*, tr. Julia Crookenden, with a Foreword by Ernest Gellner (Cambridge: Cambridge University Press, 1984).

92 The basic article is John K. Fairbank and S. Y. Teng, "On the Ch'ing Tributary System," *Harvard Journal of Asiatic Studies* 6.2 (1942), pp. 135–246; See also T. F. Tsiang [Chiang T'ing-fu], "China and European Expansion," *Politica* 2.5 (1936), 1–18. Probably the best summary is Fairbank's essay, "A Preliminary Framework," in *The Chinese World Order* (Cambridge, Mass.: Harvard University Press,1968), pp. 1–19.

93 See in particular Morris Rossabi, editor, *China Among Equals* (Berkeley: University of California Press, 1983).

94 See Kwang-chih Chang, *Art, myth, and ritual: the path to political authority in ancient China* (Cambridge: Harvard University Press, 1983).

95 Jaroslav Prusek, *Chinese Statelets and the Northern Barbarians in the Period 1400–300 B.C.* (New York: Humanities Press, 1971), p. 223.

96 Denis Sinor, "The Inner Asian Warriors," *Journal of the American Oriental Society* 101.2 (1981), 133–44, p. 135.

97 Watson, II, p. 155. Cited by Sinor, "Inner Asian Warriors," p. 135.

98 Sinor, "Inner Asian Warriors" p. 137; see also Sinor, "Horse and Pasture in Inner Asian History," *Oriens Extremus* 19 (1972), pp. 171–83.

99 *HS* 54.12a. Cited by Sinor, p. 140, where other references are given as well.

100 Watson, II, p. 161. Cited by Sinor, p. 135.

101 See Denis Sinor, "On Mongol Strategy," in *Inner Asia and its Contacts with Medieval Europe* (London: Variorum Reprints, 1977), pp. 238–49.

102 B. H. Liddell Hart followed a long tradition when he portrayed the Mongol army as "irrestible to troops far more strongly armed and numerous." B. H. Liddell Hart, *Great Captains Unveiled* (Boston: Little, Brown, and Co., 1928), p. 10. But as John Masson Smith points out, he appears to have been wrong. The nomads possessed no magical superiority in warfare: their successes appear to have depended as much on effective mobilization and leadership as on technological advantages. Chinggis, who created the Mongol world empire of the thirteenth century owed his success not to "the discovery or creation of better weapons, tactics, horses, or soldiers," but to his skill in the mobilization, "in unprecedented and usually overwhelming numbers, of the ordinary Inner Asian nomads, with their traditional military resources." John Masson Smith, Jr., "ʿAyn Jālūt: Mamlūk Success or Mongol Failure?," *Harvard Journal of Asiatic Studies* 44.2 (1984), p. 319 note 32; p. 345.

103 *HS* 94A.3759.

104 *SC* 110.2879; Watson, II.155.

105 *HS* 94B.3834.

106 The literature on these questions is enormous. The best review is by Ch'i-ch'ing

Hsiao, "Pei-ya yu-mu min-tsu nan-ch'in ko-chung yüan-yin ti chien-t'ao" in *Yüan-tai-shih hsin-t'an* (Taipei: Hsin-wen-feng, 1983) pp. 303–22. Other useful sources include A. M. Khazanov, *Nomads and the outside world*, tr. Julia Crookenden, with a Foreword by Ernest Gellner (Cambridge: Cambridge University Press, 1984); two articles by Rudi Paul Lindner, "Nomadism, Horses and Huns," *Past and Present* No. 92 (August, 1981), pp. 3–19, and "What Was a Nomadic Tribe?" *Comparative Studies in Society and History* 24.4 (1982), 689–711; Joseph Fletcher, "The Mongols: ecological and social perspectives," *Harvard Journal of Asiatic Studies* 46.1 (1986), 11–50. The argument about surplus horses is found in I. Ia. Zlatkin, *Istoriia Dzhungarskogo Khanstva 1635–1758* (Moscow: "Nauka", 1964), 41–2; while the strongest arguments for the possibility of coexistence are found in the many works of Sechin Jagchid, such as "Patterns of Trade and Conflict Between China and the Nomads of Mongolia," *Zentralasiatische Studien* 11 (1977), 177–204.

107 Khazanov, p. 81.

108 Fredrik Barth, *Nomads of South Persia: The Basseri Tribe of the Khamseh Confederacy* (Oslo University Press. London: George Allen & Unwin, Ltd., 1961), pp. 113–21.

109 For further references on this question, see: Khazanov, *Nomads and the outside world*, pp. 228–302; Barfield, "The Hsiung-nu Imperial Confederacy," pp. 45–7; Rudi Paul Lindner, *Nomads and Ottomans in Medieval Anatolia* (Bloomington: Research Institute for Inner Asian Studies, Indiana University, 1983).

110 The term was originated by Professor Thomas Barfield, of Harvard.

111 James Legge, tr., *The Chinese Classics* Vol. IV. *The She King* (reprint ed., Taipei: Wen-shih-che, 1971), p. 263. On the warfare with the Hsien-yün, see Jaroslav Prusek, *Chinese Statelets and the Northern Barbarians in the Period 1400–300 B.C.* (New York: Humanities Press, 1971), pp. 119–35.

112 See Prusek, pp. 119–35 for these points.

113 Ruth I. Meserve, "The Inhospitable Land of the Barbarian," *Journal of Asian History* 16.1 (1982), p. 53.

114 See Prusek, cited above.

115 *SC*, 43.1805–11.

116 *SC*, 8:384–385; Watson, *op. cit.*, 1:110, 235–236.

117 *Tso chuan*, Duke Hsiang, year 4. Legge, *Chinese Classics*, V, pp. 422, 424.

118 Thomas J. Barfield, "The Hsiung-nu Imperial Confederacy: Organization and Foreign Policy", *Journal of Asian Studies* 41.1 (1981), 45–61.

119 See Ying-shih Yü, *Trade and Expansion in Han China*, p. 10, n. 3.

120 Yü, *Trade and Expansion*, pp. 41–42; Watson, *Records of the Grand Historian of China* II.166, II.173; *SC* 110.2895, 110.2902; *HS* 94A.3754. Secondary sources often add that the "long wall" was to be the boundary. On this problem, see notes 49, 50, 52 above.

121 Barfield, "Hsiung-nu," pp. 54–55.

122 Yü, *Trade and Expansion*, 47–9; Barfield, "Hsiung Nu," 53; *HS* 94A.3780.

123 Barfield, 53–4.

124 Barfield, 54; Watson, *Records*, 2.176; *SC* 110. 2904; *HS* 94A.3765.

125 Yü, *Trade and Expansion*, p. 11 (translation slightly modified); *HS* 48.2240–2242.

126 See Michael Loewe, "The Campaigns of Han Wu-ti," in *Chinese Ways in Warfare*, ed. Frank A. Kierman, Jr., and John K. Fairbank (Cambridge, Mass.: Harvard University Press, 1974), 67–122.

127 For Ch'ao Ts'o see *Han Shu* 49.2276–2305; also Michael Loewe, *Records of Han Administration* (Cambridge: Cambridge University Press, 1967), volume I, p. 82; for Chao Ch'ung-kuo, see *HS* 69.2971–75; also H. H. Dubs, tr. *History of the Former Han*

Dynasty (Baltimore: Waverly Press, 1938–55), II, pp. 241–2; Michael Loewe, *Crisis and Conflict in Han China* (London: Allen & Unwin, 1974), pp. 224–7; *Records of Han Administration*, II, p. 70. More general information may be found in Édouard Biot, *Mémoire sur les colonies militaires et agricoles des Chinois* (Paris: Imprimerie nationale, 1850); P. A. Herbert, "Agricultural Colonies in China in the Early Eighth Century," *Papers on Far Eastern History* 11 (1975), pp. 37–77; and Yü-ch'üan Wang, *Ming-tai ti chün-t'un* (Peking: Chung-hua, 1965).

128 See Michael Loewe, "Han foreign relations;" also Lien-sheng Yang, "Historical Notes on the Chinese World Order," in *The Chinese World Order*, ed. John K. Fairbank (Cambridge: Harvard University Press, 1968), pp. 20–33.

129 *Hou Han shu* (Chung-hua edition), 90.2992.

130 *I-ching*, hexagram 29, *k'an*. Text in "A Concordance to the Yi Ching" (Harvard-Yenching Institute Sinological Index Series, Supplement 10, 1935), 19; one literal translation may be found in P. L. F. Philastre, *"Le Yi King,"* Annales du Musée Guimet 8 (1885), 466; quite a different reading is given in Hellmut Wilhelm, tr. *The I Ching or Book of Changes*, rendered into English by Cary F. Baynes (Princeton: Princeton University Press, 1950), 115, "Thus also rulers make use of danger to protect themselves against attacks from without and against turmoil within."

131 *SC*, 40.2885; Watson, *op. cit.*, p. 159.

132 See *Ta-hsüeh yen-i pu*. In *Ssu-k'u ch'üan shu chen pen, erh chi* (Taipei: Shang-wu, 1971) vol. 177, *chüan* 150.8b–9b, esp. 9a.

133 W. J. F. Jenner, *Memories of Loyang: Yang Hsüan-chih and the lost capital (493–534)* (Oxford: Clarendon Press, 1981), pp. 16–19.

134 *Wei shu* 54.1201.

135 *Wei shu* 54.1201.

136 *Wei shu* 54.1201.

137 *Wei shu* 54.1201.

138 *Wei shu* 54.1201–2.

139 *Wei shu* 54.1202.

140 On Northern Wei fortifications, see: *Wei shu*, 3.63; *Pei shih*, 1.34–35 *Wei shu*, 4B.101; *Pei shih*, 2.58–59. A wall was built in 484 according to the *Tzu-chih t'ung-chien* (hereafter *TCTC*) (Peking: Chung-hua shu-chü, 1956), 136.4262–63; *Wei shu*, 54.1200–02; *Pei shih*, 34.1256–57. My account follows W. J. F. Jenner, *Memories of Loyang*, esp. pp. 22–23; Le Kang, "An Empire For A City: Cultural Reforms of the Hsiao-wen Emperor (A.D. 471–99)" (Ph.D dissertation: Yale University, 1983), pp. 24–25, 32; Wang Chi-lin, "T'ung-i ch'i-chien pei-Wei yü sai-wai min-tsu ti kuan-hsi," *Shih-hsüeh hui k'an* 10 (1980), 65–86.

141 *TCTC*, 158.4920; *Pei shih*, 6.229; *Pei-Ch'i shu*, 2.22.

142 *Pei shih*, 7.249; *Pei-Ch'i shu*, 4.56.

143 *Shui-ching chu*, (*SPTK* ed.), 14.1b. *TCTC*, 166.5130; *Pei shih*, 7.253; *Pei-Ch'i shu*, 4.61.

144 *TCTC*, 167.5171; *Pei shih*, 7.254–5; *Pei-Ch'i shu*, 4.64. See also *TCTC*, 169.5232 (reference to the year 563).

145 *TCTC*, 166.5156; *Pei shih*, 7.253–54; *Pei-Ch'i shu*, 4.63.

146 *Pei shih*, 10.376; *Chou shu*, 7.120.

147 *Pei shih*, 11.405; *Sui shu*, 1.15.

148 *Pei shih*, 11.412.

149 *Pei shih*, 11.413; *Sui shu*, 1.23.

150 *Sui shu*, 1.125.

151 *Pei-shih*, 12.450–1; *Sui shu*, 3.70–71; *TCTC*, 180.5632.

152 The assertion that Sui and Northern Ch'i walls were followed by the Ming is common: See Shou P'eng-fei, *op. cit.*, p. 19b, Needham, *op. cit.*, p. 48. A photo of a Northern Ch'i wall may be found in Cheng Dalin, p. 187. The only other reference to remains of walls from this period that I am aware of is a sentence reporting that a Sui wall had been found in Ninghsia. See "Ning-hsia ching-nei Chan-kuo, Ch'in, Han ch'ang-ch'eng i-chi" in *CCPK*, 45. Caution about drawing a connection between such walls and those of the Ming is expressed in *CCPK*, p. 101.

153 *Hsin T'ang shu* 93.3818–19.

154 *TCTC* 198.6247. As rendered by Charles Hartman in *Han Yü and the T'ang Search for Unity* (Princeton: Princeton University Press, 1986), p. 120. Hartman's chapter, The Politics of Empire," is very useful. See also Le Kang, "An Empire For a City," p. 226.

155 Li Chi-fu, *Yüan-ho chün-hsien chih* (Peking: Chung-hua, 1983), 2.35; 10.262; 14.397; 14.446).

156 *Hou Han shu* 3.155.

157 See for example, Huang Lin-shu *T'ang-tai shih-jen sai-fang ssu-hsiang ch'u-kao* (Hong Kong: Tsao-yang, 1982).

158 James T. C. Liu, "Yüeh Fei (1103–41) and China's Heritage of Loyalty," *Journal of Asian Studies* 31.2 (1972), 291–7; Hellmut Wilhelm, "From Myth to Myth: The Case of Yüeh Fei's biography," in *Confucian Personalities*, edited by Arthur Wright and Denis Twitchett (Stanford: Stanford University Press, 1962), 160.

159 Edward H. Kaplan, "Yüeh Fei and the Founding of the Southern Sung," 2v. (Ph.D dissertation: University of Iowa, 1970), 435; 596–7.

160 Kaplan, "Yüeh Fei," 581.

161 Recent reports attribute the first walls in the Mu-t'ien-yü valley in Huai-jou county near Peking to the Northern Sung. See Luo Zewen (Lo Che-wen), "New Survey," *China Reconstructs* 34.3 (March 1985), pp. 8–14, p. 14.

162 See Karl A. Wittfogel and Feng Chia-sheng, *History of Chinese Society: The Liao (907–125)*, Transactions of the American Philosophical Society, NS, 36 (Philadelphia, 1946), p. 367. There are other references to "ancient long walls" (*ku ch'ang-ch'eng*) in sources from the period, e.g., *Ch'i-tan kuo-chih* (Ssu-k'u shan-pen ed.), 24.1b, 7.5b.

163 "Chin-tai ch'ang-ch'eng," in *CCPK*, pp. 77–83. Liao and Chin fortification is a tangled and important subject. For further references, see Susan Bush, "Archaeological Remains of the Chin dynasty," *Bulletin of Sung-Yuan Studies*, 17 (1981), esp. pp. 12–13.

164 See Paul Pelliot, *Recherches sur les Chrétiens d'Asie Centrale et d'Extrême-Orient* (Œuvres posthumes de Paul Pelliot. Paris: Imprimerie Nationale, 1973), p. 262; H. Desmond Martin, *Chingis Khan and His Conquest of North China* (1950: reprint New York, 1977), p. 127.

165 See Ronald Syme in the *Cambridge Ancient History* (Cambridge: Cambridge University Press, 1934) 10:340–81, esp. 353; Edward Luttwak, *The Grand Strategy of the Roman Empire* (Baltimore and London: Johns Hopkins University Press, 1976), p. 50.

166 T. R. Tregear, *A Geography of China* (Chicago: Aldine Publishing Co, 1965), p. 57.

167 Ku Tsu-yü, *Tu-shih fang-yü chi-yao* (Peking: Chung-hua, 1957), 1.432–3.

168 Owen Lattimore, *Inner Asian Frontiers of China* (New York: American Geographical Society, 1940), p. 462.

169 Lattimore, *op. cit.*, p. 462.

170 John W. Dardess, "From Mongol Empire to Yüan Dynasty: Changing Forms of Imperial Rule in Mongolia and Central Asia." *Monumenta Serica* 30 (1972–3), p. 159.

171 Larry Moses, "A Theoretical Approach to the Process of Inner Asian Confederation," *Études Mongoles* 5 (1974), 115–17.

172 Some examples include: Fang Lin-hao and Li Chü-lai, comp., *Ho-t'ao chih* (1742); Chang P'eng-i, *Ho-t'ao t'u-chih* (1917); Shao Li-tzu, *Ho-t'ao t'u-k'ao* in *Kuan-chung ts'ung-shu* (reprint ed. Taipei: I-wen, 1970) 7:1a–30b; *Ho-t'ao lüeh* in *Hsiao-fang-hu-chai yü-ti ts'ung-ch'ao* (reprint ed., Taipei: Kuang-wen, 1962) 2:0923–4. Among writings that stress the territory's strategic importance are Ch'iu Chün, *Ta-hsüeh yen-i pu* (*S.K.* ed.) 151.1b–6a; Ku Yen-wu, *T'ien-hsia chün-kuo li-ping shu*, ch. 156; Ku Tsu-yü, *Tu-shih fang-yü chi-yao* (Peking: Chung-hua, 1957) 3.2651–2657 and 2683–86; Chang Wei-hua, "Ku-tai Ho-t'ao yü Chung-kuo chih kuan-hsi," *Yü-kung*, 6.5 (1936), 9–24.

173 Hibino Takeo, "Chizu ni arawareta hou-t'ao suidō no hensen" in *Chūgoku rekishi chiri kenkyū* (Tokyo: Dōbōsha, 1978), p. 317.

174 Ferdinand von Richthofen, *Baron Richthofen's Letters, 1870–72* (Shanghai: North China Herald, n.d.); William W. Rockhill, *Diary of a Journey Through Mongolia and Tibet in 1891 and 1892* (Washington, D.C.: Smithsonian Institution, 1894); George B. Cressey, "The Ordos Desert of Inner Mongolia," *Denison University Bulletin* 28.8 (1933), 155–248.

175 Cressey, "The Ordos," p. 180.

176 Cressey, "The Ordos," p. 190.

177 A general inventory of the irrigation systems in the Pao-t'ou plain, Ho-t'ao, and the Ning-shia area as they were in the late Republic may be found in: Republic of China, Supreme Economic Council, Public Works Commission, "General Description of the Yellow River Basin," *Studies on Yellow River Project*, No. 2 (Nanking, 1947), pp. 57–66. See also E. B. Vermeer, *Water Conservancy and Irrigation in China* (Leiden University Press, 1977); George B. Cressey, "The Ordos," pp. 237–9; Theodore Shabad, *China's Changing Map: National and Regional Development, 1949–1971*, Revised ed. (New York: Praeger, 1971); "Paotowchen, the Gateway to the Northwest," *The Chinese Economic Monthly* 3.5 (1926), pp. 201–11; "Agricultural Conditions in Suiyuan," *The Chinese Economic Monthly* 3.10 (1926), pp. 413–17; and "Economic Conditions in Suiyuan Province," *Chinese Economic Journal* 13.4 (1933), pp. 385–400. Also, Fu Tso-lin, *Ning-hsia-shen k'ao-ch'a-chi* (Nanking: Chung-chen, 1934), esp. pp. 109–10; Hibino Takeo, "Chizu ni arawareta hou-t'ao suidō no hensen," in *Chūgoku rekishi chiri kenkyū*, pp. 316–329; and Anzai Kuraji, "Shinmatsu ni okeru Suien no kaikon," *Mantetsu chōsa geppō* 18.12 (1938), pp. 1–44; 19.1 (1939), pp. 14–62; and 19.1 (1939), pp. 36–68.

178 Owen Lattimore, *The Desert Road to Turkestan* (Boston: Little Brown, 1929), pp. 53–54; Chu K'e-chen, "Climatic changes in Chinese history," *Scientia Sinica* 16.2 (1973), 226–249. Also Cressey, pp. 177, 220; *China News Analysis*, No. 1148 (16 February 1979) pp. 6–7; No. 1169 (7 December 1979), p. 9; and No. 1172 (18 January 1980), p. 5; Chao Yung-fu, "Li-shih shang Mao-wu-su sha-mo-ti ti pien-ch'ien wen-ti," *Wen-wu* (1976) 2.66–82, esp. pp. 38–9.

179 *SC* 110.2885; Watson, *Records of the Grand Historian* 1.159.

180 *SC* 110.2887–8; Chang Wei-hua, "Ku-tai Ho-t'ao yü Chung-kuo chih kuan-hsi," pp. 7–18; idem, *Chung-kuo ch'ang-ch'eng chien-chih k'ao*, p. 137.

181 Chang, "Ho-hsi," p. 28.

182 *SC* 112.2961; Watson, *Records of the Grand Historian of China* II.236–7.

183 Hans Bielenstein, "The Restoration of the Han Dynasty," Part III, *Bulletin of the Museum of Far Eastern Antiquities* 39 (1967), p. 96.

184 Bielenstein, *Restoration*, III, pp. 105–9.

185 Bielenstein, *Restoration* III, 112–17 and *passim*.

186 Ch'iu Chün, *Ta-hsüeh yen-i pu*, 151.1b–2a.

187 Rafe de Crespigny, *Northern Frontier*, p. 457.

188 *Pei shih* 12.450–451; *Sui shu* 3.70–71; *TCTC* 180.5632.

189 *Chiu T'ang shu* 93.2982; *Hsin T'ang Shu* 111.4152; K'ang Le, "T'ang-tai ch'ien-ch'i ti pien-fang" (Master's thesis: National Taiwan University, 1974), 72–3; Robert des Rotours, tr. *Traité des Fonctionnaires et Traité de l'Armée* (Leiden, 1947; reprint ed. San Francisco: Chinese Materials Center, 1974), pp. 742–3.

190 *Chin shih* 134.2876–7; *Sung shih* 486.14028; translation slightly modified from Ruth W. Dunnell, "Tanguts and the Tangut State of Ta Hsia" (Ph.D dissertation: Princeton University, 1983), 27–8.

191 See the "Introduction" by Andrew Watson, ed., in *Mao Zedong and the Political Economy of the Border Region: A Translation of Mao's 'Economic and Financial Problems'* (Cambridge: Cambridge University Press, 1980), 1–50.

192 John W. Dardess, "From Mongol Empire to Yüan Dynasty: Changing Forms of Imperial Rule in Mongolia and Central Asia," *Monumenta Serica* 30 (1972–3), p. 128.

193 Dardess, "From Mongol Empire to Yüan Dynasty," pp. 128–31.

194 On the destruction of the Ta Hsia, see Francis Woodman Cleaves, tr., *The Secret History of the Mongols* (Cambridge, Mass.: Harvard University Press, 1982), p. 206; Ruth W. Dunnell, "Tanguts and the Tangut State of Ta Hsia," pp. 265–6.

195 *Yüan shih* 6.115, cited by Dardess, p. 147.

196 See Dardess, "From Mongol Empire to Yüan Dynasty," pp. 132–52 for the analysis followed here. See also, Thomas T. Allsen, "The Princes of the Left Hand: An Introduction to the History of the *Ulus* of Orda in the Thirteenth and Early Fourteenth Centuries," pp. 128–24. *Archivum Eurasiae Medii Aevi* 5 (1985 [1987]), pp. 5–40.

197 Dardess, "From Mongol Empire to Yüan Dynasty," pp. 152, 155–60 and *passim*.

198 John Dardess, *Conquerors and Confucians: Aspects of Political Change in Late Yüan China* (New York and London: Columbia University Press, 1973), 180, n. 47.

199 Dardess, *Conquerors and Confucians* pp. 31 ff.

200 The *limes* were not walls: the word's root meaning is a pathway along which troops advance, hence a military road with fortified posts and signal towers, or ultimately, a frontier. *The Oxford Classical Dictionary*, Second Edition (Oxford: Clarendon Press, 1970), p. 160.

201 Vivian Rowe, *The Great Wall of France* (New York: Putnam's 1961).

202 See Judith M. Hughes, *To the Maginot Line* (Cambridge, Mass.: Harvard University Press, 1971); Vivian Rowe, *The Great Wall of France*; for the diplomatic background, see Walter A. McDougall, *France's Rhineland Diplomacy, 1914–1924* (Princeton: Princeton University Press, 1978).

203 E. L. Dreyer, *Early Ming China: A Political History 1355–1435* (Stanford: Stanford University Press, 1982), p. 1; F. W. Mote, "The T'u-mu Incident of 1449," in *Chinese Ways in Warfare*, edited by Frank A. Kierman, Jr. and John K. Fairbank (Cambridge, Mass.: Harvard University Press, 1974), p. 251.

204 Joseph F. Fletcher, Jr. "Bloody Tanistry: Authority and Succession in the Ottoman, Indian Muslim, and Late Chinese Empires" (Paper prepared for the Conference on the Theory of Democracy and Popular Participation, Bellagio, Italy, September 3–8, 1978). p. 78.

205 Dreyer, *Early Ming China*, p. 1.

206 Dreyer, *Early Ming China*, p. 62; See also his, "The Emergence of Chu Yüan-chang, 1360–1365" (Ph.D dissertation: Harvard University, 1970), pp. 437–8.

207 Dreyer, *Early Ming China* pp. 74–6.

208 L. Carrington Goodrich, ed. *Dictionary of Ming Biography 1368–1644* (Hereafter *DMB*) (New York and London: Columbia University Press, 1976), 1293–4; Dreyer, 141–3.

209 See Fletcher, "Bloody Tanistry," especially pp. 79–83.

210 For reviews of the literature regarding the Yung-lo emperor's ancestry, see Henry Serruys, "A Manuscript Version of the Legend of the Mongol Ancestry of the Yung-lo Emperor," *Occasional Papers of the Mongolia Society* No. 8 (1972), pp. 19–29; "Sino-Mongol Relations During the Ming II. The Tribute System and Diplomatic Missions (1400–1600)", p. 22 n. 3; S. J. Shaw, "Historical Significance of the Curious Theory of the Mongol Blood in the Veins of the Ming Emperors", *The Chinese Social and Political Science Review* 20 (1937), pp. 492–8.

211 See Henry Serruys, *Sino-Jürced Relations During the Yung-lo Period (1403–1424)* (Wiesbaden: Otto Harrassowitz, 1955), and Yang Hu, ed. *Nu-erh-kan tu-ssu chi ch'i wei-so yen-chiu* (Honan: Chung-chou shu-hua she, 1982).

212 Edward L. Farmer, *Early Ming Government: The Evolution of Dual Capitals* (Cambridge, Mass.: Harvard University Press, 1976), pp. 135–6; John K. Fairbank and Edwin O. Reischauer, *East Asia: The Great Tradition* (Boston: Houghton Mifflin, 1960), pp. 327–328.

213 On the Yung-lo emperor's campaigns, see Morris Rossabi, article on Arughtai, pp. 12–15 in *DMB*; biography of Chu Ti [the Yung-lo emperor] by F. W. Mote and L. Carrington Goodrich in *DMB*, p. 360; Dreyer, pp. 174–82; also Wolfgang Franke, "Yunglo's Mongolei Feldzüge," *Sinologische Arbeiten* 3 (1945), 1–54; and "Chinesische Feldzüge durch die Mongolei im frühen 15. Jahrhundert," *Sinologica* 3 (1951–3), 81–8.

214 *DMB*, 282.

215 I have been influenced here by the treatment of Roman policy in Edward N. Luttwak's *The Grand Strategy of the Roman Empire: From the First Century A.D. to the Third.* (Baltimore and London: The Johns Hopkins University Press, 1976), especially pages 196–7; Rafe de Crespigny treats the end of the Han as being related to a rather similar failure of *wei*. See de Crespigny, *Northern Frontier: The Policies and Strategy of the Later Han Empire*, p. 417.

216 *MS* 91.2235.

217 *MSL T'ai-tsu* 78.1424–5; 80.1451–2.

218 *MS* 130.3825; 91.2235; *MSL T'ai-tsu* 81.1465–66.

219 *MS* 91.2235.

210 *MS* 41.957.

221 K'ai-p'ing, Ch'üan-ning, and Hsing-ho, *MS* 40:908–9 Ta-ning, *MS* 40.905–6 Ying-ch'ang, *MS* 40: 906–7.

222 *MS* 40:973–4.

223 *MS* 91.2236.

224 For more detail on Yüan frontier dispositions, see Dardess, "From Mongol Empire," pp. 145–9. On the Ming frontier, see Tamura Jitsuzō, "Mindai no kyū-hen-chin," in *Ishihama hakase koki kinen tōyōgaku ronsō* (Osaka: Kansai Daigaku, 1958), 290–300; and "Mindai no hoppen bōei taisei," in *Mindai Man-Mō Shi Kenkyū* (Kyoto: Kyoto University, 1963), 73–161.

225 Discussed in Serruys, "Towers," pp. 14–15.

226 *MS* 91.2236.

227 *MSL T'ai-tsung* 12.1616; 13.1699.

228 *MS* 8.2236.

229 *MSL Hsüan-tsung* 57.1358.

230 On these changes see Wu Chi-hua, "The Contraction of Forward Defences on the North China Frontier during the Ming Dynasty," *Papers on Far Eastern History* 17 (1978), 1–13; idem, "Ming-tai Tung-sheng ti she-fang yü ch'i-fang," in *Ming-tai chih-tu-shih lun-ts'ung* (Taipei, 1971), 319–48; Shimizu Taiji, "Tainei toshi no naishi ni tsukite," *Tōyō Gakuhō* 8.1 (1918), 125–41.

231 *MS* 91.2236.

232 See Ch'en Wen-shih, "Ming-tai wei-so ti chün," *Bulletin of the Institute of History and Philology, Academia Sinica* 48 (1977), pp. 177–202; Wang Yü-ch'üan, *Ming-tai ti chün-t'un* (Peking: Chung-hua, 1965), p. 225; *MS* 89.2176.

233 See Romeyn Taylor, "Yüan Origins of the *Wei-so* system," in *Chinese Government in Ming Times*, edited by Charles O. Hucker (New York: Columbia University Press, 1969) pp. 31–3.

234 See Wei Ch'ing-yüan, *Ming-tai ti huang-ts'e chih-tu* (Peking: Chung-hua, 1961); Hsiao Ch'i-ch'ing, "The Military Establishment of the Yüan Dynasty" (Ph.D dissertation: Harvard University, 1969), pp. li–lii.

235 Ray Huang, *Taxation*, p. 265.

236 *MS* 90.2204; Romeyn Taylor, "The Guard System of the Ming dynasty: Its Original Organization and Its Decline" (M.A. Thesis: University of Chicago, 1956), p. 16.

237 N. P. Svistunova, "Organizatsiia pogranichnoi sluzhby na severe Kitaia v epokhu Min," in *Kitai i Sosedi v Drevnosti i Srednevekov'e*, edited by L. S. Perelomov and S. L. Tikhvinskii (Moscow: "Nauka," 1970), p. 218.

238 On Chao Ch'ung-kuo, see: *HS* 69.2971–5; H. H. Dubs, tr. *History of the Former Han Dynasty* (Baltimore: Waverly Press, 1938–55), pp. 241–2; Michael Loewe, *Crisis and Conflict in Han China* (London: Allen & Unwin, 1974), pp. 241–2; *Records of Han Administration* (Cambridge: Cambridge University Press, 1967), II, p. 70.

239 Shimizu Taiji, "Minsho ni okeru gunton no tenkai to sono soshiki," in *Mindai tochi seido shi kenkyū* (Tokyo: Taian, 1968), 327.

240 Wang Yü-ch'üan, *Ming-tai chün-t'un*, 182–183.

241 See Morris Rossabi, "The Tea and Horse Trade with Inner Asia," *Journal of Asian History* 4 (1970), pp. 136–70; Henry Serruys, *Sino-Mongolian Relations during the Ming*: III. *The Horse Fairs (1400–1600)*, (Brussels: Institut Belge des Hautes Etudes Chinoises, 1975); Tani Mitsukata, "A Study of Horse Administration in the Ming Period," *Acta Asiatica* 21(1971), pp. 73–97.

242 On this complex subject, see: Huang, *Taxation*, pp. 189–221; Hsü Hong, "Ming-tai ti yen-fa," (Ph.D dissertation: National Taiwan University, 1972); Lee Lung-wa, "Ming-tai ti k'ai-chung-fa" *Journal of the Institute of Chinese Studies in the Chinese University of Hong Kong* 4(1971), pp. 371–493. Terada Takanobu, "Kaichūhō no tenkai," in *Mindai Man-Mō Shi Kenkyū*, edited by Tamura Jitsuzō (Kyoto: Kyoto University, 1963), pp. 163–218; Esson M. Gale and Ch'en Sung-ch'iao, "China's Salt Administration: Excerpts from Native Sources," *Asea Yon'gu* 1(1958), pp. 137–217, 2(1959), pp. 273–316; Wang Ch'ung-wu, "The Ming System of Merchant Colonization," in *Chinese Social History: Translations of Selected Studies*, ed. E-tu Zen Sun and John DeFrancis (Washington D.C.: American Council of Learned Societies, 1956), pp. 299–308.

243 Morris Rossabi, *China and Inner Asia* (New York: Pica Press, 1975), p. 23.

244 see n. 92 above.

245 Henry Serruys, "Sino-Mongol Relations During the Ming, II. The Tribute System and Diplomatic Missions (1400–1600)," *Melanges Chinois et Bouddhique* 14(1969), pp. 22–3, 24 (hereafter cited as SMRII); cf. Owen Lattimore, *Inner Asian Frontiers of China*, pp. 499–500.

246 Dardess, "From Mongol Empire to Yüan Dynasty," p. 159.

247 Franke, Feldzüge, 9–10; *DMB*, 532–3.

248 Jung-pang Lo, "Intervention in Vietnam: A Case Study of the Foreign Policy of the Early Ming Government," *Ts'ing-hua Journal of Chinese Studies* 8(1970), p. 175.

249 *MS* 28:8469–70; Hambis, *Documents*, 26–7; On the location of the battle see Franke, *Addenda*, p. 34 note 37.7.
250 *MS* 28:8470; Hambis, *Documents*, p. 28.
251 Biography by Morris Rossabi in *DMB* 1.416–20.
252 See David M. Farquhar, "Oirat-Chinese Tribute Relations, 1408–1446," *Studia Altaica* (Wiesbaden, 1957), pp. 60–8.
253 We owe chiefly to a series of Japanese scholars our present understanding of the centrality of economic issues in Ming–Mongol relations. A good summary is Hagiwara Jumpei, *Mindai Mōko shi kenkyū* (Kyoto: Dōbōsha, 1980).
254 Rossabi, "Esen," in *DMB*, 1 p. 417. David M. Farquhar, "Oirat-Chinese Tribute Relations, 1408–1446," *Studia Altaica* (Wiesbaden, 1957), pp. 60–8.
255 *MS* 327.8470; Hambis, *Documents*, p. 30; Cf. Morris Rossabi, "Notes on Esen's Pride and Ming China's Prejudice," *Mongolia Society Bulletin* 9.2(1970), pp. 31–8.
256 Mote, "The T'u-mu Incident," pp. 254–5.
257 Mote, pp. 261–2.
258 Mote, pp. 263–72.
259 *MSL Ying-tsung* 187.3774–5.
260 *Ta Ming hui tien* (hereafter *TMHT*) (1587: rpt. Taipei: Hsin-wen-feng, 1976), 130.1847.
261 *MSL Ying-tsung shih-lu* 181.3509–10; 3514–15; 3517–18. A detailed account may be found in Philip De Heer, *The caretaker emperor: aspects of the imperial institution in fifteenth-century China as reflected in the political history of the reign of Chu Ch'i-yü* (Leiden: Brill, 1986), which I follow.
262 Mote, "The T'u-mu Incident," p. 266, quoting *Ming-shih chi-shih pen-mo*, ch. 33.
263 *MS* 327.8471; 328.8502–3; Louis Hambis, *Documents sur l'histoire des Mongols a l'époque des Ming* (Paris: Presses Universitaires de France, 1969), 30–2, 103–4; Dmitrii D. Pokotilov, *History of the Eastern Mongols During the Ming Dynasty from 1368 to 1634* trans. Rudolf Loewenthal (1947: rpt. Philadelphia: Porcupine Press, 1976), 64.
264 *MS* 328.8503; Hambis, 105–6; Rossabi, *China and Inner Asia*, pp. 35–36. The movement of the Mongols into the Yellow River loop has been analyzed in two articles by Louis Hambis, "Note sur l'installation des Mongols dans la boucle du fleuve jaune," *Mongolian Studies* (1970), 167–179, and "A propos des noms de trois clans des Ordos," in *Studies in General and Oriental Linguistics Presented to Shirō Hattori on the Occasion of his Sixtieth Birthday*, ed. Roman Jakobson and Shigeo Kawamoto (Tokyo: TEC, 1970), 175–9. See also Tamura Jitsuzō "Mindai no Orudosu (Tenjun, Seika jidai)," *Tōyōshi kenkyū* (1960), 1–14.
265 *MS* 327.8472–4; Hambis, *Documents*, xv, 35–9; "Note," 168.
266 See De Heer, *Caretaker emperor*, p. 63 and *passim*.
267 *MSL Ying-tsung shih-lu* 191.3935.
268 Lo Che-wen, *Ch'ang-ch'eng*, p. 110.
269 See note 427 below.
270 SMR II, p. 135.
271 *MSCSPM*: 58.617–18 SMR II, 135–136; Hambis, 32–5.
272 See biography by Tilemann Grimm in *DMB*, 1.819–22.
273 *MSL Ying-tsung* 302.6397–8; Haneda Toru and Tamura Jitsuzō eds., *Mindai Man-Mō Shiryō* hereafter (*MMS*) 3.615; SMR II, 33.
274 *MSL Ying-tsung* 359.7148–9; *MMS* 3.694–5; SMRII, 34.
275 Ch'iu Chün, *Ch'ung-pien ch'iung-t'ai kao* 20.12a–b.
276 *MSL Hsien-tsung* 27.0537–40.
277 *MSL Hsien-tsung* 29.0585–7.

278 Quoted above, n. 100.
279 *MSL Hsien-tsung* 30.0602–4; 31.0618–19; *MS* 327.8473; Hambis *Documents*, 36. Li Hsien's biography is in *MS* 176.4673–7.
280 *MS* 327.8473; Hambis, *Documents*, 36–7.
281 *MSL Hsien-tsung* 42.0855; *MS* 327.8473; Hambis, *Documents*, 37.
282 *MS* 327.8474; Hambis, *Documents*, 37–8.
283 *MSL Hsien-tsung* 77.1496.
284 *MSL Hsien-tsung* 78.1515.
285 *MS* 118.3605.
286 *MSL Hsien-tsung* 88.1720; *MS* 327.8474; Hambis, *Documents*, 38.
287 *MS* 327.8474; *MSL Hsien-tsung* 101.1959; 103.2008; Hambis, *Documents*, 38–9.
288 *MSL Hsien-tsung* 101.1965–7; Ch'en Tzu-lung, ed., *Huang-Ming ching-shih wen-pien* (hereafter *HMCSWP*) (rpt. Taipei: Kuo-lien, 1964), 4.505–8.
289 *MSL Hsien-tsung* 101.1967–8.
290 See the fine article by Richard L. Edmonds, "The Willow Palisade," *Annals of the Association of American Geographers* 69.4(1979), p. 610 note 42. Also Inaba Iwakichi, "Mindai Ryōtō no henshō," in *Manshū rekishi chiri*, 1.460–546 edited by Yanai Watari. (Tokyo: Maruzen, 1941); Chang Wei-hua, "Ming-tai Liao-tung pien-ch'iang chien-chih yen-ko k'ao *Shih-hsüeh nien-pao* 2.1(1934), 267–73; and Satō, Hiroshi, "On the Palisade in Manchuria," *Japanese Journal of Geology and Geography* 3.3–4(1924), 167–78, all cited by Edmonds.
291 See biography by Hok-lam Chan in *DMB*, ii.1104–7; and in *MS*:172.4595–7.
292 *MS* 155.4263; *MSL Hsien-tsung* 104.2040–1.
293 *MS* 155.4264.
294 *MSL Hsien-tsung* 108.2111–13.
295 *MSL Hsien-tsung* 108.2118–20.
296 *MSL Hsien-tsung* 108.2120.
297 *MS* 327.8474; Hambis, *Documents*, 30; *MS* 155.4265.
298 *MS Hsien-tsung* 88.1720; *MS* 327.8474; Hambis, *Documents*, 38.
299 *MS* 327.8474; Hambis, *Documents*, 38.
300 *MS* 178.4736 *MSL Hsien-tsung* 93.1781–2. I am indebted to Dr. Hung-lam Chu for bringing to my attention Ch'iu Chün's "Yü Su-min Kung chuan," in *Ch'ung-pien Ch'iung-t' ai kao*, S.K. ed., 20.11b–21a; See also the biography by Hok-lam Chan in *DMB* ii.1620–4; and the account in *MS*: 178.4736–40.
301 *MS* 178.4736 *MSL Hsien-tsung* 93.1781–2.
302 *MSL Hsien-tsung* 93.1781–2.
303 See biography by Lienche Tu Fang in *DMB*, ii.1580–2; *MS*:177.4721–5.
304 *MSL Hsien-tsung* 101.1963; 102.1998.
305 *MS* 177.4724.
306 *MSL Hsien-tsung* 102.2017.
307 *MSL Hsien-tsung* 107.2070–1; 106.2083–4.
308 *MSL Hsien-tsung* 109.2123–5.
309 *MSL Hsien-tsung* 108.2110; Haneda Toru and Tamura Jitsuzō eds., *MMS* iv. 288 places this section in ch. 110.
310 *MSL Hsien-tsung* 111.2161–2.
311 *MS* 327.8566; Hambis, *Documents*, 15.
312 Luttwak, *Grand Strategy of the Roman Empire*, 46.
313 *MS* 171.4573; 327.8474; Hambis, 39–40; DMB, 1457.
314 See Chung K'an, *Ning-hsia wen-wu shu-lüeh* (Ning-hsia jen-min ch'u-pan-she, 1980), pp. 104–6; *MS*13:169.

315 *MSL Hsien-tsung* 130.2467–8; *MS* 178.4737; Hsü Ch'ien-hsüeh, *Ming shih lieh chuan* (Taipei: Hsüeh-sheng, 1970) 47.2025; *DMB*, 1622–3.

316 *Ho-t'ao chih* 4.18b–19a.

317 Chung K'an, *loc. cit.*

318 *MS* 178.4738.

319 *MS* 327.8474–5; Hambis, *Documents*, 39–40; "Note", 168.

320 *DMB*, 18.

321 *MS* 327.8478; Hambis, *Documents*, 51.

322 Serruys, SMR II, pp. 8–9.

323 *MS* 327.8477; Hambis, *Documents*, 46; Pokotilov, 100; *DMB*, 18–19.

324 *MS* 327.8482; Hambis, *Documents*, 58.

325 *MS* 181.4804–10.

326 Ch'iu Chün *Ta-hsüeh yen-i pu*, (*S.K.* ed.), 1512.1b–6a; "Fu Ho-t'ao," in *HMCSWP*, 73.106–14, 6.109–13.

327 Tamura Jitsuzō, "Kyu Shun to *Daigakuengiho*," in *Tōhō Gakkai Sōritsu Jūgo-shūnen Kinen Tōhōgaku Ronshū* (Tokyo: Tōhō Gakkai, 1962), 164.

328 See Evgenij I, Kyçanov, "Les guerres entre les Sung du Nord et le Hsi-Hsia," in *Études Song in Memoriam Étienne Balazs*, ed. Françoise Aubin (Évreux: Mouton, 1971)1.2, 101–18.

329 See biographies in *Sung shih* 312.10221–32; 314.10267–81.

330 Dunnell, "Tanguts," 125–31.

331 Ch'en Cheng-hsiang, "Ch'ang-ch'eng yü ta-yün-ho," In *Chung-kuo wen-hua ti-li* (second edition. Taipei: Mu-to, 1983), 167.

332 Wei Huan, *Huang-ming chiu-pien k'ao* (1541. Reprint edition, Taipei: Hua-wen, 1968) 5.231. (hereafter *HMCPK*).

333 *HMCPK* 5.231–2; 251.

334 Biography of Yü Tzu-chün by Hok-lam Chan in *DMB*, II, p. 1622.

335 *MS* 178.4738–9; *Ch'ung-pien ch'iung-t'ai kao* 20. 17a.

336 *MS* 327.8475; Hambis, *Documents*, 40; also see Wang Chih's biography, *MS* 304.7778–81.

337 *MS* 327.8574; Hambis, *Documents*, 41; *MS* 171.4574; *DMB*, II 1458.

338 *DMB* I, 958–9.

339 *MS* 178.4738; 155.4264.

340 *Hou Han shu* 78.2537–8. Tr. Ronald C. Egan, "The Prose Style of Fan Yeh," *Harvard Journal of Asiatic Studies* 39.2(1979), p. 348.

341 *Ch'ung-pien ch'iung-t'ai kao* 20.16b.

342 See Yü's biography in *MS* 178.4738–9; *DMB* II, 1622–3.

343 *MS* 327.8475; Hambis, *Documents*, 43.

344 *DMB* II, 1459.

345 *MS* 327.8475; Hambis, *Documents*, 43.

346 *MS* 327.8475–6; Hambis, *Documents*, 43–44; Wang Ch'i, *Hsü wen-hsien t'ung-k'ao* 232.13824–5; on the borders, see *MS* 73.1774; SMR II, n. 26.

347 *MS* 178.4744–5.

348 My treatment of the period follows the chapter, "The Cheng-te Reign, 1506–1521," by James Geiss, in the *Cambridge History of China*, vol. 7, *The Ming Dynasty*, pp. 403–39.

349 *MS* 327.8467; Hambis, *Documents*, 44; Wang Ch'i, *Hsü wen-hsien t'ung-k'ao* 232.13835–6.

350 *MSL Wu-tsung* 9.0284.

351 *MSL Wu-tsung* 17.0522–3; *MS* 198.5226–7 *Kuan-chung tsou-i* 7.42b–50a.

352 *MSL Wu-tsung* 62.0704–5; *MS* 304.7789. See also Chiang Ying-liang, "Yang I-ch'ing yü Ming-tai chung-nien chih pei-pien-chiang," *Hsin-ya-hsi-ya* 10.1 (1935), 63–78.

353 See Carney Thomas Fisher, "The Great Ritual Controversy in Ming China" (Ph.D dissertation: University of Michigan, 1977); James Geiss, "The Chia-ching reign, 1522–1566," in *Cambridge History of China*, Volume 7, pp. 440–511. My treatment of the Chia-ching period generally follows the latter: Dr. Geiss generously allowed me to consult his manuscript before it was published, and I am indebted to him for many insights and references drawn from his wide reading.

354 Shen Te-fu, *Wan-li yeh-huo-pien* (1619: Peking: Chung-hua, 1980), 2.57. My thanks to Dr. James Geiss for this reference.

355 *DMB*, I, p. 6.

356 *MS* 327.8482; Hambis, *Documents*, 58; Serruys, "Chinese in Southern Mongolia during the Sixteenth Century," *Monumenta Serica* 18 (1959), 38–9 n. 125.

357 SMR III, p. 149.

358 *MSL Shih-tsung* 137.3325; *MS* 202.5327–8; *MMS* 6.29–30; SMRII, 34. In the court politics of the period, T'ang Lung had been on good terms with Yen Sung; Hsia Yen was behind his fall. *MS* 202.5328.

359 *MSL Shih-tsung* 251.5030–34; *MMS* 6.216–18; SMRII, 54.

360 *MSL Shih-tsung* 251.5030; *MMS* 6.216; SMRII, 35.

361 *MSL Shih-tsung* 253.5072–3; *MMS* 6.229–30; SMRII, 57–8.

362 Text in Wang Shih-chi, San-yün ch'ou-tsu k'ao (late Wan-li: in Kuo-li Pei-p'ing t'u-shu-kuan shan-pen ts'ung-shu ti i chi, pt. 2, v. 11), 29b–31a; SMRII, 57–61.

363 *MS* 204.5393–5.

364 SMRII, 58.

365 SMRII, 59

366 SMRII, p. 60. I have changed Serruys's rendering of *pien* from "[Great] wall" to "border walls."

367 *MS* 198.5247; see also *MSL Shih-tsung* 313.5862–65; *MMS* 6.445–7.

368 *MS* 204.5386; *DMB*, 1303–4.

369 *MSL Shih-tsung* 307.5792.

370 *MSL Shih-tsung* 310.5824.

371 *MS* 204.5387 *MSL Shih-tsung* 316.5301–2; 323:5996.

372 *MS* 204.5387.

373 *MSL* 318.5924–8; Hsia Hsieh, *Ming T'ung-chien* (Reprint ed., Peking, Chung-hua, 1959) 58.2230–31 (hereafter, *MTC*).

374 *MS* 196.5197.

375 For a summary of the discussion, see *MSL Shih-tsung* 318.5924–8. An abbreviated text of the memorial may be found in *HMCSWP* 237.393–546. The most complete text is in Tseng Hsien, *Tseng Hsiang-min kung fu-t'ao i* (hereafter *NLP*) (1587: Kuo-li Pei-p'ing t'u-shu-kuan shan-pen-shu chiao-p'ien, 39.6).

376 So Kwan-wai, "Grand Secretary Yan Song (1480–1566?): A New Appraisal," in *Essays in the History of China and Chinese–American Relations*, ed. So, Kwan-wai and Warren Cohen (East Lansing: Michigan State University, Asian Studies Center, 1982). Professor So has also permitted me to read his manuscript, "Yen Sung yü Hsia Yen," not yet published.

377 Hsia's biography is in *MS* 196.5191–5199; Yen's in *MS* 308.7914–21.

378 *MS* 110.3356; *DMB* II, 1586.

379 *MSL Shih-tsung* 303.5476; 306.5779.

380 *MS* 196.5195.

381 Liu Ts'un-yan, "The Penetration of Taoism into the Ming Neo-Confucian Elites," *T'oung Pao* 57 (1971), 63.

382 *MTC* 58.2231.

383 *MSL Shih-tsung* 318.5927–8; *NLP* 16b–21a.

384 *MSL Shih-tsung* 282.5487.

385 *DMB* II, 1543.

386 *MSL Shih-tsung* 323.5987–8; 324.6012–13.

387 *MSL Shih-tsung* 198.5242. *MSL Shih-tsung* 324.6012–13.

388 The eleventh lunar month, 12 December 1547–10 January 1548. *MSL Shih-tsung* 325.6020; *NLP*, 21a–26b.

389 Fan Shou-chi, *Su-huang wai-shih* 1582 (manuscript copy in Gest Oriental Library) ch. 27; Chih Ta-lun, *Yung-ling pien-nien hsin-shih* 1596 (reprint ed., 2v. Taipei: Hsüeh-sheng shu-chü, 1970) entry for year 26, month 3; Shen Yüeh, *Chia-lung liang-ch'ao wen-chien-lu*, 1599 (Hishi copy; Gest Oriental Library) II.7.44a; Wu Jui-teng, *Liang-ch'ao hsien-chang lu*, (Hishi copy: Gest Oriental Library) II.12.18a.

390 On 9 September 1547, both the minister of war, Ch'en Ching, and the Nanking minister of war, Hu Shun, were impeached by censors and allowed to retire. *MSL Shih-tsung* 325.6017; 326.6031–2; 327.6033.

391 *MSL Shih-tsung* 329.6056; T'an Ch'ien, *Kuo ch'üeh* (Reprint ed., Taipei: Ting-wen, 1958), 59.3708, (hereafter *KC*).

392 *MSL Shih-tsung* 330.6073–74; *MMS* 6.516–17; *NLP*, 42a–105a; *HMCSWP* 237.393–240.546. Tseng's drawings are preserved in Mao Yüan-i, *Wu-pei chih* (1621: Ming edition in Gest Oriental Library), ch. 66.

393 *MSL Shih-tsung* 331.6079–81.

394 *HMCSWP* 237.2480. The figure is obtained by taking the cost for fifty days, deducting from it the pikemen and the 5,000 taels for other expenses, and applying it to the remainder of the year. To this figure is then added the full cost of the summer campaign, i.e. $(315/50 \times 198{,}850) + 216{,}850 = 1{,}252{,}755$.

395 Nineteenth-century estimates give the daily grain consumption of a horse as 0.03 *tan* (or about 4 pounds) and the working load of a camel as 2 *tan* (or about 266 pounds). That means it would take 1,500 camel loads of grain to feed 100,000 horses for a single day. See Denis Sinor, "Horse and Pasture in Inner Asian History," *Oriens Extremus* 19 (1972) p. 177, citing Wen-djang Chu, *The Moslem Rebellions in Northwest China 1862–1878* (The Hague: Mouton, 1966) p. 183.

396 Ssu-ma Kuang, *Tzu-chih t'ung-chien* (Peking: Chung-hua, 1956) 136.4262–3; *Wei shu* 54.1200–2; *Pei shih* 34.1256–7.

397 *MS* 198.5249; *HMCSWP* 225.2363–7.

398 *MS* 205.5423–25; *DMB*, 1252–6.

399 T'ang Shun-chih, *Ching-ch'üan hsien-sheng wen-chi* (*SPTK* ed., reprint Taipei: 1967), 8.141.44.

400 *MS* 214.5655–60; *DMB*, 1525–8.

401 Hsia Yen, "Pei-yü ch'en-hsieh shu," in *Kuei-chou hsien-sheng chi* (Ming ed. in Gest Oriental Library), 14.41a–42a.

402 *MSL Shih-tsung* 332.6087 *Chia-lung liang-ch'ao wen-chien-lu*, II.8.1a.

403 *Han Shu* 74.3136; 69.2971–6. Michael Loewe, *Crisis and Conflict in Han China* (London: George Allen and Unwin, 1974), 148–9. Early military writers paid much attention to justification (*ming*); see Christopher C. Rand, "The Role of Military Thought in Early Chinese Intellectual History." (Ph.D Dissertation: Harvard University, 1977), 182. For the quote Wei refers to, see Paul J. Lin, *A Translation of Lao-tzu's Tao-te-ching and Wang Pi's Commentary* (Ann Arbor: University of Michigan, 1977), 55. See also Rand, "Role," 148, 342.

404 Lin, tr., *Lao-tzu*, 55.

405 *Analects* XVI.. James Legge, tr., *The Chinese Classics*, I pp. 306–9.

406 The Han precedent is mentioned by commentaries, e.g. in *MSCSPM* 58.625. On Wei Hsiang, see Michael Loewe, *Crisis and Conflict in Han China* pp. 148–9.

407 *MSL Shih-tsung* 334.6122–4; 341.6201–2.

408 Charles O. Hucker, "Governmental Organization of the Ming Dynasty," in Studies of Governmental Institutions in Chinese History, ed. John L. Bishop (Cambridge, Mass.: Harvard University Press, 1968), p. 63; See also, Tamura Jitsuzō, "Mindai no Kyū-hen-chin," in *Ishihama hakase koki kinen tōyōgaku ronsō* (Osaka, 1958), 290–300; and "Mindai no hoppen bōei taisei," in *Mindai Man-Mō Shi Kenkyū* (Kyoto: Kyoto University, 1963), 73–161.

409 Wolfgang Franke, "Addenda and Corrigenda to Pokotilov's *History of the Eastern Mongols During the Ming dynasty from 1358 to 1634*," *Studia Serica*, Series A, No. 3 (Peiping: Published by the Editors, 1949), pp. 17–18.

410 *MSL* 318.5924–5; *MMS* 6.466–7.

411 Compare *TCTC* 136.4262 and *MSL Shih-tsung* 464.7840; also see *CCPK*, 118; Geil, *The Great Wall*, 77–9.

412 See "I k'uai chen-kuei ti ch'ang-ch'eng kung-p'ai" in *CCPK*, pp. 118–17 (pagination is correct – article continues on preceding page).

413 "Chia-yü-kuan chi ch'i fu-chin ti ch'ang-ch'eng," in *CCPK* p. 107; *Chia-yü-kuan shih wen-wu kai-k'uang* (Chia-yü-kuan shih wen-wu kuan-li so, 1980), 9.

414 *CCPK*, 107.

415 *CCPK*, 107; *Chia-yü-kuan shih wen-wu kai-k'uang*, 6.

416 Langdon Warner, *The Long Old Road in China* (Garden City, New York: Doubleday, Page & Co., 1926), 63–4.

417 See map in Luo Zewen *et al.*, *The Great Wall of China* (New York: McGraw-Hill, 1981), 66–7; Wu Chi-hua, "Lun Ming-tai pien-fang nei-i yü ch'ang-ch'eng hsiu-chu," *Tung-hai ta-hsüeh li-shih hsüeh-pao* 4 (1981), 37–41.

418 See Chung K'an, *Ning-hsia wen-wu shu-lüeh* (Ning-hsia jen-min ch'u-pan she, 1980), pp. 104–6; *MS* 13:169.

419 Operational Navigation Chart, People's Republic of China, ONC G-9 (Defense Mapping Agency Aerospace Center, May 1974, revised August 1980).

420 Luo, *op. cit.*, 94.

421 *Huai-nan-tzu* (Chu-tzu chi-ch'eng ed., Shanghai: Shih-chieh, 1935), 4.55; cf. *Chi-fu t'ung-chih* (1910: rpt. Taipei: Hua-wen, 1970), 69.2257.

422 Cheng Dalin, *The Great Wall of China* (Hong Kong: South China Morning Post and New China News, 1984), p. 73.

423 *Yen-ch'ing-wei chih lüeh* (1745: rpt. Taipei: Ch'eng-wen, 1970), 14.

424 Ibid, 14–15.

425 Hibino Takeo, "Kyoyōkan no rekishi chiri," in *Chūgoku rekishi chiri kenkyū* (Tokyo: Dōbōsha, 1978), 304–5; Lo, *Ch'ang-ch'eng*, pp. 93–4.

426 *MSL Ying-tsung* 254.5484; *Yen-ch'ing-wei chih lüeh*, 23.

427 Lo, *Ch'ang-ch'eng*, p. 106. Cheng Dalin describes the Chü-yung-kuan defenses as a fortress having a circumference of 6.5 kilometers, with northern and southern gates, begun by Hsü Ta, who also began the walls at Pa-ta-ling, construction of which continued until 1582. Cheng, pp. 76–8.

428 *Lin-yü-hsien chih* (1929: reprint ed., Taipei: Ch'eng-wen, 1968), 7.434–5, 13.766,769,771; Lo Che-wen, *Shan-hai-kuan kuan-ch'eng chi ch'i chien-chu k'an-ch'a-chi*," in *CCPK*, pp. 93–100; Lo, *Ch'ang-ch'eng*, p. 82.

429 Cheng Dalin, pp. 65–70.

430 Cheng Dalin, pp. 51–62.

431 Cheng Dalin, pp. 63–84.

432 "Shan-hsi-sheng ching-nei ch'ang-ch'eng chien-chi," in *CCPK*, pp. 101–6.
433 See Wu T'ing-hsieh, *Ming-tai tu-fu nien-piao*, n.d., ch.1.1a; See also Charles O. Hucker, "Governmental Organization of the Ming Dynasty," in *Studies of Governmental Institutions in Chinese History*, ed. John L. Bishop (Cambridge, Mass.: Harvard University Press, 1968), 97–100.
434 *HMCPK* 5.251.
435 Li Hsün, *Chieh-an lao-jen man-pi* (Peking: Chung-hua, 1982), 99–100 gives some examples. My thanks to Dr. James Geiss for this reference.
436 *HMCPK* 5.233; 251.
437 Mao Po-wen, who was Weng Wan-ta's superior in the Vietnam campaign, supervised the work. *MTC* 51.1921; 57.2163; *MSL Shih-tsung* 225.4688; *MMS* 6.174.
438 *HMCPK* 5.232.
439 *MSL Shih-tsung* 288.5553–5; *MMS* 6.366–7.
440 "Shan-hsi-sheng ching-nei ch'ang-ch'eng chien-chi," p. 103.
441 Serruys, "Towers," 11; 37–39; Ch'en Cheng-hsiang, "Ch'ang-ch'eng yü ta-yün ho," 168–71.
442 Serruys, "Towers," 13.
443 Serruys, "Towers," p. 13.
444 Serruys, "Towers," 16 note 17.
445 The list is from Ch'en Cheng-hsiang, "Ch'ang-ch'eng," pp. 168–71, the map *CCPK* 102.
446 *MS* 91.2241.
447 *MS* 91.2240; 198.5246–7; *MSL* 320.5946—56; *MMS* 6.476–84.
448 *MSL Shih-tsung* 298.5678–9; 5681–3. *MMS* 6.399–400; 401–2.
449 *MSL Shih-tsung* 309.5811; *MMS* 6.427.
450 *MSL Shih-tsung* 313.5868–9; *MS* 198.5247; *MMS*, 6.448–9.
451 *MSL Shih-tsung* 315.5888; *MMS* 6.452.
452 *MSL Shih-tsung* 315.5899. *MMS* 6.456 *MS* 211.5582.
453 *MSL Shih-tsung* 337.6159–60; *MMS* 6.3544.
454 "Shan-hsi ching-nei ch'ang-ch'eng chien-chi," in *CCPK*, 102–5.
455 *MSL Shih-tsung* 312.5847–50; 311.5840–1; *MMS* 6.441–3, 439–40.
456 *MSL Shih-tsung* 347.6293–7; *MMS* 6.575–9.
457 *MSL Shih-tsung* 347.6293–7; *MMS* 6.578.
458 *MS* 327.,8480–1; *MTC* (Peking: Chung-hua, 1959) 59.2264–68; Hambis, *Documents*, 55–6.
459 Wiliam Edgar Geil, *The Great Wall of China* (New York: Sturgis & Walton, 1909), 85.
460 *MSL Shih-tsung* 369.6606–7; *MMS* 6.662–3.
461 *MTC*, 60.2310.
462 *MSL Shih-tsung* 395.6952–3; *MMS* 7.54–5.
463 *MSL Shih-tsung* 432.7456; *MMS* 7.157.
464 *MSL Shih-tsung* 398.6990; *MSL Shih-tsung* 434.7487; *MMS*, 7.66; 7.160.
465 *MSL Shih-tsung* 442.7560; *MMS* 7.173.
466 *MSL Shih-tsung* 459.7761–3; *MMS* 7.226.
467 *MSL Shih-tsung* 464.7840.
468 *KC* 65.4072–3.
469 *Lin-yü-hsien chih* (1929: reprint Taipei: Ch'eng-wen, 1968), 13.766–7.
470 Luo, *The Great Wall*, 120.
471 *MSL Mu-tsung* 29.0759–0760; *MMS* 7.616.
472 *MS* 212.5614–15; Robert O. Thompson, "Defense of the Northern Frontier in Ming

China Especially the Chi-chou Area Northeast of Peking, 1569–83" (Master's thesis: University of Chicago, 1962), 70–1.

473 Ray Huang, *1587, A Year of No Significance* (New Haven and London: Yale University Press, 1981), 182; *HMCSWP* 349.736–48.

474 Huang, *1587*, p. 182; *MSL Shen-tsung* 110.2113.

475 Huang, *1587*, 182.

476 *MSL Shen-tsung* 11.0365–6; *MMS* 8.137–8.

477 *MSL Shen-tsung* 22.0584–5; *MMS* 8.187–8.

478 *MSL Shen-tsung* 23.0598–9; *MMS* 8.189.

479 *MSL Shen-tsung* 48.1098, 48.1114; *MMS* 8.272–3.

480 This point is made strongly by Thomas Barfield.

481 Mark Mancall, *China at the Center: 300 Years of Foreign Policy* (New York: The Free Press, 1984), p. 6.

482 Wolfgang Bauer, *China und die Fremden 3000 Jahre Auseinandersetzung in Krieg und Frieden* (Munich: C. H. Beck, 1980), p. 1.

483 Owen Lattimore, "Herdsmen, farmers, urban culture," in *Pastoral Production and Society*, edited by l'Equipe écologie et anthropologie des sociétés pastorales (Cambridge: Cambridge University Press and Paris: Editions de la Maison des Sciences de l'Homme, 1979), p. 481.

484 *MS* 308.7914–21.

485 I Chih, "Ming-tai 'ch'i-t'ao' shih-mo," in *Ming-tai pien-fang*, ed. Pao Tsun-p'eng (Taipei: Hsüeh-sheng shu-chü, 1968), 189–204.

486 Wang Shih-chen, *Ming-feng chi* (Shanghai: Chung-hua, 1959), 1; it should be noted that the attribution to Wang Shih-chen is uncertain.

487 *MSL Shih-tsung* 364.6483–84; Serruys, SMR III, pp. 150–1.

488 *MS* 213.5632–5633; *MS* 198.5251; *MSL Shih-tsung* 364.6994; 364.6499; 368.6589–90; SMR III, p. 151.

489 *MTC* 59:3276.

490 *MTC* 60:2279–84; *MSL Shih-tsung* 371.6621–5; *MMS* 6.664–8; SMR III, 151–3.

491 *MSL Shih-tsung* 376.6689–93; *MMS* 6.688–92; SMR III, 156–158.

492 *MSL Shih-tsung* 371.6633–35; *MMS* 6.6673–74; SMR III, 153.

493 SMR II, 62.

494 *MSL Shih-tsung* 394.6930; *MMS* 7.51; SMR III, 161.

495 *MSL Shih-tsung* 473.7939; *MMS* 7.290–1.

496 On the Vietnam campaigns, see Lo Jung-pang, *op. cit.*, 62–66; also his article, "Intervention in Vietnam: A Case Study of the Foreign Policy of the Early Ming Government," *Ts'ing-hua Journal of Chinese Studies* 8(1970), 154–82.

497 So, *Japanese Piracy*, 92.

498 Ibid., 85.

499 Pin-tsun Chang, "Chinese Maritime Trade: The Case of Sixteenth-century Fu-chien (Fukien)" (Ph.D dissertation: Princeton University, 1983), 75–8.

500 *MSL Shih-tsung* 371.6628–35; *MMS* 6.668–72; SMR III, 153, 262.

501 See A. R. Davis, ed. *The Penguin Book of Chinese Verse* (Harmondsworth and Baltimore: Penguin Books, 1962), p. 59.

502 Biography by Sun Yüen-king and L. Carrington Goodrich in *DMB*, II, 104.

503 Ch'ien Mu, "Tu Ming-ch'u k'ai-kuo chu-ch'en shih-wen-chi," *Hsin-ya Hsüeh-pao* 6.2 (August 1964), pp. 243–326. Cited by F. W. Mote, "Some Problems of Race and Nation in 14th-Century China" (Paper presented to the University Seminar on Traditional China: Columbia University, 11 March 1969), pp. 3, 5.

504 Quoted in Elie Kedourie, *Nationalism* (London: Hutchinson & Co., 1985), p. 122.

505 Andrew J. Nathan, *Peking Politics, 1918–1923: Factionalism and the Failure of Constitutionalism* (Berkeley: University of California Press, 1976), p. 38.

506 Nathan, pp. 37–44.

507 John Meskill, "Academies and Politics in the Ming Dynasty," in *Chinese Government in Ming Times*, ed. Charles O. Hucker (New York and London: Columbia University Press, 1969), 169. On this subject see also, Heinrich Busch, "The Tung-lin Shu-yüan and its political and philosophical significance," *Monumenta Serica* 14 (1949–55), 1–163; Charles O. Hucker, "The Tung-lin movement of the late Ming period," in *Chinese Thought and Institutions*, ed. John K. Fairbank (Chicago: University of Chicago Press, 1957), 132–62.

508 Meskill, "Academies," 159.

509 Meskill, 153–4.

510 *DMB*, 366.

511 Meskill, "Academies," 163–4.

512 So, *Japanese Piracy*, pp. 144–56.

513 On this connection see T'ang Hsiu-mei, "Chang Chü-cheng ti cheng-chih ssu-hsiang yü ts'e-lüeh yen-chiu" (Master's thesis: National Taiwan University, 1971), p. 150.

514 *MS* 222.5838–39.

515 *MS* 222.5839–40. SMRII, 64–7.

516 *MS* 222.5841–43. SMRII, 70–3.

517 Serruys, "Chinese in Southern Mongolia," pp. 38–9, n. 125.

518 SMRII, 68–9, n. 11.

519 SMRII, 83.

520 T'ang Hsiu-mei, "Chang Chü-cheng," pp. 132–41.

521 T'ang Hsiu-mei, pp. 141–4.

522 Huang, *1587*, 181.

523 Ray Huang, *Taxation*, 288 n. 107.

524 Wang Yü-ch'üan, *Ming-tai ti chün-t'un* (Peking: Chung-hua, 1965), 102–3.

525 The *fu-t'ao i* (cited above) was republished in 1587, five years after Chang's death, with a preface by Ch'en Wen-chu (cs. 1565), a literary figure of the late Ming who also contributed prefaces to works of Wu Ch'eng-en (ca. 1506–82) and Wang Shih-mou (1536–8, cs. 1559), the younger brother of Wang Shih-chen. See *DMB*, pp. 1305, pp. 1481, 1406–8.

526 Chiang Wu-hsiung, "Ming-mo Liao-tung pien-fang chih yen-chiu" (Master's thesis: National Taiwan University, 1978), second page (unnumbered) of introduction,

527 Albert Chan, *The Glory and Decline of the Ming* (Norman: University of Oklahoma Press, 1982), 300, apparently citing Chao I, *Erh-shih-erh shih cha-chi* (in *Ts'ung-shu chi-ch'eng chien-pien*, Taipei: Shang-wu, 1965–6), 35.739–41. c.f. Lo, "Policy Formulation," 68–9.

528 The relationship in the decision-making process between what makes sense strategically and what is desirable or feasible politically, continues to be topic of great interest to students of foreign policy. I have found an article by Philip G. Cerny particularly useful: "Foreign policy leadership and national integration," *British Journal of International Studies* 5.1 (April 1979), pp. 59–85.

529 See Michael Yahuda, *Towards the End of Isolationism: China's Foreign Policy After Mao* (London: Macmillan, 1983), p. 3.

530 See n. 92 above.

531 Mark Mancall, *China at the Center* (New York: The Free Press, 1984); Warren I. Cohen, *America's Response to China* (New York: Wiley, 1971): Yahuda, *op. cit.*, are but a few examples.

532 Yahuda, *op. cit.*, pp. xi–xii.

533 See Kuang-sheng Liao, "Linkage Politics in China: Internal Mobilization and Articulated External Hostility in the Cultural Revolution, 1967–1969," *World Politics* 28.4(1976), pp. 590–610; and *Antiforeignism and Modernization in China, 1860–1980: Linkage between Domestic Politics and Foreign Policy* (Hong Kong: The Chinese University Press, 1984).

534 Derk Bodde, tr. *Statesmen, Patriot, and General in Ancient China*, p. 61.

535 Bodde, *op. cit.*, p. 64.

536 Chia I, "The Faults of Ch'in," in William Theodore de Bary, *et al.*, *Sources of Chinese Tradition* (New York and London: Columbia University Press, 1960) 1.152.

537 *Han Shu* 64B.2831, cited by Ch'iu-kuei Wang, "The Transformation of The Meng Chiang-nü Story in Chinese Popular Literature" (Ph.D dissertation: Cambridge University, 1977). Chapter II note 56, p. 188.

538 Anne Birrell, *New Songs from a Jade Terrace: An Anthology of Early Chinese Love Poetry, Translated with Annotations and Introduction* (London: George Allen & Unwin, 1982), p. 49. These short lines are found in a number of early sources, and according to C. K. Wang, "It is probable that they were originally part of a popular ballad." They are found in the *Wu-li lun* of Yang Ch'üan (third century), where the story of Meng T'ien's cutting the earth's veins is also mentioned; also in the *Shui-ching chu* 3.7b. Ch'iu-kuei Wang, Chapter II, n. 57, p. 188.

539 Birrell, *New Songs from a Jade Terrace*, pp. 48–9. See also, *Yüeh-fu shih-chi* (SPPY ed.), 38.1a–5b.

540 Cheng Dalin, *The Great Wall of China*, p. 197.

541 Liang Heng and Judith Shapiro, *Son of the Revolution* (New York: Knopf, 1983), p. 26.

542 See Chang-tai Hung, *Going to the People: Chinese Intellectuals and Folk Literature, 1918–1937* (Cambridge, Mass.: Harvard University Press, 1985), esp. pp. 93–99.

543 James Legge, ed. and tr. *The Chinese Classics* (reprint ed. Taipei: Wen-shih-che, 1971), 5.504.

544 Ch'iu-kuei Wang, pp. 7–8.

545 Ch'iu-kuei Wang gives the following references. Deaths of wall-builders: *Sui shu* 3.70; 24.676; *T'ung-tien* 7.24b (n. 75, p. 190); widows sent to wall-builders: *Pei shih* 7.252; prisoners set free to marry them: *Pei shih* 6.229; (p. 29).

546 Two useful collections are Huang Lin-shu, *T'ang-tai shih-jen sai-fang ssu-hsiang ch'u-kao* (Hong Kong: Tsao-yang, 1982) and *Ch'ang-ch'eng shih-ch'ao*, ed. Chia-yü-kuan-shih wen-wu kuan-li-so (Chia-yü-kuan, 1981).

547 See references in Chapter 3 above.

548 *Sung shu* 43.1344; Morohashi Tetsuji, *Dai Kanwa Jiten* (Tokyo: Taishukan, 1955–60), 9.10108–9.

549 See n. 61 above.

550 Ku Chieh-kang and Shih Nien-hai, *Chung-kuo chiang-yü yen-ko shih* (Changsha: Shang-wu, 1938), 268; Hung Liang-chi and Wu Yü-chi, *Li-ch'ao shih-an* (Ch'ien-lung edition in Harvard-Yenching Library), 17.14a.

551 e.g. in "Chao yin ma sung Ch'en Tzu ch'u sai," pp. 21–2 in *Ch'ang-ch'eng shih-ch'ao*.

552 Wan Ssu-t'ung, *Hsin yüeh-fu tz'u* (1869 edition, in the collection of Harvard-Yenching Library), 20a–b. Chao I, *Tu-shih erh-shih-i shou*, in *Ou-pei shih-ch'ao*, in *Kuo-hsüeh chi-pen ts'ung-shu*, ed. Wang Yün-wu (Taipei: Taiwan Commercial Press, 1968) volume 324, p. 5. My thanks to Yong Gyu Rhew for calling this poem to my attention.

553 John Meskill, translator, *Ch'oe Pu's Diary: A Record of Drifting Across the Sea* (Tucson: University of Arizona Press, 1965), p. 141.

554 Lo, *Ch'ang-ch'eng*, p. 85.

555 Frederick G. Clapp, "Along and Across the Great Wall of China," *The Geographical Review* 9 (1920), p. 234.

556 *China Reconstructs* (North American Edition) 34.3 (March, 1985), 6.

557 See n. 66 above.

558 Gog and Magog are mentioned in Ezekiel, xxxviii.2 and Revelation, xx.8. Among basic references on Alexander's wall are: C. E. Wilson, "The Wall of Alexander Against Gog and Magog; and the Expedition Sent out to find it by the Khalif Wāthiq in 842 A.D.," *Asia Major* (1922), 575–612; Andrew Runni Anderson, *Alexander's Gate, Gog and Magog, and the Inclosed Nations*, Monographs of the Mediaeval Academy of America, No. 5, Cambridge, Mass., 1932; and K. Czeglèdy, "The Syriac Legend Concerning Alexander the Great," *Acta Orientalia Academiae Scientiarum Hungaricae* 7 (1957), No. 2–3, pp. 232–248; and J. A. Boyle, "The Alexander Legend in Central Asia," *Folklore* 85 (1974), pp. 217–228. For a summary, see Ruth I. Meserve, "The Inhospitable Land of the Barbarian," *Journal of Asian History*, 16 (1982), 75–9.

559 Rashīd ad-Dīn, *Jami' al-Tawarikh* (ed. A. Ali-zade), 1985, pp. 307–8. See Paul Pelliot, *Recherches sur les Chrétiens d'Asie Centrale et d'Extrême-Orient* (Œuvres posthumes de Paul Pelliot. Paris: Imprimerie Nationale, 1973), p. 262 for further information. My thanks to Isenbike Togan Aricanli, of Harvard, for these references.

560 Henry Yule and Henri Cordier, *Cathay and the Way Thither* (London, 1913–16), IV, 123.

561 Ammianus Marcellinus, *History*, XXIII:6,64. John C. Rolfe reads: "Beyond these lands [...], towards the east, the summits of lofty walls enclose the Seres, remarkable for the richness and extent of their country." Loeb Classical Library edition (Cambridge, Mass: Harvard University Press, 1935–39) II. pp. 384–85.

562 "A Treatise of China and the adjoyning Regions [...]" in Samuel Purchas, *Hakluytus Posthumus or Purchas His Pilgrimes*, 20v. (Glasgow: James MacLehose and Sons, 1905) XI, p. 480; "The report of a Mahometan Merchant which had beene in Cambalu: and the troublesome travell of Benedictus Goes, a Portugal Jesuite, from Lahor to China by land, thorow the Tartars Countryes," in Purchas, XII, p. 234; Louis J. Gallagher, S.J., translator, *China in the Sixteenth Century: The Journals of Matthew Ricci: 1583–1610* (New York: Random House, 1953), p. 10.

563 "Extracts of Alhacen his Arabike Historie of Tamerlan, touching his Martiall Travels, done into French by Jean Du Bec, Abbot of Mortimer," in Purchas, XI, p. 418.

564 "The troublesome travell of Benedictus Goes," p. 234; Juan Gonzalez de Mendoza, *The historie of the great and mightie kingdom of China [...]*, *Translated out of Spanish by R. Parke* (London: I. Wolfe, 1588), p. 18.

565 Gaspar da Cruz, *op. cit.* p. 485.

566 Abraham Ortelius, *Theatrum Orbis Terrarum: The Theatre of the Whole World [...]* (London: I. Norton, 1606), p. 106 and plate between pp. 106–7.

567 William W. Appleton, *A Cycle of Cathay: The Chinese Vogue in England during the Seventeenth and Eighteenth Centuries* (New York: Columbia University Press, 1951), end papers. The map was published in Speed's *Prospects of the Most Famous Parts of the World* (1627–31).

568 *China Illustrata* (Amsterdam, 1667), 218. Golius found the passage in the "exemplaire" of Abu 'l'Fidā (1273–1331). I have been unable to locate the original source. See, "Addition dv royavme de Catay, par Jacques Gool," n.p., n.d., which may be found in the rare book collection of Princeton University, No. Ex 1706.183e pt. 2, pp. 215–27. My thanks to Louise Marlow and Roy Mottaheddeh for assistance with this question.

569 Petlin's text is in John Frederick Baddeley, *Russia, Mongolia, China* (London: Macmillan, 1919), II, pp. 70–85; see page 71 for the Wall. I have seen only an English version of the text Ides wrote originally in Dutch: Evert Ysbrandszoon Ides, *A journal*

of the embassy for Their Majesties John and Peter Alexievitz [...] *over land into China* [...] (London: Printed for D. Brown and T. Goodwin, 1698), p. 73. A useful modern edition is Izbrant Ides and Adam Brand, *Zapiski o Russkom posol'stve v Kitai (1692–1695)* with introduction, translation, and commentary by M. I. Kazanin (Moscow: Glavnaia redaktsiia vostochnoi literatury, 1967). On the Mongol terminology, see G. F. Miller, *Istoriia Sibiri* (Moscow–Leningrad, 1937), I, p. 516 and E. M. Murzaev, "Opyt ob'iasneniia nezvaniia 'Krym'," *Izvestiia Vsesoiuznogo Geograficheskogo Obshchestvo* 80 (1948) No. 3, pp. 295–8, both cited by Kazanin, *op. cit.*, n. 1 to chapter XIII, p. 308. On the largely unacknowledged borrowing of Western European sinological works by Russians, see the present author's review of P. E. Skachkov, *Ocherki istorii russkogo kitaevedeniia*, in *Kritika* 15 (1979) No. 1, pp. 1–16.

570 Martino Martini, *Novus Atlas Sinensis* (Amsterdam: Blaeu, 166?), pp. 15–16.

571 Johan Nieuhof, *An Embassy from the East India Company of the United Provinces to the Great Tartar Cham* [...] Englished and set forth with their several sculptures, by John Ogilby [...] (London: printed by J. Macock for the author, 1669), p. 7, pp. 137–8. League to mile conversion is in the text.

572 Athanasius Kircher, S.J. *China monumenti qua sacris qua profanis, Illustrata* (Amsterdam: Joannem Janssonium à Waesberge & Elizeum Weyerstraet, 1667).

573 Ferdinand Verbiest, *Voyages de L'Empereur de la Chine dans la Tartarie* [...] (Paris: Estienne Michallet, 1685) 51–54.

574 Appleton, *A Cycle of Cathay*, 1.

575 The best general work on this vast topic is Donald F. Lach, *Asia in the Making of Europe* (Chicago: University of Chicago Press, 1965–).

576 A. Owen Aldridge, "Voltaire and the Cult of China," *Tamkang Review* 2.2–3.1 (1971–2), pp. 25–49, at 38–9.

577 Denis Diderot, *Encyclopédie* (1765): rpt. Stuttgart: Bad Cannstart, 1966), x. 866; John Lough, *The Contributors to the Encylopèdie* (London: Grant and Cutler, 1973), 84–5.

578 J. B. Du Halde, The General History of China (London: J. Watts, 1741), II, 76–7.

579 See Locnaeus, pp. 5, 11.

580 C. K. Wang, *op. cit.*, p. 32, quoting *Chin shu* 130.3208 and *Pei shih* 93.3604. See also Joseph Needham, *op. cit.*, IV part 3 page 42.

581 April 10, 1778. *Boswell's Life of Johnson*, 6v. ed. G. B. Hill; rev. L. F. Powell (Oxford: Clarendon Press, 1934), III, p. 269; John Bell, *A Journey from St. Petersburg to Pekin 1719–22*, edited and with an introduction by J. L. Stevenson (New York: Barnes and Noble, 1966).

582 See note 27 above.

583 George L. Staunton, *An Authentic Account of an Embassy from the King of Great Britain to the Emperor of China* [...] (London: G. Nicol, 1797), 184. See also J. L. Cranmer-Byng, ed. *An Embassy to China: Being the Journal Kept by Lord Macartney During his Embassy to the Emperor Ch'ien-lung, 1793–94* (London: Longmans, 1962), pp. 110–13.

584 *China, in a series of views, displaying the scenery, architecture, and social habits of that ancient empire* [...] (London and Paris: Fisher, Son, & Co., n.d. preface July 1843), 2v.

585 A few examples: "Visit to the Great Wall of China" (by a correspondent), *The Illustrated London News* 17.449 (October 5, 1850), 271–2; H., "The Great Wall of China," *Once a Week* 6 (7 June 1862), 668–72.

586 Ludovic, Comte de Beauvoir, *Voyage Autour du Monde*, 3v. (Paris: Plon, 1872) III, pp. 105–9. Translation quoted from *China: Nagel's Encyclopedia-Guide* (Geneva, Paris, Munich: 1973), p. 620.

587 Jonas Locnaeus, *D.D. Murum Sinensem brevis dissertatione* [...] (Uppsala: Henricus Keyser, 1694), p. 15.

588 Charles William Wall, *An Examination of the Ancient Orthography of the Jews* (London: Whittaker and Co., 1841), II, pp. 335–375.

589 O. E. von Möllendorf, "Die Grosse Mauer von China," *Zeitschrift der Deutschen Morgenländischen Gesellschaft* 35.2 (1881), 75–131, at 76.

590 Larrieu, l'Abbé, "Rapport sur La Grande Muraille de Chine ou il est prouvé que cette muraille telle qu'elle est communément décrite non seulement n'existe pas, mais même n'a jamais existe," *Revue de l'Extrême-Orient* 3 (1887), 347–63.

591 "The Great Wall Not a Myth," *The Chinese Recorder and Missionary Journal* 19.6 (June, 1888), 239.

592 E. Martin, "La Vérité sur La Grande Muraille de la Chine," *L'Anthropologie* 2 (1891), 438–44. Also in *Revue Scientifique (Revue Rose)* 48.16 (17 October 1891), 499–502.

593 Frederick J. Teggart, *Rome and China: A Study of Correlations in Historical Events* (Berkeley: University of California Press, 1939), n. 22, pp. 232–3, provides an exhaustive list of references. For its falsity, see Manfred G. Raschke, "New Studies in Roman Commerce with the East," *Aufstieg und Niedergang Der Römischen Welt* ed. Hildegard Temporini and Wolfgang Haase (Berlin and New York: Walter De Gruyter, 1978) II.9.2, pp. 604–1361, n. 101 on page 697.

594 Frances V. Moulder, *Japan, China, and the modern world economy* (Cambridge: Cambridge University Press, 1977), note 49, on pp. 209–10, quoting Shlomo Avineri, ed., *Karl Marx on Colonialism and Modernization* (New York: Doubleday, 1968), 44–5.

595 Romyn Hitchcock, "The Great Wall of China," *The Century Illustrated Monthly Magazine* 45 (November 1892–April 1893), 327–32; William Edgar Geil, *The Great Wall of China* (New York: Sturgis and Walton, 1909), p. 17: "It has been sagely remarked that this long structure, called by the Chinese scholars of the Wanlich'ang Ch'êng, or Wall of Ten Thousand Miles, could be clearly defined by the mysterious Man-in-the-Moon, if such an individual exist and if he is endowed with the same faculties which we possess." Joseph Needham, *Science and Civilization in China* (Cambridge: Cambridge University Press, 1954–) IV:3,47 states that the Wall "has been considered the only work of man which could be picked out by Martian astronomers." He follows L. Newton Hayes, *The Great Wall of China* (Shanghai: Kelly and Walsh, 1929), p. 2. The idea thus long antedates manned space flight (and in any case no astronaut has reported seeing the Wall) and probably has its origins in the great interest in Mars which was spurred by the research of the astronomers G. V. Schiaparelli and Percival Lowell.

596 22 May 1932. The text – long since disowned by Ripley International – described the Wall as "The mightiest work of man – the only one that would be visible to the human eye from the moon!" Ripley based his assertion on Adam Warwick, "A Thousand Miles Along the Great Wall of China: The Mightiest Barrier Ever Built by Man Has Stood Guard Over the Land of Chin for Twenty Centuries," *National Geographic* 43.2 (February, 1923), 113–43.

597 George L. Staunton, *An Authentic Account of an Embassy from the King of Great Britain to the Emperor of China* [...] (London: G. Nicol, 1797), 184.

598 Chang Hsiang-wen, "Ch'ang-ch'eng k'ao," *Ti-li tsa-chih* 5 (1914), No. 9, 1–3.

599 Liang Ch'i-ch'ao, *Chung-kuo li-shih yen-chiu-fa* (preface dated 1922; first published 1925. Edition used is Taipei: Taiwan Chung-hua, 1967), pp. 39, 71.

600 Sun Yat-sen, *Sun Wen hsüeh-shuo* (Taipei: Yüan-tung, 1957), pp. 38–9.

601 "Ch'ang ch'eng," 15 May 1925. *Lu Hsün ch'üan-chi* (Shanghai: Hsin-hua shu-tien, 1981) Vol. 3, pp. 58–9.

602 *Reverberations: A New Translation of Complete Poems of Mao Tse-tung with Notes by Nancy T. Lin* (Hong Kong: Joint Publishing Co., 1980), pp. 38–41. See poems by Yeh and Chu

in *Ch'ang-ch'eng shih-ch'ao*, pp. 63–64; by Ch'en Yi in Tung K'an, *Ning-hsia wen-wu shu-lüeh* (Ning-hsai jen-min ch'u-pan she, 1980), p. 106.

603 Howard L. Boorman, ed., *Biographical Dictionary of Republican China* (New York: Columbia University Press, 1967–79), 3:40–1, 266–7. See also Jay Leyda, *Dianying: An Account of Films and the Film Audience in China* (Cambridge: M.I.T. Press, 1972), p. 99.

604 Luo and Liu, "Ch'ang-ch'eng ti pao-hu," 3 April 1986, p. 2.

605 Kuo Shu-tzu, "Wan-li ch'ang-ch'eng tung-shou chung-chen Shan-hai-kuan," *Wen-wu t'ien-ti* (1982), No. 1, p. 2.

606 Chin Shou-shen, "The Great Wall of China," *China Reconstructs* 11.1 (1962), pp. 20–1.

607 Liang Heng and Judith Shapiro, *Son of the Revolution* (New York: Knopf, 1983) p. 115.

608 "Ch'ang-ch'eng pao-hu yen-chiu kung-tso tso-t'an-hui ts'e-chi," in *Chung-kuo ch'ang-ch'eng i-chi tiao-ch'a pao-kao chi* (Peking: Wen-wu, 1981), pp. 3–5.

609 Roger Garside, *Coming Alive: China after Mao* (London: André Deutsch, 1981), pp. 291–292.

610 George Carter Stent introduced the tale to England in *Entombed Alive and Other Songs, Ballads, &c. (from the Chinese)* (London: William H. Allen and Co., 1878); the limited edition is Genevieve Wimsatt and Geoffrey Chen, *The Lady of the Long Wall* (New York: Columbia University Press, 1934). On the folklorists, see Hung Chang-tai, cited above.

611 Li Yu-ning, ed. *The Politics of Historiography: The First Emperor of China* (White Plains, N.Y.: International Arts and Sciences Press, 1975), p. 163; Kuei-hsien chiao-yü-chü, *Meng Chiang-nü shih i-chu tsun-ju fan-fa ti ta tu-ts'ao* (Kuang-hsi jen-min, 1975).

612 Ellen Johnston Laing, *An Index to Reproductions of Paintings by Twentieth-Century Chinese Artists* (Eugene, Oregon: University of Oregon, Asia Studies Program, Publication No. 6, June 1984); Feng, p. 137; Ch'ien (1972), p. 97. Laing lists in addition works by Lin Chieh (1924–) in 1927 (p. 277); Wei Tzu-hsi (1915–) in 1978 (p. 427); Wu Kuan-chung (1915–) in 1981 (p. 445); and Yen Ti (1920–79) in 1956 and 1960 (p. 474). My thanks to Robert Harrist for this information.

613 William Theodore De Bary, et. al., *Sources of Chinese Tradition* (New York: Columbia University Press, 1960), 1.175–176.

614 *New York Times*, 8 October 1974, p. 43.

615 See, for example, Harrison Salisbury's book, *The Long March: The Untold Story* (New York: Harper and Row, 1985).

616 See *China Pictorial* October, 1984, 8–13; *China Reconstructs* 33.10 (1984), 20–5.

617 *China Reconstructs* 33.10 (October, 1984), 25.

618 Zhang Xinxin and Sang Ye, *Chinese Profiles* (Beijing: Panda Books, 1987), pp. 15–21, at 20.

619 See Zhang Wei, "Man Winds Up Great Wall Trek," *Beijing Review* 29.15 (14 April 1986), pp. 14–18.

620 Zhang, p. 18.

621 *New York Times*, 25 February 1972, pp. 14, 17.

622 As this book was going to press, a striking example of this process appeared in the second episode, "Destiny," of "River Elegy," a television series about Chinese culture broadcast in China early in 1988, whose critical stance tested the limits of candor. The commentator observed: "If the Great Wall could speak, surely it would tell the descendants of the Yellow Emperor, in all honesty, that it is nothing but a massive monument to tragedy, cast in its present form by historical destiny. The Great Wall can in no way represent strength, progress or glory; it is a symbol of confinement,

conservatism, impotent defence and timidity in the face of invasion. Because of its massive scale and venerable history, it has left the imprint of its grand conceit and self-deception on the very soul of the Chinese. " 'Ah, Great Wall, why do we still sing your praises?' " Quoted in Geremie Barmé, "TV requiem for the myths of the Middle Kingdom," *Far Eastern Economic Review* 141.35 (1 September 1988), p. 43.

Bibliography

Chinese and Japanese materials

Aṅzai Kuraji 安齋庫治. "Shinmatsu ni okeru Suien no kaikon 清末に就ける綏遠の
開墾." *Mantetsu chōsa geppō* 18.12 (1938), 1–44; 19.1 (1939), 14–62; 19.2 (1939), 36–68.

Aoki Tomitarō 青木富太郎. *Banri no chōjō* 萬里の長城. Tokyo: Kondō shuppansha, 1972.

Chang Ch'un-shu 張春樹. *Han-tai pien-chiang-shih lun-chi* 漢代邊疆史論集. Taipei: Shih-huo
ch'u-pan-she, 1977.

Chang Hen-shui 張恨水, *Meng Chiang Nü* 孟姜女. With illustrations by Wang Shu-hui
王叔暉. Peking: Pei-ching ch'u-pan-she, 1957.

Chang Hsiang-wen 張相文. "Ch'ang-ch'eng k'ao 長城考." *Ti-li tsa-chih* 5 (1914), No. 9,
1–3.

Chang Hung-hsiang 張鴻翔. "Ch'ang-ch'eng kuan-pao lu 長城開堡錄." *Ti-hsüeh tsa-chih*
1 (1936): 13–32; 2 (1936): 19–36; 3 (1936): 2–28.

Chang P'eng-i 張朋一. *Ho-t'ao t'u-chih* 河套圖志 (1917).

Chang Te-hui 張德輝. *Sai-pei chi-hsing* 塞北紀行, 1 ch. in *Huang-ch'ao fan-shu yü-ti ts'ung-shu*
皇朝藩屬輿地叢書. Taipei: Kuang-wen, 1968.

Chang T'ing-yü 張廷玉 *et al.*, comp. *Ming Shih* 明實 (1739). Peking: Chung-hua shu-chü,
1974.

Chang Wei-hua 張維華. "Ming-tai Liao-tung pien-ch'iang chien-chih yen-ko k'ao 明代
遼東邊牆建置沿革考." *Shih-hsüeh nien-pao* 2.1 (1934), 267–73.

   "Ku-tai Ho-t'ao yü Chung-kuo chih kuan-hsi 古代河套與中國之關係." *Yü Kung* 6.5
   (1 Nov. 1936): 9–24.

   Chung-kuo ch'ang-ch'eng chien-chih k'ao, shang pien 中國長城建置考上編. Peking: Chung-
   hua, 1979.

Chang Yü 張雨. *Pien-cheng k'ao* 邊政考 (1547). In *Chung-hua wen-shih ts'ung-shu*, Taipei:
1968–71.

"Ch'ang-ch'eng tsai kuo-shih-chung ti ti-wei 長城在國史中的地位." In *Kuo-li T'ai-wan
Ta-hsüeh shih-chou-nien hsiao-ch'ing chuan-k'an*. Taipei: Taiwan University, 1956, pp. 45–
66.

Chao I 趙翼. *Erh-shih-erh-shih cha-chi* 二十二史札記. In *Ts'ung-shu chi-ch'eng chien-pien*,
Taipei: Shang-wu, 1965–6.

   Tu-shih erh-shih-i shou 讀史二十一首 in *Ou-pei shih-ch'ao* 甌北詩鈔. In *Kuo-hsüeh chi-pen
   ts'ung shu*, vol. 324, p. 5.

Chen Te-hsiu 真德秀. *Chen Wen-chung kung ch'üan-chi* 真文忠公全集. Reprint edn, Taipei:
Wen-yu, 1968.

Ch'en Cheng-hsiang 陳正祥. "Ch'ang-ch'eng yü ta-yün-ho 長城與大運河." In *Chung-kuo
wen-hua ti-li*, edited by Ch'en Cheng-hsiang. Second edition. Taipei: Mu-to, 1983.
pp. 157–71.

   Chung-kuo wen-hua ti-li 中國文化地理. Second edition. Taipei: Mu-to, 1982.

Ch'en Jen-hsi 陳仁錫. *Pa-pien lei-tsuan* 八編類纂 (1626). Reprint edn, Taipei: Hua-wen, 1968.

Huang-Ming Shih-fa lu 皇明世法錄 (1630). In *Chung-kuo shih-hsüeh ts'ung-shu*, Taipei: 1965.

Ch'en Lun-hsü [Albert Chan] 陳綸緒. "Chi Ming T'ien-shun Ch'eng-hua chien ta-ch'en nan-pei chih cheng 記明代天順成化間大出南北之爭." *Sinological Researches* (Tokyo) no. 1 (1964), 89–112.

Ch'en Tzu-lung 陳子龍, ed. *Huang Ming ching-shih wen-pien* 皇明經世文編 (1638). Reprint edn, Taipei: Kuo-lien, 1964.

Ch'en Wen-shih 陳文石. "Ming-tai wei-so ti chün 明代衛所的軍." *Bulletin of the Institute of History and Philology, Academia Sinica* 48 (1977), 177–204.

Cheng Shao-tsung 鄭紹宗. "Ho-pei-sheng Chan-kuo, Ch'in, Han shih-ch'i ku ch'ang-ch'eng ho ch'eng-chang i-chih 河北省戰國, 秦漢時期古長城和城障遺址." In *Chung-kuo ch'ang-ch'eng i-chi tiao-ch'a pao-kao-chi*, pp. 34–9.

Ch'eng Ta-ch'ang 程大昌. *Pei-pien pei-tui* 北邊備對. Ch. 66 in Li Shih 李杕, *Li-tai hsiao-shih* 歷代小史. Taipei: Commercial Press, 1969.

Ch'eng-te-fu chih 承德府志 (1887) Reprint edn, Taipei: Ch'eng-wen, 1968.

Chi-fu t'ung-chih 畿輔通志 (1910) Reprint edn, Taipei, Hua-wen, 1967.

Chia-yü-kuan-shih wen-wu kai-k'uang, 嘉峪關市文物概況. Chia-yü-kuan, 1980.

Chia-yü-kuan wen-wu kuan-li-so 嘉峪關文物管理所, ed. *Ch'ang-ch'eng shih-ch'ao* 長城詩鈔. Chia-yü-kuan, 1981.

Chiang Mei-feng 蔣美鳳. "Yu Chia-ching nien-chien Meng-ku jen ju-ch'in ch'ing-hsing t'an-t'ao Ch'ang-ch'eng ti kung-yung 由嘉靖年間蒙古人入侵情形探討長城的功用." *Shih Yüan* 29 (1978), 31–4.

Chiang Wu-hsiung 蔣武雄. "Ming-mo Liao-tung pien-fang chih yen-chiu 明末遼東邊防之研究," Master's thesis: National Taiwan University, 1978.

Chiang Ying-liang 江應樑. "Yang I-ch'ing yü Ming-tai Chung-kuo chih hsi-pei pien-chiang 楊一清與明代中國之西北邊疆." *Hsin Ya-hsi-ya* 10.1 (1935): 63–78.

Ch'ien Mu 錢穆. "Tu Ming-ch'u k'ai-kuo chu-ch'en shih-wen-chi 讀明初開國諸臣詩文集." *Hsin-ya Hsüeh-pao* 6.2 (August, 1964): 243–326.

Chih Ta-lun 支大綸. *Huang Ming Yung-ling pien-nien hsin-shih* 皇明永陵編年信史 (1596). Reprint edn, Taipei: Hsüeh-sheng, 1970.

Chin Ying-hsi 金應熙. "Tso-wei chün-shih fang-yü-hsien ho wen-hua hui-chü-hsien ti Chung-kuo ku ch'ang-ch'eng 作為軍事防禦綫和文化會聚綫的中國古長城." Chung-kuo shih-hsüeh hui 中國史學會. In *Ti shih-liu chieh kuo-chi li-shih k'o-hsüeh ta-hui Chung-kuo hsüeh-che lun-wen-chi*, pp. 271–91.

Chiu-pien t'u-shuo 九邊圖說 (1569). In *Chung-kuo pien-chiang shih-ti ts'ung-shu*.

Ch'iu Chün 丘濬. *Ch'ung-pien ch'iung-t'ai hui-kao* 重編瓊臺會稿. In *Ssu-k'u ch'üan-shu chen-pen, ssu-chi*, Taipei: Shang-wu, 1973.

Ta-hsüeh yen-i pu 大學衍義補 (1487). In *Ssu-k'u ch'üan-shu chen pen, erh chi* Taipei: Shang-wu, 1971.

Chou K'ang-hsieh 周康燮, ed. *Ming-tai She-hui Ching-chi-shih lun-chi* 明代社會經濟史論集. Hong Kong: Ch'ung-wen shu-tien, 1975.

Chou Mi 周密. *Kuei-hsin tsa-shih* 癸辛雜識. In *Hsüeh-chin t'ao-yüan* 學津討原. Reprint edn, Taipei: I-wen, 1965.

Chou Shu-jen 周樹人 [Lu Hsün 魯迅]. *Lu Hsün Ch'üan-chi* 魯迅全集. Shanghai: Hsin-hua shu-tien, 1981.

Chu Hsieh 朱偰. "Wan-li ch'ang-ch'eng hsiu-chien ti yen-ko 萬里長城修建的沿革." *Li-shih chiao-hsüeh* (1955) 12: 17–32.

"Ming-tai chiang-yü-t'u so piao-shih ti pien-ch'iang, shih fou shih Ch'ang-ch'eng ti yen-ch'ang? Wei-shen-mo chiao pien-ch'iang? 明代疆域圖所標示的邊疆是否是長城的延長？為甚麼叫邊牆?" *Li-shih chiao-hsüeh* 8 (1956): 55–6.

"Ku ch'ang-ch'eng i-chih ti hsin fa-hsien 古長城遺址的新發現." *Wen-wu ts'an-k'ao tzu-liao* (1956), No. 11.

Chu Tung-jun 朱東潤. *Chang Chü-cheng ta-chüan* 張居正大傳. Wuhan: Hupei jen-min, 1957.

Chü-yung-kuan chih 居庸關志 (1586). In *Chung-kuo fang-chih ts'ung-shu* 中國方志叢書.

Ch'üan Han-sheng 全漢昇. "Ming-tai pei-pien mi-liang chia-ko ti pien-tung 明代北邊米糧價格的變動." *Hsin-Ya Hsüeh-pao* (1970), 9.2 (1970), 49–96.

Chung-hua wen-shih t'sung-shu 中華文史叢書. Ed. Wang Yu-li 王有力. Taipei: Taiwan Hua-wen shu-chü, 1968–71.

Chung Kan 鍾侃. *Ning-hsia wen-wu shu-lüeh* 宁夏文物述略. Ning-hsia jen-min, 1980.

Chung-kuo ch'ang-ch'eng i-chi tiao-ch'a pao-kao chi 中國長城遺迹調查報告集. Peking: Wen-wu, 1981.

Chung-kuo fang-chih ts'ung-shu 中國方志叢書. Taipei: Ch'eng-wen, 1968–.

Chung-kuo kao-ku-hsüeh wen-hsien mu-lu 中國考古學文獻目錄. Prepared by Academia Sinica, Institute of Archaeology. Hong Kong, 1979.

Chung-kuo li-shih ti-t'u chi 中國歷史地圖集. Peking, Chung-hua ti-t'u hsüeh-hui, 1975.

Chung-kuo pien-chiang shih-ti ts'ung-shu 中國邊疆史地叢書. Taipei: Lien-kuo-feng ch'u-pan-she, 1969.

Chung-kuo she-hui k'o-hsüeh yüan k'ao-ku yen-chiu-so Shen-si kung-tso tui 中國社會科學院考古研究所陝西工作隊. "Shen-hsi Hua-yang, Ta-li Wei ch'ang-ch'eng k'an-ch'a chi 陝西華陽大荔魏長城勘查記." *Wen-wu* 1980, No. 6, 481–7.

Chung-kuo shih-hsüeh hui 中國史學會. *Ti shih-liu chieh kuo-chi li-shih k'o-hsüeh ta-hui Chung-kuo hsüeh-che lun-wen chi* 第十六屆國際歷史科學大會中國學者論文集. Peking: Chung-hua, 1985.

Chung-kuo shih-hsüeh ts'ung-shu 中國史學叢書. Ed. Wei Ch'i-hsien 魏齊賢. Taipei: Hsüeh-sheng shu-chü, 1965.

Chung-wei-hsien chih 中衛縣志. (1760).

Erh shih ssu shih 二十四史. Peking: Chung-hua shu-chü, 1959–77.

Fan Shou-chi 范守己. *Huang Ming Su-huang wai-shih* 皇明肅皇外史 (1582). Manuscript copy in Gest Oriental Library, Princeton University.

Fu Tso-lin 傅作霖. *Ning-hsia-shen k'ao-ch'a chi* 寧夏省考察記. Nanking: Chung-cheng, 1934.

Hagiwara Jumpei 荻原淳平. *Mindai Mōko shi kenkyū* 明代蒙古史研究. Kyoto: Dōbōsha, 1980.

"Doboku no hen zengo – keizai mondai o chūshin to suru Min-Mō kōshō 土木の變前後 – 經濟問題を中心とする 明蒙交涉." *Tōyōshi-kenkyū* 11 (1951) 3.193–212.

Haneda Toru 羽田亨 and Tamura Jitsuzō 田村實造, eds. *Mindai Man-Mō Shiryō* 明代滿蒙史料. Kyoto: Kyoto University, 1943–59.

Hibino Takeo 日比野丈夫. *Chūgoku rekishi chiri kenkyū* 中國歷史地理研究. Tokyo: Dōbōsha, 1978.

"Kyo-yō-kan no rekishi chiri 居庸關の歷史地理." In *Chūgoku rekishi chiri kenkyū* 中國歷史地理研究, pp. 293–315.

"Chizu ni arawareta Hou-t'ao suidō no hensen 地圖に現れた後唐水道の變遷." In *Chūgoku rekishi chiri kenkyū* 中國歷史地理研究, pp. 316–329.

Ho-t'ao chih 河套志 (1742).

Hou Chih-pu-tsu-chai ts'ung-shu 後知不足齋叢書. Ed. Pao T'ing-chüeh 鮑廷爵. Reprint of Ch'ing edition. Taipei: I-wen, 1968.

Hou Jen-chih 侯仁之. "Ming-tai Hsüan-Ta Shan-si san-chen ma-shih-k'ao 明宣大西三鎮馬市考." In *Ming-tai ching-chi* 明代經濟, edited by Pao Tsun-p'eng. Taipei: Hsüeh-sheng shu-chu, 1968, pp. 189–246.

Hsi-kuan chih 西關志 (1548). In *Kuo-li Pei-p'ing t'u-shu-kuan shan-pen-shu chiao-p'ien* reels 418.4–419.1.

Hsia Hsieh 夏燮. *Ming T'ung-chien* 明通鑑 (*c.* 1870). Reprint edn, Peking: Chung-hua, 1959.

Hsia Yen 夏言. *Hsia Kuei-chou hsien-sheng chi* 夏桂州先生集. Ming edn in Gest Oriental Library, Princeton University.

Hsiang Ch'un-sung 項春松. "Chao-wu-ta meng Yen Ch'in ch'ang-ch'eng i-chih tiao-ch'a pao-kao," 昭烏達盟燕秦長城遺址調查報告. In *Chung-kuo ch'ang-ch'eng i-chi tiao-ch'a pao-kao-chi* 中國長城遺迹調查報告集, pp. 6–20.

Hsiao Ch'i-ch'ing 蕭啓慶. "Pei-ya yu-mu min-tsu nan-ch'in ko-chung yüan-yin ti chien-t'ao 北亞遊牧民族南侵各種原因之檢討," pp. 303–322 in *Yüan-tai-shih hsin-t'an* Taipei: Hsin-wen-feng, 1981.

  Yüan-tai-shih hsin-t'an 元代史新探. Taipei: Hsin-wen-feng, 1981.

Hsü Ch'ien-hsüeh 徐乾學. *Ming-shih lieh-chuan* 明史列傳. In *Ming-tai shih-chi hui-k'an* 明代史籍彙刊. Taipei: Hsüeh-sheng, 1970.

Hsü Chü-ch'ing 徐琚青. "Pei-pien ch'ang-ch'eng k'ao 北邊長城考." *Shih-hsüeh nien-pao* 1.1 (1929), 15–19.

Hsü Ch'ung-hsi 許重熙. *Hsien-chang wai-shih hsü-pien* 憲章外史續編 (1633). Reprint edn, Taipei: Wei-wen, 1977.

Hsü Hsüeh-mo 徐學謨. *Shih-miao shih-yü lu* 世廟識餘錄 (Wan-li). Reprint edn, Taipei: Kuo-feng, 1965.

Hsü Hung 徐泓. *Ming-tai ti yen-fa* 明代的鹽法. Ph.D. dissertation: National Taiwan University, 1972.

Hsü Jih-chiu 徐日久. *Wu-pien tien-tse* 五邊典則 (1630). Hishi copy in Gest Oriental Library, Princeton University.

Hsü Lun 許論. *Chiu-pien t'u-lun* 九邊圖論 (1534). In *Hou chih-pu-tsu-chai ts'ung-shu*. Taipei: 1968.

Hsüeh-chin t'ao yüan 學津討原. Ed. Chang Hai-p'eng 張海鵬. In *Pai-pu ts'ung-shu chi-ch'eng*.

Hsüeh-chin t'ao-yüan 學津討原. Taipei: I-wen, 1965.

Hsüeh-hai lei-pien 學海類編. Ed. Ts'ao Jung 曹溶. In *Pai-pu ts'ung-shu chi-ch'eng* 百部叢書集成

Huang-ch'ao fan-shu yü-ti ts'ung-shu 皇朝藩屬輿地叢書. (Ch'ing, ed. P'u shih 浦氏, comp.). Reprint edn, Taipei: Kuang-wen, 1968.

Huang Lin-shu 黃麟書. *Pien-sai yen-chiu* 邊塞研究. Hong Kong: Tsao-yang, 1979.

  Ch'in-huang ch'ang-ch'eng k'ao 秦皇長城考. Hong Kong: Tsao-yang, 1972.

  T'ang-tai shih-jen sai-fang ssu-hsiang ch'u-kao 唐代詩人塞防思想初稿. Hong Kong: Tsao-yang, 1982.

Huang Shih 黃奭. *Huang Shih i-shu k'ao* 黃氏逸書考. Reprint edn, Taipei: I-wen, 1971.

Hung Liang-chi 洪亮吉. *Shih-liu-kuo chiang-yü chih* 十六國疆域志. Shanghai: Commercial Press, 1958.

Hung Liang-chi 洪亮吉 and Wu Yü-chui 吳裕垂. *Li-ch'ao shih-an* 歷朝史案. Ch'ien-lung edition in Harvard-Yenching library.

Huo Chi 霍冀. *Chiu-pien t'u-shuo* 九邊圖說 (1569). In *Chung-kuo pien-chiang shih-ti ts'ung-shu*.

I Chih 伊志. "Ming-tai 'Ch'i-T'ao' Shih-mo 明代「棄套」始末." In *Ming-tai Pien-fang* 明代邊防, edited by Pao Tsun-p'eng. Taipei, 1968, pp. 189–204.

Inaba Iwakichi 稻葉岩吉. "Mindai Ryōtō no henshō 明代遼東の邊牆." in *Manshū rekishi chiri*, 1.460–546. Edited by Yanai Watari. Tokyo: Maruzen, 1941.

Itō Chūta 伊東忠太. *Tōyō kenchiku no kenkyū* 東洋建築之研究. Tokyo: Ryūginsha, 1943.

Jagchid, Sechin. *Pei-Ya yu-mu min-tsu yü chung-yüan nung-yeh min-tsu chien ti ho-p'ing, chan-cheng, yü mao-i chih kuan-hsi* 北亞游牧民族與中原農業民族間的和平、戰爭與貿易之關係. Taipei: Cheng-chung, 1973.

Kan-chen chih 甘鎮志 (1657). Reprint edn, Taipei: Hsüeh-sheng, 1968.

Kan-su t'ung-chih 甘肅通志 (1736). Reprint edn, Taipei, Wen-hai, 1966.

K'ang Lo 康樂. "T'ang-tai ch'ien-ch'i ti pien-fang 唐代前期的邊防." Master's thesis: National Taiwan University, 1974.

"T'ang-tai ch'ien-ch'i ti pien-fang 唐代前期的邊防." *Tung-hai ta-hsüeh li-shih hsüeh-pao* I (1977), 1–40.

Kao Wei-yüeh 高維嶽 et al., comp. *Sui-te chih-li chou chih* 綏德直隸州志 (1905). Microfilm in Harvard-Yenching Library.

Ko Shan-lin and Lu Ssu-hsien 蓋山林 陸思覽. "Yang-shan nan-lu ti Chao ch'ang-ch'eng 陽山南麓的趙長城." In *Chung-kuo ch'ang-ch'eng i-chi tiao-ch'a pao-kao-chi*, pp. 21–24.

K'ou-pei san-t'ing chih 口北三廳志 (1758). In *Chung-kuo fang-chih ts'ung-shu*, Taipei, 1968.

Ku Chieh-kang 顧頡剛. *Shih-lin tsa-shih* 史林雜識. Peking: Chung-hua, 1963.

Ku Chieh-kang and Shih Nien-hai 顧頡剛 史念海. *Chung-kuo chiang-yü yen-ko shih* 中國疆域沿革史. Shanghai: Commercial Press, 1938.

Ku Tsu-yü 顧祖禹. *Tu-shih fang-yü chi-yao* 讀史方輿紀要. Peking: Chung-hua, 1957.

Ku Yen-wu 顧炎武. *T'ien-hsia chün-kuo li-ping shu* 天下郡國利病書. In *Ssu-pu ts'ung-kan*. *Ching-tun k'ao-ku-lu* 京東考古錄. In *Hsüeh-hai lei-pien* 學海. *Jih-chih-lu* 日知錄. In *Ssu-pu pei-yao*. 四部備要.

Ku Ying-t'ai 谷應泰. *Ming-shih chi-shih pen-mo* 明史記事本末 (1658). Reprint edn, Taipei: San-min, 1969.

Ku-yüan-chou chih 固原州志 (1909). Reprint edn, Taipei, Hsüeh-sheng, 1967.

Kuei-hsien chiao-yü-chu, Kuei-hsien kung-nung shih-fan 貴縣教育局貴縣工農師範, eds. *Meng chiang-nü shih i-chu tsun-ju fan-fa ti ta tu-ts'ao* 孟姜女是一株尊儒反法的大毒草. Kuang-hsi jen-min, 1975.

Kuo-hsüeh chi-pen ts'ung-shu 國學基本叢書. Ed. Wang Yün-wu 王雲五. Taipei: Taiwan Commercial Press, 1968.

Kuo-li Pei-p'ing t'u-shu-kuan shan-pen ts'ung-shu 國立北平圖書館善本叢書. Ed. Hsieh Kuo-chen 謝國楨. Shanghai: Shang-wu, 1937.

Kuo-li Pei-p'ing t'u-shu-kuan shan-pen-shu chiao-p'ien 國立北京圖書館善本書膠片. Microfilms by Library of Congress, Washington, D.C., 1972–3.

Kuo-li T'ai-wan Ta-hsüeh shih-chou nien-hsiao-ch'ing chuan-k'an 國立臺灣大學十周年校慶專刊. Taipei: Taiwan University, 1956.

Kuo Shao-yü 郭紹虞. "Ming-tai ti wen-jen chi-t'uan 明代的文人集團." *Wen-i fu-hsing* (July 1948), 86–117.

Kuo Shu-tsu 郭述祖. "Wan-li ch'ang-ch'eng tung-shou chung-chen shan-hai-kuan 萬里長城東首重鎮山海關." *Wen-wu T'ien-ti* (1982) 1.1–2.

Li Chi-fu 李吉甫. *Yüan-ho chün-hsien chih* 元和郡縣志 (T'ang). Peking: Chung-hua, 1983.

Li Kuo-pin 黎國彬. "Hsien-tsai ti Ch'ang-ch'eng shih ho-shih chien-tsao? Ku Ch'ang-ch'eng ti i-chih tsai chin ho ch'u? 現在的長城是何時建造的？古長城的遺迹在今何處?" *Li-shih chiao-hsüeh* 3.1 (1952): 22.

Li Lung-hua [Lee Lung-wah] 李龍華. "Ming-tai ti k'ai-chung-fa 明代的開中法." *Journal of the Institute of Chinese Studies of the Chinese University of Hong Kong* IV.2 (1971): 371–493.

Li Nan 李楠. *Shan-hsi ssu-chen t'u-shuo* 陝西四鎮圖說 (1616). Microfilm of original edition in Tōyō Bunko.

Li Shih 李栻. *Li-tai hsiao-shih* 歷代小史. Taipei: Commercial Press, 1969.

Li Shu-fang 李漱芳. "Ming-tai pien-ch'iang yen-ko k'ao-lüeh 明代邊牆沿革考略." *Yü-kung* 5.1 (March 1936): 1–15.

Li Wen-hsin 李文信. "Chung-kuo pei-pu ch'ang-ch'eng yen-ko k'ao 中國北部長城沿革考." *She-hui k'o-hsüeh chi-k'an* 1979 1: 144–53; 2: 128–41.

Liang Ch'i-ch'ao 梁啓超. *Chung-kuo li-shih yen-chiu fa* 中國歷史研究法. Taipei: Taiwan Chung-hua shu-chü, 1967.

Liang Fang-chung 梁方仲. "Ming-tai ti Min-ping 明代的民兵." *Chung-kuo she-hui ching-chi-shih chi-k'an* 5 (1937): 201–234.

Liang Yü-sheng 梁玉繩. *Shih-chi chih-i* 史記志疑 (1576). Peking: Chung-hua, 1981.

Liao-tung chih 遼東志 (1537). Reprint ed. Taipei: T'ai-lien kuo-feng, 1969.

Lin Shu-hui 林樹惠. "Ming chih pei-pien pei-yü 明之北邊備禦." *Shih-hsüeh nien-pao* 3.2 (1940), 73–99.

Lin-yü-hsien chih 臨榆縣志 (1929). Reprint edn, Taipei: Ch'eng-wen, 1968.

Lo Che-wen 羅哲文. *Ch'ang-ch'eng Shih-hua* 長城史話. Peking: Chung-hua, 1963.

  "Lin-t'ao Ch'in ch'ang-ch'eng, Tun-huang Yü-men-kuan, Chiu-ch'üan Chia-yü-kuan k'an-ch'a chien-chi 臨洮秦長城、敦煌、玉門關、酒泉、嘉峪關勘查簡記. *Wen-wu* 6 (1964), 47–57.

  "Wan-li Ch'ang-ch'eng – Shan-hai-kuan, Chü-yung-kuan Yün-t'ai ho Pa-ta-ling, Chia-yü-kuan 萬里長城－山海關、居庸關、雲臺和八達嶺嘉峪關." *Wen-wu* 8 (1977), 65–74.

  "Wan-li ch'ang-ch'eng 萬里長城." *Wen-wu T'ien-ti* (1981), No. 1, 3–4.

  Ch'ang-ch'eng 長城. Peking: Pei-ching ch'u-pan-she, 1982.

Lo Che-wen and Liu Wen-yüan 羅哲文 劉文淵. "Ch'ang-ch'eng ti pao-hu, yen-chiu ho li-yung 長城的保護研究和利用." *Jen-min jih-pao* (overseas edition), 3 April 1986, p. 2, and 4 April p.2.

Lo Hung-hsien 羅洪先. *Kuang-yü-t'u* 廣輿圖 (1541). Reprint edn, Taipei: Hsüeh-hai, 1969.

Lu Kung 路工, ed. *Meng Chiang-nü wan-li hsüan-fu chi* 孟姜女萬里尋夫記. Shanghai: Shanghai ch'u-pan she, 1955.

Lu Yao-tung 逯耀東. *Lo-ma ch'ang-ch'eng* 勒馬長城. Taipei: Shih-pao ch'u-pan-she, 1977.

Lu Ying-yang 陸應陽. *Kuang-yü-chi* 廣輿記 (1600). Reprint edn, Taipei: Hsüeh-hai, 1969.

Maeda Masano 前田正名. "Hoku-i heijō jidai no orudosu sabaku minami midori michi 北魏平城時代のオルドス沙漠南綠路." *Tōyōshi kenkyū* 31 (1972): 61–89.

Mao Yüan-i 毛元儀. *Wu-pei chih* 武備志 (1621). Ming edition in collection of Gest Oriental Library, Princeton University.

Ming Shih-lu 明實錄. Reprint edn, Taipei: Academia Sinica, 1963–.

Ming-tai shih-chi hui-k'an 明代史籍彙刊. Ed. Ch'ü Wan-li 屈萬里. Taipei: Hsüeh-sheng shu-chü, 1969.

Murata Jiro 村田治郎, ed. *Kyoyōkan* 居庸關 2v. Kyoto: Faculty of Engineering, Kyoto University, 1947.

Ning-hsia chih 寧夏志 (1577). In *Pien-chiang fang-chih*, 邊疆方志. Taipei, 1969.

Ning-hsia-fu chih 寧夏府志 (1798). In *Chung-kuo fang-chih ts'ung-shu*.

Ning-hsia hsin-chih 寧夏新志 (1501). Reprint edn, Taipei: Ch'eng-wen, 1968.

Ning-hsia Tzu-chih-ch'ü po-wu-kuan 寧夏自治區博物館. "Ning-hsia ching-nei Chan-kuo Ch'in Han ch'ang-ch'eng i-chi 寧夏境內戰國秦漢長城遺迹." In *Chung-kuo ch'ang-ch'eng i-chi tiao-ch'a pao-kao-chi*, pp. 45–51.

Ning Mo-kung 寧墨公. "Ming-tai chiu-pien hsüeh-shuo chih yen-chiu 明代九邊學說之研究." *Chung-kuo pien-chiang* 1 (1942) 5–7, 11–13.

Pai-pu ts'ung-shu chi-ch'eng 百部叢書集成. Taipei: I-wen, 1965.

P'an Ch'eng-pin 潘承彬. "Ming-tai chih Liao-tung pien-ch'iang 明代之遼東邊牆." *Yü-kung* 6.3/4 (1936), 61–80.

Pao Tsun-p'eng 包遵彭, ed. *Ming-tai ching-chi* 明代經濟. Taipei: Hsüeh-sheng shu-chü, 1968.

  ed. *Ming-tai cheng-chih* 明代政治. Taipei: Hsüeh-sheng shu-chü, 1968.

  ed. *Ming-tai pien-fang* 明代邊防. Taipei: Hsüeh-sheng shu-chü, 1968.

Pien-chiang fang-chih 邊疆方志. Taipei: 1969.

Pu-ni-a-lin 布尼阿林. "Ho-pei-sheng Wei-ch'ang-hsien Yen Ch'in ch'ang-ch'eng tiao-ch'a pao-kao" 河北省圍場縣燕秦長城調查報告." In *Chung-kuo ch'ang-ch'eng i-chi tiao-ch'a pao-kao-chi*, pp. 40–4.

Shan-pei wen-wu tiao-ch'a cheng-chi tsu 陝北文物調查征集組. "T'ung-wan-ch'eng yi-chih tiao-ch'a 統萬城遺址調查." *Wen-wu* (1957) 10.52–5.

Shen Shih-hsing 申世行. *Ta Ming hui-tien* 大明會典 (1587). Reprint edn, Taipei: Hsin-wen-feng, 1976.

Shen Te-fu 沈德符. *Wan-li yeh-huo-pien* 萬曆野獲編 (1619). Peking: Chung-hua, 1980.

Shen Yüeh 沈越. *Huang Ming Chia Lung liang-ch'ao wen-chien lu* 皇明嘉隆兩朝聞見錄 (1599). Hishi copy in collection of Gest Oriental Library, Princeton University.

Shih Nien-hai 史念海. "Huang-ho chung-yu Chan-kuo chi Ch'in shih chu ch'ang-ch'eng i-chi ti t'an-so 黃河中游戰國及秦時諸長城遺迹的探索." In *Chung-kuo ch'ang-ch'eng i-chi tiao-ch'a pao-kao-chi*, pp. 52–67.

"O-erh-to-ssu kao-yüan tung-pu Chan-kuo shih-ch'i Ch'in ch'ang-ch'eng i-chi t'an-so chi 鄂爾多斯高原東部戰國時期秦長城遺迹探索記." In *Chung-kuo ch'ang-ch'eng i-chi tiao-ch'a pao-kao-chi*, pp. 68–75.

Shimzu Taiji 清水泰次. "Minsho ni okeru gunton no tenkai to sono soshiki 明初に就ける軍屯の展開とその組織." In *Mindai tochi seidōshi kenkyū*, pp. 269–328.

"Minmatsu no gunshō 明末之軍餉. In *Ishihama hakushi koki kinen tōyōshi ronsō* 石濱博士古稀記念東洋史論叢·1933, pp. 435–61.

"Mindai gunton no hōkai 明代軍屯の崩潰." In *Mindai tochi seidōshi kenkyū*, pp. 329–54.

"Tainei toshi no naishi ni tsukite 大寧都司の內徙につきて." *Tōyō gakuhō* 8 (1918), 125–41.

Mindai tochi seidoshi kenkyū 明代土地制度史研究 (Tokyo: Daian, 1968).

Shou P'eng-fei 壽鵬飛. *Li-tai ch'ang-ch'eng k'ao* 歷代長城考. (1941).

So Kwan-wai (Su Chün-wei) 蘇均煒. "Ta-hsüeh-shih Yen Sung hsin-lun 大學士嚴嵩新論." Paper presented at the International Conference of Ming and Ch'ing Studies, Nankai University, 5–8 August 1980.

Ssu-k'u ch'üan-shu chen-pen 四庫全書珍本, eleventh series. Reprint of Ch'ing originals, ed. Wang Yün-wu 王雲五. Taipei: Shang-wu, 1971–.

Ssu-ma Kuang 司馬光. *Tzu-chih t'ung-chien* 資治通鑑. Peking: Chung-hua, 1956.

Ssu-pu pei-yao 四部備要 (1936). Facsimile edn, Taipei: Chung-hua shu chü, 1965.

Ssu-pu ts'ung-k'an ch'u pien so-pen. Taipei: Shang-wu, 1967.

Ssu-pu ts'ung-k'an san-pien 四部叢刊三編. Ed. Chang Yüan-chi 張元濟. Shanghai: Shang-wu, 1935–6.

Su-chen chih 肅鎮志 (1657). Reprint edn, Taipei: Ch'eng-wen, 1970.

Su-chou hsin chih 肅州新志 (1737). Reprint edn, Taipei: 1967.

Su Hsin 蘇莘. "Ming pien-ch'iang cheng-ku 明邊牆證古." *Ti-li tsa-chih* 6 (1915), No. 15.

Sui-yüan ch'üan-chih 綏遠全志 (1907). Reprint edn, Taipei: Hua-wen, 1969.

Sun Wen 孫文 [Sun Yat-sen 孫逸仙]. *Sun-wen hsüeh-shuo* 孫文學說. Taipei: Yüan-tung, 1957.

Tamura Jitsuzō 田村實造. "Mindai no kyū-hen-chin 明代の九邊鎮." In *Ishihama sensei koki kinen tōyōgaku ronsō*, pp. 290–300. Osaka: Kansai Daigaku, 1958.

"Kyu Shun to Daigakuengiho 丘濬と大學衍義補." *Tōhō Gakkai Sōritsu Jūgo-shūnen kinen Tōhōgaku ronshū*. Tokyo: Tōhō Gakkai, 1962.

"Mindai no hoppen bōei taisei 明代の北邊防衛體制." In *Mindai Man-Mō Shi Kenkyū*, pp. 73–161. Edited by Tamura Jitsuzō. Kyoto: Faculty of Letters, Kyoto University, 1963.

"Mindai no Orudosu: Tenjun, Seika jidai 明代のオルドス天順成化時代." *Tōyōshi kenkyū* 19 (1960): 1–14.

"Aribuka no ran ni tsuite アリブカの亂について." *Tōyōshi kenkyū* 15 (1955), 171–86.

ed. *Mindai Man-Mō Shi Kenkyū* 明代滿蒙史研究. Kyoto: Faculty of Letters, Kyoto University, 1963.

T'an Ch'ien 談遷. *Kuo ch'üeh* 國榷 (*c.* 1653). Reprint edn, Taipei: Ting-wen, 1958.

T'ang Hsiao-feng 唐曉峰. "Nei Meng-ku hsi-pei-pu Ch'in Han ch'ang-ch'eng tiao-ch'a chi 內蒙古西北部秦漢長城調查記." *Wen-wu* (1977), No. 5, pp. 16–24.

T'ang Hsiu-mei 唐秀美. "Chang Chü-cheng ti cheng-chih ssu-hsiang yü ts'e-lüeh yen-chiu 張居正的政治思想與策略研究." Master's Thesis: National Taiwan University, 1971.

T'ang Shun-chih 唐順之. *Ching-ch'üan hsien-sheng wen-chi* 荆川先生文集. Taipei: Shang-wu, 1967.

Teng Yen-lin 鄧衍林. *Chung-kuo pien-chiang t'u-chi-lu* 中國邊疆圖籍錄. Shanghai: Commercial Press, 1958.

Terada Takanobu 寺田隆信. "Kaichūhō no tenkai 開中法の展開." In *Mindai Man-Mō Shi Kenkyū*, pp. 163–218. Edited by Tamura Jitsuzō. Kyoto: Faculty of Letters, Kyoto University, 1963.

"Minun ryō to tonden ryō – Mindai ni okeru henshō mindai no ichi sokumen 民運糧と屯田糧—明代における邊餉問題の一側面." *Tōyō shi kenkyū* 21 (1962): 196–217.

Tseng Hsien 曾銑. *Tseng Hsiang-min kung fu t'ao i* 曾襄敏公復套議. In *Kuo-li Pei-p'ing t'u-shu-kuan shan-pen-shu chiao-p'ien*, reel 39 (6).

Ts'ui Pao 崔豹. *Ku-chin chu* 古今注. In *Ssu-pu pei-yao*, vol. C-12.

Ts'ung-shu chi-ch'eng chien-pien 叢書集成簡編, ed. Wang Yün-wu 王雲五. Taipei: Shang-wu, 1965–6.

Tu Yu 杜佑. *Tung-tien* 通典. Shanghai: Shang-wu, 1936.

Uemura Seiji 植村清二. *Banri no chōjō* 萬里の長城. Tokyo: Sōgensha, 1974.

Wada Sei 和田清. *Tōashi kenkyū (Mōko hen)* 東亞史研究(蒙古篇). Tokyo: The Tōyō Bunko Publication Series A, No. 42, 1959.

Wan Ssu-t'ung 萬斯同. *Hsin yüeh fu tz'u* 新樂府詞. 1869 edn, in collection of Harvard-Yenching Library.

Wang Chih-ch'en 王之臣 *et al.*, comp. *Shuo-fang-tao chih* 朔方道志 (1925). Copy in Harvard-Yenching Library.

Wang Chi-lin 王吉林. "T'ung-i ch'i-chien pei-Wei yü sai-wai min-tsu ti kuan-hsi 統一期間北魏與塞外民族的關係." *Shih-hsüeh hui-k'an* 10 (1980): 65–86.

Wang Ch'i 王圻. *Hsü wen-hsien t'ung-k'ao* 續文獻通考 (1586). Reprint edn, Taipei: Wen-hai, 1979.

Wang Ch'ung-wu 王崇武. "Ming-tai ti chiang-yü yü Ming-tai ti kuo-fang 明代的疆域與明代的國防." *Hsien-tai hsüeh-pao* 1 (1947) 2.3, 31–42.

Wang Fei-tsao 王飛藻, comp. *Ta-t'ung-fu chih* 大同府志 (1776). Microfilm in Harvard-Yenching Library.

Wang Kuo-liang 王國良. *Chung-kuo ch'ang-ch'eng yen-ko k'ao* 中國長城沿革考. Shanghai: Commercial Press, 1931.

Wang Shih-chen 王世貞. *Ming-feng chi* 鳴鳳記. Shanghai: Chung-hua, 1950.

Wang Shih-ch'i 王志琦. *San-yün ch'ou-tsu k'ao* 三雲籌俎考 (Wan-li). In *Kuo-li Pei-p'ing t'u-shu-kuan shan-pen ts'ung-shu ti i chi*.

Wang Yü-ch'üan 王毓銓. *Ming-tai ti chün-t'un* 明代的軍屯. Peking: Chung-hua shu-chü, 1965.

Wang Yün 王惲. *Ch'iu-chien hsien-sheng ta-ch'üan wen-chi* 秋澗先生大全文集. In *Ssu-pu ts'ung-k'an*.

Wang Yung 王庸 and Mao Nai-wen 茅乃文, eds. *Chung-kuo ti-hsüeh lun-wen so-yin* 中國地學論文索引. National Central Library, Peiping, 1934. Reprint edn, Taipei, 1970.

Wei Huan 魏煥. *Huang-ming chiu-pien k'ao* 皇明九邊考 (1541). Reprint of Chia-ching edn, Taipei: Hua-wen, 1968.

Wen-wu pien-chi wei-yüan-hui 文物編輯委員會, ed. *Chung-kuo ch'ang-ch'eng i-chi tiao-ch'a pao-kao-chi* 中國長城遺迹調查報告集. Peking: Wen-wu ch'u-pan-she, 1981.

Wu Chi-hua 吳緝華. "Lun Ming-tai pien-fang nei-i yü ch'ang-ch'eng hsiu-chü 論明代邊防內移與長城修築." *Tung-hai Ta-hsüeh li-shih hsüeh-pao* 4 (1981), 25–47.

"Lun Ming-tai pei-fang pien-fang nei-i chih yin-hsiang 論明代北方邊防內移之影響." *Hsin-ya hsüeh-pao* 13 (1979), 363–408.

Ming-tai chih-tu-shih lun-ts'un 明代制度史論叢. Taipei, 1971.

"Ming-tai Tung-sheng ti she-fang yü ch'i-fang 明代東勝的設防與棄防." In *Ming-tai chih-tu-shih lun-ts'un*, pp. 319–348.

"Ming-tai tsui-kao chün-shih chi-kou ti yen-pien 明代最高軍事機構的演變." *Nanyang University Journal* vi (1972): 144–55.

"Ming-tai chien-kuo tui-wai ti chi-pen t'ai-tu chi chüeh-ts'e 明代建國對外的基本態度之決策." *Journal of Oriental Studies* [*Tung-fang wen-hua*] 16.1/2 (1978), 184–93.

Wu Jui-teng 吳瑞登. *Liang-ch'ao hsien-chang lu* 兩朝憲章錄 (1594). Hishi copy in collection of Gest Oriental Library, Princeton University.

Wu Sen 吳森. "Ch'ang-ch'eng ti ku-chin chi ch'i chia-chih 長城的古今和其價值." *Ch'ang Liu* 57 (1978), 22–4.

Wu T'ing-hsieh 吳廷燮. *Ming tu-fu nien-piao* 明都府年代. Republican ed., n.d., n.p., copy in Harvard-Yenching Library.

Yan I-ch'ing 楊一清. *Hsi-cheng jih lu* 西征日錄. In *Pai-pu ts'ung-shu chi-ch'eng*.

Kuan-chung tsou-i 關中奏議. In *Ssu-k'u ch'uan-shu chen-pen wu-chi* (五集). Taipei, 1974.

Yanai Watari 箭內亙 *et al.*, eds. *Manshū rekishi chiri*, 2 vols. 滿洲歷史地理 Tokyo: Maruzen, 1940.

Yang Ch'üan 楊泉. *Wu-li lun* 物理論. In Huang Shih, *Huang Shih i-shu k'ao*. Taipei: I-wen, 1971.

Yang Hu 楊暘, ed. *Ming-tai Nu-erh-kan tu-ssu chi ch'i wei-so yen-chiu* 明代奴几干都司及其衛所研究. Honan: Chung-chou shu-hua she, 1982).

Yang Shou-ching 楊守敬. *Li-tai yü-ti yen-ko hsien-yao t'u* 歷代輿地沿革險要圖 (1878–1911). Reprint edn, Taipei: Lien-ching, 1975.

Yeh Sheng 葉盛. *Shui-tung jih-chi* 水東日記. Peking: Chung-hua, 1980.

Yeh Tsu-hao 葉祖灝. *Ning-hsia ti chin-hsi* 寧夏的今昔. Taipei: Commercial Press, 1969 (1st edn 1947).

Yen Sheng 琰生. "Ku ch'ang-ch'eng ho chin ch'ang-ch'eng chiu-ching yu shen-mo pu-t'ung? Ku ch'ang-ch'eng shih-fou hai tsai? Ch'in Shih-huang so chu ti ch'ang-ch'eng shih shen-mo ch'ang-ch'eng? 古長城和今長城究竟有甚麼不同？古長城是否還在？秦始所築的長城是甚麼長城?" *Li-shih chiao-hsüeh* (1955), No. 10, p. 56.

Yen Sung 嚴嵩. *Chia-ching tsou tui lu* 嘉靖奏對錄. In *Kuo-li Pei-p'ing t'u-shu-kuan shan-pen-shu chiao-p'ien*, reel 65 (5).

Ch'ien-shan-t'ang chi 鈐山堂集 (1559). Hishi copy in collection of Gest Oriental Library, Princeton University.

Nan-kung shu-lüeh 南宮疏略. In *Kuo-li Pei-p'ing t'u-shu-kuan shan-pen-shu chiao-p'ien*, reel 40 (1).

Yen Wen-ju 閻文儒. "Ho-hsi k'ao-ku tsa-chi 河西考古雜記." *Wen-wu k'ao-ku tzu-liao* 40 (1953) No. 12, 53–70.

Yen-an-fu chih 延安府志 ed. Hung Hui 洪蕙, (1802). In *Chung-kuo fang-chih ts'ung-shu*.

Yen-an-fu chih. Yang Huai 楊懷, ed. (1504). Microfilm, *Kuo-li Pei-p'ing t'u-shu-kuan shan pen shu chiao p'ien*, 487 (5)–488 (1). Washington, D.C.: Library of Congress, 1972–73.

Yen-ch'ing wei chih lüeh 延慶衛志略 (1745). Reprint edn, Taipei: Ch'eng-wen, 1970.

Yü-lin-fu chih 榆林府志 (1686). Reprint edn, Taipei: 1968.

Bibliography

Yü T'ung-k'uei 俞同奎. "T'an wan-li ch'ang-ch'eng 談萬里長城." *Wen-wu k'ao-ku tzu-liao*
   6 (1956): 66–72.
Yung-p'ing-fu chih 永平府志 (1879). Reprint edn, Taipei: Hsüeh-sheng, 1968.

Western materials

"Agricultural Conditions in Suiyuan." *The Chinese Economic Monthly* 3.10 (1926), 413–17.
Airs de Touen-houang. Ed. P. Demiéville *et al.*, with French translation by Demiéville and an
   introduction by Jao Tsung-i. Paris: Editions du Centre National de la Recherche
   Scientifique, 1971.
Aldridge, A. Owen. "Voltaire and the Cult of China." *Tamkang Review* 2.2–3.1 (October
   1971–April 1972), 25–49.
Allom, Thomas, and G. N. Wright, *China, in a series of views, displaying the scenery, architecture,
   and social habits of that ancient empire* 2 vols. London and Paris: Fisher, Son, & Co., n.d.
   (Preface, July 1843).
Allsen, Thomas T. "The Princes of the Left Hand: An Introduction to the History of the
   Ulus of Orda in the Thirteenth and Early Fourteenth Centuries." *Archivum Eurasiae
   Medii Aevi* 5 (1985[1987]), 5–40.
Anderson, Andrew Runni. *Alexander's Gate, Gog and Magog, and the Inclosed Nations.*
   Monographs of the Mediaeval Academy of America, No. 5. Cambridge, Mass.,
   1932.
Appleton, William W. *A Cycle of Cathay: The Chinese Vogue in England During the Seventeenth
   and Eighteenth Centuries.* New York: Columbia University Press, 1951.
Aubin, Françoise, ed. *Études Song in Memoriam Étienne Balazs.* Evreux: Mouton, 1971.
Baddeley, John Frederick. *Russia, Mongolia, China.* London: Macmillan, 1919.
Barfield, Thomas J. *The Central Asian Arabs of Afghanistan: Pastoral Nomadism in Transition.*
   Austin: University of Texas Press, 1981.
   "The Hsiung-nu Imperial Confederacy: Organization and Foreign Policy," *Journal of
   Asian Studies* 41.1(1981), 45–61.
Barnes, Irene H. *Behind the Great Wall: The Story of the C.E.Z.M.S. Work and Workers in China.*
   London: Marshall Brothers, n.d.
Barrow, Sir John. *Travels in China.* Philadelphia: W. F. M'Laughlin, 1805 (German trans.
   1804; French trans. 1805; Dutch trans. 1809).
Barth, Fredrik. *Nomads of South Persia: The Basseri Tribe of the Khamseh Confederacy.* Oslo
   University Press/London: George Allen & Unwin, Ltd., 1961.
Barthold, V. V. *La Découverte de L'Asie.* Paris: Payot, 1947.
Bauer, Wolfgang, ed. *China und die Fremden: 3000 Jahre Auseinandersetzung in Krieg und Frieden.*
   Munich: C. H. Beck, 1980.
Beauvoir, Ludovic Hébert, Comte de. *Voyage Autour du Monde.* 3 vols. Paris: Plon, 1872.
Bell, John. *A Journey from St Petersburg to Pekin, 1719–22.* Ed. and with an introduction by
   J. L. Stevenson. New York: Barnes and Noble, 1966.
Bielenstein, Hans. "The Restoration of the Han Dynasty." *Bulletin of the Museum of Far
   Eastern Antiquities* 26(1954), 1–209; 31(1959), 1–287; 39(1967), 1–198.
Biot, Edouard. *Mémoire sur les colonies militaires et agricoles des Chinois.* Paris: Imprimerie
   Nationale, 1850.
Birrell, Anne. *New Songs from a Jade Terrace: An Anthology of Early Chinese Love Poetry,
   Translated with Annotations and Introduction.* London: George Allen & Unwin, 1982.
Black, Charles E. D. "The Great Wall of China." *Calcutta Review* January 1903, 34–45.
Bodde, Derk. *China's First Unifier: A Study of the Ch'in Dynasty As Seen in the Life of Li Ssu,*

265

280?–208 B.C. Leiden: E.J. Brill, 1938; reprint edn, Hong Kong University Press, 1967.

"The State and Empire of Ch'in." In *The Cambridge History of China*, vol. 1 edited by Denis Twitchett and Michael Loewe, pp. 20–102. Cambridge: Cambridge University Press.

trans. *Statesman, Patriotic, and General in Ancient China: Three Shih Chi Biographies of the Ch'in Dynasty (255–206 B.C.)*. New Haven: American Oriental Society, 1940.

Boorman, Howard, L., ed. *Biographical Dictionary of Republican China*. New York: Columbia University Press, 1967–79.

Boswell, James. *Boswell's Life of Johnson*. 6 vols. Ed. G. B. Hill, revised by L. F. Powell. Oxford: Clarendon Press, 1934.

Boyle, J. A. "The Alexander Legend in Central Asia." *Folklore* 85(1974), 217–28.

Breeze, David, J., and Dobson, Brian. *Hadrian's Wall*. Harmondsworth, England: Penguin Books, 1978.

Busch, Heinrich. "The Tung-lin Shu-yüan and its political and philosophical significance." *Monumenta Serica* 14 (1949–55), 1–163.

Bush, Susan. "Archaeological Remains of the Chin Dynasty." *Bulletin of Sung-Yüan Studies* 17 (1981) 6–31.

Carles, W. R. "Problems in Exploration II. Ordos." *The Geographical Journal* 33.6(1909), 668–79.

Cerny, Philip G. "Foreign policy leadership and national integration." *British Journal of International Studies* 5.1 (April, 1979), pp. 59–85.

Chan, Albert. *The Glory and Decline of the Ming Dynasty*. Norman: University of Oklahoma Press, 1982.

Chang Ch'un-shu. "The Colonization of the Ho-hsi Region in the Former Han Period. A Study of the Han Frontier System." Ph.D. dissertation: Harvard University, 1963.

"Military Aspects of Han Wu-ti's Northern and Northwestern Campaigns." *Harvard Journal of Asiatic Studies* 26(1966), 148–73.

Chang, Kwang-chih. *Shang Civilization*. New Haven and London: Yale University Press, 1980.

Art, myth, and ritual: the path to political authority in ancient China. Cambridge, Mass.: Harvard University Press, 1983.

Chang, Pin-ts'un. "Chinese Maritime Trade: The Case of Sixteenth-century Fu-chien (Fukien)." Ph.D. dissertation: Princeton University, 1983.

Chapin, William W. "Glimpses of Korea and China." *National Geographic Magazine* 22.11(1910).

Chavannes, Edouard, "Les plus anciens spécimens de la cartographie Chinoise." *Bulletin de l'École Française d'Extrême-Orient* 3(1903), 214–47.

Les Documents Chinois Découverts par Aurel Stein dans les Sables du Turkestan Oriental. Oxford: Imprimerie de l'Université, 1913.

trans. *Les mémoires historiques de Se-ma Ts'ien*. 5 vols. Paris: Leroux, 1895–1905.

Cheng Dalin. *The Great Wall of China*. Hong Kong: South China Morning Post and New China News, 1984.

Cheng Te-k'un. "Ch'in-Han Architectural Remains." *Journal of the Institute of Chinese Studies of the Chinese University of Hong Kong* 9.2(1978), 503–84.

Chin Shou-shen, "The Great Wall of China," *China Reconstructs* 11.1(1962), 20–4.

China: Nagel's Encyclopedia-Guide. Geneva, Paris, Munich: 1973.

"Chinese Discover 62 More Miles of The Great Wall." *The Washington Post*, 27 February 1983, A22.

Bibliography

Chu, Hung-lam. "Ch'iu Chün (1421–1495) and the *Ta-Hsüeh Yen-I Pu*: Statecraft Thought in Fifteenth-Century China." Ph.D. dissertation: Princeton University, 1983.

Chu K'e-chen. "Climatic changes in Chinese history." *Scientia Sinica* 16.2(1973), 226–49.

Chu, Wen-djang. *The Moslem Rebellions in Northwest China 1862–1878*. The Hague: Mouton, 1966.

Clapp, Frederick, G. "Along and Across the Great Wall of China." *The Geographical Review* 9(1920), 221–49.

Cleaves, Francis Woodman, trans. *The Secret History of the Mongols*. Cambridge, Mass.: Harvard University Press, 1982.

Cohen, Warren I. *America's Response to China*. New York: Wiley, 1971.

Cordier, Henri. *Bibliotheca Sinica*. Paris: E. Guilmoto, 1904–8.

"Bulletin Critique" [Review of Geil, *The Great Wall*]. *T'oung Pao*, second series, 11(1910), 690–1.

Cranmer-Byng, J. L., ed. *An Embassy to China Being the Journal Kept by Lord Macartney During his Embassy to the Emperor Ch'ien-lung, 1793–94*. London: Longmans, 1962.

Crawford, Robert B. "Eunuch Power in the Ming Dynasty." *T'oung Pao* 49(1961), 115–48.

Cressey, George B. "The Ordos Desert of Inner Mongolia." *Denison University Bulletin* 28.8(1933), 155–248.

Czeglédy, K. "The Syriac Legend Concerning Alexander the Great." *Acta Orientalia Academiae Scientiarum Hungaricae* 7(1957), No. 2–3, pp. 232–48.

d'Anville, J. B. *Nouvel Atlas de la Chine* ... The Hague: Henri Scheurleer, 1737.

Dardess, John. *Conquerors and Confucians: Aspects of Political Change in Late Yüan China*. New York: Columbia University Press, 1973.

"From Mongol Empire to Yüan Dynasty: Changing Forms of Imperial Rule in Mongolia and Central Asia." *Monumenta Serica* 30(1972–73), 117–165.

Davis, A. R., ed. *The Penguin Book of Chinese Verse*. Harmondsworth and Baltimore: Penguin Books, 1962.

De Bary, William Theodore *et al. Sources of Chinese Tradition*. New York: Columbia University Press, 1960.

de Crespigny, Rafe. *Northern Frontier: The Politics and Strategy of the Later Han Empire*. Canberra: Australian National University, Faculty of East Asian Studies, 1984.

DeGoeje, M. J. "De Mur van Gog en Magog." *Verslagen en Mededeelingen der Koninklijke Akademie van Wetenschappen* (Amsterdam), 3rd ser., 5(1888), 87–124.

de Groot, J. J. M., trans. *Chinesische Urkunden zue Geschichte Asiens* 1: *Die Hunnen der vorchristlichen Zeit*. Berlin and Leipzig: W. de Gruyter & Co., 1921.

des Rotours, Robert, trans. *Traité des Fonctionnaires et Traité de L'Armée*, 2 vols. Leiden, 1947: reprint edn, San Francisco: Chinese Materials Center, 1974.

Diderot, Denis. *Encyclopédie ou Dictionnaire raisonné* ... Facsimile of the first edition, 1751–80. Stuttgart–Bad Cannstatt: Fromann, 1966.

Dreyer, Edward L. *Early Ming China: A Political History 1355–1435*. Stanford: Stanford University Press, 1982.

Duffy, Christopher. *Fire and Stone: The Science of Fortress Warfare 1660–1860*. London: David & Charles, 1975.

DuHalde, Jean Baptiste. *Description* ... *de la Chine* ... The Hague: H. Scheurleer, 1736.

DuHalde, P. *The General History of China*, 3rd edn. London: J. Watts, 1741.

Dunnell, Ruth, W. "Tanguts and the Tangut State of Ta Hsia." Ph.D. dissertation: Princeton University, 1983.

Dyson, Stephen L. *The Creation of the Roman Frontier*. Princeton: Princeton University Press, 1985.

Eastman, Lloyd, E. *Throne and Mandarins: China's Search for a Foreign Policy During the*

Sino-French Controversy, 1880–1885. Cambridge, Mass.: Harvard University Press, 1967.

"Economic Conditions in Suiyuan Province." *Chinese Economic Journal* 13.4(1933), 385–400.

Edmonds, Richard L. "The Willow Palisade." *Annals of the Association of American Geographers* 69.4(1979), 599–621.

Egan, Ronald C. "The Prose Style of Fan Yeh." *Harvard Journal of Asiatic Studies* 39.2(1979), 339–401.

Eoyang, Eugene. 'The Wang Chao-chün Legend: Configurations of the Classic." *Chinese Literature: Essays, Articles, Reviews* 4(1982), 3–22.

Etiemble. "De la penseé chinoise aux 'philosophes' français." *Revue de Littérature Compareé* 30.4 (1956), 465–78.

Fairbank, John K., ed. *Chinese Thought and Institutions*. Chicago: University of Chicago Press, 1957.

The Chinese World Order. Cambridge, Mass.: Harvard University Press, 1968.

Fairbank, John K. and S. Y. Teng, "On the Ch'ing Tributary System." *Harvard Journal of Asiatic Studies* 6.2(1942), 135–246.

Fairbank, John K. and Edwin O. Reischauer. *East Asia: The Great Tradition*. Boston: Houghton Mifflin, 1960.

Fang Chao-ying. "The Great Wall of China: Keeping Out or Keeping In?" Talk presented at the Australian National University. Typescript, n.d.

Farmer, Edward L. *Early Ming Government: The Evolution of Dual Capitals*. Cambridge, Mass.: East Asian Research Center, Harvard University, 1976.

Farquhar, David M. "Oirat–Chinese Tribute Relations, 1408–1446." *Studia Altaica* (Wiesbaden, 1957), 60–8.

Fisher, Leonard Everett. *The Great Wall of China*. New York: Macmillan, 1986.

Fitzgerald, C. P. *China: A Short Cultural History*. London: The Cresset Press, 1935.

Fletcher, Joseph F., Jr. "Bloody Tanistry: Authority and Succession in the Ottoman, Indian Muslim, and Late Chinese Empires." Paper prepared for the Conference on the theory of Democracy and Popular Participation, Bellagio, Italy, 3–8 September 1978.

"China's Inner Asian frontier policies in the seventeenth century." Typescript: June 1982.

"The Mongols: ecological and social perspectives." *Harvard Journal of Asiatic Studies* 46.1(1986), 11–50.

Franke, Wolfgang. "Yunglo's Mongolei Feldzüge." *Sinologische Arbeiten* 3 (1945), 1–54.

"Addenda and Corrigenda to Pokotilov's *History of the Eastern Mongols During the Ming Dynasty from 1358 to 1634*" In *Studie Serica*, Series A., No. 3. Peiping: Published by the Editors, 1949.

"Chinesische Feldzüge durch die Mongolei im frühen 15. Jahrhundert." *Sinologica* 3 (1295 1–2), 81–8.

Friedland, Paul. "A Reconstruction of Early Tangut History." Ph.D dissertation: University of Washington, 1969.

Fryer, Jonathan. *The Great Wall of China*. London: New English Library, 1975.

Fuchs, Walter, "The Mongol Atlas of China by Chu Ssu-pen and the Kuang-yü-t'u." *Monumenta Serica Monograph* VIII, Peking: Fu Jen University, 1946.

Gallagher, Louis, J., S. J., trans. *China in the Sixteenth Century: The Journals of Matthew Ricci: 1583–1610* New York: Random House, 1953.

Garside, Roger. *Coming Alive: China After Mao*. London: André Deutsch, 1981.

Geil, William Edgar. *The Great Wall of China*. New York: Sturgis and Walton, 1909.

Geiss, James. "The Cheng-te reign, 1506–1521." In *Cambridge History of China*, Volume 7, pp. 403–40. Edited by Frederick W. Mote and Denis Twitchett. Cambridge: Cambridge University Press, 1988.

"The Chia-ching reign, 1522–1566." In *Cambridge History of China*, Volume 7, pp. 440–511. Edited by Frederick W. Mote and Denis Twitchett. Cambridge: Cambridge University Press, 1988.

Goodrich, L. Carrington, ed. *Dictionary of Ming Biography, 1368–1644*. New York and London: Columbia University Press, 1976.

"Great Wall Hiker," *China Daily* 25 March 1985, p. 3.

"Great Wall is Measured." *The Washington Post* 21 August 1979, A4.

"Great Wall secrets lure expert sleuths," *China Daily*, 28 April 1986, p. 4.

Guy, Basil. "The French Image of China Before and After Voltaire." *Studies on Voltaire and the Eighteenth Century* 21 (1963).

H., "The Great Wall of China." *Once A Week* 7 June 1862, pp. 668–72.

Haardt, Georges-Marie. *La Croisière Jaune*. Paris: Plon, 1933.

Haeger, John W., ed. *Crisis and Prosperity in Sung China*. Tucson: University of Arizona Press, 1975.

Hambis, Louis. "Note Sur L'installation des Mongols dans la boucle du Fleuve Jaune." *Mongolian Studies* (1970), 167–79.

Documents sur l'histoire des Mongols a l'époque des Ming. Paris: Presses Universitaires de France, 1969.

"A propos des noms de trois clans des Ordos." In *Studies in General and Oriental Linguistics Presented to Shirō Hattori on the Occasion of his Sixtieth Birthday*, ed. Roman Jakobson and Shigeo Kawamoto, pp. 167–79. Tokyo: TEC, 1970.

Hartman, Charles. *Han Yü and the T'ang Search for Unity*. Princeton: Princeton University Press, 1986.

Hayes, L. N. *The Great Wall of China*. Shanghai: Kelly and Walsh, 1929.

Heer, Ph. de. *The care-taker emperor: aspects of the imperial institution in fifteenth century China as reflected in the political history of the reign of Chu Ch'i-yü*. Leiden: Brill, 1986.

Herbert, P. A. "Agricultural Colonies in China in the Early Eighth Century." *Papers on Far Eastern History* 11 (1975), 37–77.

Higgins, Roland. "Piracy and Coastal Defense in the Ming Period: Government Response to Coastal Disturbances, 1523–1549." Ph.D. dissertation: University of Minnesota, 1981.

Hill, G. B., ed. *Boswell's Life of Johnson*, 6 vols., revised by L. F. Powell. Oxford: Clarendon Press, 1934.

Hitchcock, Romyn. "The Great Wall of China." *The Century Illustrated Monthly Magazine*, 45(1892–3), 327–32.

Hobsbawm, Eric, and Terence Ranger. *The Invention of Tradition*. Cambridge: Cambridge University Press, 1983.

Hsiao, Kung-chuan. *A History of Chinese Political Thought*. Vol. 1: *From the Beginnings to the Sixth century A.D.* Trans. F. W. Mote. Princeton: Princeton University Press, 1979.

Huang, Ray. *Taxation and Governmental Finance in Sixteenth-Century Ming China*. Cambridge: Cambridge University Press, 1974.

1587, A Year of No Significance. New Haven, Conn., and London: Yale University Press, 1981.

"Military Expenditures in Sixteenth Century Ming China." *Oriens Extremus* 17(1970), 39–62.

"The Liao-tung Campaign of 1619." *Oriens Extremus* 28(1981), 29–54.

"The Lung-ch'ing and Wan-li reigns, 1567–1620." In *Cambridge History of China*, Volume

7, pp. 511–74. Edited by Frederick W. Mote and Denis Twitchett. Cambridge: Cambridge University Press, 1988.

Huc, Everiste Régis. *Souvenirs d'un Voyage dans la Tartarie, le Thibet et La Chine Pendant Les Années 1844, 1845 et 1846.* Paris: Adrien Le Clere et Cie, 1850.

Hucker, Charles O. "Governmental Organization of the Ming Dynasty." In *Studies of Governmental Institutions in Chinese History*, ed. John L. Bishop. Cambridge, Mass.: Harvard University Press, 1968.

　The Censorial System of Ming China. Stanford: Stanford University Press, 1966.

　ed. *Chinese Government in Ming Times: Seven Studies.* New York and London: Columbia University Press, 1969.

Hughes, Judith M. *To the Maginot Line: The Politics of French Military Preparation ion the 1920s.* Cambridge, Mass.: Harvard University Press, 1971.

Hulsewé, A. F. P., *China in Central Asia.* Leiden: Brill, 1979.

Hung Chang-tai, *Going to the People: Chinese Intellectuals and Folk Literature, 1918–1937.* Cambridge, Mass.: Harvard University Press, 1985.

Ides, Evert Ysbrandszoon. *A journal of the embassy from Their Majesties John and Peter Alexievitz ... over land into China ...* London: Printed for D. Brown and T. Goodwin, 1698.

Ides, Izbrant and Adam Brand. *Zapiski o Russkom posol'stve v Kitai (1692–1695)* with introduction, translation, and commentary by M. I. Kazanin. Moscow: Glavnaia redaktsiia vostochnoi literatury, 1967.

Jagchid, Sechin. "Patterns of Trade and Conflict between China and the Monads of Mongolia." *Zentralasiatische Studien* 11 (1977), 177–204.

Jenner, W. J. F. *Memories of Loyang: Yang Hsüan-chih and the lost capital (493–534).* Oxford: Clarendon Press, 1981.

Jennings, Gary. *The Journeyer.* New York: Atheneum, 1984.

Kafka, Franz. *The Great Wall of China.* New York: Schocken Books, 1960.

Kaplan, Edward H. "Yüeh Fei and the Founding of the Southern Sung." Ph.D. dissertation: University of Iowa, 1970.

Kedourie, Elie. *Nationalism.* London: Hutchinson & Co., 1985.

Keightley, David N. "The Long Wall of Ch'i, A Preliminary Study." Unpublished ms. 1965.

Khazanov, A. M. *Nomads and the outside world*, tr. Julia Crookenden, with a Foreword by Ernest Gellner. Cambridge: Cambridge University Press, 1984.

Kierman, Frank A., Jr., and John K. Fairbank, eds. *Chinese Ways in Warfare.* Cambridge, Mass.: Harvard University Press, 1974.

Kircher, Athanasius, S. J. *China monumenti qua sacris qua profanis, Illustrata.* Amsterdam: Joannem Janssonium à Waesberge & Elizeum Weyerstraet, 1667.

Kyçanov, Evgenij I., "Les guerres entre les Sung du Nord et le Hsi-Hsia." In *Etudes Song in Memoriam Etienne Balazs.* 1.2 pp. 101–18, ed. François Aubin. Evreux: Mouton, 1971.

"La grande muraille de la Chine." *Annales de l'Extrême Orient* 3.2(1880–1), 185.

Lach, Donald F. *China in the Eyes of Europe: The Sixteenth Century.* Chicago: The University of Chicago Press, 1965.

　Asia in the Making of Europe. Chicago: The University of Chicago Press, 1965–.

Laing, Ellen Johnston. *An Index to Reproductions of Paintings by Twentieth Century Chinese Artists.* Eugene, Oregon: University of Oregon, Asia Studies Program, Publication No. 6, June 1984.

Lamar, Howard and Thompson, Leonard. *The Frontier in History: North America and Southern Africa Compared.* New Haven and London: Yale University Press, 1981.

Lamb, Harold. *The March of the Barbarians.* New York: Doubleday, Doran & Co., 1940.

Larrieu, M. l'Abbé. "Rapport sur La Grande Muraille de Chine ou il est prouvé que cette muraille telle qu'elle est communément décrite non seulement n'existe pas, mais même n'a jamais existé, suivi d'un article sur la barrière de pieux du Léao-tong." *Revue de l'Extrême-Orient* 3(1887), 347–63.

Latourette, Kenneth Scott. *The Development of China*. Boston and New York: Houghton Mifflin, 1917.

Lattimore, Owen. *Inner Asian Frontiers of China*. New York: American Geographical Society, 1940.

Studies in Frontier History: Collected Papers 1928–1958. London: Oxford University Press, 1962.

The Desert Road to Turkestan. Boston: Little, Brown, and Co., 1930.

"Origins of the Great Wall of China: A Frontier Concept in Theory and Practice." In *Studies in Frontier History: Collected Papers 1928–1958*, pp. 97–118. London: Oxford University Press, 1962.

"Herdsmen, farmers, urban culture." In *Pastoral Production and Society*. Edited by L'Equipe écologie et anthropologie des sociétés pastorales. Cambridge: Cambridge University Press and Paris: Editions de la Maison des Sciences de l'Homme, 1979, pp. 479–490.

Le, Kang, "An Empire for a City: Cultural Reforms of the Hsiao-wen Emperor (A.D. 471–499)." Ph.D. Dissertation: Yale University, 1983.

LeComte, Louis D. *Memoirs and Observations ... Made in a late journey through the empire of China*. Trans. of French edn. London, B. Tooke, 1697.

Ledyard, Gari. "Yin and Yang in the China-Manchuria-Korea Triangle." In *China Among Equals*, edited by Morris Rossabi. Berkeley: University of California Press, 1983, pp. 313–53.

Legge, James, ed. and trans. *The Chinese Classics*, reprint edn. Taipei: Wen-shih-che, 1971.

Leyda, Jay. *Dianying: An Account of Films and the Film Audience in China*. Cambridge, Mass.: M.I.T. Press, 1972.

Li Chien-nung. *A Political History of Modern China*. Stanford: Stanford University Press, 1967.

Li Ung-bing. *Outlines of Chinese History*. Shanghai: Commercial Press, 1914.

Li Yu-ning, ed. *The Politics of Historiography: The First Emperor of China*. White Plains, N.Y.: International Arts and Sciences Press, 1975.

Liang, Heng, and Shapiro, Judith. *Son of the Revolution*. New York: Knopf, 1983.

Liao, Kuang-sheng. "Linkage Politics in China: Internal Mobilization and Articulated External Hostility in the Cultural Revolution, 1967–69." *World Politics* 28.4(1967), 590–610.

Antiforeignism and Modernization in China, 1860–1980: Linkage Between Domestic Politics and Foreign Policy. Hong Kong: The Chinese University Press, 1984.

Liddell Hart, B. H. *Great Captains Unveiled*. Boston: Little, Brown & Co., 1928.

Lin, Nancy T., trans. *Reverberations: A New Translation of Complete Poems of Mao Tse-tung with Notes by Nancy T. Lin*. Hong Kong: Joint Publishing Co., 1980.

Lin, Paul J. *A Translation of Lao-tzu's Tao-te-ching and Wang Pi's Commentary*. Ann Arbor: University of Michigan, 1977.

Lindner, Rudi Paul. "What Was a Nomadic Tribe?" *Comparative Studies in Society and History* 24.4(1982), 689–711.

"Nomadism, Horses and Huns." *Past and Present* No. 92 (August, 1981), 3–19.

Liu, James T. C. *Ou-Yang Hsiu: An Eleventh-Century Neo-Confucianist*. Stanford: Stanford University Press, 1967.

"Yüeh Fei (1103–41) and China's Heritage of Loyalty." *Journal of Asian Studies* 31.2(1972), 291–7.

Liu, Ts'un-yan. "The Penetration of Taoism into the Ming Neo-Confucian Elites." *T'oung Pao* 57(1971), 31–102.

Lo, Jung-pang. "Policy Formulation and Decision-making on Issues Respecting Peace and War." In *Chinese Government in Ming Times: Seven Studies* edited by Charles O. Hucker (New York and London: Columbia University Press, 1969), pp. 41–72.

"Intervention in Vietnam: A Case Study of the Foreign Policy of the Early Ming Government." *Ts'ing-hua Journal of Chinese Studies* 8(1970), 154–82.

Locnaeus, Jonas. *D. D. Murum Sinesem Brevi dissertatione adumbratum* ... Uppsala; Henricus Keyser, 1694.

Loewe, Michael. "The Campaigns of Han Wu-ti." In *Chinese Ways in Warfare*, edited by Frank A. Kierman and John K. Fairbank. Cambridge, Mass.: Harvard University Press, 1974, p. 67–122.

Crisis and Conflict in Han China. London: George Allen and Unwin, 1974.

Records of Han Administration. Cambridge: Cambridge University Press, 1967.

"Han Foreign Relations." In *Cambridge History of China*, volume 1, edited by Denis Twitchett and Michael Loewe. Cambridge: Cambridge University Press, 1986, pp. 377–462.

"Lone Hiker Finishes Trek Along Great Wall." *China Daily* 27 February 1985, p. 3.

Lord, Winston. "A Taste for Sweet and Sour." *The New York Times*, 25 April 1984, p. A23.

Lough, John. *The Contributors to the Encyclopédie.* London: Grant & Cutler, 1973.

Essays on the Encyclopédie of Diderot and D'Alembert. London: Oxford University Press, 1968.

Lum, Peter. *The Purple Barrier.* London: Robert Hale, 1960.

Luo Zewen. "New Survey." *China Reconstructs* 34.3 (March 1985), 8–14.

Luo Zewen, Dai Wenbao, Dick Wilson, Jean-Pierre Drege and Herbert Delahaye. *The Great Wall of China.* New York: McGraw-Hill, 1981.

Luo Zhewen and Zhao Luo. *The Great Wall of China in History and Legend.* Beijing: Foreign Languages Press, 1986.

Luttwak, Edward N. *The Grand Strategy of the Roman Empire: From the First Century A.D. to the Third.* Baltimore and London: The Johns Hopkins University Press, 1976.

Maddocks, Melvin. "The Great Wall of China and other unearthings." *The Christian Science Monitor* 7 March 1983, 22.

Mancall, Mark. *China at the Center: 300 Years of Foreign Policy.* New York: The Free Press, 1984.

March, Andrew L. *The Idea of China: Myth and Theory in Geographic Thought.* New York and Washington: Praeger, 1974.

Marsden, William, tr. and ed. *The Travels of Marco Polo* ... London: Printed for the author, 1818.

Martin, E. "La Vérité sur La Grande Muraile de la Chine." *L'Anthropoligie* 2 (1891), 438–44.

"La Grande Muraille de la Chine." *Revue Scientifique (Revue Rose)* 48(1891), 499–502.

Martin, H. Desmond. *Chingis Khan and His Conquest of North China.* 1950: reprint edn, New York: Octagon, 1977.

Martini, Martino. *Novvs Atlas Sinensis* ... Amsterdam: Blaeu, 166–.

McDougall, Walter A. *France's Rhineland Diplomacy, 1914–1924: The Last Bid for a Balance of Power in Europe.* Princeton: Princeton University Press, 1978.

McNeill, William. *The Rise of the West.* Chicago: University of Chicago Press, 1963.

Meijer, M. J. "A Map of the Great Wall of China." *Imago Mundi* 13(1956), 110–15.

Mendoza. Juan Gonzalez de. *The historie of the great and mightie kingdom of China* ... Translated out of Spanish by R. Parke. London: I. Wolfe, 1588.

Meserve, Ruth I. "The Inhospitable Land of the Barbarian." *Journal of Asian History* 16 (1982), 51–89.

Meskill, John. *Academies in Ming China: A Historical Essay*. Tucson: University of Arizona Press, 1982.

Meskill, John, trans. *Ch'oe Pu's Diary: A Record of Drifting Across the Sea*. Tucson: University of Arizona Press, 1965.

Minns, Ellis H. *Scythians and Greeks: A Survey of Ancient History and Archaeology on the North Coast of the Euxine from the Danube to the Caucasus*. Cambridge: Cambridge University Press, 1913.

Morris, William, ed. *The American Heritage Dictionary of the English Language*. New York and other cities: American Heritage Publishing Co., and Houghton Mifflin Co., 1969.

Moses, Larry. "A Theoretical Approach to the Process of Inner Asian Confederation." *Études Mongoles* 5(1974), 113–22.

Mote, F. W., "Some Problems of Race and Nation in 14th-Century China." Paper presented to the University Seminar on Traditional China: Columbia University, 11 March 1969.

"The T'u-mu Incident of 1449." In *Chinese Ways in Warfare*, edited by Frank A. Kierman, Jr., and John K. Fairbank. Cambridge, Mass.: Harvard University Press, 1974, pp. 243–72.

Mote, Frederick W. and Twitchett, Denis, eds. *The Ming Dynasty, 1368–1644, Part I*. Volume 7 of *The Cambridge History of China*. Cambridge: Cambridge University Press, 1988.

Moulder, Frances V. *Japan, China, and the modern world economy*. Cambridge: Cambridge University Press, 1977.

Murzaev, E. M. "Opyt ob'iasneniia nazvaniia 'Krym'" *Izvestiia Vsesoiuznogo Geograficheskogo Obshchestvo* 80(1948) No. 3, pp. 295–8.

Mullie, Jos. L. M. "La Grande Muraille de Yen et de Ts'in." *Central Asiatic Journal* 13.2 (1969), 99–136.

Nancarrow, Peter. *Early China and the Wall*. Cambridge Introduction to the History of Mankind, Topic Book. Cambridge: Cambridge University Press, 1978.

Nathan, Andrew, J. *Peking Politics, 1918–1923: Factionalism and the Failure of Constitutionalism*. Berkeley: University of California Press, 1976.

Needham, Joseph. *Science and Civilization in China*. Cambridge: Cambridge University Press, 1954–.

New World Press and Radio Peking, eds. *Sixty Scenic Wonders in China*. Peking: New World, 1980.

Nieuhof, Johan. *An Embassy from the East India Company of the United Provinces to the Great Tartar Cham ... Englished and set forth with their several sculptures, by John Ogilby*. London: printed by J. Macock for the author, 1669.

Olschki, Leonardo. *Marco Polo's Asia: An Introduction to his "Description of the World" Called "Il Milione."* Berkeley: University of California Press, 1960.

Ortelius, Abraham. *Theatrum Orbis Terrarum: The Theatre of the Whole World ...* London: I. Norton, 1606.

"Paaotowchen, the Gateway to the Northwest." *The Chinese Economic Monthly* 3.5(1926), 201–11.

Park, Seong Rae. "Portents and Politics in Early Yi Korea." Ph.D. dissertation: University of Hawaii, 1977.

Pastoral Production and Society. Edited by L'Equipe écologie et anthropologie des sociétés pastorales Cambridge: Cambridge University Press and Paris: Editions de la Maison des Sciences de l'Homme, 1979.

273

Pauthier, M. G. *Chine ou Description Historique, Géographique et Littéraire de ce vaste empire, a'près des documents chinois* ... Paris: Firmin Didot Frères, 1844.

Pearce, Scott "The historical role of the Hsien-pei in medieval China." Unpublished MS.

Pelliot, Paul. *Recherches sur les Chrétiens d'Asie Centrale et d'Extrême-Orient.* Œuvres posthumes de Paul Pelliot. Paris: Imprimerie Nationale, 1973.

Peterson, Charles. "First Sung Reactions to the Mongol Invasion of the North, 1211–17." In *Crisis and Prosperity in Sung China*, ed. John W. Haeger. Tucson: University of Arizona Press, 1975.

Poirier, René. *The Fifteen Wonders of the World.* Translated by Margaret Crosland. New York: Random House, 1961.

Pokotilov, Dmitrii D. *History of the Eastern Mongols during the Ming dynasty from 1368 to 1634.* Translated by Rudolf Loewenthal. 1947; reprint edn, Philadelphia: Porcupine Press, 1976.

Pumpelly, Raphael. *My Reminiscences.* 2 vols. New York: Henry Holt, 1918.

Purchas, Samuel, ed. *Hakluytus Posthumus or Purchas His Pilgrimes.* 20 vols. Glasgow: James MacLehose and Sons, 1905.

Rand, Christopher C. "Chinese Military Thought and Philosophical Taoism." *Monumenta Serica* 34(1979–80), 171–218.

"The Role of Military Thought in Early Chinese Intellectual History." Ph.D. dissertation: Harvard University, 1977.

Raschke, Manfred G. "New Studies in Roman Commerce with the East." In *Aufstieg und Niedergang Der Römischen Welt*, edited by Hildegard Temporini and Wolfgang Haase. Berlin and New York: Walter De Gruyter, 1978, II.9.2, pp. 604–1361.

Republic of China, Supreme Economic Council, Public Works Commission. "General Description of the Yellow River Basin." *Studies on Yellow River Project* No. 2 Nanking, 1947, pp. 57–66.

Richthofen, Ferdinand von. *Baron Richthofen's Letters, 1870–72.* Shanghai: North China Herald, n.d.

Riftin, B. L. *Skazanie o velikoi stene i problema zhanra v kitaiskom fol'klore.* Moscow: Izdatel'stvo Vostochnoi Literatury, 1961.

Rockhill, William W. *Diary of a Journey Through Mongolia and Tibet in 1891 and 1892.* Washington, D.C.: Smithsonian Institution, 1894.

Rose, Ernst. "China as a Symbol of Reaction in Germany, 1830–1880." *Comparative Literature* 3.1(1951), 57–76.

Ross, E. Denison, "Nomadic Movements in Asia. Lecture II. – The Turks." *Journal of the Royal Society of Arts* 77(1929), 1075–86.

"The Invasions and Immigrations of the Tatars." *Journal of the Central Asian Society* 154, part 2(1928–9), 133–43.

Rossabi, Morris. "Ming China's Relations with Hami and Central Asia, 1404–1513: A Reexamination of Traditional Chinese Foreign Policy." Ph.D. dissertation: Columbia University, 1970.

"Notes on Esen's Pride and Ming China's Prejudice." *Mongolia Society Bulletin* 9.2 (1970), 31–8.

China and Inner Asia from 1368 to the Present Day. New York: Pica Press, 1975.

ed. *China Among Equals: The Middle Kingdom and its Neighbors, 10th–14th Centuries.* Berkeley: University of California Press, 1983.

Rostovtzeff, M. *Iranians and Greeks in South Russia.* New York: Russell & Russell, 1922.

Rowbotham, Arnold H. "Voltaire, Sinophile." *PMLA* 47.1(1932), 1050–65.

Missionary and Mandarin. Berkeley and Los Angeles: University of California Press, 1942.

Rowe, Vivian. *The Great Wall of France: The Triumph of the Maginot Line.* New York: G. P. Putnam's Sons, 1961.

Salisbury, Harrison. *The Long March: The Untold Story.* New York: Harper and Row, 1985.

Satō Hiroshi. "On the Palisade in Manchuria." *Japanese Journal of Geology and Geography* 3.3–4(1924), 167–78.

Schell, Orville. "The New Open Door." *The New Yorker* 19 November 1984, 86–153. *To Get Rich is Glorious: China in the 80's.* New York: Pantheon Books, 1984.

Schirokauer, Conrad. "Neo-Confucians Under Attack: The Condemnation of *Wei-hsüeh*." In *Crisis and Prosperity in Sung China,* ed. John W. Haeger. Tucson: University of Arizona Press, 1975.

Schönberger, H. "The Roman Frontier in Germany: An Archaeological Survey." *The Journal of Roman Studies* 59(1969), 144–97.

Scott, Robert Lee, Jr. "To Walk the Great Wall." *Reader's Digest 122* (April 1983), 152–235.

Serruys, Henry. "Chinese in Southern Mongolia during the Sixteenth Century." *Monumenta Serica* 18 (1959), 1–95.

"A Manuscript Version of the Legend of the Mongol Ancestry of the Yung-lo Emperor.". *Occasional Papers of the Mongolia Society* No. 8(1972), 19–29.

"Sino-Mongol Relations During the Ming, II. The Tribute System and Diplomatic Missions (1400–1600)." *Mélanges Chinois et Bouddhiques* 14(1969).

"Towers in the Northern Frontier Defenses of the Ming." *Ming Studies* 14(Spring 1982), 8–76.

"Sino-Mongol Relations During the Ming. III. Trade Relations: The Horse Fairs (1499–1600)." *Mélanges Chinois et Bouddhiques* 18(1975).

Sino-Jürčed Relations During the Yung-lo Period (1403–1424). Wiesbaden: Otto Harrassowitz, 1955.

"The Mongols in China During the Hung-wu Period (1368–1398)." *Mélanges Chinois et Bouddhiques* 11(1956–9).

Genealogical Tables of the Descendants of Dayan-Qan. The Hague: Mouton, 1958.

"Mongol Tribute Missions of the Ming Period." *Central Asiatic Journal* 11(1966), 1–96.

Shabad, Theodore. *China's Changing Map: National and Regional Development, 1949–1971.* Revised edn New York: Praeger, 1971.

Shaw, S. J. "Historical Significance of the Curious Theory of Mongol Blood in the Veins of the Ming Emperors." *The Chinese Social and Political Science Review* 20 (1937), 492–8.

Silverberg, Robert. *The Long Rampart.* Philadelphia: Chilton, 1965.

Sinor, Denis. "The Inner Asian Warriors." *Journal of the American Oriental Society* 101.2(1981), 133–44.

Inner Asia and its Contracts with Medieval Europe. London: Variorum Reprints, 1977.

"On Mongol Strategy." In *Inner Asia and its Contacts with Medieval Europe.* London: Variorum Reprints, 1977, pp. 238–49.

Inner Asia: A Syllabus. Indiana University Publications: Uralic and Altaic Series, vol. 96, 1969.

"Horse and Pasture in Inner Asian History." *Oriens Extremus* 19(1972).

Smith, John Masson, Jr. "'Ayn Jālut: Mamlūk Success or Mongol Failure?" *Harvard Journal of Asiatic Studies* 44.2(1984), pp. 307–45.

So, Kwan-wai. *Japanese Piracy in Ming China During the 16th Century* Michigan State University Press, 1975.

"Grand Secretary Yan Song (1480–1566?): A New Appraisal." In *Essays in the History of China and Chinese American Relations,* edited by So, Kwan-wai and Warren Cohen. East Lansing: Michigan State University, Asian Studies Center, 1982, pp. 1–40.

Staunton, Sir George Leonard. *An authentic account of an embassy from the King of Great Britain to the Emperor of China* ... London: G. Nicol, 1797.

Stein, Mark Aurel. *Ruins of Desert Cathay*, 2 vols. London: Macmillan, 1912.

Stent, George Carter. *Entombed Alive and Other Songs, Ballads, &c. (from the Chinese)*. London: William H. Allen and Co., 1878.

Sun, E-tu Zen, and John DeFrancis. *Chinese Social History: Translations of Selected Studies*. Washington, D.C.: American Council of Learned Societies, 1956.

Svistunova, N. P. "Organizatsiia pogranichnoi sluzhby na severe Kitaia v epokhu Min." In *Kitai i Sosedi v Drevnosti i Srednevekov'e*, edited by S. L. Tikhvinskii and L. S. Perelomov. Moscow: "Nauka," 1970.

Taylor, Romeyn. "Yüan origins of the *Wei-so* System." In *Chinese Government in Ming Times: Seven Studies*, edited by Charles O. Hucker. New York: Columbia University Press, 1969, pp. 23–40.

Teggart, Frederick, J. *Rome and China: A Study of Correlations in Historical Events*. Berkeley: University of California Press, 1939.

"The Great Wall not a Myth." *Chinese Recorder and Missionary Journal* 19(1888), 239.

Thompson, Robert O. "Defense of the Northern Frontier in Ming China, Especially the Chi-chou Area Northeast of Peking, 1569–83." Master's Thesis: University of Chicago, 1962.

Tregear, T. R. *A Geography of China*. Chicago: Aldine Publishing Co., 1965.

Topping, Audrey. "Family Reunion in China." *The New York Times Magazine* 12 February 1984, 37–40, 65, 80, 82.

Tsiang, T. F. [Chiang T'ing-fu], "China and European Expansion." *Politica* 2.5(1936), 1–18.

Twitchett, Denis and Fairbank, John K., general editors. *The Cambridge History of China*. Cambridge: Cambridge University Press, 1978–.

Twitchett, Denis and Loewe, Michael, eds. *The Ch'in and Han Empires, 220 B.C. through A.D. 220*. Volume 1 of *The Cambridge History of China*. Cambridge: Cambridge University Press, 1986.

Ujfalvy, Charles de. *Les Aryens au Nord et au Sud de l'Hindou-Kouch*. Paris: G. Masson, 1896.

Vasil'ev, L. S. "Velikaia kitaiskaia stena." *Voprosy istorii* (1971) 1, 204–12.

Verbiest, Ferdinand. *Voyages de L'Emperor de la Chine dans la Tartarie* ... Paris: Estienne Michallet, 1685.

Vermeer, E. B. *Water Conservancy and Irrigation in China*. Leiden: Leiden University Press, 1977.

"Visit to the Great Wall of China," ("by a correspondent"). *The Illustrated London News* 17.449 October 5, 1850, pp. 271–2.

Voltaire [François Marie Arouet]. *Œuvres complètes de Voltaire*. Paris: Garnier, 1878.

von Möllendorf, O. E. "Die Grosse Mauer von China." *Zeitschrift der Deutschen Morgenländischen Gesellschaft* 35.2(1881), 75–131.

Wakeman, Frederic. *The Fall of Imperial China*. New York: The Free Press, 1975.

ed. *Ming and Qing Historical Studies in the People's Republic of China*. Berkeley and Los Angeles: University of California Press, 1980.

Waldron, Arthur N. "The Problem of the Great Wall of China." *Harvard Journal of Asiatic Studies* 43.2(1983), 643–63.

Review of P.E. Skachkov, *Ocherki istorii russkogo kitaevedeniia. Kritika* 15(1979), no. 1, pp. 1–16.

"The Great Wall Myth: Its Origins and Role in Modern China." *Yale Journal of Criticism* 2.1 (October 1988), pp. 67–104.

Bibliography

Wall, Charles William. *An Examination of the Ancient Orthography of the Jews*. 2 vols., London: Whittaker and Co., 1841.

Wang Ch'ung-wu. "The Ming System of Merchant Colonization." In *Chinese Social History*, edited by E-tu Zen Sun and John DeFrancis. Washington, D.C.: American Council of Learned Societies, 1956, pp. 299–308.

Wang, Ch'iu-kuei. "The Transformation of The Meng Chiang-nü Story in Chinese Popular Literature." Ph.D.dissertation: Cambridge University, 1977.

Wang, Cheng-t'ing. *Looking Back and Looking Forward*. Typescript, n.d. in the collection of the Chinese Oral History Project, Library of Columbia University.

Warner, Langdon. *The Long Old Road in China*. Garden City, New York: Doubleday, Page & Co., 1926.

Warwick, Adam. "A Thousand Miles Along the Great Wall of China: The Mightiest Barrier Ever Built by Man Has Stood Guard Over the Land of China for Twenty Centuries." *National Geographic Magazine* 43.2(1923), 113–43.

Watson, Andrew, ed. and trans., *Mao Zedong and the Political Economy of the Border Region: A Translation of Mao's 'Economic and Financial Problems'*. Cambridge: Cambridge University Press, 1980.

Watson, Burton, trans. *Records of the Grand Historian of China*. New York and London: Columbia University Press, 1961.

Wechsler, Howard J. "T'ai-tsung (reign 626–49) the consolidator." In *The Cambridge History of China*, vol. 3, edited by Denis Twitchett and John K. Fairbank. Cambridge: Cambridge University Press, 1979, pp. 188–237.

Wegener, Georg. "Der grosse Wall von China." *Von Fels zum Meer* 14(1894), 201–9.

Wei, Winifred. *The Great Wall*. Taipei: China Publishing Co., 1963.

White, Julia Marie. "Topographical Painting in Early Ming China: *Eight Scenes of Peking* by Wang Fu." M.A. Thesis: University of California, Berkeley, 1983.

Wilhelm, Hellmut. "From Myth to Myth: The Case of Yüeh Fei's biography." In *Confucian Personalities*, ed. Arthur Wright and Denis Twitchett. Stanford: Stanford University Press, 1962.

Wilhelm, Hellmut, trans. *The I Ching or Book of Changes*. Rendered into English by Cary F. Baynes. Princeton: Princeton University Press, 1950.

Wilson, C. E. "The Wall of Alexander Against Gog and Magog; and the Expedition Sent out to find it by the Khalif Wāthiq in 842 A.D." *Asia Major* (1922), 575–612.

Wimsatt, Genevieve and Chen, Geoffrey, trans. *The Lady of the Long Wall*. New York: Columbia University Press, 1934.

Wingate, A. W. S. "Nine Years' Survey and Exploration in Northern and Central China." *The Geographical Journal* 29.2(1907), 174–200; 29.3(1907), 272–306.

Wittfogel, Karl A. *Oriental Despotism*. New Haven: Yale University Press, 1957.
  and Feng Chia-sheng. *History of Chinese Society: The Liao (907–1125)*. Transactions of the American Philosophical Society, NS, No. 36. Philadelphia, 1946.

Wright, Arthur, and Denis Twitchett, eds. *Confucian Personalities*. Stanford: Stanford University Press, 1962.

Wu Chi-hua. "The contraction of forward defences on the North China frontier during the Ming dynasty." *Papers on Far Eastern History* 17(1978), 1–13.

Yahuda, Michael. *Towards the End of Isolationism: China's Foreign Policy after Mao*. London: Macmillan, 1983.

Yu Chin, comp. *The Great Wall*. Peking: Cultural Relics Publishing House, 1980.

Yü, Ying-shih. *Trade and Expansion in Han China: A Study in the Structure of Sino-Barbarian Economic Relations*. Berkeley and Los Angeles: University of California Press, 1967.

Bibliography

Yule, Henry. *The Book of Ser Marco Polo the Venetian*. 2 vols. Second edition, revised. London: John Murray, 1875.

— and Cordier, Henri. *Cathay and the Way Thither* 2 vols. London: Hakluyt Society, 1913–16.

Zhang Buchun; Wallace, Robert E. *et al*. "Fault Scarps Related to the 1730 Earthquake, and Seismicity of the Yinchuan Graben, Ningxia Huizu Zizhiqu, China." *Bulletin of the Seismological Society of America* 76.5 (October 1986, 1253–87).

Zhang Wei, "Man Winds Up Great Wall Trek." *Beijing Review* 29.15 (14 April 1986), 14–18.

Zhang Xinxin and Sang Ye, eds. *Chinese Profiles*. Beijing: Panda Books, 1987.

Zhu Yuchao. "Fund Raising for Renovations." *China Reconstructs* 34.3(March 1985), 7.

Zlatkin, I. Ia. *Istoriia Dzhungarskogo Khanstva 1635–1758*. Moscow: "Nauka," 1964.

Glossary

A-t'ai　阿台
ai-kuo ko-ch'ü　愛國歌曲
Altan khan　阿拉坦汗
An-ta　俺答
An-ting gate　安定門
Arigh Böke　阿里不哥
Arughtai　阿魯台
Ayushiridara　愛猷識里達里

Bäg Arslan　白儿加里蘭
Bagha-achi　把漢那吉
Batu Möngke　巴圖孟克大衍汗
Bolai　孛來

Ch'a-chien-ling　插箭嶺
Chai Luan　翟鸞
Chai P'eng　翟鵬
chang [barrier]　障
chang [unit of measure]　丈
Chang Chü-cheng　張居正
Chang Fu-ching　張孚敬
Chang Jen-yüan　張仁愿
Chang Tso-lin　張作霖
Chang Wen-chin　張文錦
Chang-chia-k'ou　張家口
Chang-chia-k'ou pao　張家口堡
Chang-i　張掖
Ch'ang-an　長安
ch'ang-ch'eng　長城
Ch'ang-chou　昌州
Chao [state]　趙
Chao Ch'ung-kuo　趙充國
Chao Fu　趙輔
Chao I　趙翼
Chao Wen-hua　趙文華
Chao-ho　潮河
Chao-hsiang [king]　昭襄王（秦）
Chao-wu-ta [league, Mongolia]　昭烏達盟

Ch'ao Ts'o　晁錯
chen [garrison]　鎮
Chen Te-hsiu　真德秀
Chen-ch'üan pao　鎮川堡
Chen-hai-lou　鎮海樓
Chen-ho pao　鎮河堡
Chen-lu pao　鎮虜堡
Chen-pien pao　鎮邊堡
Chen-pien-ch'eng　鎮邊城
chen-shou　鎮守
Chen-yüan　鎮遠
Ch'en Ch'i-hsüeh　陳其學
Ch'en Ching　陳經
Ch'en Jui　陳銳（平江伯）
Ch'en Lin　陳琳
Ch'en Wen-chu　陳文燭
Ch'en Yüeh　陳鉞
Ch'en Yi　陳毅
Cheng-chou　鄭州
Cheng-te [reign period]　正德
Cheng-t'ung [emperor]　正統
ch'eng　城
Ch'eng Wan-li　程萬里
Ch'eng-hua [reign period]　成化
Ch'eng-te　承德
Chi-chou　薊州
Chi-lin　吉林
chi-mi　羈縻
Chi-nang [Jinong]　吉囊
chi-shih-chung　給事中
Chi-sun of Lu　魯季孫
Ch'i [state]　齊
Ch'i Chi-kuang　戚繼光
ch'i chih shen jui　其志甚銳
Ch'i Liang　杞梁
ch'i ming shen cheng　其名甚正
Ch'i Yü　齊譽
Chia [county]　葭

279

Chia Chüan-chih　賈捐之

Chia I　賈誼

Chia-ching [reign period]　嘉靖

Chia-chou　葭州

Chia-yü-kuan　嘉峪關

ch'iang-chün hsieh-chung　強君脅衆

Ch'iao Kuan-hua　喬冠華

Chieh-yang　揭陽

chien-pi ch'ing-yeh　堅壁清野

Chien-chou　建州

Chien-wen　建文

Ch'ien Liang　錢亮

Ch'ien Sung-yen　錢松嵒

ch'ien-hu·shou-yü-so　守禦千戶所

ch'ien-hu-so [chiliad]　千戶所

Ch'ien-lung [emperor]　乾隆

Ch'ih-kan A-li　叱干阿利

Ch'ih-feng　赤峰

Chih li　直隸

chin [catty]　斤

Chin [dynasty]　晉

chin [metal]　金

chin-i wei　錦衣衛

chin-shih　進士

Ch'in [dynasty]　秦

Ch'in Hung　秦紘

Ch'in Kuei　秦檜

Ch'in Shih-huang　秦始皇

Ch'in-wang　親王

Ching [emperor]　景帝

Ching [river]　涇

Ching-t'ai　景泰

ching-yün　京運

Ch'ing [dynasty]　清

ch'ing [unit of area]　頃

Chi'ng-fu　慶府

Ch'ing-hai　青海

Ch'ing-shui-ying　清水營

Chiu-men-k'ou　九門口

chiu-pien-chen　九邊鎮

Chiu-yüan　九原

Ch'iu Chün　丘濬

Ch'iu Luan　丘鸞

Ch'iu Yüeh　仇鉞

Ch'iu-kung chi　求貢記

ch'iung-ping tu-wu　窮兵黷武

Ch'oe Pu　崔溥

Chou [dynasty]　周

Chou Shang-wen　周尚文

Chou Shu-jen　周樹人

Chu Chang　朱長

Chu Chih-fan　朱寘鐇

Chu Ch'ung-ch'iu [Prince of Hsiang]
　朱沖烌, 襄陵王

Chu Hsi　朱熹

Chu Hui　朱暉

Chu Teh　朱德

Chu Wan　朱紈

Chu Yüan-chang　朱元璋

Chu Yung　朱永

Chu-fu yen　主父偃

Chü-yen　居延

Chü-yung-kuan　居庸關

Ch'u [state]　楚

ch'u shih kuo yu ming fou　出師果有名否

Chüan-yü　顓臾

Ch'üan-ning　全寧

chün-hu　軍戶

Chün-tu [mountains]　軍都山

Chung-hsing　中興

Chung-wei　中衛

Eastern Wei [dynasty]　東魏

erh-pien　二邊

Erh-li-kang　二里岡

Esen　也先

Etsina *see* Chü-yen

Fan Chung-yen　范仲淹

fan-li　藩籬

Fang Pin　方賓

Fei Ts'ai　費寀

Fen-i　分宜

Feng [empress]　馮后

Feng Pao　馮保

Feng Sheng　馮勝

Feng Shih-lu　馮石魯

Feng-chou　豐州

feng-huo-t'ai　烽火台

feng-shui　風水

Feng-t'ien　奉天

fu-shih　[按察副使]

Fu-t'u-yü　浮圖峪

Günbilig-mergen
　袞必里克黑爾根[濟農]

hai-k'ou　海寇

Hai-shan　海山

Hami　哈密

Han [dynasty] 漢
Han Ch'i 韓琦
Han Hsin 韓信
Han T'o-chou 韓佗胄
Han-ch'eng [county] 韓城
Han-yüan [canal] 漢源
hang-t'u 夯土
Heng-ch'eng 橫城
Heng-shan [county] 橫山
ho-ch'in 和親
Ho-lan [mountains] 賀蘭山
Ho-lien Po-po 赫連勃勃
Ho-lin [Karakorum *or* Khara Khorum] 和林
ho-pien 河邊
Ho-t'ao 河套
Hsü Chieh 徐階
Hsü Ning 許寧
Hsü Ta 徐達
Hsü-shui [county] 徐水
Hsüan [king of Chou] 宣
hsüan-an 巡按
Hsüan-hua 宣化
Hsüan-te [emperor] 宣德
Hsüan-ti [emperor] 宣帝
hsün-fu 巡撫
Hsi-an 西安
hsi-ch'ang 西廠
Hsi-chi [county] 西吉
Hsi-feng-k'ou 喜峰口
Hsi-kuan-men 西關門
Hsi-ma-lin 洗馬林
Hsi-yang-ho 西陽河
Hsia [dynasty] 夏
Hsia Yen 夏言
Hsia Yüan-chi 夏原吉
Hsiao-wen [emperor] 孝文
Hsieh Lan 謝蘭
hsien 縣
Hsien-pei 鮮卑
Hsien-yün 玁狁
hsin-ch'eng 新城
hsin-yang wei-chi 信仰危機
Hsing-chou 興州
Hsing-ho 興和
Hsiung T'ing-pi 熊廷弼
Hsiung-nu [people] 匈奴
Hsiung-nu Hsia [dynasty] 匈奴夏
hu [barbarian] 胡
Hu Shun 胡順

Hu Wei-yung 胡惟庸
Hu-han-yeh 呼韓邪
Hu-ho-hao-t'e 呼和浩特
Hu-lun-hu 呼倫湖
hua [civilized] 華
Hua Yün-lung 華雲龍
Hua-i t'u 華夷圖
Hua-ma-ch'ih 花馬池
Huai-jou 懷柔
Huai-lai 懷來
Huai-nan-tzu 淮南子
huang-ti 皇帝
Hung-chih [reign period] 弘治
Hung-liu [river] 紅柳
Hung-ssu pao 玄賜堡
Hung-wu [emperor] 洪武
Hung-yen-ch'ih 紅鹽池

i [barbarian] 夷
i hsien ho tsu yen 一銑何足言
i lao yung i 一勞永逸
I-chü [people] 義渠
Ibrahim 亦不剌; 亦不剌因
Ismā'īl 亦思馬因

Jehol 熱河
jinong 濟農
Jou-jan [people] 蠕蠕
Jung [people] 戎

K'ai-p'ing 開平
K'ai-shan-k'ou 開山口
K'ai-yüan 開原
Kan-chou 甘州
K'ang Yu-wei 康有為
K'ang-hsi 康熙
Kao Lü 高閭
Kao-chü [people] 高車
Kao-ch'üeh 高闕
Kao-tsu [emperor] 高祖
Kao-yai 高崖
kesig 怯薛
Khaidu 海都
Khoshila 和世喇
Khubilai 忽必烈
k'o-ping 客兵
Kökönor 庫庫撓爾
Kökö Temür 闊闊帖木兒
ku ch'ang-ch'eng 古長城
ku-chi 古跡

Ku-pei-k'ou　古北口
Ku-yüan　固原
K'u-yeh [river]　窟野河
Kuan-tso-ling　官坐嶺
Kuang-hsin [prefecture]　廣信
Kuang-ning　廣寧
Kuang-wu [emperor]　光武
K'uang Yeh　鄺野
Kuei-ch'i　貴溪
Kuei-hua ch'eng　歸化成
Kung-sun Hung　公孫弘
Kuo Hsün　郭勛

Lan Yü　藍玉
Lan-chou　蘭州
Lang-shan [mountain]　狼山
Lao-lung-t'ou　老龍頭
Lao-ying　老營堡
laobian　老邊
Later Ch'in [dynasty]　後秦
Latter Chou [dynasty]　後周
li [unit of measure]　里
Li Chi　李勣
Li Hsien　李賢
Li Hsing　李興
Li Meng-yang　李夢陽
Li Po　李白
Li Wen-chung　李文忠
liang [unit of measure]　兩
Liang Ch'i-ch'ao　梁啓超
Liang-chou　涼州
Liao [defense area]　遼
Liao [dynasty]　遼
Liao [river]　遼
Liao-ning　遼寧
Liao-tung　遼東
Liao-yang　遼陽
Lieh-nü chuan　列女傳
Lin-t'ao　臨洮
Ling-chou　靈州
Ling-pei　嶺北
Ling-wu [county]　靈武
liu chen　六鎮
Liu Chin　劉瑾
Liu Hsiang　劉向
Liu T'ien-ho　劉天和
Liu Ta-hsia　劉大夏
Liu-p'an [mountain]　六盤山
liu-t'iao-pien　柳條邊
Lo [river]　洛

Lo-yang　洛陽
Lu Fang　盧芳
Lu Hsün　魯迅
Lu Ping　陸炳
Lu-hua-shan　蘆花山
Lung-ch'ing　隆慶
Lung-ch'üan　龍泉
Lung-men-ch'eng　龍門城
Lung-shan　龍山

Ma Wen-sheng　馬文升
Ma-liang-shan　馬梁山
ma-mien　馬面
Ma-yi [nr. P'ing-ch'eng]　馬邑
Ma'alikhai　毛里孩
Mahmūd　馬哈木
Mao Po-wen　毛伯文
Mao Tse-tung　毛澤東
Mao-tun　冒頓
Mao-wu-su　毛烏素沙漠
men-hu　門戶
Meng Chiang-nü　孟姜女
Meng T'ien　蒙恬
Miao [people]　苗
Min [county]　岷
min-chuang　民壯
Min-sheng [canal]　民生
Ming [dynasty]　明
Ming-feng chi　鳴鳳記
Ming-sha　鳴沙
mou [unit of measure]　畝
Mu Ying　沐英
Mu-na-shan　母納山
Mu-t'ien-yü　慕田峪

Naghachu　納哈出
Nan Chung　南仲
Nan-ch'eng [palace]　南城
nei-pien　內邊
Niang-tzu-kuan　娘子關
Nieh Erh　聶耳
Ning-hsia　寧夏
Ning-wu [pass]　寧武關
Northern Ch'i [dynasty]　北齊
Northern Wei [dynasty]　北魏

Ögödei　窩闊台

Pa-ta-ling　八達嶺
Pai Kuei　白圭

282

Pai Mei-ch'u　白眉初
Pai-ch'eng　白城
Pai-ling-miao　百靈廟
Pai-teng-shan [mountain]　白登山
Pai-yang-k'ou　白羊口
Pan-sheng　板升
pao　堡
Pao-te chou　保德州
Pao-ting　保定
Pao-t'ou　包頭
Pei-chia　北假
Pei-lou　北樓
peng　崩
pien-ch'iang　邊牆
P'ien-t'ou-kuan　偏頭關
Ping-chou　幷州
P'ing-ch'eng　平城
P'ing-hsing　平刑
p'ing-lu chiang-chün　平虜將軍
Pohai [gulf]　渤海
pu shih chih kung　不世之功

sai [frontier]　塞
san shou-hsiang-ch'eng　三受降城
san ta ying　三大營
San-kuan-k'ou　三關口
Sang-kan [river]　桑乾
Shan-hai-kuan　山海關
Shan-yü　單于
Shang [dynasty]　商
Shang-tu　上都
Shen Shih-hsing　申時行
Shen-Kan-Ning　陝甘寧
Shen-mu　神木
Sheng-chou　勝州
shih　室
Shih Tao　史道
Shih T'ien-chüeh　石天爵
Shih-fo [mountain]　石佛
shu [bundle]　束
shu-yüan　書院
shui-chan　水站
Shui-ching chu　水經注
Shun-t'ien　順天
Shuo-fang　朔方
so　所
Ssu-hai-yeh　四海冶
Ssu-ma Ch'ien　司馬遷
Su Kang　蘇綱
Su Yu　蘇祐

Sui [dynasty]　隋
Sui Yü　隋昱
Sui-chou　綏州
Sun Chi-tsung [Marquis of Hui-ch'ang]
　　孫繼宗[會昌侯]
Sun Yat-sen　孫逸仙
Sun-tzu　孫子
Sung [dynasty]　宋
Sung-t'ing-kuan　松亭關

Ta Hsia [kingdom]　大夏
Ta-ning　大寧
Ta-pai-yang　大白陽
ta-pien　大邊
Ta-tan　韃韃
Ta-ting-fu　大定府
Ta-t'ung　大同
T'ai-hang [mountains]　太行山
T'ai-ho-ling　太和嶺
T'ai-tsung [emperor]　太宗
T'ai-wu [emperor]　太武
tan [unit of measure]　石
T'an Ch'ien　談遷
T'an Lun　譚綸
T'an Tao-chi　檀道濟
T'ang [dynasty]　唐
T'ang Hsiu-ching　唐休璟
T'ang Lung　唐龍
T'ang Shun-chih　唐順之
T'ang-lai [canal]　唐來
Tao-ma kuan　倒馬關
Tarim　塔里木
Ti [people]　狄
Ti-li chih t'u　地理之圖
Ti-shui-yai　滴水崖
ti-t'ai　敵臺
T'ien　天
T'ien Han　田漢
T'ien-ch'eng　天城
t'ien-hsia ti i kuan　天下第一關
t'ien hsien　天險
T'ien-shun [reign period]　天順
Tien-pien　定邊
Toghon　脫懽
Toghon Temür　妥懽帖木兒
Toghto-bukha　脫脫不花
Toghus Temür　脫古思帖木兒
Tseng Hsien　曾銑
tsung-tu　總都
Ts'ai-Yung　蔡邕

283

Ts'ui Yüan　崔元
Tu-shih-k'ou　獨石口
T'u Ch'iao　屠僑
T'u-mu　土木
Tuan-t'ou-shan　斷頭山
Tun-huang　敦煌
Tun-k'ou　墩口
tun-t'ai　墩台
t'un-t'ien　屯田
Tung Chung-shu　董仲舒
Tung-sheng　東勝
T'ung-chou　通州
T'ung-kuan　潼關
T'ung-tien　通典
T'ung-wan　統萬城
Turfan　吐魯番
Tzu-ching-kuan　紫荆關
tzu-sai　紫塞
tz'u-pien　次邊

wai-pao　外堡
wai-pien　外邊
Wan Ssu-t'ung　萬斯同
wan-hu-so　萬戶所
Wan-li [reign period]　萬曆
wan-li chih ch'ang-ch'eng　萬里之長城
wan-li-ch'ang-ch'eng　萬里長城
wang [prince]　王
Wang Chen　王振
Wang Chih　汪直
Wang Chih-kao　王之誥
Wang Chin　王縉
Wang Ch'iung　王瓊
Wang Ch'ung-ku　王崇古
Wang Fu　王復
Wang Fu [artist]　王紱
Wang Fu-chih　王夫之
Wang Hua-chen　王化貞
Wang I-ch'i　王以旂
Wang I-o　王一鶚
Wang Mang　王莽
Wang San　王三
Wang Shih-chen　王世貞
Wang Shih-mou　王世懋
Wang Yüeh　王越
Wang Yün　王惲
wang-fu-lou　望夫樓
Wang-p'ing-k'ou　王平口
wei [awesomeness]　威
wei [guard]　衛

Wei [river]　渭河
Wei [state]　魏
Wei Ao　隗囂
Wei Chiang　魏絳
Wei Ch'ing　衛青
Wei Hsiang　魏相
wei-chen hua-i　威震華夷
Wei-ning-hai-tzu　威寧海子
Wen [emperor]　文帝
Wen Yüan　聞淵
Weng Wan-ta　翁萬達
Western Chin [dynasty]　西晉
Wu Ch'eng-en　吳承恩
Wu-chou　梧州
wu-hui-ling　五灰嶺
Wu-ling [king]　武靈
Wu-ti [emperor]　武帝
Wu-wang-k'ou　吳王口
Wu-wei　武威
Wu-yüan　五原

Ya-chiao shan　丫角山
Yang [emperor]　隋煬帝
Yang [mountain]　陽
Yang Chü　楊琚
Yang Chao　楊兆
Yang Chi-sheng　楊繼盛
Yang Hsin　楊信
Yang I-ch'ing　楊一清
Yang Po　楊博
Yang Shou-ch'ien　楊守謙
Yang Shou-li　楊守禮
Yang T'ing-ho　楊廷和
Yang-ho　楊和
Yang-ho [battlefield]　陽河
Yang-ho　陽和
Yao [people]　傜
Yao Hsing　姚興
Yao K'uei　姚夔
Yeh Chien-ying　葉劍英
Yeh Sheng　葉盛
Yeh Shih　葉適
Yen [state]　燕
Yen Shih-ku　顏師古
Yen Sung　嚴嵩
Yen Yu　嚴尤
Yen-fu　延府
Yen-ho-k'ou　沿河口
Yen-men-kuan　雁門關
Yen-sui　延綏

Yin-ch'üan　銀川
Yin-shan [mountains]　銀山
Ying-ch'ang　應昌
Ying-chou　應州
Yu [northeast, near Chi]　幽
Yü Ch'ien　于謙
Yü river　御河
Yü Tzu-chün　余子俊
Yü-kuan　渝關
Yü-lin　榆林
Yü-men　玉門關

Yüan [dynasty]　元
yüan [rampart]　垣
Yüan-chou　袁州
yüan-shuai-fu　元帥府
Yüeh Fei　岳飛
yüeh-fu　樂府
Yün-chung　雲中
Yün-t'ai　雲臺
Yung-lo [emperor]　永樂
Yung-ning　永寧
Yung-p'ing　永平

Index

Allom, Thomas, 209
Altan khan, 112, 122–5, 159, 160, 164, 174–7, 185–6
Appleton, William W., 206
archaeological investigations, 5, 17, 21
Arigh Böke, 68, 69
Arughtai, 76, 87
Atlas Sinensis, 206
Ayushiridara, 74

Bäg Arslan, 84, 104, 111
Bagha-achi, 185, 186
Barfield, Thomas 234 n.110, 248 n.480
Barmé, Geremie, 254 n.622
barbarians vs. Chinese, concept of, 9, 31, 32, 43, 47–8, 56, 58, 109, 120, 179, 189, *see also hua;i*
Barrow, Sir John, 6, 208
Barsubolod, 111
Batu, Möngke, 111–12, 122
ibn-Batuta, 204
Bauer, Wolfgang, 171
Bayan, General, 86
Bell, John, 208
Beshbaliq, 68
Bodde, Derk, 17
Bolai, 93, 94, 95, 96, 98, 110
Bodai-alagh, 112
borders. *See* frontiers
boundaries of Chinese territory, question of, 2, 23, 42–3, 55, 180; *see also* frontiers
brickwork, 141, 151, 152
Büyür, Lake, 74, 105

Cambridge History of China, The, 16
capital, placement of, 38, 46, 56, 75, 158
Century Illustrated Monthly Magazine, 214
Ch'a-chien-ling, 156

Chai Luan, 136, 142
Chai P'eng, 150
Chang-chia-k'ou, 17, 18, 26, 61, 111, 146, 160
Chang-chia-k'ou-pao, 157
Chang Chü-cheng, 184–8
Chang Hsiang-wen, 214
Chang-i, 23
Chang Jen-yüan, 66
Chang Wei-hua, 18, 19, 24
Chang Wen-chin, 150
Ch'ang-an, 56, 64
Ch'ang-chou, 164
Chao, state of, 13, 15, 18, 26, 39, 64
Chao Ch'ung-kuo, 42, 83
Chao Fu, 98, 99, 103, 117
Chao-ho valley, 160
Chao-hsiang, King, 18, 19, 21, 24
Chao I, 49, 189, 202
Chao Ling, 44
Chao Wen-hua, 178
Ch'ao Ts'o, 42
chariots, 116
Chen-hai-lou tower, 216
Chen-pien-ch'eng, 161
Chen Te-hsiu, 112
Ch'en Ch'i-hsüeh, 132
Ch'en Ching, 129, 131
Ch'en Jui, 118
Ch'en Lin, 196
Ch'en Yen, 117
Ch'en Yi, 216
Ch'en Yüeh, 117
Cheng-chou (Honan), 13
Cheng-te emperor, 118, 119–20
Cheng-t'ung emperor, 88–90, 91, 92, 93, 96
Ch'eng-hua emperor, 116, 124, 131